POWER UP!

daily
devotionals
from *Sports Spectrum*
magazine

Discovery House Publishers

Books, music, and videos that feed the soul with the Word of God

Box 3566 Grand Rapids, MI 49501

Discovery House Publishers is affiliated with RBC Ministries,
Grand Rapids, Michigan.

Discovery House books are distributed to the trade exclusively by
Barbour Publishing, Inc., Uhrichsville, Ohio.

Requests for permission to quote from this book should be directed to:
Permissions Department, Discovery House Publishers, P.O. Box 3566,
Grand Rapids, MI 49501.

Interior Design by Sherri L. Hoffman

Printed in the United States of America
07 08 09 / SB / 10 9 8 7 6 5 4 3

Sports mirrors life.

In sports, you have wins. In life, you have wins.

In sports, you get hurt. In life, you get hurt.

In sports, you lose. In life, you lose.

Whether you are a weekend warrior who plays church softball, a couch potato fan who wears out the remote keeping up with your favorite teams, an aspiring star who plays point guard for your school team, or a coach who lives or dies with each play your team makes, you know how true it is that sports mirrors life.

That's what makes it possible for us to use sports analogies to teach truth about life as revealed through the truth of God's Word. For instance, when an athlete who is the 215th pick in the major league draft surprises everyone and becomes a superstar, isn't that a great illustration of what the young shepherd boy named David discovered when he was anointed king? You may not look like much to a lot of people, but you can still reach the top.

Or what about the concept of sacrifice? There aren't many better illustrations of willing sacrifice (Romans 12) than seeing an athlete give up his time, his social life, his desires, and his body to do whatever the coach asks him in order to help the team. That's a sports principle, but it is also a life principle spelled out in Scripture.

In *Power Up*, we have searched out the sport analogies for you and have directed the teaching of those analogies toward the truths of God's holy Word, the Bible. Each day you can open the pages of *Power Up* and learn at least one new truth about how God wants you to live, how you should think about our awesome God, or how you can spread the love of Jesus Christ to others. And you can do it by reading sports stories.

For the sports fan who loves God, what could be better?

Well, this. What if we allowed top Christian athletes to do the teaching?

More than half of the devotional articles in *Power Up* were written by men and women who have competed at the highest levels of sports: major league baseball, the NFL, the LPGA, the NBA, the NHL, the WNBA, college sports, the Olympics, the MLS. You'll recognize the names, and you'll enjoy the opportunity to re-live with them some of their good and bad moments.

You'll get to know the athletes a little better as they tell you about their relationship with Christ and how you can improve yours.

Each devotional also contains a number of tools to guide you spiritually. You'll see right away what lesson you are to contemplate in the **Point of Emphasis**, followed by a short Bible verse (try memorizing it) to guide your thinking. Each day you'll find a **Sports Note** that will increase your sports knowledge about the topic of the day. Accompanying that is a **Game Plan**, with two or three thought-provoking questions to help you apply the truth for the day. And finally you have **From the Playbook**, a suggested Scripture reading.

Power Up is a unique tool for spiritual growth, and we think that you'll enjoy each new day's devotional as it takes you into the world of sports to help teach you timeless and invaluable truths. And we think you'll be surprised to discover the many ways sports mirrors life.

—DAVE BRANON
MANAGING EDITOR, *SPORTS SPECTRUM* MAGAZINE

CLEAR YOUR RECORD

POINT OF EMPHASIS:
Forgiveness

"I, even I, am he who blots out your transgressions, for my own sake, and remembers your sins no more." ISAIAH 43:25

Early in my pro basketball career, I was able to fulfill a dream by purchasing a townhouse. The purchase was one of the most exciting and exhausting times of my life. To be approved for the loan, an officer pulled my credit report to see if I was worthy to receive the bank's money. When the loan officer received the credit report, though, he discovered some delinquent charges that I knew were not valid.

I had to figure out how to clear my name. This rating could cause me to have a higher interest rate. After I went to the sources of the delinquent records and got the correct information, I gave it to the loan officer, hoping it would change the outcome.

Well, it did not! I would have to wait 30 days or more for the changes to clear. Now, that was a dilemma, because I would miss a deal the homeowners were offering. I couldn't clear my own good name.

The amazingly wonderful thing about Christ is this: It is so easy to have a clean record with Him! We are guilty; yet, we can be forgiven. All we have to do is "confess our sins," because "He is faithful and just to forgive us our sins and to cleanse us from all unrighteousness" (1 John 1:9 NKJV). Once you are forgiven, you don't have to wait 30 days for clearance. In Isaiah 43:25 God said, "I, even I, am he who blots out your transgressions for my own sake; And I will not remember your sins" (NKJV).

Ask God to clear your record, and He will say, "Come now, let us reason together. Though your sins are like scarlet, they shall be as white as snow; though they are red as crimson, they shall be like wool" (Isaiah 1:18).

That will get you the home you're really looking for—the one in Glory.

—CHARLOTTE SMITH-TAYLOR, PRO BASKETBALL PLAYER

SPORTS NOTE:

Charlotte Smith was one of the first women to dunk a basketball in college play.

FROM THE PLAYBOOK: Read Ephesians 1:3–8.

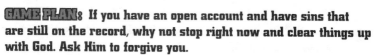

GAME PLAN: If you have an open account and have sins that are still on the record, why not stop right now and clear things up with God. Ask Him to forgive you.

LIVING THE DREAM

POINT OF EMPHASIS:
Trusting God

"I can do everything through him who gives me strength."
PHILIPPIANS 4:13

Because I began what was to be my junior year of college at Washington State in 1995 with a broken foot, my coach decided to redshirt me for the year. I had played junior college before, so my dream of playing major college football had to be put off.

That season was an uphill battle. I had to cope with surgery and the pain after a pin was placed in my bone. I had to learn to walk to classes on crutches, sometimes in the snow. The free time from football was nice; however, I couldn't just sit at home. I had to lift weights, mainly to work on my upper body strength.

SPORTS NOTE:
Dorian spent several years in the Canadian Football League with the Edmonton Eskimos after playing in the NFL.

FROM THE PLAYBOOK:
Read Genesis 33.

In 1996 I came back stronger and even faster than before. I had some exciting plays, including two fumble returns for touchdowns. I set a record with a 94-yard return against Colorado. We finished about fifth in the Pac-10, but because of that season I became well-known in the state of Washington.

The next year, I had high expectations and aspirations for the Cougars to go to the Rose Bowl. Our team had worked hard during the off-season.

The season was dramatic from beginning to end. We won the Pac-10 title, broke numerous records, and earned a trip to the Rose Bowl for the first time in 67 years. The experience was unbelievable, electrifying, and memorable. It earned us a place in Pac-10 history.

I prayed that God would go before us and prepare a path for us. My attitude was that wherever it takes us, that's sufficient for me. I gave my ability, my strength, my courage, my doubt, my uncertainties, my pride—in essence, I put myself last. God then gave me the desire of my heart. I had a successful season personally and so did our team. Thank you, Jesus!

—DORIAN BOOSE, PRO FOOTBALL PLAYER

GAME PLAN: What have you been asking God to help you with recently? Are you willing to say thank you whether you succeed or not at that goal?

THE WORD OF GOD

POINT OF EMPHASIS:
Meditating on the Bible

"Do not let this Book of the Law depart from your mouth."
JOSHUA 1:8

According to Joyce Meyer in the book *Battlefield of the Mind,* meditating on the Word of God is one of the most important life principles that we can learn.

Meditating on God's Word gives us life (Proverbs 4:20–22). When reading the Word of God, we must understand that it's simply that, a word. But once you begin "to care for," "attend to," "practice," and "study" the Word of God, it begins to minister life to you.

How?

Meditating on the Bible allows the Word to penetrate your soul and plant a seed of life. Not life itself, but a seed of life, within your heart. As you continue to read and meditate on the Word, that word begins to grow. Instruction from God's Word is one of the things the author is talking about in Mark 4:22 when he mentions "the hidden treasure of life."

Once you have revelation from God's holy Word, you then must *do.* You must act. God says, "Do not merely listen to the word, and so deceive yourselves. Do what it says" (James 1:22). Meditating on the Word should lead to action—to doing the things God wants you to do.

Daily meditate on the Word of God, and see how it changes your life. You will discover the secrets to having the abundant life (John 10:10).

—KEDRA HOLLAND-CORN, PRO BASKETBALL PLAYER

SPORTS NOTE:
On June 25, 2002, Kedra scored a career-high 28 points in a WNBA game.

FROM THE PLAYBOOK:
Read Psalm 119:97–104.

GAME PLAN: When was the last time you meditated on a passage of Scripture, squeezing out God's meaning and then seeing how to put His truth into action?

A PRAYER TO SOFTEN HEARTS

POINT OF EMPHASIS:
Praying for others

"Forgiving each other, just as in Christ God forgave you."
EPHESIANS 4:32

Forgiving is tough at times. When others mock you or put you down, the decision to turn your cheek is tough. Our heart's desire is usually to repay evil for evil. But what does Jesus say?

"Forgive [others] when they sin against you" is what Jesus told us to do (Matthew 6:14). Sometimes we lose sight of our own sin, and where the King of kings has both *brought* us from and *bought* us from.

What happens, for instance, when we try to do what is right, but get berated for it? I know this is sometimes tough to bear, especially because the sports arena can be a lonely road. For example, we hear comments when we turn our eyes from an ungodly magazine, refrain from cursing, or go to chapel or church. But Jesus says He will never leave us nor forsake us. He understands all we go through and cares about every detail of our lives!

SPORTS NOTE:
Kim was the first woman to hit a home run in a pro baseball game that pitted men vs. women.

FROM THE PLAYBOOK:
Read Genesis 33:1–11.

The next time you are persecuted for the light that beams forth from your presence—pray! And choose to forgive. You may not feel like forgiving, but our walk with God is not based on feelings. It's based on faith. We forgive because God our Father calls us to forgive. We choose to obey.

So, as you stand shagging fly balls in the outfield during batting practice, pray for those around you. God will soften your heart toward those you struggle with. With a heart like His, forgiveness will be as natural as breathing.

—KIM VOISARD, PRO BASEBALL PLAYER

GAME PLAN: Is forgiveness hard for you? Have you been working on developing a Christlike heart, one that is soft toward those who are caught in sin or who turn against you?

WHO GIVES THE INCREASE?

POINT OF EMPHASIS:
God's provision

"I planted, Apollos watered, but God gave the increase."
I Corinthians 3:6 (NKJV)

Have you ever wondered if you are bearing fruit for the Lord? This is a question I asked over and over before it was answered for me while I was a soldier in the US Army.

I was on an Army detail—helping load my unit's bags on the plane that would carry us to Saudi Arabia. On the bus ride to Altus AFB from Fort Sill, Oklahoma, I spoke about Christ to a young man who was seated next to me. Our conversation was very basic. After we got off the bus, I went to do my job. I did not see him again until two months later.

Our unit set up just outside the neutral zone in Saudi Arabia. A friend and I started a nightly Bible study. One month after the Bible study started, I saw the young man I had witnessed to. He was at the study. During the invitation he came forward and gave his life to Jesus Christ.

I observed this from the back of the meeting tent. When this man was asked how he came to Christ, he pointed back to me and said, "It was because of him." He went on to say that when he loaded the plane, someone witnessed to him; when we stopped in France, someone witnessed to him; when we stopped in Egypt, someone witnessed to him. He concluded by saying, "I knew that God was calling me to make a commitment for Him, and it began with that guy back there!

You could have mopped me off the floor as the life lesson of I Corinthians 3:6 hit me dead in the heart.

So, if you are ever in a situation where you don't think you are being effective—just remember that God is giving the increase to your good works!

—John F. Register, 2000 Paralympics silver medalist, long jump

SPORTS NOTE:
John was a world-class sprinter when a freak accident while running cost him part of a leg. Then he became a world-class paralympic athlete.

FROM THE PLAYBOOK:
Read 1 Corinthians 3.

GAME PLAN: What are some things you've done recently that you expected to bear some fruit? Could God possibly be bringing the increase but you just don't know about it?

IMAGINE GREATNESS

POINT OF EMPHASIS:
Thinking right

"If anything is excellent or praiseworthy—think about such things."
PHILIPPIANS 4:8

We think about a lot of things. If we were to transcribe every thought that went through our heads in just one day, the task would be a multi-day project.

Participation in sports gives rise to a whole different set of thoughts from everyday life. During workouts, we may be thinking about how much weight we can lift, how to implement new plays or skills, how hard to push while nursing an injury, or even where the next competitive event will take place.

SPORTS NOTE:
Jean Driscoll won the Boston Marathon wheelchair race more times than any other woman.

One skill many athletes use during training and competition is imaging. This is the ability to create mental pictures or imagery that can assist you in becoming more proficient in any area you desire. Some people use imagery to practice a technique without doing the actual movement. Others use imagery to build their confidence as they watch themselves doing what is necessary to win their event. Imagery is not magical nor does it guarantee victory, but it is an effective tool that utilizes the God-given ability to think about things that are excellent.

FROM THE PLAYBOOK:
Read 2 Samuel 7:1–17.

Imagery is often a vehicle through which athletes imagine greatness—whether they eventually achieve it or not. How gracious it was of God to design a way for us to see the goodness and the excitement of life through our mind's eye! Whether in the heat of competition or resting quietly at home, make a point to think about, as Paul put it, excellent and praiseworthy things. And don't forget, that means we need also to think about the great things God has done for us. Now, that's true greatness!

—JEAN DRISCOLL, EIGHT-TIME BOSTON MARATHON CHAMPION

GAME PLAN: How can thinking about things that are excellent strengthen your relationship with Jesus Christ? What are some not-so-excellent things that need to be eliminated from your thoughts?

FALLING SHORT

POINT OF EMPHASIS:
God's grace

"My power is made perfect in weakness." 2 CORINTHIANS 12:9

Is there a habit in your life you struggle to change? Is there something the Holy Spirit has convicted you about that needs some attention?

You're not alone. Longtime NBA center Andrew DeClercq struggled with that as well. DeClercq, who spent many seasons with the Orlando Magic, desires to honor God with his thoughts and his actions. But just as we do, he struggles.

"I have a hard time understanding why I continue to struggle with the same sins over and over again," DeClercq said. "For example, I often ask the Lord to take wrongful thoughts from me and yet I continue to have them. And at times I am easily frustrated or struggle to maintain a proper attitude. Paul's writings in 2 Corinthians give me a better perspective on how I should deal with my own weaknesses."

DeClercq often reflects on one of his favorite Bible verses, which says that God's "grace is sufficient for you, for [God's] power is made perfect in weakness" (2 Corinthians 12:9). Interesting, isn't it, that God uses our weaknesses to bring us closer to Him. And the closer we get to God the more intimate we can get in our fellowship with Him.

As we face our weaknesses, we affirm God's power, and we learn to rely on Him to help us get through our struggles. God gives us strength that has nothing to do with our performance.

Whether we play forward in the NBA or work second shift at the tool-and-die factory, the formula is the same: Our weakness can bring us closer to the power of God.

—ROXANNE ROBBINS

SPORTS NOTE:
Andrew DeClercq played college basketball at the University of Florida.

FROM THE PLAYBOOK:
Read 2 Corinthians 12:7–10.

GAME PLAN: Today take time—as much as necessary—to pray and ask God to reveal areas in your life that are not pleasing to Him. Write three action steps you can take to help correct these areas in your life.

DIVINE GUIDANCE COUNSELOR

POINT OF EMPHASIS:
The Holy Spirit

"I will ask the Father, and he will give you another Counselor."
JOHN 14:16

When I was in high school, I had a guidance counselor named Ms. Neubauer.

She was the one my friends and I ran to in times of trouble and concern, or when I needed help with making decisions about what courses to take. She even gave me advice on how to interact with my basketball coaches and teammates.

We all have plenty of times when we wonder what choices to make in life. The encouraging thing to realize is that even if we don't have a Ms. Neubauer to go to, we have someone better. We have God, who offers helpful guidance that goes beyond what any human can give. For those of us who are truly Christians and believe in Christ, we have an assurance of God's help.

God tells us that if we love Him, we will obey Him. Sure, all of us make mistakes from time to time, but if we sincerely love God, we will not keep on living a life that's displeasing to God. And He provides us with a real counselor, the Holy Spirit—kind of like having a "Ms. Neubauer" for life.

The Holy Spirit, who is called "the Spirit of truth" in John 14, leads us to truth. This includes truth in making decisions. Want to know what to do? Give God the situation in prayer, and then trust the guidance of our great Counselor, the Holy Spirit.

—TODD FULLER, FORMER NBA PLAYER

SPORTS NOTE:
While in high school, Todd Fuller played basketball for coach Bobby Jones, the former defensive star of the Philadelphia 76ers.

FROM THE PLAYBOOK:
Read John 14:15–17.

GAME PLAN: What are two tough decisions you have to make this week? Have you given them to God yet?

THE DEADLY DUO

POINT OF EMPHASIS:
Importance of friends

"Bad company corrupts good character." I CORINTHIANS 15:33

A few years ago, Greg "Cadillac" Anderson—a former NBA star—was sentenced to spend a few months in jail. He had been suckered into selling drugs while he was earning $272,000 a year to play basketball for the Atlanta Hawks.

Anderson, who picked up the nickname "Cadillac" while he was in college because he rode a bike around campus (you figure it out), knows the two most important factors that led to his illegal activity. He blames bad judgment and a poor choice of friends.

Yes, there it is again, sports fans, that deadly duo: bad judgment and bad friends. How many millions of young people do these evil twins have to snare before others will see the danger? How many lives have to be wrecked before they'll understand that making poor choices and choosing losers for friends leads to nothing but trouble?

Think about some possible poor choices:

You know that illegal drugs kill, impair, and addict. Choosing to use them is absolutely stupid.

You know that God's Word says sexual activity is reserved for marriage. Choosing to engage in it in *any other situation* will lead to regret, lack of respect, problems you cannot foresee, and a future of sadness.

Think about some possible poor choices of close friends:

Non-Christians who don't care how you believe. Christians who are dabbling in sin. Christians who don't take God seriously. Non-Christians who scoff at your love for Christ.

In each of these cases, you are asking for trouble if you let the deadly duo—or even one of the two—control your life.

—DAVE BRANON

SPORTS NOTE:
Greg Anderson scored 4,953 points in his NBA career.

FROM THE PLAYBOOK:
Read Proverbs 2.

GAME PLAN: List 10 of your closest friends. Do they (a) draw you from God, (b) draw you closer to God, or (c) give you a chance to witness about your faith?

DO THE RIGHT THING

POINT OF EMPHASIS:
Doing God's will

"Be careful to do what is right." ROMANS 12:17

It must have felt like someone dropped him on a floating piece of ice in the Antarctic. Darcy Ewing was being ignored by his fellow snowmobile racers and the media that covers the sport. It all began when his team cast him aside—placing his career in a temporary deep-freeze—because he refused to accept funding from the alcohol industry.

Darcy, who had won eight world titles and 20 national championships in snowmobile racing, was suddenly out in the cold because he couldn't feel good about receiving money from the makers of "cold ones." His wife and family supported his decision—agreeing that God wanted him to take a stand for what is right and honorable.

Darcy was off his old team, but not out of the sport. Later, during a tuneup race, a rookie driver lost control of his snowmobile and crashed into him. Darcy nearly bit off his tongue, lost some teeth, cracked two vertebras, and broke two ribs.

Undaunted, he made it to his goal—the World Championship in Snowmobiling. In the final race, Darcy took the checkered flag! He had silenced his critics and stayed true to his course.

It's not easy to do the right thing, but God will provide the strength we need. Darcy Ewing could have given in to the peer pressure of teammates and swallowed his convictions.

But he didn't.

Each day we have the opportunity to "do what is right in the eyes of everybody" (Romans 12:17)—not for our glory, but for the glory of God.

Stay true to the course. Follow God's lead. Do the right thing today.

—TOM FELTEN

SPORTS NOTE:
Darcy Ewing was killed on September 23, 2002, in an accident while riding his bicycle near his home in Big Lake, Minnesota.

FROM THE PLAYBOOK:
Read Romans 12:1–18.

GAME PLAN: Think about one area in your life where you have not been doing the right thing. Today, do what you must to correct your ways and bring honor to Jesus Christ.

IT WASN'T MY FAULT!

POINT OF EMPHASIS:
Making excuses

"The sluggard says, 'There is a lion outside!'" PROVERBS 22:13

Have you ever noticed how creative some athletes can be?

Just listen to them make excuses after an embarrassing mistake: *The court was too slippery. The sun was in my eyes. The fans were against me. I broke a string. I pulled a muscle. The other guy (team) cheated. The ref was blind.*

My all-time favorite comes from the NFL player who said he missed a field goal because—and I quote—"My helmet was too tight. It was squeezing my brain."

And we thought it was because he made a bad kick.

After a while, you find yourself wanting to shout, "Come on, guys! Enough with the excuses. Just do your best and play the game!"

Come to think of it, that's pretty good advice for those of us who are "running the race" of faith. It's easy to make excuses when we fall short of the goal. We can think of all kinds of reasons for our failures and mistakes. There's always someone or something we can blame.

But playing the blame game doesn't get us anywhere. Excuses don't fix the problem. They just waste our valuable time and keep us from focusing on the finish line. In Philippians 3:13–14, Paul said, "Forgetting what is behind and straining toward what is ahead, I press on toward the goal to win the prize for which God has called me heavenward in Christ Jesus."

Don't let excuses keep you from moving ahead in the race of life. Stay focused—and run for all you're worth!

—CHRISTIN DITCHFIELD

SPORTS NOTE: Or, as Yogi Berra supposedly said, "We made too many wrong mistakes."

FROM THE PLAYBOOK: Read Colossians 3:12–24.

 GAME PLAN: Have you been making excuses to cover your mistakes? Ask God for forgiveness instead. He'll help you overcome your failures and give you strength to run the race.

THE GREAT CHASE

POINT OF EMPHASIS:
Getting close to God

"Come near to God and he will come near to you." JAMES 4:8

A friend of mine has a one-year-old son named Skyler. He is eager for his independence but still wants Mom close at hand. She has always been his source of food and love, clean diapers, and endless snuggling. Mom is the center of his world, and he is keenly aware of her presence.

I saw this illustrated as I watched Skyler playing on the floor while his mom moved around the room. He would look over frequently to make sure she was nearby, then he'd smile and go on playing. The crisis came when Mom left the room. No more than five seconds had passed when he let out a piercing cry, as if to say, "Hey, you're too far away!" And he took off speed-crawling, chasing her with all his might.

Do you see the comparison to our relationship with God? He takes care of everything His children need, whether it's food on our plates or a trial to teach us patience. We may never realize this side of heaven just how careful He is to ensure that we are being made more like Him.

God our Father wants us to glance at Him constantly, to stay in close contact with Him. And we can be sure that if we don't, it is we who moved, unlike Skyler's mom.

"Come near to God and he will come near to you" (James 4:8). He is our safe place. All through history, He has proved that He is there for His children when they need Him. Our job is to make sure we stay in the same room with Him.

— SUE SEMRAU, WOMEN'S COLLEGE BASKETBALL COACH

SPORTS NOTE:
Sue Semrau was voted the Atlantic Coast Conference Coach of the Year in 2001.

FROM THE PLAYBOOK:
Read Psalm 62:1–8.

GAME PLAN: What is it like to stray from God? Have you done that and found the loneliness and despair? What are some things that keep you from God?

REMEMBER WHOSE YOU ARE

POINT OF EMPHASIS:
We are God's

"Know that the Lord is God. It is he who made us." PSALM 100:3

I have played basketball my entire life. I remember my elementary years playing in a league against girls who were two and three years older than I was. When I got to high school, I played varsity basketball and was the starting point guard. I was then blessed to get a scholarship to play Division I basketball at Boston College. Now I am playing in the WNBA.

With my basketball ability, I have always been in the spotlight. Many people, adults and kids, have become fans and followed my basketball career. Being someone who is watched by many, I am always challenged by my parents to "Remember Whose You Are." I am a daughter, a sister, a granddaughter, a niece, a cousin, a friend, and a teammate; but most important, I am God's! I am a believer and one who loves the Lord Jesus Christ. Therefore, I need to display a life that reflects the image of God as I strive to be more like Him. There are many eyes constantly watching me, my actions, my attitude, my life—what will they see?

God has given us as believers so much. We need to continue to pursue Him so that others can see Him through us. We need to be passionate in seeking Him and then overflowing with God's love. Whether there are many eyes on you or just a few, how are you living your life—for the Lord or for others?

Remember WHOSE You Are!

—AMBER JACOBS, WNBA GUARD

SPORTS NOTE: Amber was a third-round draft pick of the Minnesota Lynx in 2004.

FROM THE PLAYBOOK: Read Galatians 5:22–26.

GAME PLAN: Think of 10 people whose lives you touch frequently. Are they all aware of whose you are? Can they tell just by watching whose you are?

LOVING THE BALL HOG

POINT OF EMPHASIS:
Loving others

"The fruit of the righteous is a tree of life, and he who wins souls is wise." PROVERBS 11:30

SPORTS NOTE:
In 2004, Jenny's Seattle Storm won the WNBA championship. She was an assistant coach for the Storm.

FROM THE PLAYBOOK:
Read 1 Corinthians 13.

Have you ever had a teammate who did not pass the ball? How about one with a huge chip on her shoulder? How did you handle them? Most people would not pass to them, giving them that attitude right back. This is where we as Christians should see an occasion to be different. This is an opportunity for us to let God use us to change people.

If one of your teammates does not pass the ball, and then others stop passing to that person, it becomes contagious. Everyone gets preoccupied with this little subplot instead of playing as a team. One player can drastically affect an entire team. But, if you continue to pass the ball, and make an effort to pass to the ball hogs, *that* will become contagious. Teammates will see that you are continuing to be a team player and eventually will trust that they can share the ball, because they *will* get it back.

Now what about the teammate with the chip on her shoulder? Same thing applies. If you give an attitude right back, the problem gets worse. But if you continue to be nice and respectful... *eventually* others will take notice and start to change. It may take time, but if you stay consistent, teammates will see that you are different and begin to trust you.

Remember, anyone can be nice to nice people. It takes a special person, one filled with the Holy Spirit, to love people who are not nice! We are called to love people not because they love us but because *God* loves us.

Be different, and then don't be afraid to tell people why you are different!

—JENNY BOUCEK, ASSISTANT COACH, WNBA

GAME PLAN: Do you have a couple of acquaintances who get on your nerves? How can you, in the love of Christ, get close enough to help them? Do you want to?

THE PUCK STOPS HERE

POINT OF EMPHASIS:
God's grace

"My grace is sufficient for you." 2 CORINTHIANS 12:9

Don't blink . . . You're in the goal. A slap shot has blasted the puck off the ice and sent it sizzling straight at your head.

What would you do?

a. Duck. b. Snare it for an outstanding save. c. Wake up from your dream and admit you're not a pro hockey goalie.

Did you pick "a"? That's okay, I feel the same way about objects hurtling at me in excess of 100 mph. However, "c" is probably the right answer for most of us.

I mean, you have to be one tough humanoid to tend the net in pro hockey. Take Larry Dyck, for example. He played in the International Hockey League for several seasons. He was a good goalie. Tough. Determined. And legally blind in one eye since childhood.

How did Larry handle those laser-like shots at the net? "In hockey, the puck comes so fast you don't have to worry about perception," he says.

Pretty humble response, huh? In reality, this gutsy goalie played well in a position that requires lightning-quick reflexes, incredible coordination, and superb vision.

> **SPORTS NOTE:** The International Hockey League ceased play in 2001. Most of the teams joined the American Hockey League.

> **FROM THE PLAYBOOK:** Read 2 Corinthians 12:7–10.

The apostle Paul was another man who did a job well even though he was challenged by a "thorn in the flesh" (2 Corinthians 12:7). While we don't know what his affliction was, we can be sure that it was bothersome and painful. Paul pleaded with God three times to take it away, but He let it stay.

Why? Paul heard this reply from God: "My grace is sufficient for you, for my power is made perfect in weakness" (2 Corinthians 12:9).

Sometimes the things we wrestle with—physical impairments, emotional challenges, sickness—bring us to the place God wants us to be: broken and ready to do His work in His power alone.

So, keep your eyes open—and be ready at any time to stop some pucks.

—TOM FELTEN

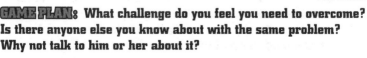

GAME PLAN: What challenge do you feel you need to overcome? Is there anyone else you know about with the same problem? Why not talk to him or her about it?

SECOND IN COMMAND

POINT OF EMPHASIS:
God's rule in our lives

"He must become greater; I must become less." JOHN 3:30

David Robinson doesn't need to play second fiddle to anyone. As one of the 50 Greatest NBA Players, a former league MVP and world champion, the talented 7'1" tower of power commanded respect.

However, "The Admiral" chose to become second in command on the San Antonio Spurs basketball team. The reason? He recognized the ability of a young hoops superstar named Tim Duncan, who came on board in 1998, and the positive effect his change had on the Spurs' team.

"It was frustrating at first, after a lifetime of getting all the shots I wanted," David says. "But with Tim's talents, you would be stupid not to let him go. The boy can really play."

SPORTS NOTE:
When David Robinson retired in 2003, he had scored 20,790 points and grabbed 10,497 rebounds in the NBA.

To understand the source of big Number 50's grace and humility, you must grasp the depth of his faith in Jesus Christ. "I would die for what I believe," he says. "I know about Jesus Christ. I know about the motivation for my life. If I'm not willing to give up my life for the Lord, then there's nothing else in my life worth standing for."

FROM THE PLAYBOOK:
John 3:26–36.

David's conviction is a true reflection of what John the Baptist stated, "He must become greater; I must become less" (John 3:30). The goal of "The Admiral's" life is to reflect with humility the glory of his Lord.

Do you seek to become lesser as Christ becomes greater in your life? Can you humbly allow another person a place of greater prominence because of your identity in Christ?

Being second in command should always be our first choice before God.

—TOM FELTEN

 GAME PLAN: Write down four key areas of your life (for example, work, family, school). Next, think about how much you reflect the "less me, more Christ" way of life in each area. Place a number from 1 (Not well) to 5 (Very well) by each word on the paper. Finally, pray for God's help in the areas where you're struggling to be second in command.

KEEPING YOUR FOCUS

POINT OF EMPHASIS:
Focusing on Jesus

"Let us fix our eyes on Jesus." HEBREWS 12:2

When standing at the free throw line, preparing to take my foul shot, I have learned one basic principle that brings success. For the split second before I shoot the ball, I must focus my eyes on one particular spot on the rim.

From years of practice, I have trained my eyes to locate this spot, focus on it and then let my body do the rest. When I get lazy in this particular action, I start to let my eyes wander and I begin to see other distractions. I might notice the fans cheering against me or see players moving into position or even notice the team mascot running down the sideline. At this point I know that I have lost my focus.

So it is the same in life. In the book of Hebrews we are told to "Fix our eyes on Jesus . . . " We need to daily remind ourselves who it is we live for and what our ultimate goal is in life.

When we give too much attention to our circumstances and surroundings, we become distracted and lose our focus. Jesus promises to give us strength if we would make Him the center of our life. Just as I must take the time to train my eyes to focus on the hoop, so must I also take the time to get away from the distractions of living and focus my mind and my eyes on the One who brings me victory in life.

—LEIGHANN REIMER, PRO BASKETBALL PLAYER

SPORTS NOTE:
Leighann played pro basketball in France for three seasons.

FROM THE PLAYBOOK:
Read Proverbs 4:25–27;
Psalm 25:15;
Psalm 141:8.

GAME PLAN: What are the distractions in my life that pull my attention away from Jesus? How can I minimize their influence on my focus time? What can I do to draw my attention to Jesus and keep it there?

EMPTY GRANDSTANDS

POINT OF EMPHASIS:
Working in the church

"The manifestation of the Spirit is given for the common good."
1 CORINTHIANS 12:7

You can play sports without spectators, but you can't play without athletes. A few years ago, a couple of high schools were having some trouble with basketball fans who refused to behave themselves during and after the contests. So to avoid trouble, the second game of the season between the two schools was played without spectators. The only people allowed in the gym were the players, the refs, the coaches, and the scorekeepers. The only sounds were the bounce of the ball, the players' comments, the shrill sound of the whistle, the blare of the buzzer, and the usual bellowing of the coaches.

SPORTS NOTE:
In 1962, 1.5 million fans watched Indiana high school tournament basketball—the most ever.

It proved that although spectators are an important element, they aren't essential.

Sometimes we get that mixed up. We think our main job is to be a spectator—especially at church. We think we've done something important by showing up and watching the action at church.

FROM THE PLAYBOOK:
Read 1 Corinthians 12:1–11.

Problem is, God never meant His followers to be spectators in the work of the church. He gave talents and skills to His followers—and those gifts are not grandstand tickets to the game of life. They are spiritual abilities to be used on the playing field of school, work, or community.

God's strategy for His work is not like a pro sports team. It does not call for all the work to be done by high-salaried professionals. Rather, every believer has his own position and role on the team. He has appropriate gifts from the Spirit to use for God's glory.

Wouldn't it be great if so many of God's people were involved in the game that the grandstands were empty!

—MART DE HAAN

 GAME PLAN: If you don't know what your gifts are, set an appointment with your pastor. He'd be glad to help you discover what God has prepared you to do.

A TENNIS BIRDIE

POINT OF EMPHASIS:
Staying fixed on God

"My eyes are fixed on you, O Sovereign Lord." PSALM 141:8

The poor bird never knew what hit it.

During the Australian Open one year, a bird was swooping around on center court—chasing a moth—as a semifinal match was being played between two doubles teams.

Suddenly, amid some hard-hitting returns, the bird flew over the court and was struck solidly by the tennis ball in play. This was a case of "bye-bye birdie." The little winged creature died instantly.

French player Julien Boutter dropped to his knees in disbelief. The startled crowd went silent. Soon, a tennis official wrapped the dead creature in a towel and removed it from the arena.

The little bird had flown blindly into the path of a lethal projectile. Its focus was on something that appeared harmless and attractive—a fluttering moth.

The apostle Paul told us where the eyes of followers of Christ should be at all times: "So we fix our eyes not on what is seen, but on what is unseen. For what is seen is temporary, but what is unseen is eternal" (2 Corinthians 4:18).

If you find yourself swooping through life, chasing after things that are "attractive" but not essential, it's likely you're in for a major hit in the days ahead.

Only by following Christ while fixing your heart and mind on Him can you avoid the dangers of an undisciplined, unfocused life.

—TOM FELTEN

SPORTS NOTE: The player who has won the most Australian Open tennis tournaments is Roy Emerson, who won it six times in the 1960s.

FROM THE PLAYBOOK: Read 2 Corinthians 4:8–18.

GAME PLAN: Make two columns on a sheet of paper. In one, write down all of your pursuits that you feel have been directed by God. In the other, list the things you are chasing after that have no real eternal value. Begin making changes if the columns clearly show the need.

GOING DOWN TO GO UP

POINT OF EMPHASIS:
Obeying God

"He will make your paths straight." Proverbs 3:6

For one young hoopster, the choice was simple. For Erin Buescher, that is. A 6'3" basketball star, she left the University of California-Santa Barbara last year—after winning three straight Big West Conference Player of the Year awards—for tiny Master's College.

Why would this likely future WNBA first-round draft pick leave the bright lights of NCAA Division I ball for the warm glow of a small NAIA school? It's simple. She wanted to draw closer to God.

Erin says that while she tasted success at Santa Barbara, inside she felt distant from Jesus Christ. "I felt like I had gotten to a place where I wasn't really happy with who I was. I felt dry inside, like a desert. Like nothing spiritual was going on."

SPORTS NOTE:
Erin was drafted into the WNBA in the second round of the 2001 draft by the Minnesota Lynx.

So, for her senior year, Erin went to a smaller, Christ-centered school to grow in her knowledge of God. "I have been blown away with what the Lord is doing with me," she said while at Master's College. "I feel like I am changing every day. The Bible and the Lord are coming alive to me like they never had before."

FROM THE PLAYBOOK:
Read Proverbs 3.

To some, it may appear that Erin took a step down. But her smile and inner peace showed that, for her, things were definitely looking up!

Are you willing to take a "step down" to follow God? If God wants us to pass up that promotion or quit that high-paying career to work with troubled youth or change schools to grow in our relationship with Him, there is only one way to reply.

"Yes, Lord."

Proverbs tells us that if we trust the Lord, He will make our paths straight. Erin has trusted Him. How ready are we to do the same? —TOM FELTEN

GAME PLAN: Write down any possible "callings" you have sensed are coming from God—new directions, work, ventures. Pray and ask God to reveal whether you should proceed in the new way(s) He has revealed. Show your list to a trusted, mature Christian friend and get his or her counsel.

LET YOUR LIGHT SHINE

POINT OF EMPHASIS:
Witnessing

"[So] that they may see your good deeds and praise your Father in heaven." MATTHEW 5:16

Though Lauren Dungy has never competed as a professional athlete, she's asked herself, "If I had a chance to be out there, what would I want people to see about me?" As the wife of NFL head coach Tony Dungy, Lauren's found that people are looking at her. They want to get something from an interview or from an afternoon with her. Lauren knows she is kind of on stage.

"When I'm asked to speak at a school function or speak in a church or other setting, people are curious about me," Lauren said. "They want to hear the inside scoop, and they're looking to me for some type of direction or inspiration. I don't want to be looked at as poised and professional when I'm on stage while behind the scenes people say, 'Oh, she just loses it.' I want my Christian faith to be something that is obvious in all areas of my life—whether I'm in the spotlight or at home with Tony and our four children."

Lauren and Tony want first and foremost to be consistent with their faith. "Our faith is something that's going to go on forever," Lauren said. "It's not a temporary thing. We don't turn it on and off. We love and serve a powerful God, and we look to Him for direction in all aspects of life. The God we serve is One we worship and give glory to every day—not just when we're with other Christians."

We are called to "let our light shine before men" (Matthew 5:16). How are you doing?

—ROXANNE ROBBINS

SPORTS NOTE:
Lauren and Tony Dungy were married in 1983.

FROM THE PLAYBOOK:
Read Matthew 5:13–16.

 GAME PLAN: Write about a time when you wanted to hide your faith in Christ but didn't. What did you see God do as a result?

CHANGED FROM THE INSIDE OUT

POINT OF EMPHASIS:
God's power to change

*"Do not conform any longer to the pattern of this world,
but be transformed."* ROMANS 12:2

For me, Romans 12:2 is a life-changing verse. These words of the apostle Paul transformed my life when I realized that there must be more to the Christian life than what I was experiencing.

Like so many Christians, I desired to live in victory. Our society tries to make us believe that victory lies in what we look like and what we own. It drives us to think that by achieving great accomplishments we will become happy and victorious. These are weapons Satan uses to destroy our destiny as believers (John 10:10).

Satan's top priority is to stop the advancements of the kingdom of God here on earth. Yet he knows how limited his power over us is. Jesus has already paid the price for our complete victory with His own blood.

For many years, I thought I needed something like a world championship in bull riding before I could be used by God. Then the Lord revealed through Romans 12:2 that all He wanted was my heart opened and my mind renewed.

I repented of my wasted efforts and for believing the lies of the enemy. Then I humbled myself and asked God to help me change.

Before I understood Romans 12:2, I actually thought I could change myself. I can't and neither can you. Even if we could change on our own, it would only be on the outside and would have only temporal results. God changes us from the inside out, and that has eternal rewards. Enter today into the magnificent process of allowing God to radically change you forever.

—SCOTT MENDES, FORMER WORLD-CHAMPION BULL RIDER

SPORTS NOTE: Scott Mendes was the 1997 Professional Rodeo Cowboys Association World Champion Bull Rider.

FROM THE PLAYBOOK:
Read Proverbs 6:23; Ephesians 4:3; 2 Corinthians 4:16.

GAME PLAN: Be honest with yourself and ask yourself this question, "Has the enemy used his tools of deception in any area of my life?" If so, are you willing to allow the Lord to show you the areas where you need to be healed?

GOING DOWN

POINT OF EMPHASIS:
Accountability

"Let us not give up meeting together." HEBREWS 10:25

I knew I was going down. My ankle had caved as I came down awkwardly on my opponent's foot. As I hit the gym floor, that familiar, unforgettable pain (I've sprained my ankles several times) radiated up my leg.

As I sat on the floor holding my quivering ankle up in the air, some of my fellow hoopsters tried to console me. Then, two of them placed my arms on their shoulders and helped me hop off the court to the locker room.

A couple of players rushed to get ice. Another filled a bucket with water for the ice. One guy ran for some Ibuprofen.

Later, more guys came in and offered encouraging words and heart-lifting banter. I felt blessed. In pain, but blessed.

Where do you go when the bottom drops out of your life? A "roached" ankle is one thing, but the pain can be unbearable when the very foundation of your life gives way. Marriage problems, child crises, job loss, moral failure—many things can drop us to the floor.

One reason God gave us the church, the body of Christ, is to provide strength and support. I had to reach for the guys who helped me get up off the gym floor. I had to open my hand and receive the care and medication being offered me.

Take the words, "Let us not give up meeting together, as some are in the habit of doing, but let us encourage one another" (Hebrews 10:25) to heart. Grow in your accountability and fellowship with strong believers in Christ.

You never know when you may go down.

—TOM FELTEN

SPORTS NOTE: The most common injury to basketball players is the sprained ankle.

FROM THE PLAYBOOK: Read Hebrews 10:19–25.

GAME PLAN: Call the Christian friend(s) who hold you accountable and help you grow in your spiritual life—thanking them for their friendship and fellowship. If you do not have a fellow believer in Christ who holds you accountable, make a list of people today and contact them this week regarding your need for mutual support and encouragement.

WORK ON THE FUNDAMENTALS

POINT OF EMPHASIS:
The basics of the faith

"For the word of God is living and active. Sharper than any double-edged sword, it penetrates even to dividing soul and spirit."
HEBREWS 4:12

In the 1980s, I played professional women's basketball for the WBL—the Women's Basketball League. Although this league is no longer in existence, to play professional women's basketball was a dream come true for me. I showed up for the first practice session with the expectation that we would learn some new advanced skills at the professional level. To my amazement, it was quite the opposite. We spent most of the first few months of practice working on the basic fundamentals of basketball.

SPORTS NOTE:
Tanya Crevier is one of the top basketball handlers in the world. She can spin 10 basketballs at once.

FROM THE PLAYBOOK:
Read Psalm 119:91–93.

Now as I go from place to place teaching the skills of basketball, I have noticed that those who are grounded in the fundamental skills of the game play the game at a higher level. When the competition gets tougher, we can rely on the fundamental skills to give us the solid foundation we need. Every skill I demonstrate in my basketball show is based on very fundamental drills.

This is also true in life. I find answers in God's Word for problem areas in my own life. I memorize that Scripture, then when the trial comes again I can defeat the enemy with the Word of God, my solid foundation—my fundamentals. The Bible says in 2 Timothy 3:16, "All Scripture is given by inspiration of God, and is profitable for doctrine, for reproof, for correction, for instruction in righteousness" (NKJV). That's as fundamental as it gets.

—TANYA CREVIER, BASKETBALL SHOWPERSON

GAME PLAN: What is your basis for life? Is it the truth of God's Word? Write down three essential truths that you will not waver from.

MAKE THE SACRIFICE

POINT OF EMPHASIS:
Sacrifice for God

"Offer your bodies as living sacrifices." ROMANS 12:1

If you know anything about basketball, you've heard of A. C. Green. Although he scored more than 12,000 points and hauled down more than 9,000 rebounds, that may not be why you're familiar with A.C. More likely, you've heard about him because of his dedication. He is the NBA's iron man, playing in more consecutive games than anyone else in the league's history.

Nothing stopped A. C. Green from getting the job done on the court. One season, while he was bearing down on the record of most straight games played, he made a huge sacrifice—he lost two teeth when an opposing player swung a vicious elbow in his direction.

SPORTS NOTE: The old NBA record for consecutive games was 906, held by Randy Smith.

Despite the injury, Green didn't miss a game—and his streak extended to 1,192 games. Between November 19, 1986, and the end of the 2001 season, A. C. Green did not miss a basketball game. A. C. presented his body to basketball as a living sacrifice.

FROM THE PLAYBOOK: Read Romans 12.

What's more exciting is that he also presented his body to God as a living sacrifice. A strong Christian, A. C. set the standard for not conforming to this world. Despite living the NBA life and being subjected to every temptation imaginable, he continued to live by biblical standards of conduct. He gave himself to God for His service—just as Paul commanded in Romans 12.

Take some time and examine some of the ways Paul said you and I should be dedicated to God (verses 2–11).

Why not follow A. C.'s lead? Give yourself up to God!

—DAVE BRANON

GAME PLAN: What is holding you back from a life of dedication? Should you ask God to remove those obstacles so you can "give it up" for Him?

THE SEARCH FOR EXCELLENCE

POINT OF EMPHASIS:
God's standards

"Those who have served well gain an excellent standing."
I TIMOTHY 3:13

Striving for excellence is the norm in the NFL. But what is the definition of excellence? Is it something quantifiable like a perfect 158 quarterback rating, or is it an undefeated season like the 1972 Miami Dolphins enjoyed?

My former coach for the Buffalo Bills, Marv Levy, had this perspective: "Winning is not our goal—excellence in preparation is our goal—winning will result." It is this perspective that I favor in both defining and striving for excellence. This is more of an inside-out approach to both motivation and success. This approach levels the playing field and radically changes who is perceived as "the best."

When we use the typical "measurable" standards, the playing field is heavily tilted toward the more talented or those with the greatest resources. When the highest value is assigned to the process, however, the focus is on those who possess virtues such as diligence, faithfulness, perseverance, and integrity. This perspective does not discount the value of measurable standards, but it does put them in their proper place.

As Christians we must be careful never to forget that God's economy is radically different from the world's. His idea of excellence is based on our relationship with God—and what lasts for eternity. Although we can strive for success, and we may achieve it along the way, we should not value it over success in God's eyes. Excellence for those of us who are serving Jesus is to value only that which lasts for eternity—a relationship with God, an understanding of God's Word, and our relationships with people.

—FRANK REICH, FORMER NFL QUARTERBACK

SPORTS NOTE:
Frank Reich played 13 NFL seasons and appeared in two Super Bowls.

FROM THE PLAYBOOK:
Read Galatians 6:1–10.

GAME PLAN: How is God's view of things different from the world's in regard to what is excellent?

IT TAKES PRACTICE

POINT OF EMPHASIS:
Spiritual growth

"Above all else, guard your heart." PROVERBS 4:23

Former pro basketball player Bill Bradley tells that at the age of fifteen he attended a summer basketball camp run by "Easy Ed" Macauley, a former college and pro star. "Just remember that if you're not working at your game to the utmost of your ability," Macauley told the assembled campers, "there is someone out there with equal ability who will be working to the utmost of his ability. One day you'll play each other. And when you do, he will have the advantage."

Bill Bradley became a US senator and a candidate for President. He says that he saw in those words a truth that went far beyond the basketball court. He took them to heart and made them the guiding principle of his life. Now, many decades later, he recalls, "The important thing about this story is the type of young man I was. When I heard those words, I accepted them. Then I immediately acted on them by putting them into practice."

What do we do when we hear the truth of God's Word? Do we remark how nice it sounds, but immediately forget it? We must, like Bill Bradley did with that basketball advice, apply it immediately to life. We must put it into practice right away, or we won't benefit from it nor please God.

Solomon told us how in Proverbs 4:20–27. He said, in effect, "Don't let wise counsel get away from you."

Are you willing to take the truths of God's Word and let them be your guiding light? Can you take God's clear words of guidance and put them into practice? It might make all the difference in your life.

—MART DE HAAN

SPORTS NOTE:
While playing at Princeton for three seasons, Bill Bradley averaged 30 points a game.

FROM THE PLAYBOOK:
Read Proverbs 4:20–27.

GAME PLAN: What happens when you read something important to you in the Bible? Do you have a way of remembering it?

ONE WAY TO CONTENTMENT

POINT OF EMPHASIS:
Contentment

"Lord, what do I look for? My hope is in you." PSALM 39:7

How long do you think the fans stayed content after the Ravens won Super Bowl XXXV on January 28, 2001? It took just one week for someone to ask me, "What about your chances of winning the Super Bowl next year?"

After 11 years of playing in the NFL and winning a Super Bowl ring, I have found that the world tries to convince me of several falsehoods. First, the world tells me that my athletic accomplishments and success on the field will bring me lasting satisfaction—but I know that over time my athletic ability will fade. Where is my hope then? Psalm 39:7 says it best. My hope is in God.

SPORTS NOTE:
In Super Bowl XXXV, Matt kicked four extra points and a field goal.

Second, the world tells me that my economic success will buy me happiness. In Ecclesiastes, wise King Solomon said that all earthly treasures are empty and meaningless. True happiness comes from knowing God, who tells us that there is no eternal hope or purpose in material things. They are all temporary.

FROM THE PLAYBOOK:
Read Ecclesiastes 4 and 12:13–14.

God's viewpoint is drastically different from the world's. I have found that fulfilling something greater than myself (like the Great Commission) will give my life eternal purpose and satisfaction. I have also found that Jesus alone can fill the void we all have in our lives.

Be prepared when the world tries to sell you the wrong message about true happiness and purpose in life. Don't buy into it! The truth is, contentment is found in Christ alone.

—MATT STOVER, NFL KICKER

GAME PLAN: What have I been depending on recently for happiness? How should I revise my opinion about finding contentment?

WHERE'S DA LOVE?

POINT OF EMPHASIS:
Christlikeness

"Add . . . brotherly kindness." 2 PETER 1:5–7

I was part of a church basketball team that was in a league with other churches in the area. All of these churches preach the whole Bible, feed homeless people, and send missionaries to foreign lands. They are dynamic and active churches that you wouldn't hesitate to be a part of.

That is, except on Monday nights at league basketball games. I've never seen more bickering, complaining, and fighting in my life. And not just from the players. Fans from each church would yell at the referee if he made a bad call. You would never have known this was a group of Christians by the display of nasty attitudes. Each week there would be name-calling and sometimes pushing, shoving, and near punches. Something had to change.

Over the summer, one of our team members heard about an opportunity to play in a basketball league at a local state prison. The night of our first game arrived, and we were taken by armed guards to the gym. To say we were nervous would be an understatement. But we realized something as the weeks went by. These convicted felons were actually nicer to us and to the referees than the folks in our church league.

It was a shock to all of us when that realization came. It makes you wonder, doesn't it? After all, where's da love?

As believers, we can't afford to let a silly game like basketball distract us from our primary mission of being Christlike and glorifying God. If we can't play ball and still live for Jesus, we need to hang up our Air Jordans.

—DAN DEAL

SPORTS NOTE:
One of the most successful programs for using basketball as an outreach activity in churches is Upward Basketball.

FROM THE PLAYBOOK:
The words of Christ in Matthew 5 are essential.

GAME PLAN: Colossians 3:12 says as children of God we should show compassion and kindness. And it says we need to offer forgiveness to anyone who has a complaint against us. If a watching world doesn't see the love in Christians, why would they be interested in the faith?

PRIDE GOES BEFORE A FUMBLE

POINT OF EMPHASIS:
Pride

"Pride goes before destruction, a haughty spirit before a fall."
PROVERBS 16:18

It's a priceless Super Bowl moment. Dallas Cowboy defensive lineman Leon Lett had just scooped up a fumble and was lumbering down the field, destined for yet another TD against the hapless Buffalo Bills.

But as large Leon mentally choreographed which dance routine to implement upon his arrival in the end zone, the Bills' Don Beebe was relentlessly chewing up yardage between them. With a lunge Beebe knocked the ball loose at the one. The pigskin rolled into the end zone and out of bounds. Bills' ball at the 20, and a prominent place for Leon Lett in the Super Bowl hall of blunders.

Although I'd most like to identify with the no-quit Beebe, I'm afraid I've got a lot of Lett-like moments in my past. Hey, everybody! Look at me! Watch what I'm doing! Oops.

Which reminds me of Haman, who wasn't satisfied with his prominent position in Persia. A troublesome Hebrew named Mordecai wouldn't pay him homage. So Haman conspired against not only Mordecai but against every Jewish person in the kingdom. Unbeknownst to Haman, Mordecai was the queen's uncle.

When the queen pointed out Haman's murderous intentions to the king, Haman wound up swinging from the very gallows he had constructed for Mordecai.

It's a rare person who doesn't struggle with pride—and that's a big problem. Such an attitude runs counter to the selfless life Jesus modeled for us.

"Pride goes before destruction," says the ancient Middle Eastern wise man, "a haughty spirit before a fall" (Proverbs 16:18). That same sage also wrote, "Let another praise you, and not your own mouth" (27:2).

That's timely advice for the football field—and for the game of life as well.

—TIM GUSTAFSON

SPORTS NOTE:
Don Beebe runs a school that helps teach athletes how to run faster.

FROM THE PLAYBOOK:
Read Esther 5:9–14; 7:1–10.

GAME PLAN: What motivates me? Honor? Prestige? Greed? What ought to motivate me? What motivated Jesus when He washed His disciples' feet? (John 13:12–17).

NIGHTMARE AT THE OLYMPICS

POINT OF EMPHASIS:
Handling disappointment

"Through all this, Job did not sin nor did he blame God."
JOB 1:22 NASB

On January 31, 2002, US Olympic skier Caroline Lalive wrote in a diary article for the *Denver Post*, "Less than 10 days. The days are passing quickly, and my dream is becoming a reality. The Olympics are . . . what many dream of most of their lives."

When the Olympics came, though, reality turned out to be more of a nightmare than a dream. In the downhill, Caroline likely had a medal-winning run going but crashed in the bottom half. The combined, her strongest event, was next, but again she fell in the slalom portion, putting her 17 seconds (roughly the equivalent of 10 years in skiing) behind the leaders. She still had one more chance in the Super-G. But five gates in she went down again. An Olympic dream—over.

When I spoke with Caroline about a month after the Olympics for *Sports Spectrum's* weekly radio program, she said, "It was tough, and I questioned a lot of things. But you have to have faith that in the long run, God's plan is going to be way better. I just need to keep trusting the Lord and submersing myself in the Word and in prayer so I can continue to draw strength from Him even in some pretty big turmoil."

SPORTS NOTE: Caroline began skiing at age 2 while living in Switzerland.

FROM THE PLAYBOOK: Read Job 1.

Have you experienced a major disappointment recently? Don't neglect spending regular time reading the Bible and praying. Caroline found help reading the Old Testament book of Job. "He must really have wondered what was going on too!" she observed. You may find help there as well.

—BRIAN HETTINGA

GAME PLAN: Make it a point to reach out to someone you know who has experienced a serious setback recently. Sincerely ask how he or she is doing and really listen. If you get the chance, let your friend know how God's Word has encouraged you during a disappointing time.

FEBRUARY 1

WHAT'S IN A NAME?

POINT OF EMPHASIS:
God's names

"I have called you by your name." ISAIAH 43:1 NKJV

Big Mac. Pistol Pete. Iron Mike. The Golden Bear. The Big Unit. The Rocket. The Admiral. The Mailman.

It's a part of our culture to nickname our favorite athletes. We like to give them special names that refer to their unique abilities or their extraordinary achievements, names that describe their stature or their personality.

Believe it or not, men and women in Bible times were named the same way! Esau means "red" or "hairy." Moses means "to draw out" (Pharaoh's daughter *drew him out* of the bulrushes). Often when someone had a special encounter with God, He gave that person a new name to reflect the change in his or her character or purpose. Abram, "exalted father," became Abraham, "father of many nations." His wife Sarai became Sarah, "princess." Jacob, "the deceiver," became Israel, "prince of God." Simon became Peter, "the rock."

The Bible gives us many different names that describe the attributes (characteristics) of God. Here are just a few: the Almighty, the Creator, Everlasting Father, Prince of Peace, Righteous Judge, the Holy One.

The Bible also tells us that one day God will give each one of us a special name—a secret name—that no one else knows. It's just between Him and us (Revelation 2:17). At that time, He will also write His own name upon us (Revelation 3:12).

But God has given the most precious name to His Son, Jesus Christ, "that at the name of Jesus every knee should bow, in heaven and on earth and under the earth, and every tongue confess that Jesus Christ is Lord, to the glory of God the Father" (Philippians 2:9–11).

That's the Name above all names!

—CHRISTIN DITCHFIELD

SPORTS NOTE:
Key to nicknames: Mark McGwire, Pete Maravich, Mike Ditka, Jack Nicklaus, Randy Johnson, Roger Clemens, David Robinson, Karl Malone.

FROM THE PLAYBOOK:
Read Isaiah 9:6; Revelation 19:16; 22:13,16.

GAME PLAN: Take a minute to jot down all of the Bible names for God that you can think of. Using your list, praise God for all the wonderful things He is.

TELL IT LIKE IT IS

POINT OF EMPHASIS:
God is the Greatest

"Jesus answered, 'I am the way.'" JOHN 14:6

Muhammad Ali is arguably the most famous boxer ever to be crowned the heavyweight champion of the world. We marveled at his combination of finesse and power. And few of us will forget his antics outside of the ring.

Ali, a deeply religious man, explained in a *Reader's Digest* interview what his faith means to him.

"It means a ticket to heaven. One day we're all going to die, and God's going to judge us, our good and bad deeds. If the bad outweighs the good, you go to hell. If the good outweighs the bad, you go to heaven."

While many of Ali's jabs hit their mark, his explanation of how to get to heaven is way off.

The God of the Bible is going to judge all of us one day, that part is true. But the good that we've done will *not* wipe out our bad thoughts and deeds. We can't possibly do enough good works to compensate for our sins. The truth is that God would declare every last one of us guilty and worthy of eternal punishment if it weren't for the sacrificial death of Jesus Christ.

Jesus Christ is the *only* ticket to heaven. We can't do a thing to resolve our sin problem, except put ourselves at the mercy of God and believe that Jesus' death KO's the penalty of our sin. It is only because of Jesus' sacrifice that God can look at those of us who have accepted that sacrifice and see us as redeemed sinners who have the righteousness of Christ (Romans 3:22).

Whether we're "The Greatest" or just a regular Joe—that's the way it is.

—JEFF OLSON

SPORTS NOTE: Muhammad Ali's birth name was Cassius Clay.

FROM THE PLAYBOOK: Read John 14:1–6.

 GAME PLAN: Write out on a sheet of paper how you would explain the way a person can go to heaven.

WHY NOT BE CONTENT?

POINT OF EMPHASIS:
Contentment

*"I know what it is to be in need, and I know what it is to have plenty.
I have learned the secret of being content in any and every situation."*
PHILIPPIANS 4:12

I often think of what one of the Dallas Cowboys said after winning Super Bowl XXX. As he sat in the locker room an hour after the game, he asked, "Now, who do we get to play next?"

That statement brings out a truth we all can easily recognize: Even our most magnificent achievements seldom bring total satisfaction and contentment. Do you have a problem with contentment? Join the team.

The famous preacher from years past, Charles Spurgeon, said, "Now, contentment is one of the flowers of heaven, and if we would have it, it must be cultivated. It will not grow in us by nature; it is the new nature alone that can produce it, and even then we must be specially careful and watchful that we maintain and cultivate the grace which God has sown in it." In other words, we gain contentment when we begin our relationship with Christ, but it is something we have to continue to work at to maintain.

In his letter to the people at Philippi, Paul said, "I have learned to be content whatever the circumstances." Clearly, there had been a time when he didn't know how to be content. However, Paul learned the secret to contentment in this life, which is found in Philippians 4:13: "I can do everything through him who gives me strength."

When we rely on the strength of God and shower Him with thanksgiving for the blessings we do have, that's when the peace of contentment will flow in our hearts. God has put us right where we are for a reason, so it is futile to dwell on the past or worry about the future.

We each need to let God work in us and use us right where we are today. We must let the peace of God bring us the contentment we long for.

—CASEY SHAW, PRO BASKETBALL PLAYER

SPORTS NOTE:
Casey's father-in-law is the longtime hoops coach at Valparaiso University.

FROM THE PLAYBOOK:
Read Philippians 4:10–13.

GAME PLAN: What circumstance or situation is causing you to feel discontent? How can God's strength help you with that?

A STRATEGY OF PATIENCE

POINT OF EMPHASIS:
Patience

"Trust in the Lord, and do good . . . and wait patiently for him."
PSALM 37:3,7

How many times have you heard a coach yell out impatiently, "Be patient! You're too anxious!"

It's so hard to wait for things to develop on the basketball court or on the soccer pitch. We want things to happen right now!

One person who knew about patience and who knew how to teach it to his players was John Wooden, legendary coach of UCLA basketball in the 1960s and 1970s. In his landmark book *They Call Me Coach*, Wooden talked about the value of patience in sports. "In game play," he wrote, "it has always been my philosophy that patience will win out. By that, I mean patience to follow our game plan. If we do believe in it, we will wear the opposition down and will get to them. If we break away from our style, however, and play their style, we're in trouble."

Wooden, a Christian gentleman who earned everyone's respect for his demeanor, was on to something that goes beyond basketball. Patience in life is even more vital than it is in hoops—especially for those who want to live for God.

Look at what Psalm 37 says. There God is saying, in effect, "Do what's right and trust Me. Regardless of how badly you may seem to be losing, just do My will and leave the outcome to Me. I'll make sure that eventually you'll be the winner."

Follow the strategy of patience. Wait on God's direction. It's a strategy that will not just keep us from beating ourselves; it will lead to victory!

—MART DE HAAN

SPORTS NOTE:
John Wooden won 664 games and lost just 162 as an NCAA coach.

FROM THE PLAYBOOK:
Read Psalm 37:1–11.

GAME PLAN: On a scale of 1 to 10, how would you rate yourself in the area of patience? What are two things you're waiting for God to do in your life right now? How can you learn to be patient?

SUPER SUNDAY BECOMES SUPER SON-DAY

POINT OF EMPHASIS:
True worship

"Worship the Lord with gladness; come before him with joyful songs." PSALM 100:2

As we prepared for Super Bowl XXXV, I was asked by a reporter to write a daily Super Bowl diary. It gave me a chance to reflect on this huge game.

For instance, as I got ready for the biggest game of my career, I found that I spent most of my time on my knees and not on my cleats. I felt that I had to surrender my insufficient strength and ask God to arm me with strength for the battle before me (Psalm 18:39).

Over the years I've been asked many times, "How can you play football on Sunday?" It was no different as we got ready for the Super Bowl. My answer has always been this: True worship is envisioning yourself at the throne of God, and it is not confined to the place you might be. The football field becomes my place of worship on Sunday as I give God the glory after each field goal attempt—make or miss.

Right before we took the field for the Super Bowl, I had the privilege of sharing in worship with many believers on my team. As Trent Dilfer led us in prayer, we looked into one another's eyes and truly had confidence. With many of us having our eyes focused on Christ, we worshiped and then went to battle unified.

Few people will ever experience the thrill of playing in and winning a Super Bowl—but we all have the opportunity and privilege to worship God at His throne anytime and anywhere.

We also have the opportunity to join Him in victory over the biggest battle ever—the battle for lost souls.

—MATT STOVER, NFL KICKER

SPORTS NOTE:
Between 1991 and 2004, Stover made 350 field goals and 431 extra points for the Browns and Ravens.

FROM THE PLAYBOOK:
Read John 4:21–24.

GAME PLAN: Where is the best place for you to worship God? Whom do you enjoy worshiping with?

DON'T JUST SIT THERE!

POINT OF EMPHASIS:
Doers of the Word

"Faith without deeds is dead." JAMES 2:26

I'm not an exercise nut. I'll probably never own anything produced by Nordic Trac. I jog once in a while, but I don't really get a kick out of it. And I do push-ups and sit-ups only when my mirror tells me I must.

I do love to play basketball. Full-court, all-out, fast-breaking style. But that's not exercise. That's just flat-out fun.

So, I'm not here to pump you up like some guy with biceps to burn. That's not why I'm telling you about a recent American Medical Association survey.

The AMA found America's teenagers to be in the worst physical shape ever. More than half of all young women and a quarter of all young men are unable to do a single pull-up, the study showed. Fifty percent of the females and 30 percent of the males were not able to run a mile in less than 10 minutes.

To fix the problem, Tom McMillen, co-chair of The President's Council on Physical Fitness from 1993 to 1997 and a former NBA player, suggested this: "Don't Spectate, Recreate!" In other words, get off the couch and into the action.

I wonder what the stats are for spiritual exercise? I wonder if there's a problem among people who spend a lot of time in pews but little time exercising their faith.

James put it like this: "Do not merely listen to the word and so deceive yourselves. Do what it says" (James 1:22). He also said, "What good is it, my brothers, if a man claims to have faith but has no deeds?" (2:14).

The Christian life is a call to action. Are you getting your spiritual exercise?

—DAVE BRANON

SPORTS NOTE: Tom McMillen scored 5,914 points during his 11 years in the NBA.

FROM THE PLAYBOOK: Read James 2:14–26.

 GAME PLAN: Today I will exercise my faith by doing these two things:

THE BEAUTIFUL GAME

POINT OF EMPHASIS:
Pleasing God

"There is no other name under heaven given to men by which we must be saved." ACTS 4:12

Which sport is best? Which is worst?

ESPN's Tony Kornheiser may speak for many Americans when he bashes soccer, but he certainly doesn't speak for all of us. I have an American friend who is quick to defend what Pele called "the beautiful game."

"Americans don't appreciate the tactical nature of soccer," he says. "Soccer is much more than scoring. A single pass can be beautiful. There's no artistry in instant gratification."

SPORTS NOTE:
Pele, whose given name was Edson Arantes do Nascimento, was the IOC Player of the Century for the 1900s.

FROM THE PLAYBOOK:
Read John 14:5–14.

Then there's baseball. My wife can't understand why I actually *want* the pitcher to hold the runner on first. She just thinks it slows down what she finds to be an already too-slow game. She prefers hockey.

The point is that we each have different tastes and preferences. And each game can be a favorite to numbers of people.

Many people feel that way about religion—that it's okay to select whichever one best suits your style.

But Jesus was emphatic in saying that you can't pick and choose religions. He knew that a fallen human race could never measure up to God's standard of perfect holiness. That's why He said, "I am the way and the truth and the life. No one comes to the Father except through me" (John 14:6).

The only way to please God is to give your heart to His Son, Jesus. He died for you, paying the penalty for your sin. And He grants eternal life to anyone who will accept Him (John 3:16).

When it comes to which sport is the beautiful game, take your pick. But when it comes to pleasing God, we can only choose the Beautiful Name.

—TIM GUSTAFSON

GAME PLAN: How do you know you truly belong to God? Read John 14:15. What (or who) helps you obey God's commands (John 14:16–17)?

WORTH WATCHING

POINT OF EMPHASIS:
Witnessing

"Say 'No' to ungodliness and worldly passions." TITUS 2:12

You would think a bunch of hard-driving hockey players wouldn't fear someone as non-threatening as a Christian. But that wasn't the case with the National Hockey League team the Washington Capitals many years ago when they acquired right-winger Jean Pronovost from the Atlanta Flames.

As soon as Pronovost joined the team, the players were warned: "Keep an eye on the new guy." He was a Christian, and to some folks in hockey, that means dangerous.

Two teammates who watched Pronovost closely were up-and-coming NHL stars Mike Gartner (who had recently moved over from the World Hockey Association) and Ryan Walter (who was in his third year in the league). As Mike and Ryan observed his life, they saw something they liked—his Christian testimony.

Soon Mike and Ryan were attending Bible studies with Jean. And in time both players trusted Jesus Christ as Savior through Pronovost's influence. Still today, though retired from the NHL, Gartner and Walter continue to witness about their faith.

SPORTS NOTE:
Jean Pronovost played in the NHL All-Star Game each season from 1975 through 1978.

FROM THE PLAYBOOK:
Read Titus 2.

What is it about genuine Christians that some people find irresistible? Paul talked about those inviting qualities in his letter to Titus. He mentioned traits like sober-mindedness (2:6), good works, integrity, reverence (v. 7), and a life that no one can speak evil of (v. 8).

If you are a Christian, does that describe you? Others are keeping an eye on you. They want to know if there's anything genuine about this idea of being a follower of Jesus.

Let's heed Paul's advice and make sure our lives are worth watching.

—DAVE BRANON

GAME PLAN: What are three characteristics you have that might attract others to Christ? Are there any negative characteristics that you might want to eliminate?

IF THEY COULD SEE ME NOW

POINT OF EMPHASIS:
God's special plans

"'Isn't he the man who raised havoc in Jerusalem?'" ACTS 9:21

In 1983, Michael Jordan had already won the NCAA basketball championship at North Carolina, was a first-team All-American, and was headed for the Olympics. That same year, a skinny, 6' 2" kid from Hamburg, Arkansas, graduated from high school with no future in basketball. In fact, his role with the University of Central Arkansas basketball team was manager. His name was Scottie Pippen.

As you know—unless you absolutely hate basketball or have been off on a work-study program to Mongolia for a couple of decades—Scottie Pippen and Michael Jordan teamed up to make one of the greatest twosomes in basketball history, winning six championships during their years with the Chicago Bulls. It didn't look like it would be possible in 1983, but Pippen became one of the best basketball players in the world.

The world is full of Scottie Pippens—people who look like they won't amount to much.

Maybe you feel that way about yourself. Perhaps you think you've failed in your career pursuits or you've not become as dedicated a Christian as you wanted to be. You figure you'll never amount to anything worthwhile. Well, don't quit. God has something special He wants to do with your life.

If we had known Saul of Tarsus before a blinding light and a voice from heaven turned his life around, we wouldn't have had much good to say about him. But what a change took place when he turned his life over to God!

What you are right now is not what you will always be. Like Saul, ask God, "What shall I do, Lord?" (Acts 22:10). Then watch things happen.

—DAVE BRANON

SPORTS NOTE:
Scottie Pippen retired at the end of the 2004 season—his 17th in the NBA. He scored 18,940 points.

FROM THE PLAYBOOK:
Read Acts 9:1–20.

GAME PLAN: On a scale of 1 to 5 (5 being the highest), have I reached the potential God gave me? What two goals should I aim for in the next few weeks?

JOY IN THE JOURNEY

POINT OF EMPHASIS:
Joyfulness

"God intended it for good." GENESIS 50:20

World-class cyclist Jacqui Lockwood says her life was changed forever in February 1997. That's when doctors discovered a grapefruit-size tumor on her heart. The diagnosis: non-Hodgkins lymphoma. As Lockwood tells it, she went from "world-class to couch-class in one week's time!" She faced months of chemotherapy and an uncertain future. It should have been devastating. But it wasn't.

"The more often I talk about it and look back on it, the more I realize how special it was," says Jacqui.

Special?

"I just had a real peace about it, that for some reason it was something I needed to go through," Jacqui explains. She was overwhelmed by the prayer support and encouragement she received from her church family and the members of her Bible-study group. Even her son's classmates and their families gathered for prayer on Jacqui's behalf. Having been a Christian for just a short time, this outpouring of love and concern was a new experience for her.

SPORTS NOTE:
When she is not cycling, Jacqui is a spine, hand, and foot specialist at Arizona State University in the Sports Medicine Department.

FROM THE PLAYBOOK:
Read James 1:2–4, 12.

"It was also a wonderful witnessing opportunity," Lockwood says. As she underwent chemotherapy, Jacqui freely shared her faith with the other patients who were "facing death head-on."

Jacqui's experience with cancer led her to re-evaluate her priorities, especially in regard to her sport. "I learned that God gives, and He can take away. On the big tandem of life, God's the captain—I'm just the stoker! Now, whenever I race, I do it for His glory."

Her bout with cancer could have been a tragic experience. But Jacqui chose to trust God—for good or for bad. She found joy in a journey that brought her to a deeper relationship with Him.

—CHRISTIN DITCHFIELD

GAME PLAN: Take a few moments to think about the tough times you've experienced in your own life. Write down what you've learned and how you've grown through those times.

JESUS AND THE WOMAN

POINT OF EMPHASIS:
The value of women

"There is neither . . . male nor female. For you are all one in Christ."
GALATIANS 3:28

Women athletes have always faced challenges when pursuing athletic goals. Many challenges have been brought on by a lack of opportunity, by clear opposition, and by an ignorance of their abilities. As a child, I was initially discouraged from pursuing my athletic dreams because of comparison to my male counterparts and because of appearances. Fortunately, things were beginning to change, and eventually women's sports were encouraged and the opportunities became limitless.

SPORTS NOTE:
LaVonna is an elementary school teacher in California.

Women during the time of Jesus faced some negative attitudes as well. Women were viewed as lesser citizens and often treated with contempt and disrespect. How uncomfortable and shocking it must have been for the men in Jesus' day, then, when He lifted women from the agony of degradation and servitude to the joy of fellowship with Him.

FROM THE PLAYBOOK:
Read the entire story of the Samaritan woman in John 4:1–26.

This is clearly demonstrated by the act of love He showed to the woman at the well. Being a Samaritan was enough to make her despised by the Jews, but being a woman further diminished her worth. Praise God that our loving Savior shared with her the spiritual water that would forever quench her thirst! He led her to the one true God—regardless of the barriers presented by society.

We must strive to do the same with people in our sphere of influence. Are you willing to come out of your comfort zone and make a difference in someone's life—especially someone society does not consider valuable?

—LaVonna Martin-Floreal, Olympic silver medalist, track

GAME PLAN: Can you think of anyone in your sphere of influence who is somehow looked down on by others? What can you do to make that person feel the love of Christ as the Savior did for the woman at the well?

NOT MY PLANS, BUT HIS

POINT OF EMPHASIS:
God's plans

"Now to him who is able to do immeasurably more than all we ask or imagine." EPHESIANS 3:20

A major fear for most athletes is injury. It is crucial for our bodies to be healthy. In February 2003, I faced this fear head on when I severely injured my ankle during a game. After sitting out for several weeks, followed by an unsuccessful attempt at returning to play, I was eventually sent for an MRI. The results were startling. A severely bruised anklebone, a small bone chip, and several other old injuries had combined to produce the extreme pain I was experiencing. The recommended solution was major surgery.

This was not in my plans. In two months I was to compete in the Pan American Games, in three months the Olympic qualifications, and I was in the middle of signing my third professional contract. I had no time for surgery and six months of rehabilitation.

Thankfully, God had something else planned. From the day I injured my ankle I prayed that God would heal me. I didn't know God's will for this specific situation, but I rested in the promise that He is able to do immeasurably more than I could ask or imagine. I waited on Him, and although there was no spontaneous, dramatic healing, God definitely answered my prayer.

Despite the doctor's prognosis, I played in both competitions, and to this day I am able to play pain-free. No surgery was needed, because I had the best doctor of all—a heavenly Healer.

When we think things are impossible, that is when God takes over.

— LEIGHANN REIMER, PRO BASKETBALL PLAYER

SPORTS NOTE:
Leighann and her husband Chad had their first child in May 2005. She played pro basketball in Europe before that.

FROM THE PLAYBOOK:
Read James 5:13–18.

GAME PLAN: What situation do you face today that is beyond your control? Is there anything holding you back from giving it to God in faith—trusting that whichever way He handles your situation, it is best. What can you do while you wait on His answer?

BEARING YOUR CROSS

POINT OF EMPHASIS:
Bear your cross

"If anyone would come after me, he must . . . take up his cross and follow me." MATTHEW 16:24

As Christians, many times we are called upon to bear our cross; to endure pain and suffering in the midst of our circumstances.

Just because we try to live according to the Spirit and not according to the flesh (Galatians 5:16–26), we are sometimes talked about, ridiculed, judged, lied about, misunderstood, and a host of other discouraging things. It is during these times that we might feel the desire to abandon God's will and begin implementing our own will. We feel "the cross" is too difficult to bear (1 Corinthians 10:13).

SPORTS NOTE:
As a prepster, Kedra played for Lutheran Northern High School in Houston, Texas.

FROM THE PLAYBOOK:
Read Matthew 16:24–28 and Mark 14:32–42.

We grow weary in doing good things, we stop listening to the Holy Spirit, and we begin listening to our own flesh. The Spirit says, "Endure," but the flesh says, "Walk away! You don't have to take this."

The Spirit says, "Be patient," but the flesh says, "I want it now." The Spirit says, "Think of those who need to hear My Word," but the flesh says, "Think of yourself."

The Spirit and our flesh are in constant battle for control of our life (Galatians 5:17–18), and if we are not connected to God through fellowship in the Spirit, we allow our flesh to lead us away from God (John 15:6).

It is through you that some may come to know Christ. As you are called to "bear your cross," put God before self, and allow Him to use you as a vessel to lead as many people as possible to Jesus.

—KEDRA HOLLAND-CORN, PRO BASKETBALL PLAYER

GAME PLAN: What is my response to the idea of bearing a cross? What did Jesus mean when He spoke the words of Matthew 16:24?

LOVE, TOMMY, AND JESUS

POINT OF EMPHASIS:
Marriage

"There is no fear in love. But perfect love drives out fear."
1 JOHN 4:18

I met Tommy Amico at a softball tournament in July 1997.

Right away I liked the qualities I saw in him. But Tommy lived in South Carolina, and I lived in Arizona. So, at the beginning, we started a friendship on the phone. Through our conversations, I was able to share God's plan of salvation with him. After attending an Athletes In Action meeting at the University of South Carolina, he met with an AIA staff member, and Tommy trusted Christ as Savior.

Through my relationship with Tommy, God has showed me that all things are possible if we allow Him to lead us and if it is according to His will. After seeing each other for less than two months total, Tommy and I were married in January 1999. On our wedding day, I felt the love that the Bible speaks about, but I have also learned through marriage that it takes work and a daily commitment to love each other.

I love my husband very much, but if I want to talk about love in the greatest sense, I have to talk about God.

God's love is the greatest. For instance, with God in our lives, we never have to worry about earning His love—or most important, losing His love. God is the true giver of unconditional love.

John tells us "God is love. Whoever lives in love lives in God, and God in him . . . There is no fear in love. But perfect love drives out fear" (1 John 4:16,18).

When I talk to people who are longing for the perfect relationship, I don't talk about Tommy and me, as happy as we are. I tell them that I know someone who will never let them down and will never stop loving them. That person is Jesus Christ, and He's waiting for us with open arms.

—LEAH O'BRIEN-AMICO, OLYMPIC GOLD MEDALIST, SOFTBALL

SPORTS NOTE:
Leah won gold medals in 1996, 2000, and 2004 while playing for the United States.

FROM THE PLAYBOOK:
Read 1 John 4.

GAME PLAN: Have you experienced God's love through Jesus Christ? If not, trust Jesus today.

IN AN INSTANT

POINT OF EMPHASIS:
Ready to meet God

"No one knows what is coming." ECCLESIASTES 10:14

Life is unpredictable. It can change in a moment. The tragic death of legendary NASCAR driver Dale Earnhardt Sr. is a harsh reminder of how life can forever change in an instant.

Think about it. Merely seconds before his untimely death in the 2001 Daytona 500, the "Terminator" listened to his crew chief screaming in his headset that his teammate Michael Waltrip and his son Dale Jr. had first and second place locked up. What a thrilling and proud moment that must have been for him. Then Earnhardt Sr.'s black No. 3 Monte Carlo slammed into turn No. 3—sending him into eternity.

Without warning, life can drastically change. What is true one moment can be completely different the next. The unpredictability of life is a powerful reason we shouldn't put off taking care of any important unfinished business.

While we may not know for sure where Dale Sr. will spend the rest of eternity, you can know about your own eternal fate. As you read this article, if you don't know for certain where you stand with God, talk about it with a Christian friend or a pastor.

If you are a believer with some unfinished business between you and another person, take care of it. If you have an unsaved friend with whom you haven't shared the gospel, begin praying and thinking of how you might do that.

Don't put important matters off any longer. Don't assume that you have plenty of time. You never know when life will permanently change—in an instant.

—JEFF OLSON

SPORTS NOTE:
Partially because of Earnhardt's death, NASCAR began using a new safety harness called the HANS system.

FROM THE PLAYBOOK:
Read James 4:13–17.

GAME PLAN: Make a list of your important unfinished business and set a goal to take care of each item on your list.

PUTTING FIRST THINGS FIRST

POINT OF EMPHASIS:
Setting priorities

"Seek first his kingdom and his righteousness, and all these things will be given to you." MATTHEW 6:33

I learned the importance of putting God first in my life fairly early in my spiritual journey.

During my senior year at the University of South Carolina, my focus in life started turning to "me." I had finished my junior year as a first-team All-American and SEC Player of the Year in golf, and I was looking forward to my senior year as being just as successful. I had big plans, and I thought I had everything mapped out for a successful year. Unfortunately, as I got more absorbed in all the things I needed to get accomplished, I forgot about the importance of keeping my daily time with the Lord.

As my senior year wore on, I completely neglected my quiet times with God, and I became discontented with my life. It wasn't that I totally forgot about God or denied being a Christian. I still went to church and hung around Christian friends. What I didn't do was spend the necessary one-on-one time with God to keep my focus on what God wanted me to do.

I was fortunate, however, to have close friends to remind me about keeping God first. After shifting my focus back to God, the things of life became less significant in the bigger frame of things. With my perspectives back in order, I was able to finish my senior year with the right mindset and place sixth in the NCAA Division I national championships.

It is not that God doesn't want us to set high goals or become successful; He does. But first, He wants to be involved with our lives, and He wants us to include Him in our successes—then He can rightfully get the glory.

—SIEW AI LIM, LPGA GOLFER

SPORTS NOTE: Siew Ai Lim finished the 2004 season Number 63 on the LPGA money list—up from 146 in 2003.

FROM THE PLAYBOOK: Read Numbers 18:8–29.

GAME PLAN: What has been sneaking its way to No. 1 in your life, shoving your relationship with God down the list? What can you do today and this week to make sure things get put back in place?

MEETING MICHAEL

POINT OF EMPHASIS:
Knowing Jesus

"But when he, the Spirit of truth, comes, he will guide you into all truth." JOHN 16:13

Several years ago, I met Michael Jordan through a prison ministry. At the time, he was a college student, and he was a guest speaker at the event.

A few years later, I was the half-time entertainment for the Chicago Bulls, and I chatted with Michael briefly several times. He would share a few personal things with me because I had known him when he was a college student, and he asked me if I was still involved with the prison ministry. That was special. I realized he still knew who I was. He knew me.

SPORTS NOTE:
You can find out about Tanya and other performing Creviers at www.crevierministries.org.

FROM THE PLAYBOOK:
Read John 3.

Fans love to know important things about their favorite athletes. When they do that, they know about them, but they don't necessarily know them like I know Michael. That was much more meaningful than just knowing about him.

On a grander scale, for 23 years of my life as a faithful church attender, I knew all about God and what Jesus had done on the cross. I knew the facts about Jesus, but I didn't know Him on a personal level. Until I trusted Him as Savior, I just knew about Him. I didn't know that once His Holy Spirit came to dwell in my own heart He would guide me in such a personal way. The Bible says in John 16:13 that the Spirit will guide you into all truth.

Now that I know Jesus, I no longer wait for a chance to see Him at a church meeting like I used to. Jesus lives inside me in the person of His Holy Spirit. I have a relationship with Him on a personal level every day of my life.

What a difference there is between knowing Jesus and knowing about Him!

—TANYA CREVIER, BASKETBALL SHOWPERSON

GAME PLAN: Think seriously about this question: Do you know Jesus in a personal way? Have you trusted Him as Savior?

THANKS FOR THE FREE GIFT

POINT OF EMPHASIS:
Putting God first

"For it is by grace you have been saved, through faith."
EPHESIANS 2:8,9

Because of the nature of sports, athletes are put under a spotlight. They perform for an audience, and they provide entertainment for society. This is what entices many to become the best at their sport. Those people want to reach stardom, and fame becomes the goal.

I by no means reached stardom in my basketball career at the University of California at Santa Barbara, but playing at the college level on a successful basketball team gave me some mild glimpses of what that success entails. Sure, it was fun to some degree, but it was also very empty. As long as we were winning and playing well, many loved us. However, as soon as we played below expectations or began losing, all our "friends" were nowhere to be found. There was a clear message to be learned: Performance is everything. In order to be liked, we had to perform well; otherwise, the stands would be empty.

It is because of this lesson that I am so acutely aware of God and His unconditional love for me. He couldn't care less if I play well or if we win the ballgame. His love for me is not based on works but on the fact that I am His child through faith in Jesus Christ. I have not done anything to receive it; it is His free gift to me, undeserved and unearned.

As a child of God I want to make my relationship with Him the No. 1 priority in my life. That's why I strive to play for an audience of one, to be aware of His presence at all times, and to desire His love and adoration only. I hope that is your goal as well.

—ERIN BUESCHER, WNBA GUARD

SPORTS NOTE:
After sitting out a couple of seasons, Erin re-entered the WNBA in 2005, playing for the Sacramento Monarchs.

FROM THE PLAYBOOK:
Read Ephesians 2.

GAME PLAN: What is the No. 1 priority in your life? If it is your relationship with God, how do you demonstrate it—not to others, but to God?

AN ATHLETE ANSWERS THE CALL

POINT OF EMPHASIS:
Strength from faith

"Abraham . . . was strengthened in his faith and gave glory to God." ROMANS 4:18–20

Catriona LeMay Doan. You say those three words in Canada, and you are sure to bring a smile to any sports fan. Catriona has wowed Canadians with her Olympic gold-medal performances in speed skating.

Interestingly, it was at the Olympics that she first realized she needed to be saved. Here's how it happened.

After Lillehammer, she saw a simple sign with the words "Athletes In Action" and a phone number. "I don't know now why I called," Catriona says with a laugh. "I guess I thought, 'I'm an athlete,' and I thought it applied to me."

Soon afterward, Catriona met with AIA staff person Harold Cooper, a friendly, fatherly man who has since become her spiritual mentor.

"Harold went through the gospel with me, but it was sort of too much all at once," the twenty-eight-year-old remembers. "He asked me if I wanted to become a Christian, and I was like, 'Well, maybe I will talk this over with [her husband] Bart first,' I was trying to postpone it. A few weeks later, though, I decided that it was the choice I wanted to make."

Since she gave her life to Christ in the summer of 1994, Catriona has established herself as the world's top female sprinter.

In all her personal victories and defeats she tries to integrate her faith with her emotions.

"My faith is a comfort, and it gives me a different reason to be doing the sport."

How does your faith give you strength? There can be no better source of power and might than to have a heart sold out to God.

—LORILEE CRAKER

SPORTS NOTE:
Catriona LeMay Doan is Leighann Reimer's (February 12) cousin.

FROM THE PLAYBOOK:
Read Romans 4.

GAME PLAN: Since I came to faith in Christ, what remarkable things have I done that I know I wouldn't have done without God's help? Make a list of five ways your faith helps you in your everyday life.

THE ENCOURAGER

POINT OF EMPHASIS:
God's encouragement

"Consider it pure joy, my brothers, whenever you face trials of many kinds." JAMES 1:2–4

I had one of the most disappointing years of my career in 2003. I had made four cuts in 14 tournaments, and for the first time in my golf career, I was in the red financially.

Times like that make me question if I need to stay the course as an LPGA player. I wondered if all the hard work I had done over the years was really working, or if I had just hit my peak. Thoughts of giving up were there.

Fortunately for me, I had a tremendous coach who continued to encourage me to keep persevering. He saw my potential and knew that I had so much more inside of me to become one of the top players on Tour. His encouragement and my continued perseverance in working on my game paid off as I had one of my most successful seasons on the LPGA Tour in 2004.

Looking back, I see how that parallels with my spiritual life. There are times when I feel like I'm getting nowhere in my spiritual journey, and I feel beaten down. I wonder if the difficulties I face in life are worth the effort I'm putting in as a Christian and a follower of Christ.

When we feel that way, the good news is that all of us as followers of Christ have an Encourager, the Holy Spirit. He's the still, quiet voice that tells us to keep going. He's the one who says we have so much more to achieve if only we stay the course. Listen to the Encourager. Persevere and keep pressing on to the finish line.

—SIEW AI LIM, LPGA GOLFER

SPORTS NOTE:
Siew Ai began 2003 by finishing second in the Malaysian Ladies Open in her homeland.

FROM THE PLAYBOOK:
Memorize Romans 15:13.

GAME PLAN: What is discouraging me right now? How much time have I spent talking to the Lord about it—and then listening to the Holy Spirit's encouraging guidance?

FINDING TRUE FULFILLMENT

POINT OF EMPHASIS:
Fulfillment in Jesus

"I consider everything a loss compared to . . . knowing Christ."
PHILIPPIANS 3:8

Many professional athletes look like they have everything—money, popularity, excitement, and security. What I've noticed through several years of observing athletes up close is that they often experience deep internal struggles. Loneliness creeps in when they spend countless nights on the road. And they face a tremendous amount of pressure to perform day after day.

Olympic silver medalist Rosalynn Sumners realizes how fortunate she was, as a figure skater, to turn pro and make a living with skating following her amateur career. But even in the midst of the glamour, she had times when she longed for circumstances to be different. Rosalynn found that money and fame didn't give her the security and sense of purpose she longed for. She found that hard to explain, even to her closest friends, because people didn't feel sorry for her when they realized how much money she made as a pro. Rosalynn didn't want sympathy, though. She simply wanted to meet the needs that go deeper than her Olympic experiences and her career—the basic needs we all have.

Several years ago she found what was missing—a personal relationship with Jesus Christ. At that point she asked the Lord to take the reins of her life. Rosalynn found that Jesus Christ is the only person she can be completely vulnerable and raw and honest with.

God alone provides ultimate fulfillment. Although you will always wrestle with various trials and times of loneliness in life, if you have put your trust in Jesus Christ, you have a friend who is with you no matter what your situation. He alone can give true fulfillment.

—ROXANNE ROBBINS

SPORTS NOTE:
Rosalynn won a silver medal in 1984 at the Winter Olympic Games in Sarajevo.

FROM THE PLAYBOOK:
Read Philippians 3:1–14.

GAME PLAN: Do you consider everything else a loss compared to knowing Christ? What does this question mean to you? Think deeply about this and ask God to show you what you might be clinging to for fulfillment instead of Him.

DO YOU KNOW HIM?

POINT OF EMPHASIS:
Knowing Jesus

"[Jesus took] the very nature of a servant." PHILIPPIANS 2:7

It was a tragic scene at Daytona International Speedway.

The man who loved to race would never race again. His life was taken in a sport that literally rides on the edge.

But Dirk Piz knew the dangers of motorcycle racing before he strapped on his helmet that day. Dirk rode in the Buell Pro Thunder series and was killed just a few weeks after Dale Earnhardt died on the same track. Dirk's unfortunate accident happened because he tried to avoid another racer who crashed in front of him. His action cost him his life, but it saved the life of another racer.

Let's talk about another terrible scene. The place was Jerusalem. There a righteous Man was found guilty in a sham trial. His punishment was execution on a cross for something He never did. But that Man didn't try to stop the execution. He knew that in dying, He would make salvation possible for the entire human race.

Do you know His name? He died pursuing the passion He has for mankind.

I don't know if Dirk Piz knew Jesus. I don't know if you do either. But you need to. You need to meet this righteous Man. He gave His life for you.

None of us can hide from the fact that one day we'll die. We all have to decide if we accept or reject Jesus. What is your decision?

—DAN DEAL

SPORTS NOTE: Twenty-nine drivers have died racing at the Daytona International Speedway since 1959.

FROM THE PLAYBOOK: Read Philippians 2 or John 3.

 GAME PLAN: Before the checkered flag signals the end of your life's race, you need to be sure of something: where you'll go when you cross the finish line.

LIFE ON THE ROAD

POINT OF EMPHASIS:
Temptation

"It is God's will that you should be sanctified." I THESSALONIANS 4:3

When former All-Star guard Mark Price was still in the NBA, he knew he was in a battle—and not just for victories. He knew he was also in a battle for sexual purity. Pro athletes have a reputation for getting themselves involved in immoral behavior, and Price wanted to avoid those problems.

Mark's high moral standards and affection for his wife, Laura, mixed with his testimony as a Christian, helped him map out an out-of-town course that left no room for immoral detours. His personal plan might be a good guide for you if you travel or are in some other way faced with those temptations. Here's Mark's plan.

SPORTS NOTE:
Mark Price released a DVD in March 2005, designed to help shooters improve their shot. It was called *The Shooter's Touch*.

"You have to be careful when you're out on the road, because there are a lot of people who will try to jump on your bandwagon, so to speak. But I think that if you want to find trouble, you have to go looking for it, and I'm not the kind of person who does that.

"First, I don't even begin to play with fire. My philosophy is that if you play with fire you're going to get burned. So if anything is questionable in any way, I stay away from it.

FROM THE PLAYBOOK:
Read 1 Thessalonians 4:1–12.

"As a Christian, I think you have to keep your spiritual senses on the alert. Satan is going to attack you subtly. If you're not aware of what's going on, you're not going to see things coming.

"I try to get with some of the other Christian guys on the team and spend time with them. We encourage each other as much as we can."

That's a plan worth trying, don't you think?

—DAVE BRANON

GAME PLAN: When do temptations most often threaten to trip you up? Write down three things that you know you lose if you would give in to those temptations?

BEATING THE ODDS

POINT OF EMPHASIS:
Facing battles

"He worshiped God." JUDGES 7:15

As figure skater Paul Wylie prepared for the 1988 and 1992 Olympics, Gideon was his hero. Gideon, a judge in the Old Testament, faced a challenge—an army that outnumbered him many times over.

God asked Gideon to trust that he would win the battle based on God's strength and not Gideon's army's strength. Eventually Gideon wound up with 300 men to fight an army that was described in Judges 7:12 as being "thick as locusts."

Sometimes we can feel outnumbered. But maybe at those times it is God's way of saying, "Let me show you that I'm going to win the victory for you . . . this will increase your faith and the faith of the people that witness it."

Prior to the Olympics Paul Wylie tasted many bitter defeats. But God allowed him to skate his best when it truly counted. The silver medal Wylie won is an unprecedented, unrepeated feat. He was the only person in skating history to win an Olympic medal without also being a national champion. Wylie saw God work through his circumstances so that when he reached the victory at the end he was pre-pared to give God the glory. Instead of being independent from God, trying to do things for His glory but without His involvement, he tried to imitate his heroes like Gideon by look-ing to God for solutions.

What type of battle are you facing? Do you feel like the odds are stacked against you? Look to the example of Gideon. Trust in God's strength. As you see Him win victories, your faith will increase.

—ROXANNE ROBBINS

SPORTS NOTE: Paul Wylie continues to skate in exhibition skating shows.

FROM THE PLAYBOOK: Read Judges 7:1–25.

GAME PLAN: Journal about the biggest challenge you've ever faced. Consider what you learned and how your faith was affected as you did or didn't trust God in the process.

TOUGH QUESTIONS FOR THE ADMIRAL

POINT OF EMPHASIS:
Salvation

"Love the Lord your God with all your heart." Mark 12:30

In 1991 a pastor visited David Robinson in the San Antonio Spurs' locker room. He told David he wanted to talk to him about Jesus. That was okay with Robinson, for he "had some questions about this Christian stuff," he recalls. But when they got together, it was the pastor who asked the tough questions. He began by asking, "David, do you love God?"

"Yeah, sure," David replied, "Who doesn't?"

"Well," said the pastor, "God gave us His Word, the Bible, to show us about Himself, to teach us about who He is. Do you read it?"

"Well, not often," David admitted.

The pastor then asked: "How much time do you spend praying—talking to God? You say you love Him. Don't you enjoy talking with Him, spending time with Him?"

David had to confess he didn't pray very much.

The pastor's words challenged him. "It made me realize I really didn't love God. You can say all you want, but if your actions don't back it up, it means nothing. My heart just broke. I started crying and I said, 'God, I'm so sorry. I've been living like You aren't real. I know You are. I can't ignore You anymore. I want to learn about You, I want to know You, I want to love You.' I started reading my Bible and praying and spending time with Him, and my whole world opened up."

Is it time we asked ourselves some of those questions the pastor asked David Robinson?

—Christin Ditchfield

SPORTS NOTE:
After retiring from basketball, David Robinson began working with Pastor Max Lucado at Oak Hills Church in San Antonio.

FROM THE PLAYBOOK:
Read Psalm 119:105 –112.

GAME PLAN: Okay, the hard part. What are your answers to those questions? And what can be done about it if the answers aren't quite right?

PLANS FOR PAUL

POINT OF EMPHASIS:
Serving God

"I press on toward the goal." PHILIPPIANS 3:14

Paul Stankowski was sweating. He was pitted against three other young golfers for a match that would determine whether he would continue PGA Qualifying School. His goal was to make the Tour in 1994, and to do that he needed to be one of two guys in the foursome to top the others.

On the first hole, a player got a birdie. The other three, including Paul, did not. This left Paul and the other two players fighting for one remaining spot.

Paul persevered and won the next hole. The Tour was in view!

Several years later, Paul Stankowski still wonders what would have happened if he hadn't won that hole. He also ponders why he had success on that fateful day. "I don't know why," he says, "except that it is for now God's place for me. I'm not saying it's His will for me. His will is for me to serve Him wherever I am. Where I am right now is on the PGA Tour."

What about the plans God has for your life? Each new day brings opportunities for you to serve God wherever you are in your career and life.

Another Paul, the apostle, wrote, "Forgetting what is behind and straining toward what is ahead, I press on toward the goal to win the prize for which God has called me heavenward in Christ Jesus" (Philippians 3:13–14).

As you persevere this day, commit yourself to serving God with all your heart. Just like with Paul the putter and Paul the apostle, God has plans for you.

—TOM FELTEN

SPORTS NOTE: Paul Stankowski won the BellSouth Classic in 1996 and the United Airlines Hawaiian Open in 1997.

FROM THE PLAYBOOK: Read Philippians 3:4–14.

GAME PLAN: Write these words on a Post-it, "Forget the past. Seek God's plans!" and place it in a prominent place where you will see it often during the day.

THE BIBLE ON THE HALF-PIPE

POINT OF EMPHASIS:
Bible as guide

"Your word is a lamp to my feet." PSALM 119:105

For pro snowboarder Louie Fountain, God's Word is a lamp on a Cab 720. A light for his 520 Mute Grab Fakie. Without the Bible, life for Louie would be a little sketchy.

But it's not just for Louie. We all need the Bible whether we ride in the half-pipe for a living or whether we wouldn't know a half-pipe from a drainpipe.

Louie was interviewed by *TransWorld Snowboarding* magazine, and the writer asked him about being a Christian. "I try to use the Bible as a guideline for life," he said, "as a kind of owner's manual, and try my best to live that." Whether you snowride or not, you need to illuminate your way with Scripture. Otherwise your day begins in shadow and ends in darkness.

Something else Louie said in the interview was insightful. "My faith is most important to me. I'm not an especially outstanding snowboarder or anything. In the process of how I've gotten here, it's obvious that God put me where He wants me. He put the desire in my heart to snowboard, so I don't think it's too contradictory to my beliefs."

Two very simple but powerful principles come out of Louie Fountain's interview: 1. Use the Bible as your guide every day; it's your owner's manual. 2. Wherever God has you, have the faith to let Him use you where you are.

Let's learn from Louie.

—DAN DEAL

SPORTS NOTE:
Louie's grandfather was a crop duster, and his dad was an airplane pilot as well.

FROM THE PLAYBOOK:
Read Hebrews 4:12–16.

GAME PLAN: If you skate, snowboard, ski, rollerblade, ride BMX or do motocross, use the two principles Louie does to build a relationship with another ripper, rider, skater, or shredder. Then let God use that relationship for His purpose.

IT DOESN'T HURT TO ASK

POINT OF EMPHASIS:
Asking God

"The Lord is near to all who call on him." PSALM 145:18

Imagine having parents who make more than a million bucks a year. One pro football player I know took home more than $1.5 million in one season. If you were that man's son, you could ask for anything you wanted, and he could give it to you.

But he wouldn't.

You see, this player is a Christian, and he wants to be wise. If his son says, "Dad, I want a motorized car," the player can't say, "I can't afford it." He and his son both know he can. But he does place restrictions and guidelines on the requests his children make. He and his wife have to decide, based on the good of the child and the good of their family, which requests to grant and why.

It's a little like that with God. As the Master of the universe, He has everything at His disposal. Like a millionaire football player, He can't say, "I can't afford it." Yet He does put restrictions on our asking—for our own good. Look at some of them:

1. Be persistent (Luke 11:5–13).
2. Ask in faith, without doubting (James 1:6).
3. Ask for the right reasons (James 4:2–3).
4. Live righteously (James 5:16).
5. Accept any answer (2 Corinthians 12:7–10).
6. Pray with thankfulness (Philippians 4:6).

Prayer is not like ordering from a catalog. Prayer is talking to God one-to-one—conversing with Him as you would talk with a loving and caring father.

When you pray in the way God has designed, it doesn't hurt to ask.

—DAVE BRANON

SPORTS NOTE:
The average salary of a major league baseball player in 2004 was $2.4 million.

FROM THE PLAYBOOK:
Read Matthew 6:5–13.

 GAME PLAN: In the past week, what specific things have you talked to God about? Were your prayers mostly taken up with requests, praise, thanksgiving, or others' needs? Are your prayers unbalanced?

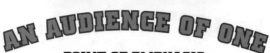

AN AUDIENCE OF ONE

POINT OF EMPHASIS:
Living for God

*"Whatever you do, work at it with all your heart,
as working for the Lord."* COLOSSIANS 3:23

The Bible tells us to "fix our eyes on Jesus, the author and perfecter of our faith" (Hebrews 12:2). This sometimes isn't as easy as it sounds.

There are a few things I have tried to do to keep my eyes on Jesus in a world filled with distractions, especially on the basketball court. One thing I do is draw a cross on my sneakers so I can always glance down to see where my true strength comes from. Another thing I sometimes do is find the brightest light in the gymnasium so I can always just look up to know that Jesus is right there with me. Finally, right before the jump ball at the beginning of the game, I walk to the center circle and with my foot I draw an invisible cross on the hardwood. This is my way of saying to the Lord, "Here I am to be used by You and for Your glory only." These serve as reminders to me that my heavenly Father is right there with me.

Christian author Os Guinness said, "I live before the Audience of One. Before others I have nothing to prove, nothing to gain, nothing to lose."

I try to live this truth out on the basketball court. Every time I step on the court, I tell myself that I am out there for one reason: to play for an Audience of One.

Whether it is in sports, school, or your job, I encourage you to live your life before an Audience of One. "Whatever you do, work at it with all your heart, as working for the Lord, not for men" (Colossians 3:23).

—CASEY SHAW, PRO BASKETBALL PLAYER

SPORTS NOTE:
Casey Shaw's wife, Dana, was an All-American basketball player at the University of Toledo.

FROM THE PLAYBOOK:
Read Colossians 3:15–24.

GAME PLAN: What are two reminders I can incorporate in my life each day to remind myself that I'm trying to please God?

TOUGH STUFF

POINT OF EMPHASIS:
Handling tough times

"Be joyful in hope, patient in affliction, faithful in prayer."
ROMANS 12:12

Playing NCAA Division I athletics is never a walk in the park. And when you play for a perennial power, it's downright tough. There's the constant pressure to win. There's the conflict between school and sports. There's the excessive attention you get from fans and the media.

When you throw an injury into all of this, it can become one maniacal mix. That's what happened to Jenny Evans, who starred as an outside hitter for the women's volleyball team at UCLA in the early 1990s.

She was forced to sit out a season with a painful right shoulder injury. During that time some of their opponents accused her of "wimping out." They implied that her year off was unnecessary—that she left her team when her abilities were sorely needed.

Just a year before, Jenny had been a *Volleyball Monthly* All-American, Volleyball Coaches Association second-team All-American, and member of the All-NCAA Tournament team.

But Jenny persevered through the injury. She came back to help UCLA have another banner season. "A lot of my drive came from knowing that God was [allowing] this trial," she said, "and I needed to please Him by being strong."

She was prepared for the tough stuff because she knew God would use it for her good. Jenny's life illustrates that "suffering produces perseverance; perseverance, character; and character, hope" (Romans 5:3–4).

Jenny said, "I was hoping . . . that through my play, people could see that God is No. 1 in my life." It's evident that people can also see Christ through her as one who is "patient in affliction."

Are you living like that?

—TOM FELTEN

SPORTS NOTE:
UCLA won the NCAA women's volleyball championship in 1990 and 1991.

FROM THE PLAYBOOK:
Read Romans 5:1–11.

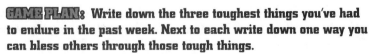

GAME PLAN: Write down the three toughest things you've had to endure in the past week. Next to each write down one way you can bless others through those tough things.

SPIRITUAL SLUMP

POINT OF EMPHASIS:
Overcoming spiritual dry times

"Will you forget me forever?" PSALM 13:1

Athletes hate slumps. They'll try anything to get out of those times when they can't hit the baseball or make a free throw or catch a pass. Baseball players change bats. Basketball players change shoes. Football players change their routine. They'll do whatever they can to find success.

Christians should hate slumps too. We should try anything to get out of those dry spells when we can't seem to pray past the ceiling, or when reading the Bible seems more frustrating than not winning a game all season.

A spiritual slump can make us feel forsaken by God. We struggle with troubling thoughts. Our hearts become sorrowful. We're sure that we're fighting a losing battle.

That was the position David found himself in as he described his situation in Psalm 13:1–2. His spiritual slump came, it seems, from a delayed response to his request for help. Yet David knew how to work his way out of the slump. First, he appealed to God (vv. 3–4), the true source of spiritual refreshment in dry times. Second, he trusted God (v. 5), the only One who knows the way out. Third, he sang God's praises (v. 6), knowing how important worship is.

In a slump? Plead with God, trust Him, and praise His name. Then get back in the game!

—DAVE BRANON

SPORTS NOTE:
Hall of Fame catcher Johnny Bench said of hitting slumps, "They're like sleeping in a soft bed. Easy to get into and hard to get out of."

FROM THE PLAYBOOK:
Read Psalm 13.

GAME PLAN: How do you know when you are going through a dry spiritual time? What are three things that can get you out of the slump?

NO MATTER WHERE

POINT OF EMPHASIS:
God's presence

"'Can anyone hide in secret places so that I cannot see him?'
declares the Lord." JEREMIAH 23:24

I had two very strange incidents happen to me in 2001. Both of them involved running into people from my home community in odd places.

The first one occurred at Conseco Field in Seattle. I was training a group of soldiers at Fort Lewis, Washington, and we decided to take in a baseball game. There were some 35,000 people in attendance. As I walked out of the exit, I heard a familiar voice call my name. When I turned around I saw Robert, one of the members of our small church in Springfield, Virginia, some 2,800 miles east of Seattle. What were the odds of that happening?

The second instance occurred in Denver. I was trying to get back to the office in Washington, DC, when my connecting flight was cancelled because of equipment failure. The next flight was the next day, so the airline put all the passengers up in a hotel. I had no way to contact my boss to let her know I was not going to be at work the next morning. However, as I sat eating breakfast the following morning, I looked up from my coffee and paper and spotted my boss walking right into the front lobby of the hotel!

I began to contemplate what all this meant.

I believe that through these highly unusual meetings God was telling me that no matter how far we go from home, He has His eyes on us. Some might see that as a bad thing—but it becomes bad only if we are doing something that is not pleasing to His sight.

Let us remember that in our Christian conduct—no matter where we are—God is watching, and maybe many others. Even when we are away from home, let our actions bring glory to His name.

—JOHN F. REGISTER, 2000 PARALYMPIC SILVER MEDALIST, LONG JUMP

SPORTS NOTE: Of his having a prosthesis left leg, Register says, "The only thing that limits me or holds me back is my mind."

FROM THE PLAYBOOK: Read Psalm 139.

GAME PLAN: Where do you go where you think no one is watching? It is at those places especially that God needs to be your guide.

SELF-ESTEEM?

POINT OF EMPHASIS:
Our value to God

"For he chose us in him before the creation of the world to be holy and blameless in his sight." EPHESIANS 1:4

Something that I hear discussed quite frequently these days is an individual's self-esteem. "We must build a positive self-esteem in our children," some will say. Where do we gain this self-esteem? Too often, I fear that we buy into the idea that our personal value is determined by a formula similar to the following: My self worth = my performance + other's opinions of me. In other words, we base our value on things like material possessions, personal achievement, popularity, our physical appearance, our intellect, or some extraordinary talent. In determining whether or not each of us is a valuable human being, we draw from this "world account." If my balance is low in these areas, I must not be worth much.

SPORTS NOTE:
In 1990, Sampen won 12 games as a pitcher for the Montreal Expos.

FROM THE PLAYBOOK:
Read Ephesians 1.

God has a significantly different set of standards upon which our value is based.

God has chosen us (Ephesians 1:4). Jesus came to this earth to seek and to save what was lost (Luke 19:10).

God has adopted us (Ephesians 1:5). Those who have placed their trust in the finished work of Jesus Christ have been adopted by God and made co-heirs with Christ.

God has accepted us (Ephesians 1:6). Though there is nothing that we can do to become acceptable to God, the righteousness of Jesus Christ is imputed to us upon our faith in Him.

God has redeemed us (Ephesians 1:7). We have been purchased and set free.

God spared not His own Son for us.

That's how much we are worth.

—BILL SAMPEN, FORMER MAJOR LEAGUE PITCHER

GAME PLAN: Which account are you drawing from? The "world account" or God's account? If you are drawing from the "world account," you are headed for bankruptcy. We do not need self-esteem. We need God-esteem. We are valuable in the eyes of the Lord, and nothing else really matters.

GIVE IT TO GOD!

POINT OF EMPHASIS:
God's control

"Cast all your anxiety on him because he cares for you." I PETER 5:7

Mary Lou Retton is happily married and living in Houston, Texas, with her husband, Shannon Kelley, and their children.

Mary Lou's fame and her personality as an Olympic champion gymnast in the 1988 Summer Games have made her a popular conference speaker and a sought-after spokesperson for a wide variety of corporations, organizations, and causes. For a number of years, she's been on the speaker's circuit, talking about winning and her Olympic experiences.

But recently, she's found herself speaking out about something much more personal. "I'm a Christian," Retton says. "I believe in Jesus Christ, who died on the cross for my sins."

Lately, Mary Lou says she's been learning about patience. "There are things I've been working on for years, asking God for His guidance and direction. But it doesn't work on my timeline; it works on the Lord's timeline. That's been very frustrating to me! I'm trying to accept that sometimes my prayers are answered 'No.' Sometimes when the Lord doesn't give me something or answer my prayer right away, He's protecting me. I may not be ready for a certain thing at this point in my life. I just have to be patient and totally trust Him."

Retton has a piece of paper taped to her desk that reads: "Good morning! This is God. I will be handling all of your problems today. I will not need your help. So, have a good day!"

"Isn't that great!" exclaims Retton. "I love it! That's what I try to live my day by, not stressing over the little things, the things that are out of our control. 'Cause we can worry ourselves sick—and worry is such a sin! Just give it to God!"

—CHRISTIN DITCHFIELD

SPORTS NOTE: In 1997 Mary Lou was inducted into the International Gymnastics Hall of Fame.

FROM THE PLAYBOOK: Read Psalm 55.

GAME PLAN: What three burdens have you been carrying around for the past couple of days? Write them on a piece of paper, pray for God to take them, and then throw the paper away.

SEX WITHOUT CONSEQUENCE?

POINT OF EMPHASIS:
Sexual morality

"The body is not meant for sexual immorality." 1 CORINTHIANS 6:13

We never dated," said the former football star. "We were never boyfriend and girlfriend. We slept together. There was no conversation."

That's the cold, hard truth detailed by one former NFL player about his sexual relationship with a woman he barely knew. Not exactly what God had in mind when he created man and woman. Nothing that even closely resembles what God designed to be shared by a man and woman—within the context of marriage.

Sadly, the sports world seems to be inundated with an increasing number of easy, casual sexual-relationship stories. Baseball, basketball, football—the sport makes no difference—all have far too many front-page sexual problems.

The thing that rarely gets mentioned in these headline-grabbing articles is the emotional and physical scar that follows an athlete's promiscuity. What about the unwanted pregnancies? We almost never hear about those. And discussing the venereal diseases that get passed from one person to the next—that's total taboo to the media. And of course no one would dare mention the spiritual and psychological problems. Yet these negative consequences of sexual sin occur on a regular basis.

Hebrews 13:4 reads, "Marriage should be honored by all, and the marriage bed kept pure."

There's a reason the Bible teaches us that sex outside of marriage is wrong. God's desire is that sex be shared between a husband and a wife to strengthen the marital bond. It was never meant as a recreational tool for a thrill-seeking athlete—or anyone else.

—ROB BENTZ

SPORTS NOTE:
One good source of information about purity is True Love Waits at www.lifeway.com/TLW.

FROM THE PLAYBOOK:
Read 1 Corinthians 6:13–20.

GAME PLAN: Is God convicting you to make a stand for purity? If so, pray right now, and ask the Father to give you strength to walk away from sexual temptation. And go one step further. Tell your closest friend about your new commitment to purity.

JULIE'S JOY

POINT OF EMPHASIS:
The value of joy

"Your joy in Christ Jesus will overflow on account of me."
PHILIPPIANS 1:26

In her freshman year at the University of Arizona, Felicity Willis began a friendship that would change her life. That's when she met softball teammate Julie Reitan. Right away, Felicity noticed something different about Julie.

"She was so happy all the time! She always had a smile on her face," recalls Felicity. "She would do just about anything for anybody."

The two teammates quickly became close friends.

But later that same year, an unspeakable tragedy struck. Julie Reitan died suddenly of complications from diabetes. Felicity was devastated. In her grief, she found herself asking a lot of questions about life and death—and her friend's faith.

"I came to realize that the reason Julie was so filled with life and so filled with joy was because of her relationship with God. I decided that was what I wanted—a personal relationship with Jesus Christ."

Willis began attending campus Bible studies and sports camps organized by Athletes In Action. It helped her get a handle on her newfound faith. Felicity says her life was changed forever by the lessons she learned from their special friendship.

"I don't take life for granted anymore, because it can be taken away from you just like that. I have an inner peace knowing that when I do die, I'll go to heaven. Now I'm just trying to live my life the way God wants me to."

Julie's joy was a testimony in life, and it was what convinced Felicity in death. As believers, do we have a convincing joy?

—CHRISTIN DITCHFIELD

SPORTS NOTE:
After college, Felicity played pro basketball in Puerto Rico and in the WNBA.

FROM THE PLAYBOOK:
Read Philippians 1.

GAME PLAN: Do your friends know you for a joy that they can trace back to Jesus?

NEW SEASON, NEW GOALS

POINT OF EMPHASIS:
Plans and God

"The Spirit intercedes for the saints in accordance with God's will."
ROMANS 8:27

One of the great things about sports is that you get to start over each season. You and everyone else begin the season exactly the same. No matter how well or poorly you played last season, when that first ball gets teed up in the first tournament of the season, everybody is at zero.

When I begin a new golf season on the LPGA Tour, I have two goals in mind as I look at my schedule and plan my year. I want to set goals that continue to push my talent forward, but I also want to keep in rhythm with the goals and direction that God has planned for me.

SPORTS NOTE:
In 2005 Wendy earned a spot on the US team for the Solheim Cup.

FROM THE PLAYBOOK:
Read about Jesus and His desire to do God's will in John 6:38–40.

At the beginning of each calendar year, I sit down and pray about what God wants to accomplish through me. In the back of my mind I have evaluated the previous year's goals, which I placed before God last year. I like to set challenging goals, but in accordance with God's will for my life. If my goals are pleasing to Him, then the Holy Spirit inside of me will allow me to feel good about my direction for each new year. I have to be comfortable with my goals on the inside before I can attain anything on the outside.

Then I can turn my goals over to God, depending on Him to guide me throughout the season—no matter what happens.

Think about the goals you set—whether it's for school, work, or family. Do you make sure to include God in your plans?

—WENDY WARD, LPGA GOLFER

GAME PLAN: What were your goals at the start of this year? Is it time for a mid-year review? What can you set as goals that you and God can work on for the rest of the year?

WHICH WAY DO I GO?

POINT OF EMPHASIS:
God's leading

"Your ears will hear a voice behind you." Isaiah 30:21

Before she was even 18, Krissy Wendell had been called the best female ice hockey player in the country. As a high school senior, Wendell scored an astonishing 166 points (110 goals and 56 assists) in 27 games. Her phenomenal success led her to a crisis of sorts when she was invited to play on the US National Women's Team.

"I really struggled with whether or not I should go to college or go out and train with the US Team for the Olympics," she recalls. "I've never spent so much time praying and trying to figure out the right decision. I kept going back and forth: 'Go to college; Don't go to college.' Ultimately my parents said, 'You need to keep praying about it and figure out what God wants you to do. When you decide, you'll know it's right because you'll have peace about it.'

"One of my favorite Bible verses is Psalm 37:4: 'Delight yourself in the Lord and he will give you the desires of your heart.' I knew I could trust God to lead me in the right path. And there's no time limit on prayer. If you pray long enough, you'll know where God is leading you."

In the end, Wendell decided to join the National Team, preparing for the 2002 Olympics. She describes the 2-year training period as a thrilling experience—the opportunity of a lifetime.

Like Krissy, we all have to make important decisions that will have a great impact on our future. God promises to give us His wisdom in every circumstance. But we have to ask!

—Christin Ditchfield

SPORTS NOTE:
In 2005, Krissy Wendell won the Patty Kazmaier Award as the most outstanding woman college hockey player.

FROM THE PLAYBOOK:
Read James 1:5 and Daniel 2:20–22.

GAME PLAN: Write down four or five decisions you need to make in the next few weeks. Pray about each one specifically, and jot down any thoughts or direction you receive over time.

SOWING AND REAPING

POINT OF EMPHASIS:
Sharing the gospel

"I planted the seed, Apollos watered it, but God made it grow."
1 CORINTHIANS 3:6

When Joe Johnson was traded to the Toronto Blue Jays in 1986, he didn't realize the impact he would have.

The following spring Joe spoke at an outreach breakfast. Jim Florada, an elderly man from Oneida, New York, attended and was moved by Joe's testimony. Later, Joe Johnson met with Jim, teammate Don Gordon, and me following a ball game. In the early hours of the morning, Joe Johnson led Jim in the sinner's prayer, and he committed his life to Christ.

God uses various people to sow the seed, others water it, but it's God who brings about the harvest. In this case, God used a pitcher to both sow the seed and see it come to fruition.

God asks only that we be sowers of the seed, His Word. He equips us to share the "good news" and provides countless opportunities to do so. Athletes have been given a unique platform from which to do this. Usually we hear of the one God uses to reap the harvest but others beforehand faithfully sowed and watered. Billy Graham's name is recognized around the world, but it was Mordecai Ham who led him to Christ.

Pray for opportunities to sow the "good news" today. You'll be amazed how God will orchestrate events and circumstances so that people are brought to Himself and He gets the glory.

—DAVID FISHER, MAJOR LEAGUE CHAPLAIN

SPORTS NOTE:
Don Gordon is involved in a ministry called Athletes Abroad for Christ.

FROM THE PLAYBOOK:
Read Psalm 126.

GAME PLAN: List three people you think need to hear the gospel from you. What do you have in common that might help start a conversation? Baseball, maybe?

SPEAKING OF SUCCESS

POINT OF EMPHASIS:
God's strength

"O Lord, I have never been eloquent." Exodus 4:10

When Mike Davis was named coach of the Indiana Hoosiers basketball team, it was a big deal. His predecessor, Bob Knight, had built up a passionate following among Indiana hoops fans.

Davis had a huge red sweater to fill. People wanted to see him fail. However, he had the courage to take the job, and he has done it well. But what might be even more courageous is the way he has worked to overcome something scarier than taking over for Knight. Davis has long had problems with public speaking.

As an elementary student, he struggled with speech. Private sessions helped him stop his severe stuttering, but the fear of hearing his voice out loud—in front of people—has not totally subsided.

So he practices and practices. He repeats difficult-to-pronounce words over and over at home with his family. Mike Davis has not allowed a speech difficulty to keep him from being a leader of men—a Division I university coach.

Another man who rose above a speech challenge was Moses. When God told him that he would confront Pharaoh and lead the people of Israel, he begged to differ—because of his lack of eloquence.

It took some strong words from God, along with the promise that "I will help you speak and will teach you what to say" (Exodus 4:12), for Moses to take the leadership role God commanded.

You may not be a Division I coach or the leader of a nation, but there may be something holding you back from leading in an area God has provided. Move forward by God's power and strength. He'll give you the words.

—Tom Felten

SPORTS NOTE: Davis was the first coach in Indiana history to begin his stay in Bloomington with three straight 20-win seasons.

FROM THE PLAYBOOK: Read Exodus 4:1–17.

GAME PLAN: Talk to a trusted friend about an area in your life where God is asking you to lead but you're reticent to do so because of fear or other factors. Commit to your friend verbally and to God in prayer your plan of action to begin leading by God's power.

TRAINING AND THINKING

POINT OF EMPHASIS:
Thinking about God

"Finally, brothers, whatever is true, . . . if anything is excellent or praiseworthy—think about such things." PHILIPPIANS 4:8

Training 25 hours a week to compete in the triathlon, I put in many miles looking at a black line on the bottom of the pool, pedaling my bike on the roads, or running trails.

I could just fritter away this time, letting my mind wander to things of this world. Or, as the verse today says, I could think about whatever is excellent and praiseworthy—all things from God.

One way to think about such things is to sing songs in your head. If you are like me, sometimes I get a song stuck in my head, and I can't get it out. Instead of this song being some catchy Top 40 tune that I just heard at the grocery store (and know only one line to!), I've taken a proactive approach to this "song in my head" problem.

I've written down the names or key phrases of my favorite songs that we sing in church or that I hear on the Christian radio station. I've taped this list to the handlebar stem of my bike and written another list under the bill of my running hat. Now like a CD changer, while training I can proactively select from my list songs that inspire me. When I ride or run up hills, I sing songs of God's power. On other days when I'm pedaling through beautiful mountains and I become overwhelmed by His incredible creation, I sing songs of praise.

What a difference it makes to think about God's power, love, and grace through song, rather than having songs dealing with things of this world floating through my head.

—BARB LINDQUIST, WORLD-CLASS TRIATHLETE

SPORTS NOTE:
In 2003, Barb was the No. 1 ranked female triathlete in the world.

FROM THE PLAYBOOK:
Read Psalm 108.

 GAME PLAN: How can you begin to program your mind with thoughts that are excellent and praiseworthy? Can a switch to Christian music do that? How much of your time do you think God-directed thoughts?

A SURE THING

POINT OF EMPHASIS:
The problem with gambling

"The desires of the diligent are fully satisfied." PROVERBS 13:4

A friend, now in his thirties, shared a story from his college days. He had been responsible in high school, saving money and even doing some investing. But when he got to college he discovered the adrenaline rush that gambling can bring.

At first, he enjoyed moderate "success," but soon he found himself on a losing streak the LA Clippers could appreciate. After several down weeks, my friend decided he needed a big winner. Just one good week and he could win it all back. He'd break even. Then he could quit.

Three games. Fifteen hundred dollars wagered. He lost it all.

My friend had to cash in his last IRA to pay his debt. In order to finish college, he joined the military. Instead of getting his degree at age 22, he finally earned it at 28. And he doesn't gamble any more.

You will search the Scriptures in vain to discover a specific prohibition against gambling. God hasn't given us a comprehensive rulebook to tell us how to behave in every situation.

SPORTS NOTE: According to one figure, Americans wager more than $2.5 billion a year on the Super Bowl alone.

FROM THE PLAYBOOK: Read Proverbs 28:19–27.

But you *will* find many principles about money in God's Word. Proverbs in particular has much to say about the proper way to build wealth. "Dishonest money dwindles away, but he who gathers money little by little makes it grow" (Proverbs 13:11). "Hard work brings a profit" (14:23). "Of what use is money in the hand of a fool?" Proverbs 17:16 asks.

Get-rich-quick schemes, whether legal or illegal, aren't advocated in Scripture. God favors honest work, careful spending habits, and generosity to the poor.

Enjoy sports, but don't waste your money gambling on an unsure thing. Learn the wise business practices of the Bible. That's the way to stay ahead of the game.

—TIM GUSTAFSON

GAME PLAN: If you bet, figure out how much money you've lost. Then vow to give that much money instead to a worthy cause.

ROCK SOLID

POINT OF EMPHASIS:
God's strength

"My hope comes from [God]. He alone is my rock and my salvation."
PSALM 62:5–8

Playing basketball at Boston College was an incredible experience for me. Our program went from not even making the NCAA tournament my freshman year to making it to the Sweet Sixteen for the first time in school history my junior year.

Finally, it was my senior year, a year during which I was challenged to lead our young team to more success. We had just finished a remarkable regular season, and the intensity was building as I realized that the next few games would be my last ever in college.

Our team was headed for the Big East tournament in Hartford, Connecticut, where 16,000 fans would be cheering on the UConn Huskies, the dominating team in the Big East Conference.

I was nervous. All I wanted in my college career was to win the Big East tournament—to be the best in the conference. It was here that I called upon the Lord to give me the strength and confidence that I needed throughout this tournament. In Him alone I felt as if I could overcome anything. With that strength, I led our team to win four games in four days, including beating UConn.

God used His words to give me assurance that I could rely on Him as my rock, strength, fortress, and refuge. He would remain stable, and He would not be shaken; therefore, I felt I could not be shaken. I went into the Big East tournament thinking there was no one or no team that could stop me and my team from doing something extraordinary—and that was to win the tournament.

When you are not feeling confident, or you are a little nervous, or you need an extra boost—seek God. You will find assurance in Him, as He is our steady rock. You may not win the big game, but you know that God will give you strength for any challenge.

—AMBER JACOBS, WNBA GUARD

SPORTS NOTE:
When Amber graduated from Boston College, she was the fourth-leading scorer in BC history (1,544 points).

FROM THE PLAYBOOK:
Read Psalm 62.

GAME PLAN: What is coming up in your life that looks as insurmountable as the UConn Huskies? How are you preparing to lean on God's strength?

LIVE OUT THE DREAM

POINT OF EMPHASIS:
God's care

"Delight yourself in the Lord and he will give you the desires of your heart." PSALM 37:4

All my life I have wanted to play hockey for Canada. This desire was even stronger for me than the desire to play in the NHL. Professional hockey came first when I was drafted by the Winnipeg Jets. Because I was only 18 at the time, I was still eligible to play in the World Junior Championship, and had a good shot at making Team Canada that year. But the Jets had their reasons for not sending me back to Juniors, and I was devastated. I felt that I had been robbed of my big chance to play for Canada.

Fast-forward almost eight years to the spring of 2003. Because my team had finished out of the playoffs, I was available for the World Championships. This time I was free to jump at the invitation offered me to join Team Canada. I was blessed with the opportunity to live out my dream while playing with an amazing group of talented athletes. And I was even able to contribute a few points along the way to our capturing the gold medal.

God may not care about a hockey tournament, but He does care about what matters to His children. I still have a lot to learn about waiting on God and understanding His timing, but I have trusted God with all of me, including my hopes and desires. I will continue to trust Him to govern those desires, and I am learning that He truly delights in blessing me, even as I delight in knowing Him.

—SHANE DOAN, NHL CENTER

SPORTS NOTE: Shane was a member of the Canadian team that took silver at the 2005 World Hockey Championships in Austria.

FROM THE PLAYBOOK: Read Ephesians 1:3–6.

 GAME PLAN: Do you recognize any times when God has fulfilled a desire? Is there an unfulfilled desire that you have in your heart today? How much time do you spend focusing on God because of the desire, compared with the time you spend simply wanting to know Him?

DO YOU HAVE THE SEAL?

POINT OF EMPHASIS:
The Holy Spirit

*"Having believed, you were marked in him with a seal,
the promised Holy Spirit."* EPHESIANS 1:13

It's Tuesday and I'm driving to the golf course for my practice round. As I drive through the front gate, I hold up my money clip. The security guard waves and allows me to pass.

The LPGA Tour money clip is a powerful piece of metal. It has my name inscribed on it, along with these words: Ladies Professional Golf Tour. It signifies that I am a member of the Tour, and it enables me access to anywhere I wish around the tournament site. When I wear my money clip, I receive both respect and a right of passage. It's my seal of approval stating that I am a professional golfer.

Unlike the money clip that I had to earn, I have another seal of approval that I experience in my life. This one I got because of nothing I did. When I accepted and trusted Jesus Christ as my personal Savior, God sealed me with His Holy Spirit. This seal gives me full and direct access to God, His promises, and His power.

God tells us in Ephesians 1:14 that the Holy Spirit "is a deposit guaranteeing our inheritance until the redemption of those who are God's possession—to the praise of his glory." For those of us who have trusted Jesus Christ, the seal of the Holy Spirit signifies that we are one of God's children.

Do you have that "seal"? Is the Holy Spirit your guarantee? Don't go anywhere unless you have it!

—TRACY HANSON, LPGA GOLFER

SPORTS NOTE:
Tracy had a story published in *Chicken Soup for the Soul* in 1999.

FROM THE PLAYBOOK:
Read these passages about the Holy Spirit: Ephesians 1:12–14; 2:18, 22; 4:3–4; 6:17–18.

GAME PLAN: Please make sure you are sealed with God's Holy Spirit. If you've never asked Jesus Christ into your life to forgive you and to save you, do so now. God will mark you "with a seal, the promised Holy Spirit" (Ephesians 1:13).

CAN'T BE LOST

POINT OF EMPHASIS:
Security in Jesus

"If God is with us, no one can defeat us." ROMANS 8:31 (PARAPHRASE)

I have the greatest golf ball in the world," said Bob as he put his ball on the tee. "It can't be lost."

Mike, his playing partner, was surprised. "How is that possible?" he asked.

Excitedly, Bob told Mike about his remarkable dimpled friend. "If you hit it into the sand, it beeps. If you hit it into the water, it floats. If you want to play golf at night, it glows."

"That sounds like a great ball," said Mike. "Where did you get it?"

"Oh, I found it in the woods," Bob responded.

Obviously, that magical golf ball wasn't all it was cracked up to be. Although it was supposed to be impervious to being lost, it wasn't.

What is not true of any golf ball I've ever played (especially those special water-seeking balls I keep buying), though, IS true of us as genuine believers in Jesus Christ. If we have put our sincere faith in Christ to save us from the penalty of our sin and redeem us through his death, burial, and resurrection, we can never be lost. No beeper. No glowing. Just eternal safety in the hands of our great and awesome God.

Contemplate these words of hope and help from the pen of the apostle Paul. "For I am convinced that neither death nor life, neither angels nor demons, neither the present nor the future, nor any powers, neither height nor depth, nor anything else in all creation, will be able to separate us from the love of God that is in Christ Jesus our Lord" (vv. 38–39).

No, we will never be lost.

—DAVE BRANON

SPORTS NOTE:
An inventor who lives on Long Island, New York, has invented a golf ball with a beeper to help you locate it if it is lost.

FROM THE PLAYBOOK:
Read Romans 8:28–39.

GAME PLAN: If you have put your faith in Jesus Christ, do you sometimes think you are far from God and you fear that you have somehow gotten "out of the loop" with Him? What do you have to do at that point, knowing that God still has you in His hand?

A MUCH BETTER PLAN

POINT OF EMPHASIS:
God's timing

"We know that in all things God works for the good of those who love him, who have been called according to his purpose." ROMANS 8:28

It was March 1996, and the American Basketball League announced it was going to start its inaugural season in October. I was in my senior year at Boise State University, and I wanted to turn my dream into reality. I was going to try out.

So when my senior year ended, I went to work on my game. I was practicing so much that I actually began to dream about my shot! I practiced with the BSU players as tryouts grew closer. One day, about halfway into a practice, I made a cut up the court and felt a "snap" in the back of my knee. I hobbled off the court and went straight to the team doctor.

He X-rayed my knee and found a bone spur. The snap I felt was actually my hamstring catching on the spur. The doctor ordered an MRI on my other knee (which had tendonitis), figuring it was a good idea to have both checked at the same time.

The tests showed that my tendon was so badly degenerated the tendon was pulling away from the bone. The doctor said that he needed to do surgery. That would mean a six-month recovery—preventing me from trying out for the ABL.

Although God's Word is extremely comforting, it doesn't always negate the depression one feels when an amazing opportunity has just been missed. That's why it's important to have a relationship with the Lord, to tell Him how you feel and to lean on Him for support. It was during that confusing time that I needed Him more than ever. I was angry, confused, and devastated. I prayed and begged for understanding.

Little did I know that the ABL would fold in a few years and that the WNBA would be the lasting league. But God knew. I believe it is because of His perfect timing, rather than mine, that I became a member of the WNBA.

—TRICIA BADER BINFORD, FORMER WNBA GUARD

SPORTS NOTE:
The ABL suspended operations in December 1998. It had begun play in 1996.

FROM THE PLAYBOOK:
Read Proverbs 2:3–5.

GAME PLAN: What situation recently has caused you to wonder where God is? Have you considered that God is looking at the long view of your life and has even this under His control?

MARCH 19

IN TRAINING

POINT OF EMPHASIS:
Training spiritually

"No discipline seems pleasant at the time." HEBREWS 12:11

Why am I doing this? I asked myself that question a thousand times while I was trying to get in shape for a 25K (15.5 mile) run.

It would have been easy to quit. I'll confess that occasionally I gave in, indulged, and wimped out when the weather wasn't so great. Over the long haul, though, I was making progress. Excess pounds were coming off and my legs and lungs were getting ready.

Race day blew in with a brisk north wind and the temperature in the low 40s. With about 3,000 others, I took off at the sound of the starter's gun. Nearly 2 hours later, I crossed the finish line—mission accomplished! It was the greatest feeling.

If you've ever tried out for a sport and gone through training for competition, you know exactly what I'm talking about.

The author of the letter to the Hebrews used athletic word pictures when he discussed the difficult process of becoming more like Christ and living for Him.

It's not an easy process. We have to resist temptations that can trip us up or slow us down (Hebrews 12:1). We have to persevere. We have to keep our eyes on the goal (vv. 2–3). We have to endure hardship and God's loving discipline (vv. 4–11), which is designed to make us the kind of people He can use to make a positive difference in the world (vv. 10–11).

With a goal so grand and noble, nothing in life is too bad to endure. The pain will be worth all we gain.

—KURT DE HAAN

SPORTS NOTE:
Kurt De Haan, managing editor of *Our Daily Bread,* was a veteran of several 25K races. He died on August 28, 2003, at age 50 while training at lunchtime.

FROM THE PLAYBOOK:
Read Hebrews 12:1–11.

GAME PLAN: What sports have you been involved with, willingly or unwillingly? How important was training/conditioning? How are you "working out" spiritually to be better prepared for the challenges of each new day?

RIDING TANDEM

POINT OF EMPHASIS:
Trusting God

"Fix [your] eyes on Jesus." HEBREWS 12:2

In the spring of 1999, Mike Sweeney, first baseman of the Kansas City Royals, was still more prospect than power hitter. The Royals were looking for a way to trade him, and as one of the team's coaches told Mike, "You have a zero percent chance of staying here."

Sweeney felt the pressure of uncertainty bearing down on him.

"I was on my knees when I saw the vivid picture of my life," Mike says. "It was a picture of a tandem bicycle. I was on the front seat of the bike trying to steer where I was going. And it struck me, 'That's why I feel all this pressure, because I'm trying to steer.' I cried my eyes out that evening. It was a time of brokenness, a time when I said, 'God, I cannot do this on my own. I realize I've been trying to do this baseball thing for years.'"

Sweeney realized that he had been trying to handle his baseball situation alone. "That night, my prayer was, 'Lord, I don't know where I'm going to go, but it's time for me to get on the back seat. I realize that with You on the front seat of the tandem bicycle, You're going to steer me wherever You want to steer me, and I'm going to get on the backseat and pedal my heart out. I'm going to keep my eyes focused straight ahead on you.'"

As it turned out, the Royals didn't trade their prospect, and Sweeney spent the next two seasons establishing himself as one of the best hitters in baseball.

When we peddle alone, the task is nearly impossible. But when we let God be in control and keep our eyes on Jesus we can stop worrying about the outcome.

—VICTOR LEE

SPORTS NOTE:
In 2002, Mike Sweeney batted .340 for the Kansas City Royals.

FROM THE PLAYBOOK:
Read: Hebrews 12:1–6.

GAME PLAN: What is the uncertainty that troubles your life? Are you trying to steer or are you letting God control things in His way? See if you can put yourself in Mike Sweeney's prayer.

WHO ARE YOU PLAYING FOR?

POINT OF EMPHASIS:
Playing for God

"Do it all for the glory of God." I CORINTHIANS 10:31

As a freshman, Becky Varnum led her high school tennis team to the Colorado state championships, capturing the singles title herself. This impressive accomplishment brought great expectations with it.

"Everyone started saying, 'You can do it four years in a row!' It put a lot of pressure on me," Varnum recalls. "It was hard to look that far into the future. I tried to just take it one match at a time."

The strategy worked. One match at a time, she captured four consecutive state championships. She graduated with a phenomenal record of 68–0. She never even lost a set!

But the pressure only increased. On the national junior tennis circuit, the competition was more intense. Varnum tasted defeat regularly. She worried that her ranking wasn't good enough for a college scholarship. She was afraid of letting her friends and family down.

After one especially disappointing loss, Becky's mom asked her a question: "Who are you playing for?"

Becky answered, "Well, I'm playing for my coach, because he's put a lot of time into me, and I'm playing for myself, because I need to go to college, and . . ."

Mom interrupted: "You need to be playing for the glory of God!"

Becky's mom reminded her of this simple truth: All God asks is that we do our best for Him—and leave the results in His hands. This truth brought peace and strength to Becky. It can do the same for you!

—CHRISTIN DITCHFIELD

SPORTS NOTE:
Becky Varnum finished her college career at Notre Dame with a singles mark of 92–66.

FROM THE PLAYBOOK:
Read Philippians 2:1–11 and Colossians 3:16–17.

 GAME PLAN: Who are you playing for? What motivates you today? Ask God to help you do everything for His glory, and trust Him with the outcome.

THE MONEY GAME

POINT OF EMPHASIS:
Money choices

"Do not be overawed when a man grows rich." PSALM 49:16

What are we to make of all this money? Some athletes make more money than the yearly GNP of small countries. Their salaries in a two-week period rival our yearly take. Their homes seem like small city-states.

The psalmist didn't know about multi-year contracts by talented baseball, basketball, hockey, or football players, but he did know about rich people. Apparently there were some pretty wealthy people in his day, and the danger then was the danger now: We can easily get sidetracked by spending too much time worrying about somebody else's money.

So the psalm writer put those rich folks' wealth in perspective. He told us first that we shouldn't be overly impressed with their homes or their bank accounts—for they are only temporary. And besides, the rich person is just as mortal as the next guy. No matter how fancy his stuff is, he can't take it with him, Psalm 49:17 reminds us.

As the psalmist concludes the chapter, we learn this: The difference between a rich person who succeeds and one who doesn't is this: Does he have "understanding"?

Not money, but understanding. That should be our goal. That should drive our desires and inform our choices. Gaining a clear understanding of God and His purposes for us and for this world—that's what must motivate us.

Understanding. Rich or poor, we all must have it.

—DAVE BRANON

SPORTS NOTE:
In 2004–2005, the New York Knicks team salary was $104,657,559. They won 33 games.

FROM THE PLAYBOOK:
Psalm 49:16–19.

 GAME PLAN: Which would you rather have—an understanding of God's purposes for you or a ton of money? If your perspective is different from the writer of the psalm, how can it change?

STEPPING DOWN TO STEP UP

POINT OF EMPHASIS:
Trusting God

"Trust in the Lord with all your heart and lean not on your own understanding." PROVERBS 3:5

After high school, I went to the University of California at Santa Barbara on a basketball scholarship. I discovered that playing Division I hoops is similar to working a full-time job. The joy I had once experienced through basketball was soon gone. Worse than that, my relationship with the Lord slowly deteriorated, draining the joy from my life.

The success our team was experiencing was far from gratifying. We were ranked in the Top 10 in the country, we won three consecutive conference titles, and I was named Most Valuable Player of the league three times. But I never felt emptier. Things looked good on the outside, but on the inside I was dying. I knew I wouldn't be able to last much longer. I knew I needed a change.

I was familiar with a small Christian college near LA, and through my mom's prompting, I decided to check it out. I made the call, and within three days I was on the campus of The Master's College, checking into my dorm. The Lord wanted me to take the first step, and when I did, He opened the floodgates. I left my huge Division I university for a small 1,000-person, Christian college in the NAIA.

Many people thought I had thrown away my chance to play in the WNBA. But when the draft came, I ended up with the Minnesota Lynx.

God wants us to trust Him. Sometimes we have to make choices that aren't popular in the world's eyes, but if we are seeking to please God, He will take care of us and provide what He knows we need. It's hard to take that first step when certainty is not guaranteed, but doing so forces us to turn to Him and trust that He is over all.

—ERIN BUESCHER, WNBA GUARD

SPORTS NOTE:
Erin Buescher averaged 17 points a game while at UC Santa Barbara and The Master's College.

FROM THE PLAYBOOK:
Read Proverbs 3.

GAME PLAN: What are two areas in which you are finding it hard to trust God? What can help you to make that leap to trust Him?

FAITH & FRISBEE

POINT OF EMPHASIS:
The danger of idols

"You shall not make for yourself an idol." DEUTERONOMY 5:8

Ya gotta love throwing a Frisbee. Whether it's playing a game of Ultimate Frisbee or just winging the disc with a friend, it makes for a great time.

The inventor of the world's favorite flying toy would have agreed. However, "Steady" Ed Headrick took Frisbee appreciation a good way beyond mere enjoyment. The celebrated saucer creator once said, "We used to say Frisbee really is a religion—'Frisbyterians,' we'd call ourselves. When we die, we don't go to purgatory. We just land up on the roof and lay there."

Sadly, Ed Headrick did die in 2002. Was Frisbee truly his hope? His "religion"?

Believers in Jesus Christ have to be careful about what takes priority in their lives. A thing as simple as playing Frisbee can become a "religion" and an idol.

One of the Ten Commandments God gave to Ancient Israel was to "not make for yourself an idol." He didn't want anything to replace His place in the hearts and lives of His people.

God requires the same from you and me. It may not be Frisbee, but have you allowed sports to become an idol in your life? Is playing, watching, or following a sport taking more of your precious time than it should?

If your answer is "Yes" to either of those questions, it's time to change. Confess to God your struggle, and seek His forgiveness and help.

Sports can be a fun pastime, but before God it must never become idol time.

—TOM FELTEN

SPORTS NOTE:
The game of Frisbee is named after the Frisbee Pie company, whose pie tins were first used as the flying objects of the game.

FROM THE PLAYBOOK:
Read Deuteronomy 5:1–22.

GAME PLAN: Take 5 minutes to think and pray about what the idols are in your life. Write them down. Ask a trusted friend to hold you accountable in getting those "idols" into proper perspective.

PRIORITY CHECK

POINT OF EMPHASIS:
Keeping priorities straight

"Seek first his kingdom and his righteousness." MATTHEW 6:33

Can a person who is truly dedicated to a sport keep other priorities straight? After all, someone who is pursuing excellence has so many things to think about.

There's training, which takes careful preparation and immense dedication. And there are affiliations—either with a team or with sponsors, coaches, trainers, and others. There's travel to practices and competitions. There's time that must be spent working on equipment, doing interviews, and pumping iron.

Consider the training regimen Barb Lindquist must endure. Barb is one of the top triathletes in the United States. In a recent year, she was the Triathlete of the Year. She must have a one-track mind.

Or not. Listen to what she says about her priorities.

"My relationship with Jesus permeates everything," says Barb. "It's who I am. It's in every part of my life, because it is my life."

"I feel [triathlon] is my mission field," says Barb. "I get to spread God's Word to other athletes, to the media, and to people around the world.

"My first priority is my relationship with Jesus. My second priority is my relationship with my husband, Loren, and my third priority is my job, or the triathlon. Even though the triathlon is my third priority, that doesn't mean I won't be the best triathlete I can be. But I also know that if my first two priorities aren't in line, I'll never be the best triathlete I can be."

How we list our priorities tells how we view God's place in our lives. We need a priority check. We need to think it through and make sure the right Person is No. 1.

—ROB BENTZ

SPORTS NOTE:
Barb Lindquist was a member of the US Olympic team in 2004.

FROM THE PLAYBOOK:
Read: Matthew 22:37–39.

GAME PLAN: This isn't easy, but list the five most important things in your life. Don't try to be super spiritual, but be honest with yourself. Now write down how that list should look.

CHOOSE YOUR FRIENDS WISELY

POINT OF EMPHASIS:
Choosing good friendships

"Walk with the wise." PROVERBS 13:20

LPGA golfer Tracy Hanson chooses to spend the majority of her time with people who encourage her to stay true to her Christian beliefs. She avoids close friendships with people who tempt her to do things she knows are wrong.

College friends and her friends on the LPGA Tour have walked with Tracy through the hard and fun times in life. But most important, they have helped her grow in her Christian faith. Tracy's faith has taught her that her worth is from Jesus Christ—and only Him—not from how she performs on the golf course.

SPORTS NOTE:
The leader of the LPGA Tour Bible study for many years has been Cris Stevens.

FROM THE PLAYBOOK:
Read Titus 2:1–8.

"Recognizing Jesus Christ as the source of my true value has helped stabilize my emotions and has given me a bigger perspective of what life is all about," Tracy says. "It's not just about golf and what I do on the golf course. It's about relating with Christ and with people."

"Fortunately, on Tour I'm able to get together with other Christian women. We meet weekly for Bible study, fellowship, and prayer. I am grateful for these relationships and for older mentors who show how to stay strong in the Lord and to experience His grace and comfort in good and difficult times."

Tracy knows that "He who walks with the wise grows wise, but a companion of fools suffers harm" (Proverbs 13:20). Whether she's at home or on the road with the LPGA Tour, Tracy looks to God for wisdom to know whom she should spend time with.

What a great example! We each need to recognize the impact other people have on our choices and the way we view ourselves. That will help us choose friends who lead us closer to God, not farther from Him.

—ROXANNE ROBBINS

GAME PLAN: What kind of messages do your friends send you about your value to God? Today, thank a friend or mentor who has helped you better understand God's deep love for you.

BROKEN CONTRACTS

POINT OF EMPHASIS:
Keeping covenant with God

"You are not my people, and I am not your God." HOSEA 1:9

Suppose the owner of a pro basketball team were to walk into the locker room one day and begin to write the word "Lo-Ammi" on the outside of select players' lockers? No, he wouldn't be helping to advertise a cleanser. He would be cleaning house.

He would be writing "Not my people" on those lockers, and in doing so he would be breaking the contract he and the players had signed. Before the season, the owner had agreed to pay the player a certain amount of money. Until that contract is legally ended or changed, the owner has an obligation to the player. He can't arbitrarily tell him he's not on the team.

The contract must be dealt with.

In the 8th century B.C., God had to deal with a covenant he had made with the people of Israel. And he did it by writing "Lo-Ammi." That was the name given to Gomer's second son, and it indicated that because of disobedience by the people, He was declaring the covenant void. It said, "You are not my people."

The covenant said they were God's special ones, but the disobedience of the people caused them to lose privilege.

If sin can make God cancel a covenant He has with His people, it is clearly something not to trifle with.

If we are redeemed by Jesus' blood, we can never be kicked out of God's family, but sin can still cause a break in our fellowship with God. And that's clearly not somewhere any child of God wants to go.

—DAVE BRANON

SPORTS NOTE:
In 1997, Kevin Garnett signed the largest contract in NBA history: 6 years for $126 million.

FROM THE PLAYBOOK:
Read Hosea 1.

GAME PLAN: If you were being totally honest with God right now, what would be three areas of your life that need to be changed because they contain disobedience to Him and His Word?

THE DISEASE OF ME

POINT OF EMPHASIS:
Dealing with pride

"The Lord detests all the proud of heart." PROVERBS 16:5

Former NBA coach Pat Riley, writing in his book *The Winner Within*, tells about the 1980 World Champion Los Angeles Lakers. After winning the NBA Finals that year, they were recognized as the best basketball team in the world.

Within weeks of their opening game of the next season, Magic Johnson tore cartilage in his knee and was out for three months. The remaining players played their hearts out and were winning 70 percent of their games without Magic but were totally ignored by the press until the return of their star guard. The players were so resentful that eventually the morale of the entire team collapsed, the guys turned on each other, the coach was fired, and they lost their opening game of the playoffs. Riley said, "Because of greed, pettiness, and resentment, we executed one the fastest falls from grace in NBA history. It was the 'Disease of Me.'"

Whether you are an athlete or not, the vice of pride is the ground in which all other sins grow. It can weasel its way into our lives and destroy relationships and communities. C. S. Lewis said, "Pride is essentially competitive—is competitive by its very nature—while the other vices are competitive only, so to speak, by accident. Pride gets no pleasure out of having something, only out of having more of it than the next man."

Do you find yourself playing the comparison game? Do you look at other people's abilities or possessions and feel resentment toward them? Not even Jesus could take pride in His abilities, but rather He said, "I can of mine own self do nothing." In Proverbs 18:12 we read, "Before his downfall a man's heart is proud, but humility comes before honor." Don't let the Disease of Me spring up in your life!

—MOLLY GRETZINGER

SPORTS NOTE:
Pat Riley won more than 1,100 games as an NBA coach.

FROM THE PLAYBOOK:
Read Proverbs 16:5,18; 18:12; 29:23.

 GAME PLAN: Ask God to search your heart and see if there is any offensive way in it. Confess to Him the people or things that you wish were yours.

HIGH GOALS

POINT OF EMPHASIS:
Setting spiritual goals

"We make it our goal to please him." 2 CORINTHIANS 5:9

Steve Fossett sets some seriously high goals. For years he chased the lofty dream of becoming the first person to fly solo in a balloon around the world. After six failed attempts and millions of dollars spent, he finally floated into the record books with a successful 15-day flight in 2002.

Fossett was interviewed immediately after achieving his global goal. Note what he said, "I still have other challenges I want to accomplish." His new "challenge" was to break the record for altitude in a glider. In fact, it was his hope to glide one day at 100,000 feet—at the doorstep of outer space.

The man is one high-flying goal setter!

You may not have the burning ambition to fly where only Steve Fosset dares, but there is a goal you should be pursuing. As a believer in Jesus Christ, you are called to please Him in the way you live your life.

The apostle Paul wrote about this goal in 2 Corinthians. We are to please Jesus (5:9), he wrote, and to do this we must "live by faith, not by sight" (v. 7).

Are you allowing things of this world to guide your steps? Are your eyes fixed on high hopes of material success?

Instead of focusing on what can be seen, turn your eyes to spiritual riches. Strive to grow in your relationship with God through prayer and studying His Word. Tell others about your Lord. By doing so, you will please Him.

Now, that's a goal worth pursuing!

—TOM FELTEN

SPORTS NOTE: Fossett's trip took him from June 19 until July 2.

FROM THE PLAYBOOK: Read 2 Corinthians 5:1–11.

 GAME PLAN: Write down five goals for your life. How does 2 Corinthians 5:9 affect how you go after them?

NOTHING LIKE THE RING?

POINT OF EMPHASIS:
God's importance

"I consider everything a loss compared to the surpassing greatness of knowing Christ Jesus." PHILIPPIANS 3:8

I wanted a ring. A championship ring—that ultimate trophy that would always be on me, and that would always speak to my greatness. I thought, "If I could ever have that, I wouldn't need anything else."

Sometimes God gives us what we want just to show us how futile and foolish these "idols" can be.

While playing for the Kentucky Wildcat basketball team, I was a part of two national championship teams. Both teams were awarded with championship rings.

I can still remember my foolishness just moments after receiving my rings. Very slowly and deliberately, I would slide those rings on my finger, truly expecting to immediately be different or better or something. This was what I had convinced myself would complete my life even more than Christ already had.

But nothing ever happened. Still to this day those rings have yet to change my life. They are pretty, heavy, and shiny. But that is about it.

It doesn't matter what our idols are or how innocent they may seem. God is a jealous God, and he will not share us with anything else. The good news is that whether we know it or not, our heart beats only for the pleasure of knowing God through Christ.

The problem is, we are so easily fooled into thinking that it's enough for Him to be Savior. But we are created to know Him—not just use Him for salvation. There is nothing created that can fill what only the Creator can.

No ring. No thing. Just God.

—CAMERON MILLS, FORMER PLAYER, UNIVERSITY OF KENTUCKY BASKETBALL

SPORTS NOTE:
Cameron Mills scored 365 points during his four-year career at Kentucky. He shot 47 percent from three-point range.

FROM THE PLAYBOOK:
Read Philippians 3.

GAME PLAN: List three things that you think would absolutely complete your life if you had them: A car? A degree? An award? A championship? Think of how that compares with knowing the God of the universe.

TRUE CONFESSION

POINT OF EMPHASIS:
Confession of sin

"They stood in their places and confessed their sins." NEHEMIAH 9:2

Athletes do not get into more trouble than other citizens. It just some-times seems that way. The fact that their indiscretions are announced on *SportsCenter* does make those difficulties appear to be much more serious.

What is most bothersome about athletes or anyone else who is convicted of a violation are those times when they don't seem to know how to face up to their error. How often have we heard publicized athletic indiscretions dismissed with something like, "Well, it wasn't that big a deal." Or, "I just made a mistake." Or, "They're just out to get me."

People who make those kinds of remarks after being caught doing wrong—even if those people are us—need to spend some time studying the prayer of confession of the Israelites in Nehemiah 9.

These people knew they had done wrong, and they fessed up. Of course, this was not always how the Israelites reacted, but their response in this instance is something we can learn from.

Let's look at what they did: They fasted and put on sackcloth. They separated themselves from outsiders. They confessed their sins. They read the Scriptures. They wor-shiped and praised God.

Sin is an ugly sight in God's eyes. No matter how much we try to clean it up, we can never make sin anything but an affront to God.

And because it is so offensive to God, our best action is to mirror the response of the Israelites (well, skip the sackcloth). We need to take sin seriously and confess it sincerely.

It may not make *SportsCenter*, but it will sure get God's attention.

—DAVE BRANON

SPORTS NOTE:
SportsCenter first went on the air on September 7, 1979.

FROM THE PLAYBOOK:
Read Nehemiah 9.

GAME PLAN: Is there a sin that you have stashed away in your life's attic? Haul it out and confess it.

BE A FOOL

POINT OF EMPHASIS:
Fool for Christ

"We are fools for Christ." 1 CORINTHIANS 4:10

Suppose you're a quarterback. Not just any quarterback—you're the field general of one of the best college football teams in the country. You're returning to a team that has a chance to win the national championship. Everybody loves you—except your gridiron rivals, of course.

Now suppose you get named to a prestigious All-America team. You're offered an all-expenses-paid weekend getaway to Arizona for a photo-shoot in a prominent magazine. First-class treatment for a first-rate player. Would you turn it down?

SPORTS NOTE:
College Football News called Danny one of the Top 100 college football players of all-time.

Danny Wuerffel did. As the golden-armed gunslinger of the Florida Gators in 1996, Wuerffel declined the honor of being a national magazine's first-team All-America quarterback. It seems the publication's philosophy is strongly at odds with his own Christ-following convictions. You see, the magazine is *Playboy*.

"I'm sure there's a good bit of the population out there that would think I'm silly for doing this," Wuerffel admitted. "But there's also a good bit of the population that would understand that's not the type of person I would want to portray myself as."

FROM THE PLAYBOOK:
Read 1 Corinthians 3:16–23.

The apostle Paul was familiar with the kind of people who would call Danny Wuerffel "silly." Conventional wisdom—the false wisdom Paul warned of in 1 Corinthians 3:19—says, "So what if you don't agree with *Playboy*. Take their money and run." Fortunately, Danny decided to pass.

Paul cautioned against being fooled into thinking we should be "wise by the standards of this age" (v. 18). He knew that God's wisdom is infinitely higher than human wisdom. We are not to follow the lead of the world—even when our refusal makes them think we're fools.

—TIM GUSTAFSON

GAME PLAN: What motivates your decisions? Is it God's wisdom? Are you concerned that people might think you're silly for honoring God's standards? What are three things you are trying to avoid but most people think you are silly to avoid? How does this help your relationship with God?

WHY BE AFRAID?

POINT OF EMPHASIS:
Overcoming fear

"Be strong and courageous. Do not be terrified." JOSHUA 1:9

One March 31, 2003, I stood on the mound at Comerica Park on opening day. Television cameras were focused on my teammates and me, and 40,000 Tiger fans were waiting for me to throw the first pitch. As a child I dreamed of a moment like this, but suddenly it was a reality.

I was nervous. No, I was scared.

Yet, God *commands* us not to be scared or worried, because He is with us *wherever* we go, including the baseball field. We can rest in the peace of the Lord with the knowledge that His presence surrounds us.

When we are overwhelmed with the circumstances of our life, we can be assured of this promise made by God to Joshua. Repeatedly in His Word, God tells us not to be afraid. When the disciples were traveling by boat, a fierce storm approached and they were worried they would surely drown. They woke Jesus and He immediately calmed the water and winds. He then asked the men, "Why are you so afraid? Do you still have no faith?" (Mark 4:40).

Many of us spend too much time worrying about the outcome of our situations. Will I get a win tonight? Will my children grow up and love the Lord? Follow Joshua's example. Continue to keep the faith and you will be "prosperous and successful" (Joshua 1:8) in the things that count the most—spiritual things. Then practice the faith you have been given and experience the grace God provides when He calms the mightiest winds in our lives.

He is always with us and assures us that we are never alone, whether it is in front of 40,000 people or by ourselves.

—MIKE MAROTH, MAJOR LEAGUE PITCHER

SPORTS NOTE:
Mike and Brooke Maroth won the 2004 Bill Emerson Good Samaritan Award for their work in starting food recovery efforts.

FROM THE PLAYBOOK:
Read Joshua 1.

GAME PLAN: What makes you afraid? Do you really think God can help you with that fear? It's a matter of faith and trust to go ahead of your fears by giving them to God.

HUMILITY'S STRENGTH

POINT OF EMPHASIS:
Seeking humility

"Clothe yourselves with humility." I PETER 5:5

Do you think you'd notice if a 360-pound man with 22-inch biceps, 35-inch thighs, and a 62-inch chest entered the room? Do you think you'd be aware of someone at the table having a dinner that consists of three T-bone steaks, a baked potato with butter, cheese, and sour cream, a salad, and two glasses of grape juice? Do you think you'd be conscious of some guy in a parking lot picking up cars and walking with them?

SPORTS NOTE:
Shane Hamman's favorite sport is golf.

FROM THE PLAYBOOK:
Read a story Jesus told about two men—one humble and one proud—in Luke 18:9–14.

Yes, you'd notice weightlifter Shane Hamman, the strongest man in America. Shane is big (his sister-in-law says his thigh was bigger than her belly when she was nine months pregnant), hungry (he says, "I can eat whatever I see"), and strong (he has hoisted 1,008 pounds—the equivalent of three refrigerators—in the squat).

But according to Huey Long, the city manager in Shane's hometown, something else makes Hamman distinctive. Long says, "A lot of times super athletes are arrogant and their personal lives are out of control. But Shane's a humble young man, and that sets him apart."

About his abilities Shane says: "God has given them to me, and I should use them for His glory, not mine." That's humility.

Okay, maybe you can't lift a refrigerator, but something sets you apart. Is it humility? First Peter 5:5–6 says, "All of you, clothe yourselves with humility toward one another, because, 'God opposes the proud but gives grace to the humble.' Humble yourselves, therefore, under God's mighty hand."

No matter what we're known for, we need to make humility what sets us apart.

—BRIAN HETTINGA

GAME PLAN: In the Bible, humility means having an adequate view of God and an accurate view of ourselves. Next time you're tempted to boast, remember who gave you your abilities and opportunities. It's a whole different way of looking at life.

EVEN IN LOSS

POINT OF EMPHASIS:
God's help during difficulties

"May the name of the Lord be praised." Job 1:21

Becky Short was only a freshman when she qualified for the women's NCAA swim championships. When she mounted the starting blocks, her Auburn University team was in first place. It was the first time in history that Auburn women had led the meet, the first time every teammate had earned an All-American honor, and the first time an Auburn swimmer had broken an American record.

It was truly Auburn's shining moment. All Becky had to do was help her relay team finish in the Top 8 in prelims. A national title would be sure to follow. Under the pressure, though, Becky false started. Her relay team did not advance, and Auburn finished fourth overall.

Becky left the pool and hid, crushed that she had cost her team the championship. Her coach, David Marsh, found Becky and said she needed to return to the team. "That was the last place I wanted to be," Becky says. "How could they love me? I had let them down so terribly. But when I returned I found comfort, love, and encouragement."

Marsh took Becky aside. "He forgave me and reminded me that Jesus taught us to rejoice in our sufferings," Becky says. "Coach Marsh shared Job 2:10 with me, which says, 'Shall we accept good from God, and not trouble?' He added, 'The Lord gave and the Lord has taken away; may the name of the Lord be praised.'" (Job 1:20). This enabled her to work through the disappointment. The very next week she helped Auburn qualify for the world championships.

Even in loss, God is there. Look for Him.

— Roxanne Robbins

SPORTS NOTE:
In March 2004, Becky Short set an NCAA record in the 50-meter freestyle (24.69 seconds).

FROM THE PLAYBOOK:
Read Job 1–2.

GAME PLAN: Think of a time you felt you failed. What did God teach you through that time?

SHARING YOUR FAITH

POINT OF EMPHASIS:
Telling of God's grace

*"If I were still trying to please men, I would not be
a servant of Christ."* GALATIANS 1:10

For most of my life, soccer was my primary focus and No. 1 priority. Unfortunately, even though I was experiencing success in the sport I loved, my quest to experience peace and happiness was futile. I reached the pinnacle of American soccer when I was drafted to play in Major League Soccer in 1996. My dream had been realized.

My search for peace, however, grew ever more elusive. The peaks and valleys of pro athletics were consuming me, and my life was full of turmoil.

SPORTS NOTE:
After retiring from the MLS in 2003, Grafer played for the Long Island Rough Riders in the United Soccer League in 2005.

FROM THE PLAYBOOK:
Read Galatians 1.

After suffering through a painful and humiliating performance on the soccer field in 1998, I began to question the emphasis I was placing on my career. I began to understand that, over time, my focus had been taken off God and placed on soccer, damaging the relationship that had provided me with peace and happiness earlier in life.

Eventually, I came to understand that peace is only attainable through Christ. I started to place my life in God's hands, not in the tumultuous events of my soccer career. I still face daily struggles, but through God's grace and a deep relationship with Jesus Christ, I experience much more peace and joy then ever before. Even after retiring from the game I love in November 2003, I still feel the joy.

And now, as did Paul in Galatians 1:13–24, I have a story to tell. Paul's testimony saved many people in the early stages of the church. I have seen my story help all kinds of people in their personal faith journeys.

Take some time to formulate your own story of faith. Then tell it to others to help them find salvation in Jesus Christ.

—PAUL GRAFER, FORMER MLS GOALIE

 GAME PLAN: Have you ever written down your story for others to read? Try it, and you'll see how God has helped you—and how He can help others.

APRIL 6

SELF TALK

POINT OF EMPHASIS:
Positive talk

"For his mouth speaks from that which fills his heart."
LUKE 6:45 NASB

As a golfer and a golf broadcaster, I often chuckle when "self-talk" is let out by some of our more extroverted players.

Perhaps unlike any other sport, golf allows the greatest opportunity for "self-talk." The average round of golf takes about 4 hours, but only about 2 minutes is actually spent hitting shots. The difference is often described as the "inner time," a period when a player loses himself in the mire of his conscious and subconscious thoughts. Much of this thought time is used up in talking to oneself. I have often heard such statements after a shot as "You idiot!" "Why did you hit it over there?" "I quit!" "I'm a hopeless case!" I even heard Tiger Woods once say to himself, "You are the worst golfer in the world!" Ah, Tiger, can I disagree?

Players use self-talk as a motivating force. Certainly it is that way with Tiger Woods. He doesn't really mean that he thinks he's the worst golfer in the world, but he says things like that to propel himself to reach a higher level of commitment and concentration.

Proper "self-talk" can have a direct positive bearing on performance and thus increase confidence. Not just in golf, but in life. That's because what comes from the mouth comes first from the heart. Our faith in Christ should cause us to tell ourselves positive things that can spur us on to live as He wants us to. Use godly self-talk to propel yourself toward the actions God wants in your life.

—BOBBY CLAMPETT, TV GOLF ANALYST

SPORTS NOTE:
Bobby Clampett won the 1982 Southern Open on the PGA Tour.

FROM THE PLAYBOOK:
Read 2 Peter 1:5–7.

GAME PLAN: When you're challenged, what kind of advice are you giving yourself? When facing difficult situations, are you leaning on God's Word to fill your thoughts or are you trusting in yourself?

SORE LOSER

POINT OF EMPHASIS:
The value of humility

"Do nothing out of selfish ambition." PHILIPPIANS 2:3

James Brendan Connolly wasn't a sore loser. In fact, completely the opposite. He was a winner on one of the world's greatest stages.

In the first modern Olympic Games in 1896, Connolly won gold for the United States in the triple jump. He had become the first medal winner of the modern Olympic Games in Athens. He later took second place in the high jump and third place in the long jump.

SPORTS NOTE:
James Brendan Connolly was on the RMS Republic when it was rammed by another ship in 1909. More than 1,500 people, including Connolly, were rescued; six people died.

FROM THE PLAYBOOK:
Read Philippians 2:3–18.

With all the Olympic success Connolly had, it seems rather odd that he would write a book about being a poor loser. But as long as there's been competition, there's been a problem with our perception of losing. Back in 1908 Connolly wrote *The English as Poor Losers*. His main idea was that a pompous attitude has no place in athletics. If you think that your race, intelligence, or social status makes you superior to other people, then your arrogance will make you a poor loser.

To a poor loser, congratulating the other team is out of the question. You've got excuses a mile-long why you didn't win. All because you're too full of pride to graciously accept the fact that another athlete is better than you are that day.

There's another book that talks about this issue. It's the Bible—specifically Philippians 2:3. Humility should mark our lives. Not only will this make us gracious losers in those few occasions when we don't win but this inspired knowledge from the Bible will also make us modest, respectful champions in the game of life.

—DAN DEAL

GAME PLAN: Are you an athlete? Find your schedule of upcoming games. Look down the list and pray for your next opponent. Ask God to help them do well and be safe from injury.

STICKING OUT ALL OVER

POINT OF EMPHASIS:
Influence of Jesus

"Let your shine before men, that they may see your good deeds and praise your Father." MATTHEW 5:16

My four-year-old niece, Alison, went with me to a nearby high school to speak and demonstrate basketball skills to the students. On our way, I glanced over at her. She was dressed in a little warm-up suit, but I noticed that big tears were running down her cheeks. Quietly, she wiped them away.

I asked, "Alison, are you okay?"

She said, "My eyes are making me sad." I was surprised that she would have this feeling, because we would be only twenty minutes from her home.

To get her mind off this, I asked, "What do you think we should tell these people today?"

She said, "Let's tell them how to get Jesus in their hearts." In her four-year-old way, she told me that we needed to tell them to ask Jesus to forgive their sins, and then ask Him to come into their hearts. Wow! Proverbs 23:26 says, "My son, give me your heart and let your eyes keep to my ways."

A little later Alison asked me, "Aunt Tanya, how big is Jesus?"

To help her understand, I said, "Probably about as big as your dad."

With a puzzled look she said, "Aunt Tanya, when we ask Jesus into our hearts, isn't He going to stick out all over?" I laughed to myself.

Then I decided that she's right. I thought of Matthew 5:16, which says, "Let your light shine before men that they may see your good deeds and praise your Father in heaven." When Jesus is Lord of our lives, He permeates our thoughts, producing righteous actions and righteous words. In other words, He "sticks out all over."

—TANYA CREVIER, BASKETBALL SHOWPERSON

SPORTS NOTE:
Tanya played for two years in the old Women's Basketball League. She graduated from South Dakota State University.

FROM THE PLAYBOOK:
Read Matthew 28:18–20.

GAME PLAN: What are three specific ways you can influence others to consider the claim of Christ? Can you find three people for whom you can let your light shine?

WHO WANTS THE BLESSING?

POINT OF EMPHASIS:
God's blessing

"All these blessings will come upon you and accompany you if you obey the Lord your God. " DEUTERONOMY 28:2

This was the hurdler's first and last junior high school state championship competition, and she wanted to win this race.

Her family, team, and coach were there to support her—confident in her ability. She was ready to run the best race of her life. She warmed up and answered the call to check in. Somehow, though, she missed the check-in. When the official called the names of the girls who would be racing, hers was not called.

Desperate, she ran to her coach for help. The meet director informed her coach that she had been told where to go, and she didn't show up. A miscommunication had taken place, and she was out of the race before it had even started. Devastation flooded the athlete, the team, her family, and her coach. All the hours of hard work were dashed because she did not respond correctly to the call, thereby putting her out of position for the race when called upon. The blessing of victory had escaped her.

How many times have God's blessings escaped us because we did not heed His call? Or we were not obedient to His will? How many missed opportunities have we passed because we did not respond correctly to His call? Blessings come when obedience to the voice of the Lord positions us to receive. We are all called to run the race of life, but we must obey the rules and not disqualify ourselves from the prize. Run your race to obtain the prize.

—MADELINE MIMS, OLYMPIC MEDALIST, TRACK

SPORTS NOTE:
Madeline Mims was inducted into the National Track and Field Hall of Fame in 1984.

FROM THE PLAYBOOK:
Read Deuteronomy 28 and 1 Corinthians 9:24–27.

 GAME PLAN: "Father, help me to run the race of life by qualifying through Your Son, Jesus Christ. May I hear Your voice through Your Holy Word and obey You in all I do and say. Then, I will be positioned for the blessing of the prize and thereby bless others. Amen."

MORE THAN YOU CAN HANDLE

POINT OF EMPHASIS:
God's providence

"When I am weak, then I am strong." 2 CORINTHIANS 12:10

At age 21, LPGA pro Terry-Jo Myers was stricken with interstitial cystitis—a rare and painful bladder disease. For 11 years, she lived in constant and excruciating pain, keeping her condition a secret from everyone but her family.

When new medications relieved her pain, Terry-Jo planned a big "comeback," only to suffer two serious back injuries, both requiring surgery. After that, though, Terry-Jo was healthy again. She decided not to keep her struggles a secret. Whenever she has the opportunity, she tells her story in the hope of encouraging others who face difficulties of their own. Often, after hearing her speak, someone will exclaim, "I guess God never gives you more than you can handle!"

Terry-Jo understands what they mean. But she has to disagree. "It's *always* more than you can handle!" she says. "You're not ever supposed to get to where you don't need Him."

The truth is, there's no way we can handle the challenges of this life on our own, no matter how hard we try. God wants us to learn to depend on Him daily.

In 2 Corinthians 12:8, the apostle Paul talked about his struggle with a problem he called a "thorn" in his flesh: "Three times I pleaded with the Lord to take it away from me. But he said to me, 'My grace is sufficient for you, for my power is made perfect in weakness.'"

Is there something in your life that you can't handle? A problem you can't solve? Praise God for it! Because when we're weak, He is strong. God's grace really *is* sufficient. Let Him be your strength today.

—CHRISTIN DITCHFIELD

SPORTS NOTE:
In 2001, Terry-Jo won the Daytona Beach, Florida, Kiwanis Foundation Humanitarian of the Year Award along with fellow golfer Dottie Pepper.

FROM THE PLAYBOOK:
Read 2 Corinthians 12:7–10 and Philippians 4:12–13.

 GAME PLAN: What is the biggest challenge you face today? Do you realize you can't handle it without God? Ask Him to help you with this situation. Pray for strength and grace.

THE RIGHT PERSPECTIVE

POINT OF EMPHASIS:
Perspective on life

"A crown that will last forever." I CORINTHIANS 9:25

Two hundred and twenty-five million dollars. A quarter of a billion dollars. That's how much major league teams have agreed to pay shortstop Alex Rodriguez over the course of his contract.

When you break down the numbers, it looks something like this: 25.2 million dollars a season; $155,000 a game; $17,000 an inning; $42,000 every at-bat—whether he hits a home run or strikes out.

When I heard about the contract, my first thought was, "Why can't that be me?"—a thought that was quickly followed by, "Can somebody in Major League Baseball say 'salary cap!'"

Instead of becoming envious or getting on a soap box, however, perhaps it's better to use the news of this contract to remind ourselves of the bigger picture.

Heaven offers every believer in Jesus Christ a lucrative "contract" too. Consider a few terms of this contract.

First, the length of the contract isn't a mere 10 years. It's eternal. It never ends (1 Corinthians 9:25).

Second, the value of the contract can't be measured in monetary terms. It has a value that is beyond description or comprehension.

Third, the health benefits are out of this world. The Bible says that there will be "no more death or mourning or crying or pain" (Revelation 21:4).

Let's keep life in perspective. Life this side of heaven continues to be filled with heartache and struggle—a fact that no salary can change, but let's remember that our "light and momentary troubles are achieving for us an eternal glory that far outweighs them all" (2 Corinthians 4:17).

A quarter of a billion dollars is nothing compared with an eternity with God in heaven.
—JEFF OLSON

SPORTS NOTE:
Rodriguez signed his huge contract with the Texas Rangers in 2000. They paid him until he was traded to the New York Yankees.

FROM THE PLAYBOOK:
Read Psalm 73.

GAME PLAN: Without minimizing your struggles, make it a point to remind yourself of the rewards God has promised to give you through Jesus Christ. Let the hope of what awaits you in heaven power you up.

NAPOLEON'S PASSION

POINT OF EMPHASIS:
Passion for God

"Let us do good to all people." GALATIANS 6:10

Napoleon Kaufman was just 27 years old when he walked away from professional football.

His body wasn't injured. His million-dollar contract was in place for the 2001 season, so there were no contract "issues" to get hammered out. Napoleon's Oakland Raiders were coming off an AFC West championship season, and the team was primed to be one of the best in the conference—with a legitimate shot at the Super Bowl. And Kaufman has had plenty of individual success in the NFL, rushing for more than 1,000 yards in a season as recently as 1997.

So exactly what was it that pulled the former University of Washington star away from the gridiron? The answer might surprise you. It was Napoleon's passion for ministry!

Kaufman's agent, Cameron Foster, told ESPN, "He loves football, but I guess he loves ministering more."

Kaufman, known in college for his speed, shifty moves, and hard-charging lifestyle, gave his life to Jesus Christ after he began his NFL career. Then he became an ordained minister, and he has sought to let the love of Jesus Christ flow through him and into the lives of others. Obviously, Napoleon believed he could do that more effectively by not playing football.

As Christians, we should all have a similar passion for reaching out and ministering to others.

In the gospel of Matthew, our Lord Jesus told the disciples about reaching out to those in need. He said, "Whatever you did for one of the least of these brothers of mine, you did for me" (25:40).

Perhaps that's why Napoleon loves ministering so much, because he knows that he's serving his Savior.

—ROB BENTZ

SPORTS NOTE: From 1995 through 2000, Napoleon Kaufman rushed for 4,792 yards. His best year was 1997, when he gained 1,294 yards.

FROM THE PLAYBOOK: Read Matthew 25:31–46.

GAME PLAN: Why not volunteer one hour of your time each week for the next month to your church or to a local ministry.

SURPRISING BOLDNESS

POINT OF EMPHASIS:
Bold witness

"Enable your servants to speak your word with great boldness."
ACTS 4:29

In my first year of racing I got to stay at a race venue with another triathlete. Sue had been at the top of the racing circuit for the previous few years. I was this shy rookie who couldn't believe her good fortune of staying with this legend.

One night Sue was flicking through the TV channels and stopped on *Touched by an Angel*. It was just at the point when the angel was lit up by God's light and was revealing herself to the woman she was assigned to help. Sue made some comment about this show being for "those crazy born-again Christians."

Well, somewhere out of this shy triathlete came the statement: "I'm a born-again Christian, and Jesus actually says in the Bible that 'no one can see the kingdom of God unless he is born again' (John 3:3)." I don't know who was more shocked at this boldness, her or me. I think it was me! When those words came out of my mouth, I sort of stepped out of myself and said, "Who is THAT girl!"

Up to this point I thought of my faith as a very personal thing. I was not bold in speaking God's truth, as I felt threatened by what others might think. To be bold with Sue was definitely out of my character. But that's the point. It was God's character and the guidance of the Holy Spirit enabling His servant to speak boldly.

The Lord can use the closeness that sports creates between competitors as a non-threatening way for each of us to speak His truth with great boldness.

—BARB LINDQUIST, WORLD-CLASS TRIATHLETE

SPORTS NOTE:
Barb Lindquist's coach and manager of her career is Loren Lindquist, her husband.

FROM THE PLAYBOOK:
Read 2 Corinthians 5:11–21.

GAME PLAN: When in the past few days have you had a chance to be bold for Jesus and found your mouth glued shut? What can help to make sure the boldness Barb showed comes out next time?

DON'T BE ANXIOUS

POINT OF EMPHASIS:
The peace of God

"By prayer and petition . . . present your requests to God."
PHILIPPIANS 4:6

American pole-vaulter Pat Manson is a three-time gold-medal winner at the Pan American Games. Yet despite his success with the pole, he finds plenty to be anxious about in life. That's why one of his favorite Bible passages is Philippians 4:6–7.

"I love it when the Bible says, "Do not be anxious about anything," Manson explains. "Absolutes, like the word *anything,* are challenging.

"It's easy in Olympic level athletics to get really nervous about things. Two weeks before the 2000 Olympic Trials, I had a severe hamstring tear. That's one of the worst injuries that could happen. It would have been easy to freak out and get anxious. Then I recalled Philippians 4:6–7, which I had committed to memory. I was reminded again, 'Do not be anxious about anything.' There have been many times I've relied on that verse. In life in general, I apply it all the time. It's a great tool to have on hand when the going gets tough.

"The second part of the verse is what you're supposed to do instead of being anxious. We're supposed to, through prayer and petition, make our requests known to God. We are also supposed to maintain a thankful attitude. And then, it promises that the peace of God will be with you."

Take it from a man who understands all about the ups and downs of life—and of sports. If a guy who jumps 18 feet in the air can learn not to be anxious, we should listen to him.

—ROXANNE ROBBINS

SPORTS NOTE:
Pat Manson won a bronze medal in the 1998 Goodwill Games.

FROM THE PLAYBOOK:
Read Philippians 4:4–9.

GAME PLAN: Is there something you're struggling to trust God with? Take time today to pray and make your requests known to God. Keep a journal to record how you see God move through this situation.

GIVE IT ALL TO GOD

POINT OF EMPHASIS:
Trusting God

"Commit to the Lord whatever you do, and your plans will succeed."
PROVERBS 16:3

In April 1994, I traveled to Boston, Massachusetts, for the Boston Marathon. I had won this prestigious event the previous 4 years, and I was more excited than ever to be returning to this race.

Three days before the marathon, I went out to eat with several people at a local restaurant. The next morning, I woke up feeling dizzy and nauseated. A phone call from a friend informed me that seven other people in our party of fourteen were dealing with the effects of food poisoning too.

The day before the marathon, I was still feeling bad, and I was beginning to despair as I thought about the next day's event. As I read my Bible, I came across Proverbs 16:3, which says, "Commit to the Lord whatever you do, and your plans will succeed." I knew this was not a guarantee of success, but right then and there I committed my race to God. I would leave the "success" part up to Him.

Amazingly, though I felt like pulling out of the race on several occasions, I won my fifth straight Boston Marathon and broke the world record in the women's wheelchair division with a time of 1 hour, 34 minutes, 22 seconds. That record still stood as the racers competed in the spring of 2005.

Since that event, I have committed everything to God: every workout, race, interview, speaking engagement, and whatever else. When I give every situation to God, the pressure is off me, regardless of the outcome.

—JEAN DRISCOLL, EIGHT-TIME BOSTON MARATHON CHAMPION

SPORTS NOTE:
Jean has been awarded two honorary doctorate degrees: one from the University of Rhode Island and one from the Massachusetts School of Law.

FROM THE PLAYBOOK:
Read 1 Corinthians 1:4–9.

GAME PLAN: Why should you commit everything to God? What are the guarantees? What does it suggest about your relationship with Him?

FOCUS ABOVE

POINT OF EMPHASIS:
Focus on God

"Do not worry about tomorrow, for tomorrow will worry about itself." MATTHEW 6:34

It was the beginning of April 2004, and the WNBA draft was coming up in a couple of weeks. So many thoughts were running through my head. Would I be drafted? What team would I go to? Am I good enough to make the team? Will I like my teammates and coaches? How would I adjust to a new environment?

It was a very stressful time and a scary situation. My college career at Boston College had gone well, but now it was time to look at the future. In a few weeks I could possibly be going to the WNBA, or I could be trying to find a job in the real world. It was all so exciting yet so nerve-racking at the same time. What was going to happen?

As I look back on it now, I know I worried way too much throughout these weeks. After being drafted in the third round by the Minnesota Lynx and then making the team, I asked myself why I had worried and made myself become so stressed and anxious. After all, the Lord knew His will for my life and what the outcome would be.

This was a good lesson for me to remember. It reminded me to keep my eyes on the Lord and to only worry about today. God is in total control, and He will provide; all we have to do is seek Him, and He will take care of the rest.

So, when you are feeling overwhelmed about situations in the future, remember to seek God and obey His ways. Do not let your worries about tomorrow affect your relationship with the Lord today!

—AMBER JACOBS, WBNA GUARD

SPORTS NOTE:
On April 17, 2004, Amber was the 33rd player chosen in the WNBA draft.

FROM THE PLAYBOOK:
Read Matthew 6:25–34.

GAME PLAN: What are you worrying about today? Does worrying change anything? If this situation entails action, take it. If it entails waiting, then turn it over to God and let Him handle it. If He needs your help, He'll let you know. Note how many times the word "worry" appears in the Playbook passage.

&%*$#@*!!

POINT OF EMPHASIS:
Using good language

"The mouth of the fool gushes folly." PROVERBS 15:2

"I been waitin' forty-five minutes for a blankety-blank pizza. That's too blankety-blank long." That was the flame-broiled reply from a fellow pizza store patron after I calmly said, "Sure taking a long time for the pizza, isn't it?"

Later that evening, I was watching a baseball game on TV. The umpires, those normally stellar icons of accuracy and perfection, blew a couple of calls. Missed 'em by a mile. Next thing I knew, I could hear tens of thousands of fans yelling in the background, "&%*$#@*&!"

SPORTS NOTE:
NASCAR has fined its drivers 25 points in the Nextel Cup standings for using bad language in interviews.

FROM THE PLAYBOOK:
Read James 3:1–12.

That same week, I overheard some Christian kids talking about something they didn't like. "That *blanks*," they complained, using a term that was not long ago considered filthy enough to get kids kicked out of school for uttering.

So what's the big deal? Does it really matter, anyway? Don't we have more important things to consider than a few naughty words? Well, if we take the Bible seriously, no.

How can we ignore verses like these: "It is shameful even to mention what the disobedient do in secret" (Ephesians 5:12). "Nor should there be obscenity, foolish talk or coarse joking, which are out of place" (5:4). "You shall not misuse the name of the Lord your God" (Exodus 20:7). "You must rid yourselves of . . . filthy language" (Colossians 3:8).

We can't always avoid hearing bad language—especially in sports. But if we understand that "filthy language" dishonors God, we'll begin to see how important it is that we keep our own words clean. We'll avoid letting ourselves become so conditioned that bad words don't bother us anymore.

—DAVE BRANON

GAME PLAN: What are some words you find yourself using that you know are not honoring to the Lord? How can your relationship with God help you keep your language clean? Do you think you can watch movies and TV with bad language and not have it affect you? Can you justify that stance biblically?

THE POWER OF VISION

POINT OF EMPHASIS:
God's best

"Where there is no vision, the people perish; but he that keepeth the law, happy is he." PROVERBS 29:18 KJV

The words of Proverbs 29:18 present a truly powerful principle.

All anyone has to do is watch the evening news or read their local newspaper to see that we are experiencing an epidemic of people who seem to have no vision for their lives. This is deeply troubling when one understands that the rest of the verse clearly states these very people will perish. Vision is a necessity in life if you are to be all that God created you to be.

Over and over in my life, I saw myself wearing the gold buckle long before I was crowned a world champion bull rider. I believe the desire I had as a small boy to be the best bull rider in the world was first placed into my heart by the Spirit of God.

Of course, I would have many hard and painful years of sacrificing to see my dream come to pass, but the most wonderful thing was how God never forsook me (Hebrews 13:5) and always provided me with His strength. He gave me the dream, and He led me down the proper paths to fulfill that desire. And finally, He gave me the perseverance to continue attempting to win the world title. My prayer concerning that championship is that God alone receive all of the glory.

Many things in life will come against your true purpose—which is to fulfill God's will. However, you must never give up on what you feel God wants you to do for Him. It is like a blueprint for your life, and it will keep you on track if you will stay before the Father with a pure heart and keep that deep desire to obey Him.

God wants nothing but the very best for your life (Proverbs 37:4). Start today by making a commitment to Jesus, then do all you can to experience the power of doing God's will in your life.

—SCOTT MENDES, BULL-RIDING WORLD CHAMPION

SPORTS NOTE:
Scott taped a TV program once called *How to Be a Rodeo Rider.* Read about it at www.tmwmedia. com/tellmehow.html.

FROM THE PLAYBOOK:
Read Matthew 12:33–35; Romans 12:2; Ephesians 4:22–24.

GAME PLAN: Are you willing to pay the price to see God's vision for your life fulfilled?

RUNNING A RACE OF FAITH

POINT OF EMPHASIS:
Running the race

"Let us throw off everything that hinders and the sin that so easily entangles." HEBREWS 12:1

At the age of 10, Tim Howard was diagnosed with Tourette's Syndrome—a neurological disorder classified by physical and visual tics. Having Tourette's was not easy for a young boy, but fortunately, Tim was blessed with the gift of athleticism and the strength to overcome his disability. By keeping his faith strong and his eyes on the prize, Tim was able to weather the difficult moments associated with his affliction and use his gifts to impact kids and fans positively.

SPORTS NOTE:
Paul Grafer and Tim Howard were teammates with the MLS MetroStars before Howard was signed by Manchester United.

FROM THE PLAYBOOK:
Read Hebrews 12.

Tim has overcome the debilitating aspects of Tourette's and is now living a dream as goalkeeper for the most famous and prestigious soccer club in the world, Manchester United Football Club. He uses his Tourette's and the exposure he gets as a famous soccer player to encourage others in their faith.

Hebrews 12 encourages all of us to "throw off everything that hinders and the sin that so easily entangles" so we can "run with perseverance the race marked out for us." By keeping his eyes fixed on Jesus, Tim has persevered through the inhibiting symptoms of his disease, run the race with endurance, and reaped worldly and eternal rewards for his faithfulness.

So, "let us fix our eyes on Jesus, the author and perfecter of our faith," so we can also run with endurance and perseverance. Jesus was the ultimate example of an enduring and persevering servant of God throughout His life. By following His example, we show our love for Him and we store up rewards in heaven.

—PAUL GRAFER, FORMER MLS GOALIE

GAME PLAN: What sometimes feels like a weight or encumbrance on your shoulders? Have you asked God to help you throw off that weight? What else can you do to make sure you're not running around with extra weight on your shoulders?

SHINE LIKE A BIG OLD STAR

POINT OF EMPHASIS:
Witnessing for Christ

"Humble yourselves, therefore, under God's mighty hand." I PETER 5:6

Do you long to be the star on your team? As highly driven athletes, sometimes we push too hard to attain perfection and be the star. We lose our perspective on the kingdom of God.

I remember hearing a testimony from a minor league baseball player, and it really challenged me. I was asking if he was getting much playing time. His answer to me was, "No, God has me in the bullpen."

I was a little confused. Why would God want him on the bench? Is that success? My perspective was way off! I was amazed at how content this player was to be on the bench. He was content because he was more concerned with God's plan than his own. He was God's light in the bullpen.

God has a purpose for every situation. We need to humble ourselves daily, seek after God, and keep His perspective. He will give us peace and give us opportunities to shine for His glory, not our own.

I love the second part of I Peter 5:6! It says, "he may lift you up in due time." This lifting up may not be from a physical standpoint, but then again it might.

I believe that God allowed me to be the first woman to hit an out-of-the-park home run in the history of baseball. It was to be used for His glory, and it was a way for my Father to bless His child. It has given me great opportunity to shine bright for Him.

May we all long to be the brightest star in the kingdom of God. Matthew 5:16 tells us, "Let your light shine before men, that they may see your good deeds and praise your Father in heaven." We never shine brighter than when we are reflecting God's glory.

—KIM VOISARD, PROFESSIONAL BASEBALL PLAYER

SPORTS NOTE:
Kim Voisard played centerfield for the Colorado Silver Bullets from 1994 through 1997. The team was the first professional women's baseball team in the US since 1954.

FROM THE PLAYBOOK:
Read Matthew 5:13–16.

GAME PLAN: Name three specific ways you can shine bright for God—showing others the light of God's presence. Then plan to make those three things happen.

THE LAVAR LEAP

POINT OF EMPHASIS:
Temptation

"Prepare your minds for action . . . " 1 PETER 1:13

When the Washington Redskins made Penn State linebacker LaVar Arrington the second overall pick in the 2000 NFL Draft, they expected big things. You know, punishing tackles, huge hits, and of course the famous "LaVar Leap"— where he hurdles the line of scrimmage to meet the ball carrier mid-air. When LaVar showed up for training camp, though, the Redskins got something they didn't expect.

SPORTS NOTE:
In 2001, LaVar had 82 tackles and three interceptions for the Washington Redskins.

FROM THE PLAYBOOK:
Find out how Peter suggests you "prepare your mind" by reading 1 Peter 1:13–25.

You see, Arrington skipped the opening week of training camp while embattled in contract negotiations. When he finally did report for his new job, he wasn't in physical or mental condition for the rigors of his first NFL camp.

It showed up in his first preseason game as a Redskin when Arrington missed tackles, played tentative instead of aggressive, and met nothing but air on his first NFL "LaVar Leap."

It took just one preseason game to help LaVar realize that he was not prepared mentally or physically. "I'll never let that happen again," said an embarrassed Arrington. And then, apparently, he headed for the weight room.

While you probably won't meet a 210-pound ball carrier in midair in front of 50,000 screaming fans any time soon, you too need to be prepared. You will run into some fierce competition. Your opponent's name is Temptation. He may not look as menacing as Jerome Bettis hurdling toward you from the backfield, but he's every bit as powerful. And he's ready to take you down—today.

Don't let Temptation catch you unprepared!

—ROB BENTZ

GAME PLAN: Select a Bible verse—maybe 1 Peter 1:13. Got one? Now strive to memorize that verse today! Keep it at the forefront of your mind when your opponent comes to challenge you.

APRIL 22

FUSSY MECHANICS

POINT OF EMPHASIS:
Christian living

"Continue to work out your salvation." Philippians 2:12

Have you ever hung out in the garage area at a NASCAR race?
If you have, you understand this statement: Those boys sure do love to tinker!

Whenever I've nosed around all those cars, I've been impressed with all the fussing, fidgeting, manipulating, and worrying that goes into getting the cars ready for the race.

The crews change tires like we change stations on the car radio. And it doesn't take much more than a whim for them to replace the whole engine—as late as a half-hour before the race.

They aren't satisfied to take the car that qualified two days earlier and park it until the race begins. Not even the crew with the fastest qualifying time is happy. They adjust and tinker till the last second.

There's a valuable principle behind this. As I think about how much more relaxing it would be for a crew to be satisfied with the car and pull up a chair for a nap, I think of how often we as followers of Jesus do just that.

It happens when we decide to let things stay as they are spiritually, perhaps thinking we're ready to face the world. Or we grow too busy because of a long list of activities.

NASCAR crews are relentless in their effort to make things better. We should have the same dedication in our effort to develop a closer relationship with God. We can do that by doing what the pros do. Create a checklist that we go over each day, asking ourselves about our prayer life, our relationships, and our outreach.

If we do that, we can really see things move fast.

—Dave Branon

SPORTS NOTE: The Wake Forest University's Babcock Graduate School of Management has sent its MBA students to the Richard Petty Ultimate Racing Experience to learn NASCAR pit crew techniques and thus study teamwork.

FROM THE PLAYBOOK: Read Philippians 3:12–4:1.

 GAME PLAN: Make a five-point checklist for your life. Every day for a week, look it over. Where there need to be adjustments, do some spiritual tinkering.

ONLY ON SUNDAY?

POINT OF EMPHASIS:
Thinking about Sunday

"Live as children of light." EPHESIANS 5:8

One controversy in professional sports today is the matter of prayer on the field. Sometimes after a big play or a victory, a player will drop to his knees and thank God. Some people object to this practice.

One newspaper writer suggested that the playing fields should be off-limits to such religious practices. He said that anything having to do with God should be confined to church. To him, it's "absolutely ridiculous" for people to talk to God anywhere else.

SPORTS NOTE:
Professional baseball was not allowed on Sunday in Philadelphia until 1934. Sunday baseball was first permitted in the major leagues in 1902 in Chicago, St. Louis, and Cincinnati.

FROM THE PLAYBOOK:
Read Ephesians 5:8–21.

As Christians, we would disagree with this kind of thinking. But we sometimes give the impression by our behavior that we believe it. We set Sundays aside to worship and serve God, but then we act as if the rest of the week is ours to do with as we please.

Now here's the point that nonbelievers fail to understand: For the believer in Jesus Christ, living for God is a 24-hours-a-day, 7-days-a-week proposition. Notice Paul's teaching in Ephesians 5. When he talked about walking "as children of light" (v. 8), he wasn't referring only to the way we behave in church on Sundays. When we are filled with the Spirit, we will exemplify compassion, kindness, humility, forgiveness, thankfulness, and love. Not just for an hour or two on Sunday, but all the time.

The Christian life is not for Sunday only. It's a day-to-day, all-the-time way of life—even on the playing field.

— DAVE BRANON

GAME PLAN: Think about what part of the week finds you acting least like a Christian. Dedicate that time period to God, and ask Him to make you godly even then.

TICKED

POINT OF EMPHASIS:
Anger

"Do not make friends with a hot-tempered man." PROVERBS 22:24

I like to play golf. I'm terrible at it, but it's fun. Most of the time, anyway. There have been moments when I got so mad at that little white ball I lost control. I threw things I shouldn't have thrown and said things I shouldn't have said. I was ticked.

It even happens to the best players. A reporter once asked PGA golf pro Craig Stadler why he had a new putter. He said, "Because the last one didn't float too well."

Maybe you've seen the TV commercial where a guy loses it on the course after a bad shot. He grabs some clubs and flings them into a nearby pond. His rage still wasn't satisfied so he picks up the whole bag and heaves that into the water. Then he finds out it was his friend's bag of clubs. Oops.

That's what can happen when you get so mad you lose control. Believe me, I know. You probably do too. It can happen with anything you do, not just golf.

We've all felt the pain caused by anger that's out of control. That's why the Bible's words about control are so helpful. It says the Spirit of God can control the response of emotions like anger (Galatians 5:16–21). All we need is the desire to let Him have control. God alone can calm the rage when we're ticked.

We need the self-control of His Spirit. This will not be easy for us, but it is possible. I find hope in knowing that.

—DAN DEAL

SPORTS NOTE:
One expert suggests that instead of getting angry and wrapping your 9-iron around a tree, keep a notebook and write down everything that is going wrong. Take out the anger on the writing implements.

FROM THE PLAYBOOK:
Look at Ephesians 4 after you've read Galatians 5. Good stuff!

GAME PLAN: Write down what makes you lose control of your anger. Then read the two Scripture passages in the Playbook. Let it sink in, and jot down how God can help you control the very things that make you mad.

WHOSE POWER IS IT?

POINT OF EMPHASIS:
God's power

"Not by might nor by power, but by my Spirit," says the Lord.
ZECHARIAH 4:6

In a previous devotional (April 13) I mentioned *Touched by an Angel*, the TV program. Today, we'll talk about Touched By an Angel—the real thing. We read in Zechariah 4:6 that an angel of God gave a word for Zerubbabel through the prophet Zechariah.

Zerubbabel was in charge of rebuilding the temple of Jerusalem after the Jews returned from captivity in Babylon. The angel was speaking words of encouragement to Zerubbabel, as the rebuilding process had been slow at best. Through the angelic visitor, God reminded Z that the people's might and power wouldn't be able to do the job alone. The Lord said it was only through working in His Spirit that the temple at Jerusalem would be rebuilt.

As athletes we are led to believe that the toughest, strongest, and even meanest will survive and win. Yes, sometimes we can win a race on just our own brute strength and sheer muscular power, but winning is not the sole purpose of racing. Only things done in the Spirit have any lasting, eternal significance.

Shouldn't that be the goal in all we do? We won't grow in our relationship with God by relying on our own might and power. God can lead us, encourage us, and mold us into the champions—both in and out of competition—that He wants us to be. It is from doing this that we become champions for God.

— BARB LINDQUIST, WORLD-CLASS TRIATHLETE

SPORTS NOTE:
On her Web site, Barb says, "I know that God has blessed me with athletic talents and it's my greatest desire to use those talents to glorify Him, not me."

FROM THE PLAYBOOK:
Read Zechariah 4.

GAME PLAN: Feeling inadequate? Join the club. Then turn it over to God to give you the strength and power you need.

HOLY COW!

POINT OF EMPHASIS:
Holiness

"Be holy, because I am holy." I PETER 1:16

Legendary baseball announcer Harry Caray made the phrase "Holy Cow" famous. "Holy Cow! He struck him out!" he would say. We also hear people talk about "Holy Toledo!" (If you live there, you know it's not true.)

But when it comes to true holiness—well, it's a far cry from animals or cities. The concept of being holy is something we need to examine with seriousness and concern. How can we not? Scripture clearly quotes God as saying, "Be holy, because I am holy."

We also read these pronouncements about holiness in the Bible: "You ought to live holy and godly lives" (2 Peter 3:11). "Make every effort to live in peace with all men and to be holy" (Hebrews 12:14). "God . . . has saved us and called us to a holy life" (2 Timothy 1:8–9).

Sounds monklike, doesn't it? There is no doubt, though, that God has put holy living out there as a goal we are to reach for.

So, what does it mean? Here's what an 18th-century Christian writer named William Law said about it: "This, and this alone, is Christianity, a universal holiness in every part of life, a heavenly wisdom in all our actions, not conforming in the spirit and temper of the world but turning all worldly enjoyments into means of piety and devotion to God."

In a society that doesn't think much of Christian piety and devotion to God and His Word, this is a double challenge. But it is possible.

Cows aren't holy and neither is Toledo. But you can be.

—DAVE BRANON

SPORTS NOTE:
Harry Caray spent 53 years as a major league baseball broadcaster. He called games for the St. Louis Cardinals, Oakland A's, Chicago White Sox, Chicago Cubs.

FROM THE PLAYBOOK:
Read Hebrews 10:1–10.

GAME PLAN: Do you equate holy with "no fun" and "boring"? How can you think differently? Do you know anyone whose life seems to be marked by the kind of holiness you'd like to experience?

CLEANING FISH

POINT OF EMPHASIS:
Fishing

"'Who can forgive sins but God alone?'" LUKE 5:21

One of the worst parts of fishing is cleaning your catch. It's a dirty job, but someone has to do it.

In my family, that someone is usually me. I'll never forget the time my wife and I went fishing in Tampa Bay. It was one of those fishing trips where everything clicked. Fish after fish struck our bait. By the end of the day, our arms ached from fighting and landing dozens of fish, but I didn't care. I was having too much fun—until it came time to clean the fish. Then the fun ended and the work began.

Jesus knew a lot about fishing. He lived on the Sea of Galilee, where many of his friends made their living catching fish. In fact, he invited his fishermen friends to trade in their nets and become fishers of men. And by extension, he invites us to take up the same task—fishing for men. He wants us to seek out those we might lead to Him for rescue.

One of the best things about being a fisher of men is that we don't have to clean what we catch. God does the cleaning (Luke 5:21; 1 John 1:9). Of course, we are called at times to invite people to change by playing the role of encourager or confronter, but it's not our job to "clean" or change anyone. That's God's business.

To a fisherman (both marine and human) such as I am, it's a relief to know that I don't bear the responsibility to "clean" those I have the privilege of seeing firsthand place their faith in Christ. My job is simply to cast the net.

—JEFF OLSON

SPORTS NOTE:
The largest freshwater fish in the world that is accessible to anglers is the Nile perch. The largest one caught weighed 232 kilograms (510 pounds) on Lake Victoria.

FROM THE PLAYBOOK:
Read Luke 5:1–11.

GAME PLAN: Set a goal to become a better fisher of men. How can you find better ways to lead friends to Jesus—and let Him do the clean-up?

ARE YOU SUPERSTITIOUS?

POINT OF EMPHASIS:
Trusting God

"You must be blameless before the Lord your God."
DEUTERONOMY 18:13

Baseball players are often superstitious. They become involved in all kinds of odd behavior in the belief that it will help them play better.

When Babe Ruth ran in from the outfield, he always stepped on second base just for good luck. Willie Mays kicked it for the same reason. Manager Leo Durocher rode in the back seat of the team bus to break a losing streak. Other baseball superstitions include never changing bats after two strikes, not changing uniforms during a winning streak, tapping the plate three times with the bat, and not stepping on the foul line.

Lefty O'Doul, a pitcher for the Yankees in the 1920s, said, "It's not that if I stepped on the foul line it would really lose the game, but why take a chance?" He must have believed deep within himself that if some supernatural power was available, he wanted its help.

Harmless rituals? Some say yes. But superstitions reveal something about the object of one's trust, and in some cases they are even tied to occult practices.

The Bible warns against trusting unknown forces that work behind the scenes. Those who trust in Christ must reject the idea of luck or chance. God is all-knowing and sovereign over the events of our lives, and He wants us to trust Him alone.

—DAVE EGNER

SPORTS NOTE:
Another famous baseball superstition: Hall-of-Famer Wade Boggs always ate only chicken on the day of a game.

FROM THE PLAYBOOK:
Read Deuteronomy 18:9–22.

GAME PLAN: What superstitions do you have? Why? How does God view superstitions?

TRAVELING THE DARK ROAD

POINT OF EMPHASIS:
God's guidance

"I will lead the blind by ways they have not known." ISAIAH 42:16

I came to know the Lord as my Savior on April 29, 1989. I was in the ninth grade, and I was invited to church through a bus ministry in Tacoma, Washington. That's where I trusted Christ.

I attended Henry Foss High School and was very involved with sports, particularly football and basketball. As I went through high school, I was a standout and was sent letters of interest by all types of colleges.

My biggest challenge, however, was to pass the SAT or ACT. By a very small margin, I failed every time. I was very discouraged.

I knew my path was changing from what I expected it to be. I decided to attend Walla Walla Community College. I figured going there for 2 years would pave the way for me to transfer to Washington State University.

It was a dark road—different from what I had dreamed it would be when I became a Christian. I can remember asking myself why I had to be in a community college, and was there truly a point to this path? I figure that I'm a new born-again Christian, and God seems to be dragging me through the dark. It didn't make sense.

Then God gave me a footnote through Isaiah 42:16, "I will lead the blind by ways they have not known, along unfamiliar paths I will guide them; I will turn the darkness into light before them and make the rough places smooth. These are the things I will do; I will not forsake them."

I got my answer! The way seemed dark, but with God's guidance and presence, I knew I would find the way.

— DORIAN BOOSE, PRO FOOTBALL PLAYER

SPORTS NOTE:
After Dorian Boose was cut from the NFL, he worked in a warehouse before getting a chance to play in the Canadian football league.

FROM THE PLAYBOOK:
Read Exodus 13:17–22.

GAME PLAN: What dark road are you traveling right now, wondering when things are going to start looking brighter? Are you willing to go along that path holding on to God's hand?

HOPE IN THE MIDST OF SUFFERING

POINT OF EMPHASIS:
Hope in suffering

"A bruised reed he will not break." MATTHEW 12:20

Dave Dravecky knows suffering.

At the peak of his major league baseball career, Dravecky lost his pitching arm to cancer. The illness was so severe, the arm had to be amputated.

Now Dave works in a ministry that enables him to reach out to others who are suffering. To others going through difficult times, Dave says, "You may feel like a bruised reed—stooped, battered, about to snap off . . . Jesus sees your frailty, and far from despising it, He longs to lift you up. Or maybe you feel like a smoldering wick—depleted, gasping for air, nearly spent. Jesus wants to rekindle your flame and help you to burn brightly once more. So have no fear. Approach the Savior with confidence. And be astonished at how expertly His gentle hands can remake your life" (from Matthew 12:20).

Dave lost his baseball career, but he was given a new opportunity. He and his wife Jan started "Outreach of Hope," which reaches out to cancer patients, amputees, and their families. Through "Outreach of Hope" Dave and Jan draw from their own experiences with suffering to help others understand the depth of God's love and His Word in the most hurtful of times.

If you, like Dave, know suffering, take his words to heart. "Approach the Savior with confidence." Then watch Him give you a hope you didn't know was possible.

— ROXANNE ROBBINS

SPORTS NOTE:
When Dave Dravecky was a child, his two baseball heroes were Sandy Koufax and Vida Blue.

FROM THE PLAYBOOK:
Read Matthew 12:15–21.

GAME PLAN: What loss in your life has God turned to gain? How can you draw from your own experience to help others who may be facing a similar trial?

A SIGN OF GREATNESS

POINT OF EMPHASIS:
Rejoice with the rejoicers

"Rejoice with those who rejoice; mourn with those who mourn."
ROMANS 12:15

Forty thousand fans were on hand at Oakland Coliseum on May 1, 1991, when Rickey Henderson broke Lou Brock's career stolen base record with his 939th successful base theft. According to *USA Today*, Lou, who had left baseball in 1979, had followed Henderson's career and was excited about his success. Realizing that Rickey would eventually set a new record, Brock said, "I'll be there. Do you think I'm going to miss it now? Rickey did in 12 years what took me 19. He's amazing."

SPORTS NOTE:
Rickey Henderson, who made his major league debut in 1979, was still playing professional baseball in 2005—at the age of 46.

The real success stories in life are with people who can rejoice in the successes of others. What Lou Brock did in cheering on Rickey Henderson should be a way of life in the family of God. Few circumstances give us a better opportunity to exhibit God's grace than when someone succeeds and surpasses us in an area of our own strength and reputation.

FROM THE PLAYBOOK:
Read Romans 12:9–16.

If we have not entrusted ourselves to God's care and provision, this will be difficult to do. If we're not drawing grace from our relationship with Jesus Christ, we will turn green with envy rather than flushed with shared happiness.

What is a better test of our relationship with Christ than to be happy for the success of others? What is a better evidence of the goodness of God than when He enables us to be glad when others do well?

Let's "rejoice with those who rejoice."

— MART DE HAAN

GAME PLAN: Write a note to someone today, telling that person what good things he or she has done.

GOD HAS PLANS FOR YOU

POINT OF EMPHASIS:
God's plans are good

"I have . . . plans to prosper you and not to harm you."
JEREMIAH 29:11

During her 18-year professional tennis career, Zina Garrison won 14 titles and became one of 12 women to win 500 matches. At age 26 she reached a No. 4 world ranking and became the first African-American tennis player since Althea Gibson in 1958 to reach a Grand Slam final. Also one of the finest doubles players in recent history, Zina and her playing partner, Pam Shriver, won gold in the 1988 Seoul Olympics.

After Zina retired from pro tennis, her life took a dramatic turn. "I went through a series of struggles for a couple of years," Zina says. "Now, however, I can see that despite the pain, it was really an awesome pilgrimage. My faith in God grew even stronger because in the midst of all the trials and tribulations I faced, He was there. I grew to understand that God would always pull me through. Even if no one else is there for me, Jesus always is. When I thought I couldn't get through or didn't have anyone there, I would pray and later on see how things materialized. Everything didn't always turn out the way I wanted it to, but in God's timing things always did work out."

Garrison has come to a new place spiritually. The 2000 US Olympic tennis coach has accepted that life does not always go the way she plans it, but she now has confidence that God is in control. As she looks ahead, she can more patiently wait on His leading and then make the most of the opportunities God brings her way.

Like Zina, we must put our trust in God in front of any plans we have—for we know He wants what is best for us.

— ROXANNE ROBBINS

SPORTS NOTE:
Zina wrote a book called *My Life in Women's Tennis*. It was published in 2000.

FROM THE PLAYBOOK:
Read Jeremiah 29:11–14.

 GAME PLAN: Write in your journal about something that didn't go the way you wanted it to. How did God turn the situation into good?

READY FOR A CHANGE?

POINT OF EMPHASIS:
The free gift of salvation

"While we were still sinners, Christ died for us." ROMANS 5:8

My swimming career has been a catalyst for personal development ever since I was young. But the greatest lesson I learned came after the swim season ended during my freshman year at the University of Texas.

Despite all the success I had experienced through my sport, I was floundering emotionally and physically. I was juggling heavy partying, training, and studying. Eventually I ended up with a severe, undiagnosed illness. I was in bed for two weeks, and I felt like I was at the bottom of the barrel. Unable to move, I took time to reflect. When I did, I recognized a need for change in my life.

God brought me to a place where I had to look up at Him. He slowed me down, and I was able to listen to Him. He gave me faith and courage to respond to His truth—that Jesus Christ is who He says He is. The reality of who Jesus Christ is and His credibility were overwhelming to me. I knew the right thing to do was to trust Him.

After acknowledging intellectually that Jesus Christ is God, I prayed—thanking Him for dying on the cross 2,000 years ago to pay for my sins. I asked Christ to enter my heart and to be the Lord of my life.

You too can accept God's free gift of forgiveness and eternal life through His Son, Jesus Christ. Isn't it time for a change?

—JOSH DAVIS, OLYMPIC GOLD MEDALIST, SWIMMING

SPORTS NOTE:
Josh Davis was the only athlete at the 1996 Olympic Games in Atlanta to win three Olympic gold medals.

FROM THE PLAYBOOK:
Read Romans 5.

GAME PLAN: Have you ever accepted Jesus Christ as your Savior? As Josh did, please stop and consider the possibility.

ASLEEP ON THE JOB

POINT OF EMPHASIS:
Stay alert

"Wake up! Strengthen what remains." REVELATION 3:2

One thing an umpire is supposed to do is pay attention. He can't be daydreaming or scanning the stands for his wife or figuring his income tax with his ball/strike counter. It's his job to keep his eye on the ball at all times. When he doesn't, a fiasco will probably follow.

It was a minor league game somewhere in Texas. The score was tied in the bottom of the ninth. (Isn't this the way baseball stories are supposed to go?) Texarkana had a runner at third and the batter had two strikes on him. (Feel the tension building?) As the Sherman pitcher came to the plate with the pitch, the runner at third took off for home. Quickly the home plate area was a swirl of activity as the ball, the runner, the batter, and the umpire all congregated amid the flying dust.

The runner appeared to slide across the plate with the winning run. But wait! No sooner had the safe call been given than the Sherman manager was nose-to-nose with the umpire. If the pitch is a strike, he explained, then the batter is out and the run doesn't count. When he asked the umpire if the pitch was a ball or a strike, all the befuddled masked man could say was, "I don't know. I was busy watching the runner, and I didn't pay attention to the pitch." You can imagine the scene that followed that confession.

That distraction caused the umpire a lot of grief. His main responsibility was to call balls and strikes, yet he let the runner take precedence, and he ignored the pitch.

Often we do something like that. The requirements of daily living, even though they might be good, distract us from our primary goal of serving Christ and living for Him. It's tough to keep our eye on pleasing the Lord while taking care of everything else at the same time. But we can do it if we don't fall asleep on the job. — DAVE BRANON

SPORTS NOTE: An umpire starting out in the minor leagues makes around $1,800 a month. In the majors, the salaries range from $84,000 to $300,000 a year.

FROM THE PLAYBOOK: Read Revelation 3:1–6.

GAME PLAN: If serving and pleasing God is my No. 1 goal, do I spend enough time each day making sure I accomplish that? What good things in my life could distract my attention from God?

A PERSPECTIVE ON FAILURE

POINT OF EMPHASIS:
Figuring out failure

"And we know that in all things, God works for the good of those who love him." ROMANS 8:28

According to Mulligan's Rules of Golf: "No matter how badly you are playing, it is always possible to play worse."

But after the final hole of the 1991 Ryder Cup, I think it would have been hard to convince Bernhard Langer that it could get worse. The Ryder Cup is the Super Bowl of golf, and Langer was in the anchor position for the European team. He and Hale Irwin of the US were the last players on the course.

Irwin had bogeyed the 18th, and Langer was faced with a 6-foot putt for par to win the match and retain the Cup for Europe. The Ryder Cup came down to the last putt on the last hole in the last match on the last day. But in that moment of a lifetime, Bernhard Langer tasted failure. His putt slid over the right edge of the hole and stayed out. Langer said, "All I could feel was pain, agony, and disappointment."

Fortunately, Bernhard Langer understands that failure is an event, not a person. Because of his personal relationship with Christ, he was able to look at the experience from an eternal perspective and cope with it. Later he commented, "I looked at it this way. There was only one perfect Man in this world, and they crucified Him. All I did was miss a putt."

Are you having a hard time getting past a failure? You know, God has a history of helping people who have failed. In all things, God works.

—BRIAN HETTINGA

SPORTS NOTE:
Bernhard Langer was elected to the World Golf Hall of Fame. He was inducted in 2002. He won the Masters in both 1985 and 1993.

FROM THE PLAYBOOK:
Read Romans 8.

GAME PLAN: Hebrews 11 is God's "Hall of Faith," but every person listed experienced a major failure in life. It takes enormous faith to believe that our failures are for the greater good.

GIVING GOD THE HONOR

POINT OF EMPHASIS:
Honoring God

"Those who honor me I will honor." I SAMUEL 2:30

Have you ever picked up a *Sports Illustrated* and been pleasantly surprised to find a story about an athlete who embraces the Christian faith? Have you been refreshed when you turned on the television and observed a person testifying about the role Jesus Christ plays in his or her life? Why did this affect you?

First, it probably surprised you to observe someone's faith articulated through the mainstream media. And it put a smile on your face because you knew thousands of people could be seeing a glimpse of our Savior. Many Christian athletes talk openly to the media about their relationship with Christ. Other Christian athletes, even when given the right opportunity, will choose not to acknowledge God publicly. They may refrain because they are young believers and not yet strong enough to handle the public expectations that accompany statements of faith. Or reporters may not ask them a question that gives them room to mention faith.

There are many legitimate reasons Christian athletes may not mention their faith each time a microphone is placed in front of them. Realizing this, 2000 USA Olympic heptathlete Dee Dee Nathan says she knows there are times when she must rely on actions and not words. Her goal, however, is never to be embarrassed about talking about her Savior. "I pray for boldness and confidence to proclaim the gospel," Nathan says. "I lean on the second part of I Samuel 2:30, which says, 'Those who honor me I will honor, but those who despise me will be disdained.'"

How will you choose to honor God today?

—ROXANNE ROBBINS

SPORTS NOTE:
Dee Dee Nathan was the first female athlete from Indiana University to compete in the Olympic Games.

FROM THE PLAYBOOK:
Read Psalm 15.

 GAME PLAN: When was the last time you had a chance to articulate your faith in Christ but held back because of embarrassment? Talk to the Lord about the situation and ask Him to give you wisdom and boldness to know when and what to say in the future.

MOM, THE HERO

POINT OF EMPHASIS:
Thanking Mom

"Listen to your father and mother." PROVERBS 1:8 (PARAPHRASE)

When ESPN *Baseball Tonight* commentator Harold Reynolds was growing up in Corvallis, Oregon, an NBA player named Gus Williams was his hero. Harold wanted to be like Gus. He tied his shoes the same way, wore the same number, and wore one wristband just like Gus.

One day Harold was lying in bed with a severe stomachache. That was when Harold began to notice the difference between heroes and role models. It wasn't Gus, his sports hero, who came into his room to take care of him. It was Harold's mother.

Harold stopped looking to athletic accomplishments to determine whom he wanted to pattern his life after. Instead, he tried to emulate people with strong character who were doing things of lasting value.

From his mother, Harold learned about love as he experienced her unconditional love for him. Within that love she taught him responsibility and respect. When he was five years old, for example, he tried to steal a candy bar. His mom made him go back to the store and explain what he did. Harold never stole again. He was held accountable for his actions. That type of responsibility brings growth in character.

That experience also showed Harold the meaning of restoration. His mom knew that confessing to the store manager would break him. She allowed him to go through that process. He learned, and later in his life, he recognized that he needed to be restored in his relationship with God. He trusted Jesus as His Savior.

Take a moment today and think of all the great things like that your mother has done for you. Then tell her thanks for the amazing lessons you learned at her feet.

—ROXANNE ROBBINS

SPORTS NOTE:
Harold Reynolds' best season as a hitter was 1989 when he hit .300 for Seattle with 184 hits.

FROM THE PLAYBOOK:
Read Proverbs 1:7–9 and Ephesians 6:1–3.

 GAME PLAN: List a few of the values you have learned from the mother the Lord has blessed you with. Then tell her thanks.

GOAL!

POINT OF EMPHASIS:
True love

"The goal of this command is love." I TIMOTHY 1:5

Pedro Zamballa stopped, took aim, and kicked the soccer ball to the right of the open goal . . . on purpose. Why would someone intentionally miss a shot?

The reason Pedro drove the ball away far right has a lot to do with a goal Paul wrote about in I Timothy—the goal to show love (v. 5).

You see, the fleet-footed forward recognized that the goalie for the other team had been knocked unconscious just before Pedro made his move. So, instead of kicking an easy goal, Pedro booted the ball away and encouraged medical personnel to help his fallen opponent.

What would you have done?

In the heat of the battle, it's amazing that Pedro chose to show love—on two counts. First, he showed love for a fellow human being. Second, he communicated a true passion for the purity of the game of soccer by not "stealing" an easy goal.

Each day we face opportunities to take advantage of situations and people for our own advantage. Paul counseled Timothy to encourage fellow-believers in Christ not to teach false things and to avoid "meaningless talk."

Paul implored Timothy to put off what may gain an advantage—but is not admirable or true—for a life of love. A life that reflected the love of God.

Today, if you're tempted to "steal a goal" or take advantage of someone for personal gain, stop and reflect on what true love in Christ is all about. You may have to do what some will criticize if you want to achieve a greater goal.

—TOM FELTEN

SPORTS NOTE:
Zamballa was playing soccer in the Spanish League when he made his altruistic move.

FROM THE PLAYBOOK:
Read 1 Timothy 1:1–7.

GAME PLAN: Write down five goals you would like to achieve today. Then write the word *Love* by each goal that jibes with God's ultimate goal—to love Him and others.

WHAT'S THE PURPOSE?

POINT OF EMPHASIS:
The ABCs of Salvation

"I am the way and the truth and the life." JOHN 14:6

Legendary jockey Pat Day, who has recorded more than 8,000 career victories, tells his story.

The early part of my riding career was like a roller-coaster ride. There were some great highs in my success, but there were also some horrible lows brought about by drug and alcohol abuse, broken relationships, and a lack of appreciation for the ability God had blessed me with.

I thought it was all coming together in 1982 when I won the national riding title. I thought reaching that pinnacle of success would give me long-lasting joy and contentment. I was wrong.

After a few weeks of celebrating, I awoke from my drug-and-alcohol-induced stupor and found that the thrill of victory was gone. This caused me to ask questions about life. Why was I here? What was my purpose?

I found that the answer to my questions rested in a personal relationship with God through His Son, Jesus Christ. But how do we come to Jesus?

1. Admit that you are a sinner. Romans 3:23 says, "For all have sinned and fall short of the glory of God."

2. Believe that Jesus Christ died on the cross for your sins. First Peter 3:18 says, "For Christ died for sins once for all, the righteous for the unrighteous, to bring you to God."

3. Confess Jesus Christ as your Lord and Savior. Romans 10:9 says, "If you confess with your mouth, 'Jesus is Lord,' and believe in your heart that God raised him from the dead, you will be saved."

When I accepted Jesus as my Savior, He forgave me of my sins, delivered me from the bondage of drugs and alcohol, saved my marriage, and gave my life new meaning! Have you trusted Him?

—PAT DAY, JOCKEY

SPORTS NOTE:
Pat Day has more than 8,000 victories as a jockey, including the 1992 Kentucky Derby.

FROM THE PLAYBOOK:
Read John 3.

GAME PLAN: Have you put your faith in Jesus? He is the only way to eternal life.

MUCH GIVEN, MUCH REQUIRED

POINT OF EMPHASIS:
Giving back to God

"It is required that those who have been given a trust must prove faithful." I Corinthians 4:2

Despite the many perks and rewards of a life as high-profile and prosperous as major league pitcher John Smoltz has enjoyed, there's still a price that must be paid for all this fame and fortune. "With every business there are decisions and pressures," says Smoltz, "but in baseball it's hard because everyone thinks they know who I am. But all they really know is based on the press's coverage and representation of me." Smoltz says, "I have been robbed of my privacy and a protected family life. This lifestyle is definitely not conducive to good family time, because you are constantly being pulled in so many different directions. People think that if you have enough money nothing else matters, and they will do whatever it takes to get it."

For Smoltz, the biblical principle that puts all this in perspective is the one that says, "To whom much is given, from him much will be required" (Luke 12:48).

His friends know he takes this thought seriously. "John is extremely compassionate and loyal," says Smoltz' good friend Jeff Foxworthy, "and he would do anything for his friends."

In the spring of 1999, then-Braves third base coach Ned Yost received word that his dad lay dying in a hospital in California and that if Ned wanted to see him again he needed to move quickly. John took care of everything for Ned and purchased a ticket for him to fly home. "John is a man of integrity," says Yost, "and getting to know him has been one of the highlights of my career."

Wouldn't that be a great thing for others to say about each of us?

—Barb Cash

SPORTS NOTE:
John Smoltz was part of a group of parents who started a new Christian school in the community in which he and his wife, Dyan, and their family live.

FROM THE PLAYBOOK:
Read 1 Corinthians 4:1–7.

 GAME PLAN: Contemplate this question: Are you more of a giver or a taker? In this life, are you pouring back into your world as much as you are getting out of it?

GOD HAS NO GRANDCHILDREN

POINT OF EMPHASIS:
Personal faith

"Choose for yourselves . . . whom you will serve." JOSHUA 24:15

Growing up, WNBA superstar Ruthie Bolton spent a lot of time shooting hoops. Basketball was one of the few games she and her nineteen siblings could all play together! When Ruthie proved to be a gifted athlete, she was following a family tradition (several of her brothers and sisters were successful college athletes). In a sense, the same was true of her Christian faith. Ruthie's father was a pastor; so are five of her brothers.

But no one gets into heaven because of his or her family's faith. A relationship with Jesus Christ isn't something you can inherit. As Joshua explained to the children of Israel, serving God is a personal decision. It's something you have to choose for yourself.

Ruthie discovered this truth soon after she graduated from high school. "When I was seven, I had asked Jesus to be my Savior," she says. "But later on, I wondered if I was just living right because I had to. It wasn't really optional at our house," she explains. "I wondered how it would be when times got tough, or when I was out on my own. In college, I found myself facing all kinds of obstacles, all kinds of challenges. When I reached back to draw on the faith and values that my father had instilled in me, then I realized that God really had saved me and that He really was with me!"

What about you? Can you truly call your faith your own?

—CHRISTIN DITCHFIELD

SPORTS NOTE:
Ruthie won gold medals at the Olympics, the Goodwill Games, and the World University Games during her long basketball career.

FROM THE PLAYBOOK:
Read Joshua 24:14–18.

GAME PLAN: Can you recall a specific time when you made the choice to receive Jesus Christ as your personal Savior and live for Him? If not, do it today!

READY OR NOT!

POINT OF EMPHASIS:
Ready to meet God

"Whoever believes in the Son has eternal life." JOHN 3:36

It was a tragedy that rocked the motor racing community.

On May 12, 2000, nineteen-year-old Adam Petty was killed during a practice run for a Grand National Race in New Hampshire. No one expects a nineteen-year-old to die. No nineteen-year-old wakes up in the morning thinking, "Today may be my last day on this earth." Few adults do, for that matter.

But sooner or later, it happens to all of us. The Bible says we're all "destined to die once, and after that to face judgment" (Hebrews 9:27). Unless Jesus returns first, every one of us will one day die. None of us knows how and when our time will come. For most of us, it will be a complete surprise. And then we will face judgment. We will be called to account for our sins and failures. We will have to pay the penalty—unless we have put our faith in Christ.

Jesus died on the cross to pay the penalty for us. If we believe in Him and receive His forgiveness, our sins have already been paid for and we can face the judgment without fear. Jesus explained, "I am the resurrection and the life. He who believes in me will live, even though he dies; and whoever lives and believes in me will never die" (John 11:25).

As a young man, Adam Petty had put his faith in Christ and received God's free gift of eternal life. And though he had no idea that May 12, 2000, would be his last day here, he was ready.

Are you?

—CHRISTIN DITCHFIELD

SPORTS NOTE: Adam's parents, Kyle and Pattie Petty, established Victory Junction Gang Camp, a camp for kids in Randleman, North Carolina.

FROM THE PLAYBOOK: Read John 3:1–17.

GAME PLAN: If you haven't already received Christ as your Savior, shouldn't you do so today? Take time right now to invite Him into your life. Confess your sins, receive His forgiveness, and enjoy the gift of eternal life.

EAGLES ON THE RISE

POINT OF EMPHASIS:
Strength from God

"Those who hope in the Lord will renew their strength." ISAIAH 40:31

In basketball, point guard is the toughest position on the court. Not only do you have to call the play, tell players what to do and where to go, and keep the tempo, but you also have to handle the ball while a defender is pressuring you. Many teams are successful because they have a great point guard who runs the show.

A good point guard allows everyone else to feel relaxed and comfortable, takes the pressure off others, and steps into a leadership role. I love being a point guard and having that control and command. However, there are times throughout my basketball career when I feel as if I cannot handle the role of being a point guard. I feel a weight on my shoulders and a built-up pressure that causes stress and anxiety.

Where will I find the energy, the stamina, and the mental toughness needed to lead my team at the point guard position when that happens? I know I cannot afford to be exhausted and overwhelmed, but I am. However, God is never too tired nor too busy to help, listen, and be my source of strength.

When you are feeling engulfed by stress or feeling uneasy because of a tough assignment ahead—stop, breathe, and pray. Although you are weary, God's power and strength never fade. As I have learned time and time again, we need to look to the Lord to renew our strength. He knows that we are overwhelmed with pressures and stress throughout the day or through the circumstances He puts us through. Yet we have a hope and joy in the Lord that allows us to call upon Him—regaining strength and soaring "like eagles" in His love (Isaiah 40:31).

—AMBER JACOBS, WNBA GUARD

SPORTS NOTE:
Amber hit two game-winning shots in the 2003 NCAA tournament for Boston College.

FROM THE PLAYBOOK:
Read Isaiah 40:27–31.

GAME PLAN: What's your stress factor? Is it as Amber describes in her job as a point guard—sometimes overwhelming? Have you thought about turning it over to God?

WALK DIFFERENTLY

POINT OF EMPHASIS:
Walking as Christians

"Blessed are you when people insult you." MATTHEW 5:11

I had been a member of the US Army track and field team for five years. One of my outside missions was to teach a Bible study. There were five of us who felt that calling. Most of our teammates called us all kinds of names from "Holy Rollers" to "Jesus Freaks."

The hour drive to track and field practice was always interesting. There were only four 15-passenger vans that took the 57-member team to practice each day. The non-Christians in our van wanted control over the radio to listen to their music. On the return trip, they would scramble to other vans because I would play either sermons or Christian music.

By the time the camp was halfway through, there were just the six Christians in our van on the way home. Each one had his or her own seat! The others were riding illegally with sometimes 16 to 18 soldiers per van.

Now, some of them did come to their senses after seeing each of the "Holy Rollers" having their own seat. We allowed them to still listen to their tapes on the way up, but they listened to ours on the way back. One of them even started liking what we were playing! Imagine that!

God tells us that we are not like the rest of the world. He has called us out to walk differently. People are going to call us names, but we have to show compassion for them just as Christ shows compassion for us. I relished the title of "Holy Roller," because it built up my treasure in heaven. Plus, we were holy and rolling in that van!

—JOHN F. REGISTER, 2000 PARALYMPIC SILVER MEDALIST, LONG JUMP

SPORTS NOTE:
While in college, John was a three-time All-American in track and field. In 1994, he injured his left leg while jumping hurdles, and had to have it amputated.

FROM THE PLAYBOOK:
Read Matthew 5.

GAME PLAN: In what ways do people find your faith something to make fun of? How have you been able to turn that into something positive?

STOP AT THE START

POINT OF EMPHASIS:
Anger

"Starting a quarrel is like breaching a dam; so drop the matter before a dispute breaks out." PROVERBS 17:14

On May 15, 1894, the Baltimore Orioles visited Boston to play a routine National League baseball game against the Beaneaters at South End Grounds. But what happened that day was anything but routine.

The Orioles' John McGraw got into a fight with Boston third baseman Tommy Tucker. Within minutes all the players from both teams had joined in the brawl. The warfare quickly spread to the grandstands. Among the fans the conflict went from bad to worse. Someone set fire to the stands, and the entire double-decked ballpark burned to the ground. Not only that, but the fire spread to 107 other Boston buildings as well.

SPORTS NOTE:
The 1894 Baltimore Orioles had seven players who eventually were elected to the Baseball Hall of Fame, including Wee Willie Keeler.

The book of Proverbs tells us to stop conflict before it turns into a flood of anger (17:14). It's difficult to take back words. A raised gun, a fist, and a voice are all alike—they are easier to lift up than to put down.

Because of God's love for us, He pleads with us not to play with the fire of unnecessary conflict. He understands the danger of strife. We may think a little conflict makes life (including sports) more interesting. But the Lord wants us to think otherwise.

FROM THE PLAYBOOK:
Read Proverbs 26:17–21.

Father, help us to heed Your warning. Help us to understand the terrible potential of conflict. When a desire to lash out at someone rises up within us, help us to stop at the start—so that we don't damage both ourselves and others.

—MART DE HAAN

GAME PLAN: When have I spoken or acted in anger? What would have happened if I had held my tongue or stopped my hand? What is the advantage of a "soft answer" (Proverbs 15:1)?

MAY 16

NEVER ALONE

POINT OF EMPHASIS:
Experiencing God's presence

"Where can I go from your Spirit? Where can I flee from your presence?" PSALM 139:7

I'm standing on the baseline alongside the rest of my Cleveland Rockers teammates in New York's Madison Square Garden as the National Anthem is being sung. As I stand there with my hand across my heart, I am reminded of the importance of the song and its comforting sound.

Several years before, I was standing next to different teammates listening to an unfamiliar anthem. That was in Launceston, Tasmania, the little island off the bottom of Australia. I headed "Down Under" to play professionally the winter following my senior year in college. It was there that I truly realized the necessity of my relationship with Jesus Christ.

Although I accepted Christ when I was eleven, I never gave complete control over to Him. I always had my family to lean on in times of need.

That comfort zone suddenly changed when I boarded a 14-hour flight to Australia. Now placed in a situation completely on my own, I learned what it meant to be alone. I chose to turn to the Lord and open my Bible. I began to study the meaning behind the verses. I found a nice Baptist church that took me in as one of their own. But most important, I continued to pray. God was there. I could feel His presence, His comfort, compassion, and love. The Lord's Spirit overfilled my heart.

SPORTS NOTE:
Tricia spent parts of five seasons in the WNBA with Utah and Cleveland. Her high game was 10 points against the New York Liberty in 1998 while with the Utah Starzz.

FROM THE PLAYBOOK:
Read Psalm 139.

I made the effort to seek Him. That's all it took. I realized He was always there. I just hadn't been paying much attention.

Jesus Christ is in my life and heart everywhere I go. Whether I was in Orlando, Florida, or Tasmania, I knew I was not alone.

—TRICIA BADER BINFORD, FORMER WNBA GUARD

GAME PLAN: Are there some places you go where you feel Jesus is not with you or is not as close? What can you do to make sure that doesn't happen?

WHO CALLS THE GAME?

POINT OF EMPHASIS:
God's judgment

"'Let him who accuses God answer him!'" Job 40:2

During an afternoon baseball game way back in 1915, American League umpire Bill Guthrie was working behind the plate. The catcher for the visiting team wasn't overly impressed with Guthrie's work, so he repeatedly protested his calls.

According to a story that appeared in the *St. Louis Post-Dispatch*, Guthrie endured this irritation for three innings. Finally in the fourth inning, he had had enough. When the catcher started to complain, Guthrie stopped him. "Son," he said gently to the catcher, "you've been a big help to me calling balls and strikes, and I appreciate it. But I think I've got the hang of it now. So I'm going to ask you to go to the clubhouse and show them how to take a shower."

The Bible character Job and that catcher had something in common. Job too had been complaining about calls he didn't think were fair. In his case, the umpire was God. After listening to Job's objections, the Lord finally spoke out of a violent storm.

Suddenly things came into perspective for the patriarch. God was gentle with Job, but He was also firm and direct. The Lord asked him the kind of questions that bring finite man back to his original size. The patriarch listened, stopped complaining, and found peace in surrendering to God.

Heavenly Father, we don't make sense when we complain about Your fairness. Help us to be like Your Son Jesus, who trusted You without complaining, even to the point of dying on the cross.

—Mart De Haan

SPORTS NOTE:
In 1910, Frank Chance, the manager of the Chicago Cubs, was the first person kicked out of a World Series game for arguing with the umpire.

FROM THE PLAYBOOK:
Read Job 40:1–14.

GAME PLAN: For every complaint you come up with in the next couple of days, balance it out with one aspect of God's greatness. See if that doesn't put the complaint in a different light.

BEGIN THE DAY THE RIGHT WAY

POINT OF EMPHASIS:
Fellowship with Christ

"In the morning, O Lord, you hear my voice; in the morning I lay my requests before you." PSALM 5:3

In the midst of all the challenges I faced when I was general manager of the Los Angeles Dodgers, one of my greatest battles was to maintain a consistent fellowship with Jesus Christ. That is, to live every day as Christ would have me live, seeking His wisdom and comfort constantly. No one does it perfectly, but I did have a plan.

There's only one right way to start the day, and that's in fellowship with Him. I mean time on my knees in prayer and time in the Word. I try to begin it with Him, though I can't say I'm always successful.

Once I've laid the foundation by starting my day that way, I don't ever feel that I get too far from His presence. In meetings, or before I did an interview, I prayed. I found myself praying continuously during the day.

I believe strongly in Proverbs 3:5–6, "Trust in the Lord with all your heart and lean not on your own understanding; in all your ways acknowledge Him, and He will make your paths straight."

I knew I couldn't do that job without Christ. I needed wisdom. I needed so many things that only He could provide. There were so many demands on my time, and so many opportunities to make the wrong decisions and go down the wrong path. So I had to begin the day the right way, then constantly talk to Him and listen to Him throughout the day.

When I trust and depend on Him, He provides me with confidence and peace of mind. No matter if you are the GM of a great baseball franchise or working at GM making great cars, the plan works.

—KEVIN MALONE, FORMER GENERAL MANAGER, LOS ANGELES DODGERS

SPORTS NOTE:
Malone was the general manager of the Montreal Expos before he was named the LA Dodgers' GM in 1998.

FROM THE PLAYBOOK:
Read Psalm 55:1, 2, 16, 17, 22.

GAME PLAN: How did you start the day today? Would a daily checklist help remind you to talk with God?

MAY 19

REAL HOPE

POINT OF EMPHASIS:
Hope in Christ

"We wait for the blessed hope—the glorious appearing of our great God and Savior, Jesus Christ." TITUS 2:13

It has been said that as oxygen is to the lungs, so hope is to the human heart. We need hope. What is real hope? Perhaps you can recall an occasion in your past when you failed to study for an exam. When someone asked you whether or not you passed, you responded, "I hope so." That type of hope could better be described as baseless optimism. Because you did not properly prepare for the exam, you have no reasonable grounds for confidence that your desires will be fulfilled. You are simply exercising wishful thinking.

SPORTS NOTE: Mostly a relief pitcher in the early 1990s with the Expos, Royals, and Angels, Sampen twice pitched in more than 50 games (1990 and 1993).

FROM THE PLAYBOOK: Read Titus 2.

Biblical hope is trustful expectation. It is the confidence that God will do what He said He would do. Titus 2:13–14 reads, "while we wait for the blessed hope—the glorious appearing of our great God and Savior, Jesus Christ, who gave himself for us to redeem us from all wickedness."

What do you draw hope from? What is it that keeps you going and gives you reason to live? Many people rely on false hope or simply on wishful thinking. They may depend upon wealth, possessions, accomplishment, good deeds, or their righteousness. While these may temporarily energize us, there is no sustaining ability for the long term, much less for eternity.

Peter writes in 1 Peter 1:3, "In his great mercy he has given us new birth into a living hope through the resurrection of Jesus Christ from the dead." Real hope can only be found through our faith and trust in the death, burial, and resurrection of Jesus Christ. If we are placing our hope in anything else, it is simply wishful thinking.

—BILL SAMPEN, FORMER MAJOR LEAGUE PITCHER

GAME PLAN: List three things that give you hope. Sometimes we need things that give us something to look forward to. How can you make sure your key hope is in God?

THE HUGGERS

POINT OF EMPHASIS:
Compassion and love

"Greet one another with a holy kiss." ROMANS 16:16

All right. Now that I've got your attention with all this mushy stuff about hugging and kissing, let's get down to business. I have an important point to make.

Nearly 3,000 athletes take part in the summer games of Michigan's Special Olympics. The slogan of the Special Olympics is this: "Caring is more important than winning." This is especially true of those competitors who are mentally impaired.

The events at the Special Olympics are like any other track meet—with one major difference. At the finish line is a group of volunteers the Olympic Committee calls "huggers." Their job, in addition to calling out the winners, is to encourage one of the competitors throughout the race and to greet him or her at the finish line with a big hug. The real secret to the success of the games is love.

These huggers remind me of what's going on in Romans 16. There Paul gave special recognition to the men and women who had been "running the race" for the Lord so diligently in Rome. He didn't flatter them or heap praise on them. He didn't give them a trophy for "Best Church Worker in the World." But he did remember them by name. He gave them confidence by approving their work.

> **SPORTS NOTE:**
> The mission of the Special Olympics is to "provide year-round sports training and athletic competition in a variety of Olympic-type sports for children and adults with intellectual disabilities."

> **FROM THE PLAYBOOK:**
> Read Romans 16:1–16

Paul would have made a good "hugger." (Actually, the text mentioned kissing, but you know how cultures change.) Perhaps you can be that kind of encourager too. Let a friend know how much you appreciate it when he or she compliments you. Express appreciation to a co-worker who's been especially kind. Somehow, let the love of Jesus show through. Make those around you feel like winners.

—MART DE HAAN

GAME PLAN: Get out the old stationery and write a note to someone who needs a written hug from you.

THE CURSE OF IMPERFECTION

POINT OF EMPHASIS:
Imperfection

"What I want to do I do not do, but what I hate I do." ROMANS 7:15

One of the most exciting major league baseball games I ever saw came excruciatingly close to being one for the record books. One mistake, however, turned it into just another game. In fact, that game, which came within one pitch of being a part of baseball lore, has gone unrecorded in record books of the game's past.

Milt Wilcox of the Detroit Tigers was pitching against the Chicago White Sox. He retired the first 26 batters. With two outs in the last inning, he was just one man away from a perfect game. If he could get the last out, he would be only the eleventh pitcher in more than 100 years of major league baseball to throw a game in which no one reached first base. But White Sox batter Jerry Hairston ruined everything. He slapped a hit against Wilcox, and the Detroit pitcher missed his hallowed place in history.

Perfection eludes all of us. We get up in the morning determined to get it right today, but before we know it we've done something that is not quite right in God's eyes. The same thing happened to God's servants in the Bible. As we observe great biblical characters, we can see how tough it is to achieve perfection. For example, Paul, the greatest missionary ever, admitted that he sometimes did what he knew he shouldn't do (Romans 7:15).

When we fall short, it's our responsibility to confess our sins to God and accept His mercy. Our sin should also remind us that we need Jesus Christ our Savior and the forgiveness He offers.

When the curse of imperfection hits, we can learn from it, confess our sins, and keep on growing.

—DAVE BRANON

SPORTS NOTE:
When David Cone pitched a perfect game for the New York Yankees in 1999, he threw just 88 pitches, and 68 of them were strikes.

FROM THE PLAYBOOK:
Read Psalm 32.

GAME PLAN: What area of your life is giving you the most trouble? That is, what is pointing out your imperfections? What happens to your relationship with God when you sin?

LET GOD WORK ON YOU

POINT OF EMPHASIS:
God's transforming power

"Yet, O Lord, you are our Father. We are the clay, you are the potter; we are all the work of your hand." ISAIAH 64:8

So many people put a delay on giving their lives to Christ because they feel they have to get right first. The reality is this: We cannot get ourselves right before God. We must humble ourselves and come to Him, knowing that He is the author of perfection. The change that we desire can be accomplished only through Jesus Christ.

Then there are some people who refuse to believe because they think the person they were yesterday is the person they have to be today. This limiting belief will keep them imprisoned to their past mistakes and limitations. When we come to Christ as we are, we relinquish our power and allow Him to reconstruct our lives.

One great example of that in Scripture is the concept that God is the potter and we are the clay. The more we yield to Him, the more He is able to shape and mold us into what He wants us to be.

Another illustration of our need to be connected to God is in John 15, where Jesus says, "I am the true vine, and my Father is the gardener. He cuts off every branch in me that bears no fruit . . . Remain in me, and I will remain in you. No branch can bear fruit by itself; it must remain in the vine" (vv. 1–4).

All we have to do is come to Him as we are. The transformation of our old selves into spiritual beings is a process. If we allow God to do the transforming in our lives, we can rest assured that we will be all that God created us to be.

—CHARLOTTE SMITH-TAYLOR, WNBA FORWARD

SPORTS NOTE:
Charlotte hit one of the most exciting shots in NCAA women's basketball history—a buzzer-beating three-pointer that gave the North Carolina Tar Heels the 1994 NCAA title.

FROM THE PLAYBOOK:
Read more about the vine and the branches in John 15:1–14.

 GAME PLAN: Have you surrendered your life to Christ completely to let Him mold you and help you bear fruit? If not, you need to do that.

ACHE 1: HOW'S YOUR ATTITUDE?

POINT OF EMPHASIS:
Godly attitude

"Your attitude should be the same as that of Christ Jesus: Who being in very nature God, did not consider equality with God something to be grasped." PHILIPPIANS 2:5

All athletes share one element of sports: pain. Whether it is the soreness of a weekend warrior who did too much, a Little Leaguer whose team lost the championship game, or a pro athlete who pushed himself too hard—they all feel the aches and pains of athletic competition.

The Christian life is compared to an athletic event in the New Testament (Acts 20:24; Romans 9:3; 1 Corinthians 9:24; Galatians 2:2; 5:7; 2 Timothy 4:7; Hebrews 12:1), an event that sometimes can seem painful. Over the next four days we will examine four attributes of Christian maturity that will help keep our perspective when trouble hits. These attributes can be remembered through the acronym "ACHE."

SPORTS NOTE:
Kyle Abbott was a first-round draft pick in 1989. He was the ninth player chosen that year.

FROM THE PLAYBOOK:
Read Philippians 2:1–11.

Attitude is the first attribute we will examine. The dictionary defines attitude as "one's disposition, opinion or mental set." In Philippians 2:5–8, Paul encourages us to have the Christlike mindset of humility. In this way, Paul reminds us that we can be our own biggest enemy. When we focus on our own needs, it is easy for us to have a selfish attitude. If this is our way of thinking, we miss the point of the Christian message.

Jesus Christ is to be our example as we grow in maturity. He never considered His own needs, but He obeyed the Father in doing His duty of going to the cross on behalf of humankind. As a result, God will exalt Him so that everyone will honor Jesus in the resurrection.

This example is given to us so that we also will demonstrate humility and consider others better than ourselves. That's the right attitude.

—KYLE ABBOTT, FORMER MAJOR LEAGUE PITCHER

GAME PLAN: When do you struggle with your attitude? Isn't it most often when something happens that doesn't go your way? That's an attitude of immaturity.

ACHE 2: ARE YOU CONCENTRATING?

POINT OF EMPHASIS:
Zeal for Christ

"I press on toward the goal to win the prize for which God has called me." PHILIPPIANS 3:14

The second letter in ACHE that reminds us of how to keep our perspective during difficult times is C—for **Concentration**.

When trials arise, how do you handle them? In Philippians, Paul writes to churchgoers who were suffering persecution for their faith. In fact, Paul himself wrote from a prison cell. His advice to his readers (and to us) is to face trials joyfully. This is not something we do automatically. It takes patience and practice. Our responsibility is to remain focused and to keep the prize of heaven before us.

In Philippians 3:12–14, Paul instructs us to "press on." In verses 13 and 14 he writes, "I do not consider myself yet to have taken hold of it. But one thing I do: Forgetting what is behind and straining toward what is ahead, I press on toward the goal to win the prize for which God has called me heavenward in Christ Jesus." Paul continued to maintain a single-minded focus on his future. The New Living Translation renders it this way, "I am focusing all my energies on this one thing: Forgetting the past and looking forward to what lies ahead, I strain to reach the end of the race and receive the prize": eternal life with Christ.

In sports, we use the term "in the zone" to describe the ultimate in concentration. Paul desired to be in the zone in regard to his Christian life.

Has anything replaced the zeal you once had for Christ? Take Paul's advice and lay it aside and pursue "the goal."

— KYLE ABBOTT, FORMER MAJOR LEAGUE PITCHER

SPORTS NOTE:
Kyle pitched in 57 games during his major league career, starting 22 of them.

FROM THE PLAYBOOK:
Read Psalm 42.

 GAME PLAN: What do you spend most of your time concentrating on? Is God even in the Top Five? What are a couple of ways you can increase your concentration on God?

ACHE 3: DO YOU HAVE HOPE?

POINT OF EMPHASIS:
Hope in God

"Our citizenship is in heaven." PHILIPPIANS 3:20

Paul gives us some practical advice for handling trials.

As we continue to look at the acronym ACHE, we can see that in order to have the right **Attitude** and maintain **Concentration**, we move to the letter H—**Hope**. The message of Christianity is one of hope. Because Jesus rose from the dead, we can be assured that God can do anything in our lives.

In Philippians 3:18–21, Paul compares unbelievers and believers and tells believers that they are citizens of heaven. We should live with hope that no matter what happens in our lives God will transform us into the glorious body in which we will live forever.

SPORTS NOTE:
Kyle made just one error in his four years in the major leagues.

If our hope is based on anything other than Jesus Christ, then that hope is vain. This is because the power that raised Christ from the dead is the same power that is available to us. God's desire is for us to have proper perspective when we face trials.

FROM THE PLAYBOOK:
Read Hebrews 6:13–20.

In comparison to eternity with Him, anything we face in life is minor. Paul said, "I consider everything a loss compared to the surpassing greatness of knowing Christ Jesus my Lord, for whose sake I have lost all things. I consider them rubbish, that I may gain Christ and be found in him, not having a righteousness of my own that comes from the law, but that which is through faith in Christ—the righteousness that comes from God and is by faith. I want to know Christ and the power of his resurrection and the fellowship of sharing in his sufferings, becoming like him in his death, and so, somehow, to attain to the resurrection from the dead" (Philippians 3:8–11).

—KYLE ABBOTT, FORMER MAJOR LEAGUE PITCHER

GAME PLAN: What do you think hope means in a spiritual context? Do you have the absolute sure hope of eternal life? With faith in Christ, you can.

ACHE 4: ARE YOU MAKING AN EFFORT?

POINT OF EMPHASIS:
Diligence

"Continue to work out your salvation." PHILIPPIANS 2:12

The final letter in the acronym ACHE is E for **Effort**.

In Philippians 2:12–16, Paul reminds us that we must "continue to work out our salvation with fear and trembling." The greatest part of this message is that God "works in us to will and to act according to his good purpose" (Philippians 2:13). This tells us that when the circumstances of our life make it the most difficult to follow God, He is the one sustaining us. This is the effort that we are to give. Our responsibility is to maintain fellowship with Him, so that we can be vessels of His grace to others.

A second aspect of this verse that is related to our witness for Christ is that we are to "Do everything without complaining or arguing" (v. 14). The image Paul presents when we make this kind of effort is that we shine like stars. People watch the way we behave. People do not care what we say if our actions do not bear the same witness. With this in mind, the effort that we make to keep the proper attitude, concentrating on the goal, with the hope of our heavenly citizenship before us, allows us to demonstrate Christlikeness to an unbelieving world.

This is why Paul was able to remain joyful in spite of troubling circumstances. He withstood the aches of life with the ACHE of Jesus Christ. It was his mindset, his goal, his hope, and his endeavor. This is how we also can achieve victory no matter what circumstances we face.

— KYLE ABBOTT, FORMER MAJOR LEAGUE PITCHER

SPORTS NOTE:
After his baseball career ended, Kyle became a Baseball Chapel representative—chaplain for the Texas Rangers.

FROM THE PLAYBOOK:
Read James 2:14–26.

GAME PLAN: Have you come to grips with the fact that you cannot do anything to earn your salvation, yet God expects us to not be lazy in our faith? What are you doing as a witness of your faith to others?

UNMISTAKABLE SUCCESS

POINT OF EMPHASIS:
Success in perspective

"Since through God's mercy we have this ministry, we do not lose heart." 2 CORINTHIANS 4:1

What would you think of a baseball player who played seven seasons without hitting the ball into fair territory? One of the best players of all time, Mickey Mantle, did the equivalent of that. His walks and strikeouts add up to more than 3,400 trips to the plate (seven seasons' worth!)

Or what would you think of an inventor who failed hundreds of times in his experiments? Thomas Edison, perhaps the greatest inventor in American history, spent many long months failing before he found a filament that would stay lit in his incandescent light.

The lesson behind these experiences is clear: We have to look beyond failures and keep persevering.

I can't think of a better example of someone who persevered despite apparent failure than the apostle Paul. His list of failures would lead most of us to quit. For one, the people in a church he founded in Corinth stumbled badly. For another, he went to prison numerous times. Throw in the shipwrecks, beatings, and betrayals (2 Corinthians 11:23–27), and you could have a picture of defeat. Yet Paul's ministry is remembered for its unmistakable success.

Let's learn to look past our failures. We should learn from them, that's for sure, but we shouldn't let them stop us. Because of God's mercy, we need not lose heart (2 Corinthians 4:1).

—DAVE BRANON

SPORTS NOTE:
Mantle struck out 1,710 times during his career. He also had 2,415 hits and 536 home runs.

FROM THE PLAYBOOK:
Read:
2 Corinthians
4:1–12.

GAME PLAN: How have you handled recent failures in your life? What would God have you do when things go south?

TARA'S TIPS

POINT OF EMPHASIS:
Living for God

"I seek you with all my heart." PSALM 119:10

When tennis teen Tara Snyder joined the WTA Tour, she expected to become a big star. Instead, Snyder suffered some tough losses, made some embarrassing mistakes, and felt like giving up. But she persevered. Four years later, she earned her first title and cracked the Top 50 in the rankings.

Even with all its challenges, life on the Tour has been a great experience for Tara. Here's what she says she learned:

1. Stay focused. "Sports are so competitive! To reach the top you really have to be motivated, even driven, to give it your best every day."

2. Surround yourself with positive, spiritual people. "My boyfriend, my coach, and my agent are all Christians. They don't put a lot of pressure on me to win or make money. They want to see me grow spiritually. They encourage me and pray for me, and their support keeps me headed in the right direction."

3. Ask God. "When I'm struggling with something personally or trying to make tough decisions about my schedule or my career, I pray. Waking up in the morning and going to bed at night—even sitting on a plane, I ask God to show me what He wants me to do. He knows what's best."

4. Most important, put Him first. "Before tennis, before anything else in my life, my faith in God comes first. I know that when I put my trust in Him, everything else will take care of itself."

Tara has learned some valuable lessons we all can apply to our lives!

—CHRISTIN DITCHFIELD

SPORTS NOTE: In 2002, Tara won the ITF/ Frisco-USA title on the Women's Tennis Association Tour.

FROM THE PLAYBOOK: Read Psalm 119:9–16, 33–37.

GAME PLAN: Look over Tara's tips and see which ones you can apply to your life today. Or make your own list of three or four life lessons you've learned lately.

POINT OF EMPHASIS:
God's plan

"Just as you share in our sufferings, so also you share in our comfort." 2 CORINTHIANS 1:7

Casey Martin wanted to ride a golf cart, and the PGA didn't want him to. So he made a federal case out of it. In a 7–2 ruling handed down in May 2001, the United States Supreme Court ruled that Martin could compete in PGA events using a golf cart.

Martin was born with an extremely rare defect called Klippel-Trenaunay-Weber Syndrome, which hinders blood from circulating properly in the leg. Walking, especially over long periods of time, is very painful, and Casey lives with an increased risk of fractures and possible amputation because of his leg's brittle bone structure.

SPORTS NOTE:
Nike sponsors the Casey Martin Award, which is given to an athlete who has overcome challenges and disabilities.

FROM THE PLAYBOOK:
Read 2 Corinthians 1:3–11.

Melinda Martin, Casey's mom, says she taught her son and his older brother Cameron that God doesn't make any mistakes in our makeup.

"He doesn't make us any less of a person. He allowed that defect in Casey's leg, but He has given him so many other good things," she says. "He is a straight-A student, plays the piano, has a very quick wit, and has a lot of friends. Sometimes when we don't know our weaknesses, we don't learn our gifts."

Because of the publicity over the use of a golf cart, Martin has had ample opportunity to display his wit along with his Christian testimony during his hundreds of media interviews surrounding his landmark legal victory.

"I have peace that God did this for a reason, and that He is in control. But to be honest, there is a lot of pressure," he says. "The media pressure is on me all the time, and I'm dealing with stuff I've never dealt with before."

It's no mistake that Casey has a bad leg, and he's learning every day new ways God is using this difficulty for His glory.

—ART STRICKLIN

GAME PLAN: What difficulty are you dealing with? Write down three ways God can use it for His glory.

DRIVEN

POINT OF EMPHASIS:
A challenge to fathers

"Fathers . . . bring them up in the training and instruction of the Lord." EPHESIANS 6:4

Bill Vukovich was the greatest driver you've never heard of. In 1953 and 1954 the "Mad Russian" won two straight Indy 500 races. His aggressive racing style and cool demeanor made him a fan favorite.

Then, in 1955, tragedy struck. As the 36-year-old was attempting to take his third straight Indy 500, on the 57th lap, he became involved in a multi-car crash that ended his life.

The driven attitude he possessed was passed on to his son, Billy. In 1968 Junior won the Rookie of the Year after his seventh place finish in the same race that made his father famous. In 1973 he finished second at the Brickyard.

Billy II passed the race gloves on to Billy III, who was named Rookie of the Year for his 14th-place finish at the 1988 race. Sadly, Bill Vukovich's grandson died just like his grandfather. In 1990, he died from injuries sustained in a sprint-car crash.

There is often a common thread, or tread in the Vukovich's case, that weaves its way through families. The interests shared from father to son are taught and caught.

That's why dads need to grasp the importance of steering their children toward God and His Word. Paul implores men to "bring them up in the training and instruction of the Lord" (Ephesians 6:4) and "be strong in the Lord and in his mighty power" (v. 10).

If you're a father, realize that you're going to be strong in something—work, sports . . . something. Carefully consider your ways. Be driven in leading your kids to the deeper truths of Christ.

If not, they'll be poorly prepared for the race of life.

—TOM FELTEN

SPORTS NOTE:
Bill Vukovich said the only way to win at Indy was to "keep your foot on the throttle and turn left."

FROM THE PLAYBOOK:
Read Ephesians 6:1–10.

 GAME PLAN: If you are a dad, spend time today talking about a principle from Scripture with your children. If you're not a dad, talk with your father (or a father figure) about God and His Word today.

OFFENSIVE "D"

POINT OF EMPHASIS:
Loving others

"He who refreshes others will himself be refreshed." PROVERBS 11:25

One of the strangest soccer games of all time occurred during a World Cup match between Barbados and Grenada in 1994. Before the game, Barbados knew its mission: Win the game by two goals to advance to the next round.

So, with 5 minutes to go and opponent Grenada playing great defense, they were in trouble. Barbados was ahead 1–0, but they were afraid they couldn't get that second goal. So one of the Barbados players dribbled to his own goal and scored for Grenada!

"Why?" you ask.

Well, the wily Barbados brain trust knew that if the game ended in a tie, it would be decided by penalty kicks, and the team that wins that way is awarded (you guessed it) a 2–0 victory!

Grenada did not like that strategy. So they began kicking the ball into their own net! The remaining minutes of the game became a surreal display of both teams defending the *other* team's goal. Somehow, the game did end in a tie and Barbados did get their 2–0 penalty-kick win.

While we would never promote such free-spirited giving on the soccer pitch, we as Christians must be willing to give generously in a way that is hard for others to understand.

Jesus said, "Love your enemies and pray for those who persecute you, that you may be sons of your Father in heaven" (Matthew 5:44–45). That may mean looking out for others to our own detriment—giving up much more than the equivalent of an "own goal"—to help someone else.

Go into today ready to live by God's strategy—loving those people who show you none.

—TOM FELTEN

SPORTS NOTE:
Despite their best efforts, neither Grenada nor Barbados made it to the World Cup tournament in 1994.

FROM THE PLAYBOOK:
Read Matthew 5:38–48.

GAME PLAN: Write down the names of three people who have mistreated you lately. Next, write down the way you have responded to their behavior. Finally, write down the way you feel Christ would have you think and act regarding the trio.

MENTORS AND FRIENDS

POINT OF EMPHASIS:
Mentoring

"Now you are the body of Christ, and each one of you is a part of it."
I CORINTHIANS 12:27

When I first arrived on the scene in the LPGA, I was fortunate to be able to get to know mature Christian golfers such as Betsy King and Barb Mucha. They were just what I needed, because they helped me understand the golf scene as a Christian—with the right perspective.

Barb was an especially key Christian friend my first few years on Tour. Now I can return the favor to others. I feel compelled to mentor the rookies coming out on the Tour and give them a sense of security and support as their sister in Christ.

I have invited numerous rookies to our Bible Fellowship for a chance to meet some of the players in a noncompetitive setting. A few years ago I invited Jamie Hullett to join me for Fellowship. Jamie can come across as very shy and quiet. She seemed to enjoy the message and the fellowship, but because of how quiet she was I didn't know she was already a Christian. She is a very strong follower of Christ and just goes about her walk in a quiet manner.

One year I invited Jody Niemann-Dansie to the group. Jody was not a Christian but through some mentoring by Siew Ai Lim, Jody and her husband, Bryan, became Christians that summer. I simply bridged the gap and befriended Jody by going to dinner and playing practice rounds with her. Then Siew Ai, who has much more mentoring knowledge than I do, had one-on-one Bible study times with Jody.

That's how the body is supposed to work—all working toward a common cause: to let others know the great love Christ has to offer us.

—WENDY WARD, LPGA GOLFER

SPORTS NOTE:
Wendy and her husband, Nate Hair III, have a cattle ranch in the state of Washington.

FROM THE PLAYBOOK:
Read 2 Timothy 2:1–15.

GAME PLAN: List three people you might be able to mentor over time. What steps can you take to begin to help them grow spiritually?

LESSONS FROM THE BENCH

POINT OF EMPHASIS:
Listening to God

"I waited patiently for the Lord." PSALM 40:1

Some players get discouraged when they feel they don't get enough playing time. Rob Smith is not one of them.

Smith is a former midfielder for the Columbus Crew in Major League Soccer, and he says his lack of playing time actually contributed to his putting his faith in God.

Smith, from Wilmington, Delaware, said he was frustrated during his second season in Columbus because he found himself on the bench more than on the playing field. "It really hurt my pride," he says.

It was during this time of discouragement that a friend led him to faith in Jesus Christ. "I understood God's grace after that," Smith said. Then in January 1998, his wife of just over a year followed in the faith.

"Things don't go perfect in life, but God always works it out somehow, and our relationship has changed so much for the better," he says. "When I do play, I play for God, and when I'm not playing, I try to be a good example and support the team."

Of his stint with the Crew, Smith said, "I feel God brought me here for a reason. If not getting enough playing time is an avenue for me to be a good witness, then I'll accept that and keep working hard."

Sometimes, it seems, God takes us out of the situation we would prefer to be in so He can teach us something we didn't know. We must be listening for God's direction—waiting patiently to see how He is working to draw us closer to Himself.

—DEL DIDUIT

SPORTS NOTE:
Rob Smith played his college soccer at the University of South Carolina.

FROM THE PLAYBOOK:
Read Galatians 1:11–18.

 GAME PLAN: Have you been sidelined recently for some reason? What might God be teaching you?

STICKING TO A COMMITMENT

POINT OF EMPHASIS:
The value of commitment

"Simply let your 'Yes' be 'Yes.'" MATTHEW 5:37

On Monday, June 3, 2002, minor league pitcher Mike Maroth of the Toledo Mud Hens made a commitment to be a guest on the Saturday, June 8, *Sports Spectrum* radio show. Maroth would go one-on-one with *SS* radio host Chuck Swirsky.

Minor league baseball was the show's scheduled theme. The former University of Central Florida product had spent parts of the previous four seasons on late-night bus rides hoping that someday he would get a shot at the big leagues.

On Friday, June 7, Maroth got the call he had always dreamed of—he was going to the big leagues!

The Detroit Tigers had summoned the young left-hander to start Saturday night's game against the Philadelphia Phillies. Family, friends, his agent, and others would be flying in from around the country to see Maroth take the mound for the very first time as a major league player. What a day it would be!

But what about his prior commitment to the *Sports Spectrum* radio show? Surely the staff at *SS* would understand if he backed out. They wouldn't force him to keep his word on such a huge day, would they?

Sports Spectrum didn't have to.

Mike Maroth chose to live out his faith in Jesus Christ in a tangible, Bible-based way. He put the words of Matthew 5:37 into practice, "Simply let your 'Yes' be 'Yes,' and your 'No,' 'No.'"

Mike remained true to his word. He kept his prior commitment to be a guest on *SS* radio. Maroth's "Yes" was truly his "Yes." What a great way to start a big league career!

—ROB BENTZ

SPORTS NOTE: Midway through the 2005 season, Mike Maroth was the all-time leader in wins by a pitcher at Comerica Park in Detroit.

FROM THE PLAYBOOK: Read Matthew 5:33–37.

GAME PLAN: Are you a person who keeps your word? Can your family, friends, and co-workers trust your word? Ask them. If you don't like the answer they give, pray to God and ask Him to make you a person of integrity who remains true to your word.

STICK OUT YOUR TONGUE!

POINT OF EMPHASIS:
Using the tongue wisely.

"I will . . . keep my tongue from sin." PSALM 39:1

How could you tell when Michael Jordan really had his game going? In a 1989 playoff game against the Cleveland Cavaliers, after making a hanging free-throw-line jump shot over Craig Ehlo, he jumped and repeatedly punched the air. He had his game going then. Or against the Portland Trailblazers in the 1992 NBA Finals when he had just drained his sixth three-pointer in the first half of Game 1, he turned to television commentators and with palms up, shrugged his shoulders. He definitely had his game going then. But what was the most consistent signal that Michael was feeling it, and something special was about to happen?

Sure—his tongue came out. Get your camera ready, because when MJ sticks his tongue out, a poster photo op is imminent.

How can you tell when Christians really have their game going? Well, according to the New Testament writer James, they stick out their tongue in a different way.

When others are gossiping and being critical, a Christian with his or her game face on uses the tongue to encourage. When tempted to use angry, cutting words, a Christian who is playing well responds with kindness and restraint. The most consistent signal of a Christian living under the Spirit's control is this: Using the tongue for good rather than evil.

If someone snaps a picture during one of your conversations today (with your spouse or one of your children or a co-worker or a friend or a store clerk), what will your tongue be doing?

—BRIAN HETTINGA

SPORTS NOTE:
Through the end of his career with the Chicago Bulls (before joining the Washington Wizards), Michael Jordan had a total of 25 game-winning shots.

FROM THE PLAYBOOK:
Read James 3:2–12.

 GAME PLAN: Eavesdrop on a couple of conversations today. Listen carefully to the words people around you use. Pay close attention to how the words are spoken. Choose a person you'd like to be like, and a person you don't want to be like. Ask God to help you be His person when you stick out your tongue.

JUNE 5

SHARE THE GOOD NEWS

POINT OF EMPHASIS:
Witnessing

"Let your light shine before men." MATTHEW 5:16

As he accepted the winner's trophy at the 1989 French Open, 17-year-old Michael Chang addressed the crowd at Roland Garros in Paris. He thanked everyone who had played a part in his phenomenal success. He concluded by thanking Jesus Christ, saying, "Without Him I'm nothing!" Along with the cheers came boos and whistles. TV commentators, coaches, and even other players criticized him for "dragging his religion into everything." They advised him to keep his personal beliefs to himself.

But Chang was unfazed by the response. He continued to speak about his faith at every opportunity, giving God the glory for his success. "I've just received so much joy, so much love, and so many blessings from the Lord," he explains. "When something good happens to you, you want to share it with people!"

When we think about it that way, sharing our faith should be the most natural thing in the world. The Gospels give us plenty of examples of people who encountered Jesus and couldn't help but share the good news.

> **SPORTS NOTE:**
> When Michael won that match in 1989 to capture the French Open, he became the youngest player to win that prestigious tournament. He defeated Stefan Edberg.

> **FROM THE PLAYBOOK:**
> Read Matthew 5:13–16 and 28:18–20.

- The shepherds witnessed His birth and then told everyone they could find.
- When Jesus called Andrew to be His disciple, Andrew went to get his brother, Simon Peter.
- Philip found his friend Nathaniel and brought him along.
- The Samaritan woman called her whole town to come and meet Jesus. Good news is exciting—you just have to share it!

Take time today to tell others what Jesus has done for you. Share the good news!

—CHRISTIN DITCHFIELD

GAME PLAN: Write down the names of two or three friends who don't know Christ. Begin praying that God will give you the opportunity to share the good news with them.

"SACRIFICE MYSELF?"

POINT OF EMPHASIS:
Sacrifice

"Greater love has no one than this, that he lay down his life for his friends." JOHN 15:13

Ever camp out on a city street?

Some 300 Detroit hockey fans did that a few years ago. The Red Wings were skating for the Stanley Cup, and true-blue fans were willing to sacrifice their comfort by sleeping and standing on the cold concrete to get tickets.

Many fans spent 2 days in the great outdoors at the ticket office in downtown Detroit. But many became unhappy campers when the last tickets were sold before they reached the window.

One woman burst into tears and said, "I'm not rich, and I tried so hard to get tickets. I was hoping to surprise my husband." (He might have thought something was up when she was missing for a couple of days.)

A 19-year-old, who did manage to snag a few tickets, had a more self-centered focus. "I felt bad for my buddies behind me who didn't get tickets," he said, "but what am I going to do, sacrifice myself? I can't do that!"

What a contrast in attitudes.

Before we send this guy to the penalty box, however, we need to consider our own lives. How often do we sacrifice ourselves for others? What's our first thought when we're presented with an opportunity to serve: "No way!" or "Sure!"

Our Savior gave the ultimate in self-sacrifice for us—He laid down His life. Jesus said, "Greater love has no one than this, that he lay down his life for his friends" (John 15:13).

Christ sacrificed it all—even for the people who hated Him. Consider what Christ has done for you. Then ask yourself: Am I willing to sacrifice myself?

Your life is your answer.

—TOM FELTEN

SPORTS NOTE:
Through 2005, the Detroit Red Wings had been in the Stanley Cup finals 17 times.

FROM THE PLAYBOOK:
Read Romans 12:1–8.

GAME PLAN: A food bank, a missions trip, an evangelism campaign: Which of these or other activities will I get involved in?

USE YOUR TALENTS

POINT OF EMPHASIS:
Using talents

"Whatever you do . . . [do it] as working for the Lord."
COLOSSIANS 3:23

Christian music icon Michael W. Smith remembers when the Cincinnati Reds were the top team in sports. As a young boy Michael and his dad made many trips from their West Virginia home to Ohio to watch the "Big Red Machine" play. At the time, Reds player Pete Rose was Michael's hero. Michael admired Rose's sheer drive, intensity, and love for the game.

"I looked up to him because I saw his commitment and determination to excel in a sport so important to him. Pete's passion for baseball helped inspire my passion for what I do," Michael says. "I remember watching Rose and thinking, 'I want to be that way about God. I want to be that way about my family, and I want to be that way about everything I do.' Not that I've always achieved that. Sometimes I get complacent and lazy, and I don't give it my best. But my passion has helped me live out a verse in the Bible that tells us that whatever we do we're to work at it as 'working for the Lord'" (Colossians 3:23).

Like all baseball fans, Michael was sad to learn about Rose's problem with gambling. But he never forgot the lessons he learned from watching Rose play baseball with zeal. As Michael has devoted his passion for music to the Lord, he's been blessed, and he has been able to encourage thousands of people to respond to God's love and plan for their lives.

Do you work hard to develop the talents God has given you? Are you doing things wholeheartedly as to the Lord?

—ROXANNE ROBBINS

SPORTS NOTE:
When Michael W. was a Little Leaguer, he was so good that his coach thought he might become a major leaguer someday.

FROM THE PLAYBOOK:
Read Colossians 3:12–25.

GAME PLAN: List an area where you have been slacking off with your talents instead of using them in a way that glorifies the Lord. Is fear or laziness holding you back? Ask God for faith and strength to start giving your best.

THERE IS MORE

POINT OF EMPHASIS
Life's changes

"God had planned something better for us." HEBREWS 11:40

Did you know that Babe Ruth started his major league career as a pitcher? That's right. In his first six seasons, the man who eventually became legendary for hitting 714 home runs was an ace southpaw.

From 1915–17, Ruth won 65 games for the Red Sox, more than any left-handed pitcher in the majors. He also holds the record for the longest complete game win in World Series history. In 1916, he pitched 14 innings in a victory over the Brooklyn Dodgers.

While Ruth was a highly successful pitcher, he didn't turn into a major home run threat until he made the change from pitcher to outfield. In fact, Ruth hit only 49 home runs before he switched positions after joining the New York Yankees in 1920.

SPORTS NOTE:
Babe Ruth is the only player to hit 3 home runs twice in a World Series game (1926 and 1928).

A major change can be unsettling. It can force us out of our comfort zone and into the unknown. Still, a change is often the very thing we need to become more of who we are truly meant to be.

That's what happened to Moses. Although he was orphaned as a baby, he eventually became a member of Egypt's royal household (Exodus 2:10). Life seemed to be going well, but God had other plans. Changes were on the horizon that would eventually shape him into a powerful leader who would lead God's people out of slavery and on to the Promised Land (Deuteronomy 34:10-12).

FROM THE PLAYBOOK:
Read the stories of change in Hebrews 11.

Sometimes God calls us to make a significant change, even when life appears to be going well, because He has something more in mind.

—JEFF OLSON

GAME PLAN: Ask God how He might be using some of the changes in your life to lead you to something more. Set up a two-month plan to make those changes.

DON'T LET IT GO TO YOUR HEAD

POINT OF EMPHASIS:
Talents from God

"Consider everything [else] a loss." PHILIPPIANS 3:8

Since making the USA Women's Basketball National Team and starring in the WNBA, Ruthie Bolton has lived a life that women athletes used to only dream about. She and her teammates have traveled the world, received lucrative endorsements, jogged with the President, and won two Olympic gold medals.

If you were in Ruthie's, or another star athletes' shoes, how would you keep the success, money, and awards in perspective? Wouldn't it be easy to let it all go to your head?

To stay grounded, Ruthie clings to the truth of Philippians 3:8, which says, "I consider everything a loss compared to the surpassing greatness of knowing Christ Jesus my Lord, for whose sake I have lost all things."

"My spiritual background and being a Christian has really helped me as far as keeping a great attitude and realizing I can't take this too seriously," Ruthie says. "I need to take basketball seriously to a certain point, but also realize this is all background music. The most important thing is to do right and please God."

By "background music," Ruthie means basketball is something that has added happiness to her life but does not make up the core of who she is. She uses a musical analogy to describe her perspective on sports because she is also a gifted singer. Performing gospel songs at various venues is a way for Ruthie to give thanks for a Christian faith that has enabled her to deal with life's pressures.

What talents has God given you? How can you use those talents for His glory?

—ROXANNE ROBBINS

SPORTS NOTE:
Ruthie was the 16th child of Rev. Linwood and Leola Bolton. Eventually, she would have 19 brothers and sisters.

FROM THE PLAYBOOK:
Read Philippians 3:1–11.

 GAME PLAN: Is there something in your life that is overshadowing your walk with the Lord? If so, ask God to help you prioritize your thoughts and time so that you can fully experience the surpassing greatness of knowing Christ.

JUNE 10

GET TOGETHER WITH GOD

POINT OF EMPHASIS:
Time with God

"My heart says of you, 'Seek his face! Your face, Lord, I will seek.'"
PSALM 27:8

You make it look so easy and graceful."

I have heard this comment about my golf swing many times. Often my response is this: "I have played golf for many years, hitting thousands of golf balls, stroking thousands of putts, and competing in several hundred tournaments."

SPORTS NOTE:
In 2002, Tracy attended the Winter Olympics, where she handed out Jesus pins as a way of witnessing.

FROM THE PLAYBOOK:
Read Psalm 34:1–10 to discover some of the benefits of spending time with God.

I say that because I have practiced and spent mountains of time developing a graceful swing. It just didn't happen the first time I played golf. I have chosen to spend time honing my golf skills and in return I have been blessed with the opportunity to play professionally. When I don't spend time practicing, I find it difficult to stay consistent on the course. So I must spend time practicing daily to stay competitive.

I believe the same principle applies to our relationship with God. A strong relationship with Him does not just spring up overnight. One of the reasons God wants us to spend quality time with Him is so that we can get to know Him better.

We can do that by studying and reading the Bible, and by learning from mature Christians. Just as I must listen carefully to my golf coach in order to improve my game, we must also spend time talking to and listening to God. Through intimate moments with Him we grow, we change, we're encouraged, and we find rest. The psalm writer David said, "My heart says of you, 'Seek his face!' Your face, Lord, I will seek" (27:8).

Seek His face daily and allow your spirit to be refreshed and renewed.

—TRACY HANSON, LPGA GOLFER

GAME PLAN: Have you spent time with God today? Get out your schedule right now and set aside **30 minutes** for each of the next **5 days** to enjoy God's company. Read Scripture, pray, or just listen to God.

MIXED SIGNALS

POINT OF EMPHASIS:
Hypocrisy

"Do not be yoked together with unbelievers." 2 CORINTHIANS 6:14

You would think the American Cancer Society would be more careful. But someone wasn't paying attention to details when the ACS decided to hold a benefit night in conjunction with a professional tennis tournament.

That sounds pretty safe, tennis being excellent exercise for a healthy heart and all. Things started to turn embarrassing, though, when the ACS discovered that a major tobacco company was sponsoring the competition. Although they weren't aware of it, officials of the society had committed themselves to selling 500 tickets to an event that was named after a well-known brand of cigarettes. By the time they found out, it was too late.

So, here was a group that was asking people to quit smoking, yet sending out publicity that portrayed a young woman with a tennis racket in one hand and a cigarette in the other. It was a classic example of mixed signals.

Just as cigarettes and the American Cancer Society don't mix, neither do Christians and some of our entanglements. For example, if you start dating a person who has no interest in God or biblical morality, you are sending mixed signals.

Paul stated in 2 Corinthians 6:14 that God's children must restrict their close fellowship to those who see things as they do. Why? Because righteousness and wickedness have nothing in common. Whenever there are mixed signals, the message is garbled.

Remember, God's Word says that Christ and His enemy have nothing in common. So, let's be careful not to be "yoked together" with those who favor Satan's agenda over the Lord's.

—MART DE HAAN

SPORTS NOTE: The National Center for Chronic Disease Prevention and Health Promotion estimates that there are 430,000 smoking-related deaths in the United States in a year.

FROM THE PLAYBOOK: Read 2 Corinthians 6:14–16.

 GAME PLAN: List your five closest relationships. If any of those people are not fellow believers, how can you try to win them over without compromising your standards?

YOU NEED TEAMMATES

POINT OF EMPHASIS:
Christian unity

"Though all its parts are many, they form one body."
1 CORINTHIANS 12:12

We as Christians are called to be good "teammates." This applies not only in the arena of athletics but also in our day-to-day lives.
What makes a good teammate in God's eyes?

• A good teammate sees the big picture, which is not about self-satisfaction and individual honors, but rather the goal of the group.

• A good teammate is someone who puts the team's goals ahead of his or her own and is unselfish in serving others with respect.

• A good teammate has complete faith in the leader and is obedient.

• A good teammate does everything with diligence, passion, joy, and appreciation.

• A good teammate knows his or her role and performs his or her best, without envy or pride.

SPORTS NOTE:
Jenny Boucek played for the Cleveland Rockers of the WNBA in 1997.

FROM THE PLAYBOOK:
Read 1 Corinthians 12:12–27.

We all have different roles and different talents that God specifically gave us to use for His purposes on His team! We must know our roles and use our talents for His purposes, knowing that however big or small that role, we all are an important part of the body of Christ.

We all need each other, and we all are needed for the proper functioning of His kingdom.

—JENNY BOUCEK, ASSISTANT COACH, WNBA

GAME PLAN: What kind of a teammate are you? Do people see you as self-centered or others-centered? When you talk, do you mostly talk about you, or do you allow others to feel important? What can you do to be a better companion, teammate, sister, brother, wife, husband, friend?

GOD IS IN CONTROL

POINT OF EMPHASIS:
God's control

"Do not be anxious about anything." PHILIPPIANS 4:6

It was getting down to crunch time. I was on the USA national volleyball team, and we were only one month away from our Olympic qualifying tournament.

I realized my priorities were a bit mixed up when I received a call from my doctor just minutes before I was to leave for practice. She told me that a mole removed from my chest had come back positive for malignant melanoma. My first reaction was, "Can we take care of this in about a month?" She replied, "This could be life-threatening." I was shocked by her words.

After she explained the seriousness of melanoma, I understood that this was something I needed to take care of immediately. I realized I was letting volleyball consume my life.

The next week was filled with uncertainties. I had surgery to remove the cancer and some lymph nodes. The severity of the melanoma would not be determined until the biopsy reports came back.

During this long week of uncertainty, I found tremendous peace in knowing that God was in control. Philippians 4:6–7, which has become my favorite verse, gave me God's amazing comfort. It says, "Do not be anxious about anything, but in everything, by prayer and petition, with thanksgiving, present your requests to God. And the peace of God, . . . will guard your hearts."

SPORTS NOTE:
Val's husband, Hunter, is one of the top triathletes in the world. He has twice represented the United States in the Olympics.

FROM THE PLAYBOOK:
Read Philippians 4:4–9.

Through God's grace, I received His peace, I knew He was in control and He carried me through. My surgery was a success! The cancer was contained, and it had not spread. Three weeks later and all stitched up, I was able to help my team qualify for the 2000 Olympics. I learned to rely more on God through this trying experience and always put Him first.

—VAL KEMPER, FORMER MEMBER, US NATIONAL VOLLEYBALL TEAM

GAME PLAN: What are you facing that has you frightened or uncertain? Have you begun to give that to God in prayer?

JUNE 14

BORN-AGAIN CHAMPIONS

POINT OF EMPHASIS:
Keeping your eyes on Jesus

"Run in such a way as to get the prize." I CORINTHIANS 9:24

In this society of competitiveness and winning at all cost, it is a common misperception that Christians are too nice to be good athletes. I often hear new believers struggling with how to be competitive as a Christian. Yes, your perspective on sports will change once you are born again, but it should not prevent you from being a champion. In fact, it should help you!

Once you realize that winning is not the most important thing, and anything less is a failure, it takes the pressure off. Getting bogged down in the pressures of performance and results is the fall of many athletes. Many of the factors that go into the end-result are out of your control.

What *is* in your control is doing everything to the best of your ability. Keeping your eyes on Christ and focusing on pleasing Him—that's running the race to get the *real* prize.

God gave us talents so we could use them to glorify Him. He wants us to be awesome! He blesses us so that we can bless other people and bring glory to Him. We need to recognize the gifts He gave us and use them for His will, knowing that they are from the Lord, our maker.

All athletes want to win, and that is okay. But remember that sometimes it is not part of His master plan for us to win the game on earth. But He wants us to compete as if we are striving for the ultimate prize—eternity!

—JENNY BOUCEK, ASSISTANT COACH, WNBA

SPORTS NOTE:
In 1998, Jenny was named the top basketball player in Iceland, but she injured her back and had to retire before completing the 1998 WNBA season.

FROM THE PLAYBOOK:
Read 1 Corinthians 9:19–27.

GAME PLAN: Is there anything in your life that you think is a specific skill or knowledge or ability God gave you to serve Him? How have you used that skill in the past week to glorify God?

LOOKING FOR JOY IN THE RIGHT PLACE

POINT OF EMPHASIS:
Security in Christ

"When anxiety was great within me, your consolation brought joy to my soul." PSALM 94:19

One night during my rookie year with the Minnesota Lynx, we played in Madison Square Garden against the New York Liberty in front of 14,000 people. The game was close, and the lead seesawed back and forth.

As the game wound down to the final moments, we were behind by just two points, and I was still on the floor. Suddenly, I found the ball in my hands with less than 10 seconds to go. I drove to the basket and got fouled with 6 seconds left. Talk about unexpected! Here I was at the free throw line with our team's last chance to tie the game as 14,000 people screamed at me. And trust me, they weren't yelling encouragement.

I stepped to the line and shot the ball—then watched in horror as it missed the rim, the backboard, and the net. I was a pro basketball player who had been playing ball for twelve years, and I had air-balled the easiest shot in the game.

We had a chance at an upset, and I blew it. I felt worthless. I had let down the team, the coaches, the fans, and myself.

I learned a valuable lesson through this experience. I had allowed my desire to be a successful athlete overrun my desire to be a child of God—pleasing in His sight. I had fallen into the trap of believing that my identity and self-worth depended on how well I performed on the court. That's just not true.

Because of Calvary, my salvation is secure. My security is in Christ. Sure the sting of choking in crunch time was no fun, but it was a good reminder that my performance is not where my true joy comes from. My joy is found in Jesus—the delight of my soul.

—ERIN BUESCHER, WNBA GUARD

SPORTS NOTE:
Erin enjoys surfing and is a member of the Christian Surfers organization.

FROM THE PLAYBOOK:
Read Philippians 2:1–18.

GAME PLAN: What error have you made recently that made you forget that your worth is in Jesus, not in your performance? What can you learn from Erin's experience?

THE ETERNAL TEAM

POINT OF EMPHASIS:
Working together

"Though one may be overpowered, two can defend themselves. A cord of three strands is not quickly broken." ECCLESIASTES 4:12

Kobe Bryant, Gary Payton, Karl Malone, and Shaquille O'Neal. The Los Angeles Lakers line-up seemed more like an All-Star team. You would think such a star-studded team would be a sure bet to win the championship. But here they were in Game 5 of the 2004 NBA Finals—down by 28 points to the Detroit Pistons. They were going to lose and Detroit would be the NBA champions. How could this happen? How did this team of "All-Stars" lose to the Pistons, a team with no real superstars?

SPORTS NOTE:
David Thompson had a vertical leap of 44 inches when he was in college and the pros.

FROM THE PLAYBOOK:
Read Ephesians 2:11–22.

If you take a look at how both teams approached the game, you can see why the Pistons were victorious. Some of the players on the Lakers' squad seemed to be more concerned with their own individual performances than with the team's success. Basically, they were not playing as a team. At times they looked lost on the court—as if they had never played together before. The Pistons, on the other hand, had a strong front. They banded together as a team and shut the Lakers down.

It is important to be on Jesus' team because no single person can defeat the devil. We cannot win that battle on our own. But teamed with Jesus Christ and a great Playbook—the Bible—we can WIN! We shouldn't stop there. As Christians we need to encourage one another and work together for God's glory. Alone we are helpless, but together we are unbeatable!

—DAVID THOMPSON, FORMER NBA STAR

GAME PLAN: What does it mean to you to be a team player in God's kingdom? Who are you teaming up with to get something accomplished? What goals do you have for the people you are working with?

POSITIVE PARENTING

POINT OF EMPHASIS:
Parenting

"You . . . bring the punishment." JEREMIAH 32:18

The youth soccer league referee took a deep breath and struggled to maintain his composure. Throughout the game he had endured inappropriate comments and critiques from one of the head coaches.

Repeatedly, the ref confronted the coach, who would look back at him like a snake staring down a rodent—smirking and hissing.

The game continued, but so did the verbal volleys from the sideline. Finally, the ref, a dignified man in his forties, said, "That's it, you're gone." The coach was asked to leave the game . . . and his team . . . forever.

Two players strode off with the angry coach. They were his sons. The trio was known throughout the soccer league as being focused on one thing—winning at all costs. Now, they were all off the team.

It's a sad reality that the mistakes fathers and mothers make can affect their children. The prophet Jeremiah was inspired by God to write these words, "You show love to thousands but bring the punishment for the fathers' sins into the laps of their children after them" (Jeremiah 32:18).

Although we might not have the same residual difficulties that father-son problems caused in Jeremiah's day, the words and actions of parents *will* greatly influence their children. If you're a parent, reflect on the ways you have been acting toward your spouse, your children, fellow church members, neighbors, and co-workers. Would you want your kids exhibiting the same behavior?

Look to the God of love and compassion, the God of "great purposes" and "mighty deeds" for your inspiration. Don't do anything that will bring harm to those who are looking to you for guidance.

—TOM FELTEN

SPORTS NOTE: In June 2005, the LA Galaxy of Major League Soccer held a Soccer Dad Appreciation Night in a game with Real Salt Lake.

FROM THE PLAYBOOK: Read Jeremiah 32:17–23.

 GAME PLAN: Catch someone you love doing something right today. Encourage your child, spouse, or friend with positive words and actions.

DAD'S HAT

POINT OF EMPHASIS:
Fathers

"Honor your father." EPHESIANS 6:2

Amid the celebration, there was tragedy.

It was the opening ceremonies of the 1992 Summer Olympic Games in Barcelona, Spain. One by one the teams entered the stadium and paraded around the track to the cheers of 65,000 people. But in one section of Olympic Stadium, shock and sadness fell as Peter Karnaugh, father of United States swimmer Ron Karnaugh, was stricken with a fatal heart attack.

SPORTS NOTE:
In 1997, at the age of 31, Ron became the oldest US swimmer to be a member of the national team. By that time, he had also become a medical doctor.

FROM THE PLAYBOOK:
Read Ephesians 6:1–4.

Five days later, Ron showed up for his race wearing his dad's hat, which he carefully set aside before his competition began. Why the hat? It was the swimmer's tribute to his dad, whom he described as "my best friend." The hat was one his dad had worn when they went fishing and did other things together. Wearing the hat was Ron's way of honoring his dad for standing beside him, encouraging him, and guiding him. When Ron dove into the water, he did so without his dad's presence but with his dad's help.

There are many ways to honor our fathers, as Scripture tells us to do. In a world in which far too many dads have opted out of the day-to-day responsibilities that are part of fatherhood, it is more vital than ever to pay homage to the men who shape our lives in so many ways. One way to do that, even if they're no longer with us, is to show respect for the values they taught us.

What can you do for your dad today to show him the kind of honor Ron Karnaugh demonstrated and the apostle Paul was talking about?

— DAVE BRANON

 GAME PLAN: Is your dad sure that you appreciate his contributions to your life? Have you told him? What is the best thing your dad ever taught you?

THE IAMT PRINCIPLE

POINT OF EMPHASIS:
Seek restoration

"Go ... just between the two of you." MATTHEW 18:15

Ernie Lombardi sure could hit, but he couldn't run! Lombardi is the only catcher to win two batting titles, but Ernie's lack of speed was also legendary. In fact, infielders could play him so deep that Lombardi once confessed that Dodgers' shortstop Pee Wee Reese "was in the league 3 years before I realized he wasn't an outfielder."

Lombardi won his first batting title with Cincinnati in 1938, hitting .342 and winning NL MVP honors. However, after struggling at the plate in 1941, Reds general manager Warren Giles sent him to the Boston Braves, only to have the slow-footed but hard-hitting catcher win the second of his batting titles with a .330 average.

The two had argued publicly, mainly over salary issues, Lombardi calling Giles "the old goat." Decades later, the still bitter Giles, himself an influential member of the Hall of Fame, successfully lobbied against Lombardi's election to Cooperstown. Only after both men passed away did the Veteran's Committee name Ernie to the Hall.

What a sad commentary that they would both go to the grave holding tightly to their grudge. Neither was willing to go to the other to attempt to restore their relationship.

In Matthew 18, Jesus talked to His disciples about how to handle those times when we experience disagreements with others. The process of healing a broken relationship doesn't begin by waiting for the other person to come to you. It begins with the *"It's Always My Turn"* principle. Although every situation may not get resolved, you are responsible to start the process that can lead to forgiveness and restoration. Remember, IAMT.

—BRIAN HETTINGA

SPORTS NOTE: Lombardi hit over .300 in 10 of his 17 major league seasons.

FROM THE PLAYBOOK: Read the 4-step process of confrontation, repentance, forgiveness, and restoration Jesus outlined in Matthew 18:15–20.

GAME PLAN: Do you really want people to remember you for your ability to hold a grudge? Apply the IAMT principle to a disagreement you have with someone this week.

MVP

POINT OF EMPHASIS:
Christian qualities

"Filled with the fruit of righteousness that comes through Jesus Christ—to the glory and praise of God." PHILIPPIANS 1:11

Remember the year the voting for the NBA's Most Valuable Player was so close? It was the 1988–89 season, and Magic Johnson won the award by just a few votes over Michael Jordan.

How did the leading scorer that year not win the MVP trophy? The answer is this: the MVP award is not solely for a player's outstanding individual play. Basketball is a team sport. The MVP must be a player who not only can score points but also can inspire his or her teammates to excel in their abilities on the court. In that particular season, Magic met that criterion more than Michael.

SPORTS NOTE:
Michael Jordan was MVP of the NBA five times: 1988, 1991, 1992, 1996, and 1998. Magic Johnson won the award three times: 1987, 1989, and 1990.

If you think about it, this happens within the realm of Christianity. The church is one body, one team. Oh sure, there are some names of people in a church that we recognize more than others. But each of us as members must be a good teammate—a most valuable parishioner, so to speak. Eight qualities will help you achieve award-winning status with the one person whose vote really counts.

FROM THE PLAYBOOK:
Read Philippians 1:1–11.

- Initiative – be a self-starter with contagious energy
- Vision – see beyond the obvious, look for new objectives
- Unselfishness – let go of the control and quest for glory
- Teamwork – involve and inspire others
- Faithfulness – don't give up, season after season
- Enthusiasm – bring excitement to what you do
- Discipline – maintain good character regardless of the odds
- Confidence – security, faith, and determination

The challenge we face in being an MVP begins with the qualities we choose. And let's hope it's a close vote among all the people in the church.

—DAN DEAL

GAME PLAN: What characteristics do I have that can really be an asset to my church? How can I use them to help?

A PROMISE KEPT

POINT OF EMPHASIS:
Service for God

"Your hearts must be fully committed to the Lord." I KINGS 8:61

It was every college basketball star's dream—being chosen as the first pick in the NBA Draft.

But David Robinson wouldn't join the San Antonio Spurs right away. He insisted on completing his 2-year service commitment to the Navy first. He had given his word, and he would not go back on it—no matter how tempting the offer. Robinson understood the importance of keeping a commitment.

Those of us who are Christians—like David—have committed our lives to Jesus Christ. We've received forgiveness for our sins and the gift of eternal life. And in return, we've promised to "love, honor, and obey"—to serve Him with our whole hearts. It's a commitment some of us have a hard time keeping.

Times get tough or temptation comes knocking, and we forget all about the promise we made. Or worse yet, we choose to ignore it. We go back on our word and back to a lifestyle that displeases God. Some Christians in Bible times had the same problem. The apostle Paul wrote to them: "You were running a good race. Who cut in on you and kept you from obeying the truth?" (Galatians 5:7).

God is faithful to all His promises (Psalm 145:13). He keeps His commitment to us, and He expects us to do the same. Jesus said, "No one who puts his hand to the plow and looks back is fit for service in the kingdom of God." (Luke 9:62)

Are you "fit for service" in God's kingdom? Are you keeping your commitment to Him?

—CHRISTIN DITCHFIELD

SPORTS NOTE:
When David Robinson enrolled at the Naval Academy, he was 6' 4" tall and had very little basketball experience. By the time he graduated, he was a 7-footer.

FROM THE PLAYBOOK:
Read Luke 9:57–62 and Hebrews 12:1–13.

GAME PLAN: If you haven't kept your commitment to Christ, take a moment now to ask God's forgiveness. Rededicate your life to Him and ask Him to help you keep your promise.

MASTERING YOUR THOUGHTS

POINT OF EMPHASIS:
Guard your thoughts

"For the sinful nature desires what is contrary to the Spirit."
GALATIANS 5:17

Learning to use mental visualization techniques to improve athletic performances has been a breakthrough method for many athletes trying to reach the highest levels of their sport. Michael Jordan spent hours visualizing successful performances, high-flying dunks, and fade-away jumpers to help him become the greatest basketball player of all time.

SPORTS NOTE:
Some proponents of sports visualization say that with mental rehearsal, minds and bodies become trained to actually perform the skill imagined.

FROM THE PLAYBOOK:
Read Galatians 5.

In the same way that athletes can improve their abilities by mastering their minds, we can also improve our lives and our relationship with God by using our minds properly. Guarding our hearts and minds from worldly trash is encouraged in several places in the Bible. Guarding our minds will improve the quality of our lives and deepen our relationship with God.

The only way to overcome our sinful nature and the temptations of this world is to "live by the Spirit" (Galatians 5:16). The next verse reads, "For the sinful nature desires what is contrary to the Spirit, and the Spirit what is contrary to the sinful nature." Our sinful nature and relationship with God cannot coexist successfully. One or the other must be sacrificed.

Martin Luther said, "You can't keep a bird from flying over your head, but you can keep it from building a nest in your hair." By God's grace, we can keep our thoughts pure so impurities do not build a nest and reside in our minds.

Submit your thoughts to the authority of Christ. "Guard your heart, for it is the wellspring of life" (Proverbs 4:23). Master your thoughts by giving them to the Master.

—PAUL GRAFER, FORMER MLS GOALIE

GAME PLAN: What does it mean to guard your mind? How can you, in a very practical way, guard your mind and heart? What are some influences that tend to fill your mind with things that are not pleasing to God? Any plans to slow down those influences on your heart?

THINK FIRST, TALK LATER

POINT OF EMPHASIS:
Think before talking

"He who guards his mouth . . . keeps himself from calamity."
PROVERBS 21:23

Sometimes it's not what you say that causes problems—it's when you say it. Just ask Dave Andrews.

Andrews was the public address announcer for a minor league baseball game when Abilene Prairie Dogs manager Charley Kerfeld went into a rage over being tossed out of the game for arguing with umpire Mel Chettum (yes, that's an umpire's real name). Kerfeld proceeded to trash the dugout—throwing bats onto the field. Then he got into it with the umpire again, yelling things to the man in blue, who was standing 100 feet away.

The team's media relations director was afraid Kerfeld might be saying some things the fans didn't need to hear, so he instructed Andrews to read a promotional announcement.

Andrews grabbed the microphone and said over the loudspeakers, "We'd like to thank Lens Crafters for providing the sunglasses for tonight's promotion."

That's all ump Mel Chettum needed to hear. He turned toward the press box, pointed to Andrews, and kicked him out of the game.

"I couldn't believe it," said Andrews. "We honestly didn't think about it." He hadn't even made the connection between thanking an eyeglass company at the same time the manager was questioning the umpire's vision.

We all make similar mistakes from time to time. We talk before we consider who might be hearing what we say, or who we might hurt in the process.

Scripture is clear that it is best to show restraint before we talk—to think through the consequences of our words.

Think first, talk later. It'll keep you out of trouble.

—DAVE BRANON

SPORTS NOTE:
Charley Kerfeld, who was 6' 6" tall, pitched for the Houston Astros and Atlanta Braves in the late 1980s and early 1990s.

FROM THE PLAYBOOK:
Read Proverbs 10:19 and 17:27–28.

GAME PLAN: Is there anyone I have hurt recently with my tongue? How can I make it up to that person?

HOLD ON!

POINT OF EMPHASIS:
Hold on to God

"You need to persevere." HEBREWS 10:36

Imagine what it would be like to be an Olympian, proudly representing your country at the Opening Ceremonies—smiling and waving to more than 100,000 people as they cheer for you.

Perhaps you would even finish in the Top Three and receive a gold, silver, or bronze medal.

Picturing yourself as a famous Olympic athlete can be fun, and if you're an athlete it can motivate you to work hard. No matter how lofty your goal, though, things come up that cause you to feel like quitting.

But even the excitement of the goal is not always enough to keep you going. LaVonna Floreal, 1992 100-meter hurdles Olympic silver medalist, remembers what it was like to pursue Olympic dreams when she felt like giving up. To block distractions, she would focus on a target and work everything else around that mark. In her words, "it's like having a circle with a point in the middle that you can always see unless you turn your back away from it."

Endurance is perseverance. It is pressing on when you want to stop because of obstacles, trials, or ridicule. LaVonna learned how to endure hardships as an athlete in order to reach her goal. Still today, she applies the disciplines she learned as an athlete to her Christian walk and her goal of glorifying God.

Each day we face temptations and obstacles that can cause us to sin or falter in our walk of faith. Yet as a successful athlete continues to persevere, so should we. "Let us hold unswervingly to the hope we profess," the author of Hebrews says (10:23). When we do that, nothing can stop us from doing what God wants us to do.

—ROXANNE ROBBINS

SPORTS NOTE:
In 2002, LaVonna was inducted into the University of Tennessee Lady Vols Hall of Fame.

FROM THE PLAYBOOK:
Read Hebrews 10.

GAME PLAN: Today, list three worthy goals and three things you need to do to reach those goals. Ask God to help you stay disciplined so you can finish the task and bring Him glory in the process.

THREE TIPS FOR SUCCESS

POINT OF EMPHASIS:
Suggestions for success

"Oh, Lord, hear my prayer." PSALM 143:1

While I was waiting for the NBA draft to take place in New York City in 2003, a reporter asked me how I was handling my anxiety as the minutes ticked down toward when I would find out who I would play for in the NBA. I told him, "I rely on God for everything. It's hard to always pray about every situation. But I know He's there with me even when I think about things. I know He's thinking about them with me." Prayer helped me during that time.

So did friends. I had a friend from high school, Ben Chamberlain, with me as well as a friend from Central Michigan University, Whitney Robinson. Also, my brother Mike was with us. Then, after the draft took place and the Los Angeles Clippers had selected me, we all joined my family at a restaurant to celebrate.

Then I knew what would happen in the next few years—I would be living in Los Angeles and playing at Staples Arena. I would be near my agent, Rob Pelinka, who is a Christian, and I would have Ben there with me to keep me accountable.

But I knew I would still have to be careful what I did. Just as in college, there would be women and teammates who would want me to do negative things, but I knew it wasn't beneficial to me. The devil gets the best of you sometimes. When that happens, you just have to come back the next day harder and stronger.

With help from prayer, dependable friends, and good decisions, I hope to be the kind of player and role model who can please God during my NBA career.

—CHRIS KAMAN, NBA CENTER

SPORTS NOTE:
Chris's agent, Rob Pelinka, played basketball for Michigan in the Fab Five era.

FROM THE PLAYBOOK:
Read Proverbs 17:17.

GAME PLAN: What would you say the three weapons against trouble would be in your life? How often do you use them? How valuable are your friends to you in helping you keep on track?

LOOK BEHIND THE CLOUDS

POINT OF EMPHASIS:
God's provisions

"The Lord God is a sun and shield; the Lord bestows favor and honor." PSALM 84:11

After flying quite a bit one summer while playing for the Washington Freedom in the Women's United Soccer Association, I was reminded of the sovereignty of God over and over again.

As always I grabbed a window seat—they are the best seats. There's just something about being up in that sky, gazing out the window, and seeing God's splendor. The plane had just taken off. I turned to look out the window. It was another dreary, rainy day. But as we climbed to a greater altitude, we were soon breaking through the gray clouds. To my amazement, my eyes were suddenly fixed on a brilliant sunrise.

On other flights, I would glance out the window and I wouldn't be able to see anything. There would just be the dreary clouds of a lingering storm. It was during those times that I had to remind myself of the beauty I had seen earlier. A blue sky really was out there, even though I couldn't see it at that moment.

God will take you through tough times, but He will always bring you back to the realization of His sovereignty and His care for you. There is always a blue sky.

I have learned that if God is going to teach you something He is going to "live you through it." At the end of trying times, whether it was a loss, an injury, or another struggle, I became stronger knowing I had survived. I kept my sites on what I knew to be true.

When you look out the window of a plane, you may see clouds and rain—but remember what that blue sky looks like. The sun is still shining, even if you can't see its rays. Comfort, peace, and confidence will rest in your heart.

—AMANDA CROMWELL, COLLEGE SOCCER COACH

SPORTS NOTE:
During her WUSL career, Amanda became soccer coach at the University of Central Florida. In 2004, she was named Coach of the Year by the National Intercollegiate Soccer Officials Association.

FROM THE PLAYBOOK:
Read Psalm 84:10–12.

GAME PLAN: What clouds are blocking your view of God's provision and love? How can your trust in God help you see past them?

RIDING THE WAVES

POINT OF EMPHASIS:
Hold tightly to Christ

"But when he asks, he must believe and not doubt." JAMES 1:6

Margo Oberg is a five-time world champion surfer who lives and rides the water in Hawaii. She's had some serious surf encounters, but none quite as scary as the time she almost "bought it" when she was 16. It all began after Margo wiped out on a humongous wave.

Here are Margo's own words: "Below the wave it looks like a mini-tornado, and you spin around and then usually come up. But sometimes there's so much pressure that you grope for the top and there's no way up."

That's what happened on this not-so-sweet-16 occasion.

Panic set in, and Margo started swimming for the surface—not realizing that she was actually heading straight down. She became delirious and nearly blacked out.

Miraculously (she believes God brought her up), her motionless body began to rise to the surface like a cork. She was able to flounder onto shore.

Margo wouldn't have that panic problem today. She's ridden the waves long enough to relax and not freak out when a wave turns her upside down.

You get a lot of stuff thrown at you every day—new ideas, odd philosophies, touchy emotional issues. Do you sometimes feel like a wave being driven by the wind? Do you feel as if you're swimming down instead of up?

Hold tightly to your faith in Christ. Pray to Him. Acknowledge that He "does not change like shifting shadows" (James 1:17). The more you do, the easier it is to avoid getting drowned with strange ideas.

Surf's up!

—TOM FELTEN

SPORTS NOTE: Margo is a member of the Hawaii Sports Hall of Fame and was named one of the Top 100 Women Sports Figures of the twentieth century.

FROM THE PLAYBOOK: Read James 1:1–18.

GAME PLAN: What do you need to do to become better at recognizing and avoiding wrong "waves"?

NUMBER 3

POINT OF EMPHASIS:
Learning from Scripture

"There are three things that are too amazing for me."
PROVERBS 30:18

Now pinch-hitting for Solomon, Number 3, Aaaaa-guuur!"
Now, I realize it's a little silly to suggest that Agur was wearing Babe Ruth's number as he stood in for the great wise Solomon, but you have to admit, the man liked the number 3.

He talks about "three things that are never satisfied," "three things that are too amazing," "three things [under which] the earth trembles," and "three things that are stately in their stride." He does throw in a list of two, and even his list of three usually turns to four, but Agur was nothing if not a statistician of the first order. He would have kept score at baseball games. He liked to make lists.

Agur was using a standard device called the numerical proverb. It occurs earlier in Proverbs in chapter 6, and some even say Jesus' Beatitudes had this kind of numerical form. Here, when Agur mentions "three things . . . four" and lists a fourth item, it is that final one that is he is emphasizing.

Although the clear teaching of Agur's words is not abundantly evident, we can deduce from his listings the importance we should place on looking deeply and appreciatively at the world around us. God has created a remarkable, varied world, and we need to honor God by noticing it.

There are three, nay four things to get from Agur's words: The writer's humility, God's flawless Word, falsehoods are detestable, and God's creation is inspiring.

In any ballpark, that's a home run for No. 3.

—DAVE BRANON

SPORTS NOTE:
On October 9, 1916, Babe Ruth pitched 14 innings as Boston beat Brooklyn in a World Series game.

FROM THE PLAYBOOK:
Read Proverbs 30.

GAME PLAN: People love lists. Why not list "Three Things That Amaze You" in God's world. Or "Three Things That Will Keep You Close to God."

BOAST IN THIS

POINT OF EMPHASIS:
God's greatness

"He chose the lowly things of this world . . . so that no one may boast before him." I CORINTHIANS 1:28–29

I'm the greatest," heavyweight champion Muhammad Ali boasted often during his heyday.

This sort of proclamation is not all that rare in sports today. Any athlete knows that having confidence in your abilities is crucial to personal success in your sport. If you doubt that you have what it takes, you'll often fail. However, moving from quiet confidence to bragging or boasting is a journey the Christian—whether an athlete, an accountant, or an architect—simply should not take.

The obnoxious boasting that spews from the mouth of an athlete is clearly rooted in a heart filled with pride. This heart of pride and arrogance is what the apostle Paul wrote against in his letter to the church in Corinth. In spite of the pious attitude of the Corinthian believers, Paul told them they had nothing in themselves to boast about. He wrote to challenge them to see that only by God's grace did they have anything to boast about at all.

In I Corinthians 1:27–29 Paul wrote, "But God chose the foolish things of the world to shame the wise; God chose the weak things of the world to shame the strong. He chose the lowly things of this world and the despised things—and the things that are not—to nullify the things that are, so that no one may boast before him."

SPORTS NOTE: Muhammad Ali won the heavyweight title 20 times.

FROM THE PLAYBOOK: Read 1 Corinthians 1:26–31.

What does this mean for you and me? Basically, don't boast about things such as your athletic prowess, your good looks, your successful career, or your moral lifestyle. God is the One who gives these things to you. He is the One who has chosen to use you for His purposes. He deserves the credit.

So if you must boast, boast in the Lord! —ROB BENTZ

 GAME PLAN: Use today's journal space to write down three primary ways that God has blessed you. Once you have your items listed, spend a few moments in prayer thanking Him for how He has gifted you.

LEAN ON GOD

POINT OF EMPHASIS:
Depend on God's strength

"In all your ways acknowledge him." PROVERBS **3:6**

As a child, Olympian Wilma Rudolph suffered through polio, double pneumonia, and scarlet fever, which caused her to lose the use of her left leg. From the age of six she wore a brace. A doctor told Wilma's mother that rubbing her daughter's leg might help. So every day Wilma received four leg-rubs from her brothers, sisters, and mother. Eventually she graduated from a brace to an orthopedic shoe, and she joined her brothers playing basketball whenever she could.

One day, Wilma's mother returned home and found her daughter playing basketball without her brace. Five years later, Wilma had developed into a star runner and at age sixteen qualified for the US Olympic team. She went on to win three gold medals in 1960—in the 100- and 200-meter dashes and the 4 x 100 meter relay.

Wilma refused to lean on the understanding that she was crippled. As a result she went on to greatness.

Proverbs 3:5–6 says, "Trust in the Lord with all your heart and lean not on your own understanding; in all your ways acknowledge him, and he will make your paths straight." When you face a challenge, meditate on this verse. Write down your understanding of your situation and consider whether you're leaning on it. One way to tell if you're leaning on your understanding is by the actions you're taking or paralysis you're experiencing as a result.

For example, you might be afraid to go on an overseas mission trip. It's okay to be cautious, but instead of leaning on the unknown as you make decisions, you need to acknowledge God with your concerns.

Learn to lean on God, and watch things really take off.

—ROXANNE ROBBINS

SPORTS NOTE:
Wilma Rudolph was 54 when she died of brain cancer in 1994.

FROM THE PLAYBOOK:
Read Proverbs 3.

 GAME PLAN: As you make decisions today, big or small, ask, "Am I trusting myself, or am I trusting God completely?"

CAN YOU OUTGIVE GOD?

POINT OF EMPHASIS:
Stewardship

"Bring the whole tithe into the storehouse." MALACHI 3:10

In my first year as a professional golfer, my church had voiced a need for a family that urgently needed financial help. I felt a nudging to contribute to the benevolent fund, but I was unsure of the amount I should commit. After some thought and prayer, I decided I would give 10 percent of my next check to the fund on top of my regular tithe. Considering that the biggest check in my professional career until then was $2,000, I didn't think much of it.

In the very next tournament I played, I finished tied for second place and took home the biggest check of my career—$4,000. Now I was in a little bit of a dilemma. I was expecting to give around $200 to this fund, but now 10 percent would mean I would have to double that.

To make my decision even more difficult, I had not told anyone about my vow. Furthermore, I was sure that whatever I did contribute would have been received with thanksgiving. I decided to write the check for $400 and send it off immediately—before I could have second thoughts. As I was leaving for the next tournament, the family I was staying with for the week put a card in my car just before I pulled out.

Once I arrived at my next destination, I opened the card and found $500 in cash along with several prepaid calling cards. They had no idea of my commitment to God, but God knew.

You can never outgive God. This does not mean that in order for God to bless you, you have to give money to the church. It's not about us—it's about Him. He wants us to be faithful in the stewardship of the resources He gives us—and to honor our commitments.

—SIEW AI LIM, LPGA GOLFER

SPORTS NOTE: On June 6, 2004, Siew Ai had her biggest golf payday, finishing second at the Kellogg-Keebler Classic in Illinois.

FROM THE PLAYBOOK: Read Leviticus 27 and Malachi 3. Consider how those Old Testament standards should fit into your world today.

GAME PLAN: What about this idea of tithing? Is it a habit in your life? Could it be possible that it is the least God expects of us?

TRUSTING IN GOD

POINT OF EMPHASIS:
Trusting God

"For everyone who asks receives; he who seeks finds." LUKE 11:10

During the closing prayer of our pre-game chapel before an MLS game in my last season, our chaplain asked God to give our team the supernatural power to know which way the ball was going while we were on the field. Initially, I shrugged off this prayer and did not put much faith in God's desire to be a part of this aspect of our lives.

Toward the end of the game, with the 1–0 score perilously hanging in our favor, our opponents maneuvered down the field in an effort to equalize the score. With a great deal of congestion in front of my goal, I struggled to see the ball and was concerned that if a shot was taken, I wouldn't be able to make the save.

Fortunately, I caught a glimpse of the advancing forward's body motion and his wind up, so I knew he was going to shoot. Somehow, I correctly dove to my right and was able to parry the shot away to safety.

I gave thanks to God. I immediately believed that He provided me with the ability to know the side of the goal that the ball was headed for—not for my benefit or the benefit of the team—but to prove that there are no prayers that should be "shrugged off." He showed me that no prayer, no matter how big or small, goes unheard.

Trusting God is not easy. But by developing a relationship with Him through prayer, we can have confidence that He is always there.

Luke 11:10 says, "For everyone who asks receives; he who seeks finds; and to him who knocks, the door will be opened." Ask. Then trust God—no matter what His answer might be.

—PAUL GRAFER, FORMER MLS GOALIE

SPORTS NOTE:
As do the other major sports leagues, many MLS teams have a chaplain who conducts chapel services for the players.

FROM THE PLAYBOOK:
Read Matthew 6:5–12.

GAME PLAN: When was the last time you prayed with faith, believing that God was definitely listening and ready to answer? What do you conclude when your prayer isn't answered directly and clearly in line with what you asked? Do you still trust?

GIVING IT YOUR BEST

POINT OF EMPHASIS:
Preparing to share the gospel

"Always be prepared to give an answer." 1 PETER 3:15

In order to give the best effort we are capable of, we are required to prepare properly.

As a pitcher, I must prepare for each start in order to perform at the top of my game. I prepare myself physically, mentally, and emotionally on my day to pitch but also on the 4 days in between. I construct a "game plan" or strategy against the team I will face. If I am well prepared, I am able to approach each start with full confidence. If I neglect this responsibility or do not give a full effort, I will most likely struggle and not be able to pitch to the best of my ability.

This concept also applies to our witness as a follower of Christ. Preparation of our testimony not only affects our personal relationship with the Lord but also our ability to influence others for Christ. If we are not equipped with the Word, we may not be prepared to help others discover a personal relationship with God through Jesus. Giving an answer for what we believe demands that we read the Bible and communicate with God through prayer on a daily basis.

God does not want us to keep our faith to ourselves. He desires for us to share what Christ has done in our lives with those who do not know Him and those who need to be encouraged. When we do, we give others the opportunity to know Jesus Christ as their Lord and Savior.

Commit to proper preparation, and you will be confident in sharing the hope He has given you when provided with opportunities.

—MIKE MAROTH, MAJOR LEAGUE PITCHER

SPORTS NOTE:
Mike Maroth pitched in college for the University of Central Florida.

FROM THE PLAYBOOK:
Read Paul the apostle's testimony in Acts 22.

GAME PLAN: Have you ever written down your testimony so that when you have a chance to share it with someone, you'll know what to say? Try it this week. Then read it to a Christian friend who can help you say it even better.

IS GOD RIGHT-HANDED?

POINT OF EMPHASIS:
God's love and care for us

"Your right hand, O Lord, was majestic in power." EXODUS 15:6

One summer during my teenage years, my good friend Larry decided to become left-handed.

I don't know what got in to him, but whenever we would practice basketball, he practiced left-handed. Maybe he thought he could end up being ambidextrous. All he ended up being was cut from the basketball team.

Being left-handed sometimes looks inviting. When I batted against future major leaguer Don Gullett in high school, I was convinced that lefties were unhittable. At least he was. He pitched a perfect game against my team.

SPORTS NOTE:
Don Gullett was 109–50 as a major league pitcher—fourth best winning percentage all-time among 100-or-more game winners.

I have a naturally right-handed nephew who bats left-handed because my brother taught him to bat that way since he was little. His power-hitting high school career from the first-base side verified that decision.

So, I have nothing against left-handedness. But there is something intriguing about Isaiah 41:10. It says of God, "I will uphold you with my righteous right hand."

The reference to God's right hand doesn't mean what we think of when we discuss which hand we pitch with, but it has significance. In Exodus 15:6, we see that God's right hand is "majestic in power." In Psalm 20:6, His right hand has "saving power." And in Psalm 89:13, we see that God's right hand is "exalted."

FROM THE PLAYBOOK:
Read Isaiah 41:10–13.

These examples of metonymy, the use of a part to speak of the whole, don't mean that right-handedness is better. Instead, it reminds us of some of God's remarkable attributes.

Righteous, majestic. He saves. He is exalted.

What an awesome God we serve! How often do we praise Him for His hand of blessing?

—DAVE BRANON

GAME PLAN: How have you seen God work in your life? Where do you look to see God's majesty and power? What praise song helps you to recall God's awesomeness?

WHEN GOD ASKS THE QUESTIONS

POINT OF EMPHASIS:
Trusting God

"We are hard pressed on every side, but not crushed; perplexed, but not in despair; persecuted, but not abandoned; struck down, but not destroyed." 2 CORINTHIANS 4:8

While playing with the Washington Freedom in the United Soccer Association, I tried to bring my best to everything I did. That was my approach in every game, every practice, every chapel, and every encounter with family and friends.

You never know when it's going to be your last day at the stadium. This was a concept I learned back in 1996.

That year I tore my ACL 6 months before the Olympics. I questioned God when that happened. I wanted to know: "Why did You allow this to happen? Why do I have to go through this right now? Why did it turn out this way?"

You know what happened next? I came to my senses and realized that God asks us questions also. He asks, "Why did you ignore Me this morning? Why don't you trust Me? Why don't you spend time with Me? Why can't you be satisfied with just Me?"

There were times during the summer of 2001 when I felt a bit like Play-Doh. I was being pushed and pulled, squeezed and pounded in all different directions, in all areas of my life. The reality of this is that although the Play-Doh goes through all these changes, it never loses its consistency, it never loses its toughness, and it never loses its identity. It is still Play-Doh.

Same thing with us. We may go through some trials, some struggles, but it doesn't change who we are in Christ. We still have our identity in Christ. We can still trust Him.

I had to learn to trust Him, be satisfied with Him, and spend quality time with Him. That is how I dig in and stay focused. God gets me through the pushes and pulls, and that allows me to bring my best to every situation.

—AMANDA CROMWELL, COLLEGE SOCCER COACH

SPORTS NOTE: For a short period of time, Amanda played in the United Soccer Association during the off-season while coaching the University of Central Florida soccer team during the college season.

FROM THE PLAYBOOK: Read 2 Corinthians 4:8–9.

GAME PLAN: What are some of the questions you sometimes ask God? What are the answers He wants from you?

A WALK WITH GOD

POINT OF EMPHASIS:
Walking with God

"Enoch walked with God." GENESIS 5:24

What is a walk with God?

A quick glance around the world of sports reveals many elder statesmen who have been "walking with God" for a long time.

Men like Florida State football coach Bobby Bowden, Hall of Fame baseball broadcaster Ernie Harwell, and legendary college basketball coach John Wooden have left a godly example of what it means to live a life of faith in Jesus Christ. These men have walked with God in the public arena of high-profile sports.

Bowden, a veteran of more than 40 years of gridiron coaching, has put together many successful game plans. Fact is, Bowden has won more than 350 games at the Division I level—that puts him among the top two Division I coaches in the history of college football!

While Bowden has had a great deal of success on the field, his life away from football has also been a success. He's walked with God faithfully for more than 40 years.

The faithful lives of men like Bowden, Harwell, and Wooden is reminiscent of Old Testament hero Enoch. There are only a few details about this man of God in the Bible, but the information we are given about Enoch in Scripture is that he "walked with God" for a very long time.

What can we learn from Enoch (and our more contemporary examples like Bowden, Harwell, and Wooden)?

We can learn that faith is a lifelong journey. It's a journey filled with both high and low points. A walk with God is a life of faith that carries on from day-to-day, week-to-week, month-to-month, and from year-to-year. It's a life-long thing.

Keep walking!

—ROB BENTZ

SPORTS NOTE:
Legendary announcer Ernie Harwell trusted Jesus Christ as Savior after listening to Billy Graham present the gospel.

FROM THE PLAYBOOK:
Read the story of Enoch in Genesis 5:21–24.

GAME PLAN: Is your walk of faith getting old? Are you getting bored on your spiritual journey? Hang in there! Keep in mind, you're in a marathon—not a sprint. The Christian life is something that has plenty of ups and downs along the way. Remember, a lengthy "walk with God" is the goal.

LOSING ON A WINNING TEAM

POINT OF EMPHASIS:
Using God-given talent

"He who has begun a good work in you will carry it on to completion until the day of Christ Jesus." PHILIPPIANS 1:6

Renee was only in high school, but she displayed Olympic potential. One of the fastest 200-meter runners in the US, the only thing holding her back was that she never took responsibility for her God-given talent—she was extremely lazy. Consequently, she did not develop the confidence she needed.

The day came when Renee's team competed at the US National Track & Field Championships. The team qualified to run in the 800-meter medley finals. She would be running the third leg—200 meters. Waiting to run the final 400 meters was a runner who held the 400-meter world record. If Renee could hand off the baton in second place, the anchor runner could bring home a victory.

The gun fired and everything was going perfectly when Renee took the baton in third place. As the fourth runner waited for the handoff, she figured Renee would pull them up to second, and she would go after first place. Poised to receive the baton, she watched helplessly as one runner after another went past. The whole field went by before she saw Renee slowly coming off the curve, holding her side.

She knew that Renee had decided not to run, and she was faking an injury. When the pressure was on, Renee had no confidence. She hadn't trained to win. Surprisingly, the team pulled out a victory, but as the others celebrated, Renee became the loser on a winning team.

God gives all of us unique gifts and talents. But just like Renee, if we don't develop them, we may become losers among winners. Colossians 3:23 tells us to do everything "heartily, as to the Lord" (NKJV). When we develop our gifts and talents to glorify Him, victory is ours. We are never losers in the eyes of Jesus.

—MADELINE MIMS, OLYMPIC MEDALIST, TRACK

SPORTS NOTE:
Madeline Mims was a four-time Olympian—winning a gold medal in the 1988 Games in the 800-meter race.

FROM THE PLAYBOOK:
Read Psalm 27.

GAME PLAN: "Father, I repent of any slothfulness in my life that will cause me to lose out on experiencing the blessings You have for me. My hope and confidence are in You, my beloved Creator and God. I praise You with my life."

NEED A SHOWER?

POINT OF EMPHASIS:
Spiritual cleanliness

"Do not conform any longer to the pattern of this world, but be transformed by the renewing of your mind." ROMANS 12:2

After a game or a match we feel pretty grimy, don't we? We are in dire need of a shower with lots of soap!

Well, think about all the dirt in the world from a spiritual standpoint. Every day we are confronted by sin around us. We see it, smell it, and sense it even from afar. The ability to detect sin is a trait our heavenly Father gave us when we became His. As we live in this world, we have to battle the dirt on a daily basis.

Should we remain grimy? Not at all. Just as we take a shower physically to remove the dirt of our athletic competition, we need a spiritual shower to remove the grime of life. Daily we need to come to the Father and cleanse our heart and mind. We need to repent and be washed clean. It's a privilege we have as a child of God—free forgiveness.

As we are cleansed, we then need to fill our minds with God and His truth! If we don't, then the dirt we picked up from the world filters into our mind.

Where do we dwell? Where do our minds dwell? Psalm 119:11 says, "I have hidden your word in my heart that I might not sin against you." Philippians 4:7 says, "The peace of God, which transcends all understanding, will guard your hearts and your minds in Christ Jesus."

With all the spiritual dirt in the locker room, on the playing field, and in the hotel rooms—cover your hearts, renew your minds, and dwell on God and His precious truth! Be clean.

—KIM VOISARD, PRO BASEBALL PLAYER

SPORTS NOTE:
In 1996, Kim hit a home run against a men's team of All-Stars from the Cape Cod League—the first such home run by a woman.

FROM THE PLAYBOOK:
Read Psalm 51, which is David's plea for forgiveness when he got himself filthy with sin.

GAME PLAN: What grime is most likely to stick to you? Which of the world's sinful offerings affects you the most? Spend some time asking God to clean those things off you and protect you.

HOW TO GET UP WHEN YOU'RE DOWN

POINT OF EMPHASIS:
Overcoming trouble

"Give, and it will be given to you." Luke 6:38

Do you ever feel a little down? As athletes, we go through a lot of intense emotions. Our confidence ebbs and flows. How do you handle the down times? Do you feel sorry for yourself? Do you let excuses justify your behavior? Do you let your problems affect the whole team?

When you find yourself in a bad mood, the best way to get out of the funk is to lift other people up. Instead of moping in practice and bringing negative energy around the team, make an extra effort to cheer for your teammates and give them compliments. If you do, you will not only keep from letting your selfish issues affect the team, but you will also feel better. God will honor that, and He will give you an unexplainable joy.

Give and you will receive. Give good energy and you will get good energy. Give negative energy and that is what you will get.

Don't depend on others to make you happy. You are in control of your moods and how you handle circumstances. Sometimes you may not feel like being in a good mood, but if you fake it, you will start to feel it. And in the meantime, you may just lift someone else up and brighten his day.

Helping others is one of the best remedies for the blues. Don't give to get, because God knows your heart. But if you give with a pure heart, you will be sure to receive!

—Jenny Boucek, assistant coach, WNBA

SPORTS NOTE:
While in college at the University of Virginia, Jenny was a two-time GTE Academic All-American while being the team's Player of the Year twice.

FROM THE PLAYBOOK:
Read Proverbs 11:23–31.

 GAME PLAN: Whose day can I brighten today? Who needs that extra touch of kindness?

THE EYES OF A SPY

POINT OF EMPHASIS:
Finding God

"I call to the Lord, who is worthy of praise, and I am saved from my enemies." PSALM 18:3

For a few weeks every summer, my assistant coaches and I go out recruiting in gymnasiums nationwide. You could say that we're "spying on" the great players. Since many of them have incredible physical talent, our job is to see through to their character. We want to know who they are in times of adversity and how they approach the game.

Have you ever read in the Bible about Joshua, Caleb, and the twelve spies? It's a captivating story that begins when twelve leaders are selected to spy out the Promised Land and report back to their people, the Israelites. What they saw was an abundance of food, a fertile land "flowing with milk and honey," just what God had promised them. But unexpectedly, they also saw fortified cities and extremely large men like giants. So ten of the spies allowed fear into their hearts and convinced the Israelites that there was no hope in trusting God. But two men stood strong and insisted that there was hope, that God was true to His word. They saw through the unexpected obstacles to the truth of God's promise.

Often, I watch players to see how they react when unexpected things happen. What about us? How do we respond when life throws a curve at us? Do we tremble with fear? Do we stand strong in what we believe even when we're standing alone?

Unbelief looks at obstacles that stand in the way; faith looks at the God who is able to overcome those obstacles. The eyes of a good spy see God in every situation.

—SUE SEMRAU, WOMEN'S COLLEGE BASKETBALL COACH

SPORTS NOTE:
Sue played college basketball at the University of California-San Diego, where she was the 13th top scorer in school history.

FROM THE PLAYBOOK:
Read Numbers 13.

GAME PLAN: What obstacles are standing in your way today? Obstacles that prevent you from trusting God completely?

REALIGNED PRIORITIES

POINT OF EMPHASIS:
Following God's leading

"There are different kinds of gifts, but the same Spirit."
1 CORINTHIANS 12:4

By the time I was a seventh grader, I knew the Lord had blessed me with the gift of speed. I decided to make the most of my gift. I committed myself to the game of basketball.

By following this work ethic, I made it to the WNBA. I was a member of the Utah Starzz and living my dream. Then lightning struck! I was cut by the Starzz midway through my second season. I was devastated. I felt as if I had failed.

Reflecting on that time, I realize I didn't fail in my effort. I had worked hard and used the gifts God had blessed me with as much as I could. Where I failed, however, was in my priorities. I had been using my gifts for my personal glory and determining my success and failure based upon society's standards. What should have mattered was how I used my talent for God's glory, and I hadn't done that. God, however, knew how to help me realign my priorities.

I had been at home in Boise, Idaho, for two weeks when I received a call to play for the Cleveland Rockers. Upon arriving in Cleveland, I went to chapel with our chaplain, Alice Simpson, before my first game. She and one other Rockers player were the only other two in attendance. I wondered why God would take me away from Utah, where I had been surrounded by other Christians, and place me among so many non-believers.

I did not then know God's intentions. But a short year after my arrival in Cleveland, seven of the eleven players on my team were attending chapels regularly. Teammates were reading devotionals on airplanes. I have used this special gift and brought non-believers to Christ. This, to me, has been well worth the sorrow I faced for such a short time and has also been the best victory I could ever win. —TRICIA BADER BINFORD, WNBA GUARD

SPORTS NOTE: The Utah Starzz moved to Texas in 2003 and became the San Antonio Silver Stars.

FROM THE PLAYBOOK: Read 1 Corinthians 12.

GAME PLAN: Is God pointing you in a direction that feels uncomfortable? Could it be that He has some grand things in store for you if you would follow Him?

QUIT COMPLAINING... START THANKING

POINT OF EMPHASIS
Be thankful

"Give thanks in all circumstances." I THESSALONIANS 5:18

NASCAR Craftsman Truck Series driver Kelly Sutton has overcome multiple challenges to become one of the few women to excel in the male-dominated sport. And the obstacles have not all been gender related. Sutton has also had to jump extraordinary physical hurdles because she has Multiple Sclerosis (MS).

Sutton, the only NASCAR driver in history to race with MS, told *Sports Spectrum* writer Jim Gibbs, "I like challenges, and MS is just a part of my life. It's like a bump in the road or a bump on the racetrack, and you've got to find ways to get over it.

"I've just incorporated it all into my daily routine," she says, "which is nothing really special. I just eat healthy foods and work out. In the off-season, I work with a trainer and try to maintain good health throughout the year. I do like to swim, and I try to do that as much as I can. But I also train with weights. Not so much to build muscles but to build endurance in the muscles."

Sutton doesn't complain about her afflictions. Instead she embraces the opportunity to glorify God by giving thanks for what she can do. She lives out I Thessalonians 5:16–18, which says, "Be joyful always; pray continually; give thanks in all circumstances, for this is God's will for you in Christ Jesus."

If you feel that you've been a complainer recently, today choose instead to thank God and entrust your future to Him.

—ROXANNE ROBBINS

SPORTS NOTE:
If you want to find out more about Kelly Sutton, you can go to her Web site at www.kellygirlsutton.com.

FROM THE PLAYBOOK:
Read 1 Thessalonians 5:12–28.

GAME PLAN: Think about a person who overcame physical setbacks to excel in a sport. Take a few minutes to talk to this person about the situation. What can you learn from his or her example?

PLUGGERS, FOOZLES, AND SKYSCRAPERS

POINT OF EMPHASIS:
Understanding key words

"It is God's will that you should be sanctified." I THESSALONIANS 4:3

Baseball used to be the most popular sport in the land.

And in the game's heyday, some of the best writing in journalism came from baseball writers. The scribes invented all kinds of colorful new ways to describe the action on the field. After all, if you have to describe more than 150 games, you must be creative.

For example, fans were once called *pluggers*, a stupid play on the field was a *foozle*, and a fly ball was dubbed a *sky-scraper*. The dugout was the *dog kennel*, and a curveball was a *mackerel*.

Those words have gone the way of the doubleheader, day World Series games, and ERAs under 3. They no longer are a part of the vocabulary of baseball fans.

If we aren't careful, we might lose some of the most important words of the Christian faith as well. Words like *purity*, *sanctification*, and *holiness*. These words are threatened with extinction because of the inconvenience they cause us.

It's not easy to be holy in a world that pushes the enve-lope of permissiveness at every turn. It's tough to be set apart (sanctified) when fewer and fewer of our friends care about that distinction. It's hard to remain sexually pure when there's such a lack of discretion in sexual matters.

SPORTS NOTE:
The first great baseball writer was Henry Chadwick, who came up with the plan for scoring baseball games. He wrote the first hardcover baseball book. It was called *The Game of Baseball.*

FROM THE PLAYBOOK:
Read 1 Thessalonians 4:1–12.

It doesn't matter if we don't have *pluggers*, *foozles*, and *skyscrapers* in baseball anymore. But we can't afford to lose words like *purity*, *sanctification*, and *holiness*. We need to keep these words on our lips and in our lives. They are words from God Himself. And He never changes what He has in mind for us.

—DAVE BRANON

 GAME PLAN: Think through the next week of your life. Are there some places you plan to go where purity, sanctification, or holiness will be compromised? How can a change of plans keep your heart closer to where it should be?

ALL-STAR ACTION

POINT OF EMPHASIS:
Demonstrating Compassion

"The Lord is gracious and righteous, our God is full of compassion." PSALM 116:5

A few years ago, shortstop Omar Vizquel of the Cleveland Indians was headed for his very first All-Star Game appearance.

He was on a jet bound for Denver where the big game would be played. As he was en route, he noticed a girl standing in coach at the back of the plane, trying to maintain her balance in the aisle.

The girl, Rachel Dando, had injured her knee in a softball tournament and was wearing a massive brace. By standing—avoiding a squeeze play between narrow airplane seats—she had some relief from her discomfort.

SPORTS NOTE:
Omar made the All-Star team in 1998, 1999, and 2002.

Omar made a beeline to Rachel, offering her his seat in first class.

Rachel was delighted. She stretched out her big old brace and flew the friendly (and now much more comfortable) skies to Colorado.

Omar sat in coach and mixed with the fans.

FROM THE PLAYBOOK:
Read Zechariah 7:9–13.

Omar's great assist is a reflection of what God revealed of Himself through a "pinch-hitter"—a prophet named Zechariah. God wanted His people to "show mercy and compassion to one another. Do not oppress the widow or the fatherless, the alien or the poor" (Zechariah 7:9–10). Unlike Omar, the people didn't listen. They turned a deaf ear to the Lord and a cold shoulder to those who needed help. God was furious. He no longer listened to them or their needs. He turned His face away.

God is serious about compassion. He wants you and me to look for those who are hurting, down, or on the outside—to extend a hand of compassion. To show some All-Star acts of God's love and kindness.

—TOM FELTEN

GAME PLAN: In the last month how have you shown compassion and love to others who are less fortunate? What tangible act of kindness can you do this week for someone—showing the love of God?

KEEP JUMPING!

POINT OF EMPHASIS:
Trusting God

"Those who know your name will trust in you, for you, Lord, have never forsaken those who seek you." PSALM 9:10

Often God reveals to me magnificent truths through my family. Such was the case a few years ago with my oldest son, Grayson. He is the future extreme biker of the family and in a word, *fearless*. At the age of 3 he would jump off our foyer steps into my arms. Never sensing that I was nervous, he would always spring into the air like a flying squirrel with a big smile on his face.

Then came that fateful day that most fathers have experienced—the day things didn't go as planned. My son jumped from way above only to feel my hands slide across the back of his legs. I had dropped him. He landed headfirst on the hardwood floor with a loud thud.

Turning to pick him up in terror, I just wanted to see him moving his arms and legs, which he did. He cried in my arms for about 5 minutes. My wife Kym brought me some ice in a towel that I held on his head. Thank you, Father, that he was okay.

After I wiped away the tears, I began to walk into the family room thinking to myself "Never again." I noticed he didn't follow me, so I walked back into the foyer to make sure he had recovered. And there he was—standing on the seventh step again with a big smile on his red streaky face and a big knot on his head. He mouthed the words "Got me?" And before I could answer he was in mid-flight again.

Faith says "I believe in you." Trust says more. Trust says, "You are good!" Because my Father in heaven has given me the life of His Son, Jesus, I know He is good. Therefore, I will jump!

—PAUL BYRD, MAJOR LEAGUE PITCHER

SPORTS NOTE:
While pitching for LSU, Paul helped the Tigers get to the College World Series three straight years.

FROM THE PLAYBOOK:
Read Psalm 40:1–4.

GAME PLAN: What situation are you in that says you need to jump in faith, trusting that Jesus will support you?

WHO GETS THE FOCUS?

POINT OF EMPHASIS:
Focus on God

"Set your minds on things above, not on earthly things."
COLOSSIANS 3:2

It was the 1968 Olympic Games in Mexico City, and I was waiting to go out to the track to run my first round in the women's 800-meter race. A reporter from my hometown had somehow made it through security. "Hi, Madeline. Everyone back home sends good wishes to you. We're real proud of you and surprised at what you've accomplished here."

I was puzzled. I had been the best female 800-meter runner in the world for the last two years. What was so surprising about my competing at the Olympic Games?

He continued, "Madeline, we're glad you've made it this far, but do you think you will make it?" The sting of his words numbed my mind. What did he mean? I hadn't considered the idea that I wouldn't make it, whatever IT was.

Before he could finish his sentence, I sharply turned, looked him in the eye, and said, "I have learned that everybody here has come to win, and I'm no different. So you just watch me."

As I walked away I began to think about what the reporter said. I had worked hard to get to this place in my life, yet I was now fighting doubt and fear.

I prayed, and God reminded me that I was beautifully and wonderfully made. Confidence again soared through my being as I remembered that my Creator had made me an athlete to glorify Him. I began to focus on paying my vows to the Lord in the presence of all His people. I won my heat, my semi-finals, and then the finals for the gold medal.

If we focus our attention on the purpose God intended for our lives, we will never lose focus of who we are, and the reason we do what we do.

—MADELINE MIMS, OLYMPIC MEDALIST, TRACK

SPORTS NOTE:
In 1968, Madeline ran the 800-meter race in 2:00.9 to win the gold medal.

FROM THE PLAYBOOK:
Read: Psalms 139; 116; and 117.

GAME PLAN: "Father, may I always bring glory to You by being what You have made me to be. You have blessed my life to be a blessing to others. I will only become what You have purposed me to be, for Your workmanship on my life is enough in Christ Jesus."

WHAT HAS YOUR ATTENTION?

POINT OF EMPHASIS
Focus on God

"But you didn't pay a bit of attention to me, Jacob. You so quickly tired of me, Israel." ISAIAH 43:22 (THE MESSAGE)

It was the 2004 US Open women's quarterfinals. Crowds gathered to watch tennis champions Svetlana Kuznetsova and Nadia Petrova play match after match, competing at the top of their game.

And then came the rain. What was left of Hurricane Frances washed over the National Tennis Center in Flushing Meadows, New York, suspending games and rerouting players to different courts. Kuznetsova and Petrova were assigned to Court 11—the outside venue, where there were, by actual count, only thirteen people in the stands. The attention of fair-weather tennis fans had quickly been diverted.

Scripture itself is saturated with stories of people who too easily stopped paying attention to what they were supposed to be watching. Samson, Esau, Saul, Solomon, and even King David all lost sight of God. They turned their attention to other things. God pleaded with the people of Israel. "'Return, faithless Israel,' ... 'I will frown on you no longer, for I am merciful'" (Jeremiah 3:12). Despite their faintheartedness, God was still devoted to saving His people.

Are you easily diverted by life's circumstances? Could you be a fair-weather fan when it comes to following Jesus? Although following God may sometimes feel unpopular, too hard to pursue, or even somewhat like sitting in the rain, the pursuit is still worth it! When you do get distracted, remember that God is still committed to you. Turn your attention back to Him today.

—MOLLY GRETZINGER

SPORTS NOTE: Svetlana Kuznetsova won the 2004 US Open, giving the Russian tennis player her first Grand Slam title.

FROM THE PLAYBOOK: Read 2 Samuel 11:1–27. Read about David's distraction.

GAME PLAN: What activities in your life distract you from focusing on Jesus? Decide today to spend ten more minutes with Jesus instead of serving that "distraction."

DON'T FORGET THE SMALL THINGS

POINT OF EMPHASIS:
God and small things

"I thank my God every time I remember you." PHILIPPIANS 1:3

It was Saturday afternoon, and I just hung up the phone with Mom. I asked her to tell me she loved me, something I had never had to do before. But, something in my spirit prompted me to make sure I heard her say, "I love you, Honey."

Mom was in her ninth month of battling melanoma cancer, and her body was wearing out rapidly. I called home every day to talk with her. As the days passed, the conversations became shorter and shorter.

The day after my perplexing conversation, I received a call from home. It was my sister telling me that mom had died a few hours earlier. I was stunned, speechless and paralyzed.

In my state of shock, I thought back to that conversation the day prior. God knew that I needed to hear those words one more time. He created a memory that I can hold on to during the times when I miss mom and I long to pick up the phone and just say, "Hello."

It's easy to forget to thank God for the blessings He's given me in my life. But the one gift I will continue to thank Him for is the remembrance of my mother's last words to me.

It may seem like a small thing, but it'll stick with me for years and years to come.

Remember to "Devote yourselves to prayer, being watchful and thankful" (Colossians 4:2). And thank God for the small things.

—TRACY HANSON, LPGA GOLFER

SPORTS NOTE:
Tracy has an active speaking ministry, addressing groups such as the Fellowship of Christian Athletes, College Golf Ministry, and church youth groups.

FROM THE PLAYBOOK:
Read Psalm 136 and think about the many things for which we can praise God.

GAME PLAN: Write down five "small" things you were thankful for this past week. Spend time in prayer talking to God and thanking Him for these blessings.

WHAT IS GOD'S PLAN?

POINT OF EMPHASIS:
God's plan

"'For I know the plans I have for you,' declares the Lord."
JEREMIAH 29:11

After training with the USA National Volleyball team for almost four years, the big day finally arrived. The final cut for the 2000 Olympic team was about to happen. I felt confident. My fitness level was at its peak. My dream was about to come true.

There were 15 girls in the room as the head coach revealed which 12 players would travel to Sydney for the 2000 Olympics. He listed the names and left the room.

I thought there was a mistake. Where was my name? Perhaps he left it off accidentally. I counted the names. There were 12 names, and Val Sterk was not listed. How could this be? Some of the players on the list had been with the team for only a couple months; I had been there for years! My heart was broken; my dreams, crushed. Suddenly, the thousands of hours in the gym, the sweat, the tears—it all became meaningless.

My dream to play volleyball in the Olympics was shattered. Why had God put me through this for four years just to be cut at the very end? I spent a long time in prayer, and finally I began to realize that sometimes our plans don't match God's plan. Proverbs 19:21 says, "Many are the plans in a man's heart, but it is the Lord's purpose that prevails."

SPORTS NOTE: While playing volleyball at Michigan State in the 1990s, Val was a two-time first team All-American.

FROM THE PLAYBOOK: Read Jeremiah 29:4–13.

The day I was cut from the Olympic team was also the day I had my first date with Olympic triathlete Hunter Kemper. Our relationship developed quickly, and I was given the opportunity to travel with his family to Sydney to support him and my volleyball teammates at the Olympics.

That disappointing day in 2000 had a bright ending. Three years later, I would marry the man of my dreams, Hunter Kemper. Now I know why God had me at the Olympic Training Center all those years. God's plan truly is the best.

—VAL KEMPER, FORMER MEMBER, US NATIONAL VOLLEYBALL TEAM

GAME PLAN: Where do you think God's plan has gone awry? Have you prayed and asked God to reveal what He is doing?

HANG ON FOR THE RIDE OF YOUR LIFE

POINT OF EMPHASIS:
Trust God

"Where the Spirit of the Lord is, there is freedom."
2 CORINTHIANS 3:17

If I had my choice of what to do on a hot summer day, I'd go out on a beautiful lake and water-ski. It's one of my all-time favorite activities. If you've ever water-skied, you can imagine how it relates to being a follower of Jesus Christ.

In water-skiing, simply getting up on the skis is a tremendous feat. It's a matter of having a good stance and letting the boat do the work. Similarly, trusting Christ to be our Master can be a very difficult choice, because pride, in its various forms, throws us off balance. But when we choose Christ, we put ourselves in position to receive His free gift of salvation, and the Holy Spirit does the work of changing us on the inside and out.

Once you get up on the skis, the ride is almost effortless. In fact, there is an area behind the boat, called the wake, which fans out, and if you ski straight and stay within this area, the ride is smooth and few waves will trouble you. Likewise, many believers stay in their comfortable place spiritually. They shy away from challenges and risks for fear of making mistakes or looking silly. But Christ calls us to experience life to the fullest. "Where the Spirit of the Lord is, there is freedom" (2 Corinthians 3:17). He wants us to get out of the wake, to slalom the waters of life with enthusiasm.

We need to trust God. After all, He's driving.

—SUE SEMRAU, COLLEGE WOMEN'S BASKETBALL COACH

SPORTS NOTE:
Water skiing was invented at Lake City, Minnesota, in 1922 by Ralph Samuelson.

FROM THE PLAYBOOK:
Read Acts 21 for an example of how Paul kept leaving his comfort zone to reach people.

GAME PLAN: What are three non-comfort zone things you think God wants you to do this week? Keep track of them and keep yourself accountable to complete them.

WHY SPORTS?

POINT OF EMPHASIS:
Learning from sports

"Be conformed to the likeness of his Son." ROMANS 8:29

Sports—why do people play them? Why do people follow them with such fervor? What is the motive?

Athletes have a multitude of reasons for playing sports—it could be because they are good at it, they need a college scholarship, they want to please their parents, they like to compete, or they like recognition. Sports fans might follow sports because games are a form of recreation, they love the sport, they live vicariously through their favorite athlete, or because they love the thrill of winning and losing.

I believe sports are a microcosm of life. All of the elements of life are condensed into a few months of high-intensity growth. Athletes are confronted with physical, mental, and emotional strain. They have to persevere under trial, to discipline themselves, to recover from failure and defeat—and to do it all with grace. We often forget that God allows us to participate in sports to show us who we are and how much we need Him.

God is more concerned with who we become as we play sports than what the score of the game is. And for some people, sports are the best way to learn about life.

Even the apostle Paul used sports. He reminded us that life is like running a race and that we are to run in such a way as to get the prize. We are to have purpose and discipline as we progress spiritually. For the Christian, playing sports is another tool God can use to teach us how to live a holy life.

—MOLLY GRETZINGER

SPORTS NOTE:
Each year, major league baseball has an attendance of more than 70,000,000 fans.

FROM THE PLAYBOOK:
Read 1 Corinthians 9:24–27.

GAME PLAN: Why are you interested in sports? Is your motive tied to this world and its pleasures or does it have eternal significance?

JULY 22

COMPETITIVE AND CONTENT?

POINT OF EMPHASIS:
Contentment

"I have learned to be content whatever the circumstances."
PHILIPPIANS 4:11

Contentment for a competitive athlete seems like a contradiction. Most athletes are encouraged by coaches to strive only toward winning. The development of a winning attitude is paramount in attaining great success. Often any hint of a negative attitude is a sure sign of defeat. Because of this, many are faced with winning at all costs.

As an athlete, I struggled with being satisfied in any situation. The truth is . . . I wanted to win! Losing was not an option for me. Consequently, I would put a lot of pressure on myself if I lost a race. This is not difficult to do in an individual sport such as track and field. Your sole reliance is not on a team, but on yourself. Not until I learned this principle of contentment did I truly succeed as an athlete.

One example occurred during my return to competition after a 14-month absence from the sport. Prior to this point in my career, winning and losing was the focus of my heart. Like many, I found my self-worth in what I accomplished on the track. Slowly, I became dissatisfied if I didn't accomplish my goals. After my layoff from competition, the Lord began to mold my heart toward satisfaction in Him. His plan for my life began to unfold as I looked toward His face. Because of this new focus, He graciously gave me my heart's desire of an Olympic medal.

Although I still struggle with contentment in my life, I forever have a reminder of His power, which is available when my focal point is on Him.

—LAVONNA MARTIN-FLOREAL, OLYMPIC SILVER MEDALIST, TRACK

SPORTS NOTE:
LaVonna's husband, former Olympian Edrick Floreal, is a college track coach.

FROM THE PLAYBOOK:
Read 1 Timothy 6:6–10.

GAME PLAN: What are three areas of your life for which you lack contentment? What do you try to do to find the joy you so much desire? How often do you include God in your search for contentment?

A BRANCH WITH NO VINE

POINT OF EMPHASIS:
Abiding with Christ

"Apart from me you can do nothing." JOHN 15:5

Now that we are in the middle of the baseball season, I want you to think with me about one of the tools of the trade, a baseball glove. What does a baseball glove do? What if you put a glove out at second base or in center field by itself? What would the glove do? Do you think that it would make any defensive plays? The fact is, a baseball glove, by itself, is not terribly valuable.

However, if you put a hand in the glove, particularly the correct hand, it can do some amazing things. It can increase the reach and range of a fielder in catching fly balls or fielding ground balls. The glove enables the fielder to make plays that would otherwise be impossible. The same glove that is seemingly worthless by itself becomes invaluable when worn and directed by the appropriate hand. Interestingly enough, the potential of the glove never changed. The only thing that changes is the one who is guiding the glove.

God says that each of us is similar to that glove in that we all have great potential, but not without Him. He says that without Him, we can do nothing of any eternal significance. Without God and the empowerment of the Holy Spirit, we struggle to find meaning and purpose and significance in life. Just like a baseball glove, we have great potential. But without the guidance of the hand of God, we will never reach that potential.

Are you trying to accomplish things apart from Christ? You will be frustrated and unsuccessful in the end. Jesus said you can do *nothing*. Or, are you remaining in Him, producing fruit that will last for an eternity?

—BILL SAMPEN, FORMER MAJOR LEAGUE PITCHER

SPORTS NOTE:
Bill Sampen, who played in the majors from 1990 through 1994, attended MacMurray College in Jacksonville, Illinois.

FROM THE PLAYBOOK:
Read John 15.

GAME PLAN: Do you believe that you have great potential? What is the best way to achieve that potential? By yourself or with God's help?

YA GOTTA PAY THE PRICE

POINT OF EMPHASIS:
The price of glory

"I consider that our present sufferings are not worth comparing with the glory that will be revealed in us." ROMANS 8:18

I have yet to meet a football player who loves training camp. Some training camps are worse than others, depending on the length, the coach, and the weather, but one thing is sure during training camp: suffering. It is a test of the will, a test of endurance. Twice a day in the sometimes 100-degree heat you put on the pads and go out to practice and knock the snot out of each other. Sometimes you wake up in the morning and feel like you can barely walk, but somehow, you find the strength to push yourself through two more practices.

So why do we do it? Why do we choose to suffer? It is for the glory of the season; the chance to be a part of something great. Even during a championship season there is suffering. Even during a winning effort there is pain. But there are few things that are as fulfilling as knowing that the price for victory was extremely high, but you paid it and won.

It is interesting what man is willing to endure for glory that is so fleeting. The glory of a win or a winning season only lasts a short while. Yet God calls us to share in His *eternal* glory. Yes, we may have to suffer as players on His team, but it is only the suffering that precedes a glorious victory! Would we rather sit comfortably on the sidelines watching, or step on the field and pay the price of victory?

—BOB CHRISTIAN, NFL RUNNING BACK

SPORTS NOTE:
Bob Christian played 133 games during his NFL career from 1993 through 2002, rushing for 831 yards and scoring 12 touchdowns.

FROM THE PLAYBOOK:
Read Romans 8:18–27.

GAME PLAN: What are you facing that seems unbearable? Is it something you are doing for God's glory or your own? It'll be much more valuable when you see it as something that can lead others to know God better.

WHAT'S IN A NAME?

POINT OF EMPHASIS:
Becoming a better person

"You will be called . . . Peter." JOHN 1:42

Fishing enthusiasts. I know you exist. Admit it. You love the thrill of a perfect cast, a bent pole, and pulling in the "big one."

You are in good company. We don't know if Jesus actually wet a line or not, but He did hang out with a group of fishermen. One, in particular, was quite a character. He was impulsive, outspoken, and unpredictable. Most of us know him as Peter. But before he met Jesus, he went by the name of Simon.

When Jesus first saw him, He changed his name to Peter, which meant "a rock" (John 1:42). Why did Jesus mess with his name? In biblical times, it was frequently hoped that a person would take on the meaning of his or her name. Peter wasn't a rock of a person when he first met Jesus. But Jesus didn't merely see him for who he *was*—a hotheaded choleric who would tuck his tail in and run when the chips were down. He also saw him for who he *could be*—a rock, a trusted follower He could count on.

Are there things about you that you wish were different? Maybe even your name?

Perhaps deep down inside you wish you were less angry and more patient. Maybe you wish you were less afraid of what others think and more courageous to stand up for what you believe. Changing your name won't help, but changing your outlook will.

Remember that Jesus looks at you the way He looked at Simon Peter. He sees both who you are *and* who you could be for others and for God. And He will help you become the person He wants you to be.

—JEFF OLSON

> **SPORTS NOTE:**
> In a typical year, an estimated 35 million people spend about $38 billion on fishing goods and services in the United States, according to the US Fish and Wildlife Services.

> **FROM THE PLAYBOOK:**
> Read Philippians 1:6.

 GAME PLAN: Name some aspect of your character that you would like to see changed and begin to pray for God's help to make you change.

FLAME DROPPER

POINT OF EMPHASIS:
Live by the Spirit

"So I say, live by the Spirit." GALATIANS 5:16

Never, ever drop a torch. Especially if the torch happens to be the Olympic flame.

Just ask Harley Sheffield.

He will forever be known as the ultimate *flame dropper*. You see, Harley was pedaling his bicycle across the Tacoma-Narrows Bridge when his rear tire slipped and the Olympic Torch—on its cross-country ride to the 1996 Games in Atlanta—did a two-and-a-half-in-the-pike-position off the back of his bike and shattered on the pavement.

Poor Harley.

Fortunately for him, the "mother flame" was still burning steadily in a trailing van. They lit a replacement torch and the Olympic symbol was back in business.

Harley's plight reminds me of how we sometimes extinguish the work of the Holy Spirit in our lives. Christ gave us the Holy Spirit to counsel, comfort, and guide us—but when we sin, the work He performs in our hearts is stifled. In essence, we drop the flame.

As believers in Christ, though, we are still *indwelt* by the Holy Spirit. But we, during times of sin and turning away from God, no longer are *filled* with the Spirit. In Galatians 5, we read that the fruit of "the Spirit is love, joy, peace, patience, kindness, goodness, faithfulness, gentleness and self-control" (vv. 22–23).

Look over that list again. If you are not experiencing those evidences—the fruit—of the Holy Spirit in your life, maybe it's time to examine how you've been led astray by sin. It's time to repent.

Don't drop the flame. "Live by the Spirit, and you will not gratify the desires of the sinful nature" (v. 16).

Keep that flame burning!

—TOM FELTEN

SPORTS NOTE:
The Olympic torch is historically lit at Mount Olympus in Greece—allowed only to be lit by the sun using a mirror.

FROM THE PLAYBOOK:
Read Romans 8:1–17.

GAME PLAN: Sit down with a close friend and ask him or her to tell you which fruits of the Spirit appear to be present in your life. Read the whole list one by one!

MICKEY MANTLE AND FRIEND

POINT OF EMPHASIS:
Witnessing to a friend

*"If you confess with your mouth, 'Jesus is Lord,' and believe . . .
you will be saved."* ROMANS 10:9

New York Yankee great Mickey Mantle was a man who lived for friendships. Some friends seemed to bring out the best in the Mick; some did otherwise. But there was one friend Mickey knew he could depend on for the things that mattered most: Bobby Richardson, former Yankee second baseman.

Mickey Mantle was aware of his mortality. At age 42, he became the Mantle male who had lived the longest. He saw his father die at age 40. Later, his son would die at age 36. So when teammate Roger Maris died in 1985, Mantle approached Richardson and asked him to preside at his own funeral. Not that Mickey was ill at the time. He was just 53, but he realized he had not taken very good care of himself.

Mickey knew that what he feared in dying, Richardson had peace about. Throughout their friendship since the mid-50s, Bobby had gently reminded Mantle about the importance of making peace with God.

In August 1995, just five days before Mantle was to die, he asked that Richardson visit him. When Richardson arrived, his friend knew he was dying.

Mickey looked up at his teammate with those hollow eyes and said, "Bobby, I've been wanting to tell you something. I want you to know that I've received Christ as my Savior."

Richardson gently went through the plan of salvation with Mickey and reminded him that to be saved a person must confess his sins and put his faith in Christ's sacrifice. Quietly Mickey said, "That's what I did."

It had been forty years since Mick and Bobby had become friends. But it was a friendship that in the end would pay off for eternity.

—DAVE BRANON

SPORTS NOTE: Bobby Richardson was the Most Valuable Player of the 1960 World Series.

FROM THE PLAYBOOK: Read Romans 10:1–15.

GAME PLAN: Do you have a friend who, like Mickey Mantle, needs Jesus as Savior? Does that friend trust you enough to believe what you say about matters of faith? How can you share the gospel with him or her?

THE BEST IS YET TO COME

POINT OF EMPHASIS:
God's work in our lives

"He who began a good work in you will carry it on." PHILIPPIANS 1:6

Madeline Manning Mims was a member of four Summer Olympic teams. In 1968 she won gold in the women's 800 meters, setting Olympic, American, and world records. She was the first American woman to break the 2-minute barrier in the 800 meters.

Today Madeline serves as an official chaplain for professional and Olympic track athletes. Frequently she shares the value Philippians 1:6 has had in her life. It says, "Being confident of this, that he who began a good work in you will carry it on to completion until the day of Christ Jesus."

Speaking of this verse, Madeline says, "This Scripture has been an encouragement to me during my active athletics and in the everyday race of life. My confidence is not based on my talents, gifts, or hard work alone, but on what God has done for me, to me, in me, and through me. When I meditate on the fact that what He has started in me is a good work that is constantly being processed into a finished work, I am encouraged to keep obeying His will for my life.

" 'He's not finished with me yet' and 'The best is yet to come' are ideals that I trust as I anticipate my future. It helps me to know that no matter how short I may fall of His glory, God will never give up on me. This knowledge gives me confidence."

How exciting that is—to live with the anticipation that God is not finished and that He has even greater things in mind for us.

—ROXANNE ROBBINS

SPORTS NOTE:
Madeline is an accomplished gospel singer in addition to being a popular speaker for Christian groups.

FROM THE PLAYBOOK:
Read Philippians 1:3–11.

GAME PLAN: How has God changed your life and heart this past year? Thank Him in advance for the good work He will complete in your life.

ALONE TIME

POINT OF EMPHASIS:
Getting alone with God

"He went up . . . by himself to pray." MATTHEW 14:23

Have you ever dreamed of cracking a walk-off three-run homer in the bottom of the ninth inning to send your team home happy? How about draining the game-winning three-pointer with thousands of fans watching?

What athlete hasn't spent some time dreaming about such scenarios?

In order to put yourself in the hero position, you've got to do something first—every athlete has to put in some "alone" time.

Whether you're working on dribbling drills or shooting free throws, you've got to put in some significant time—just you and your "rock." (Or your baseball bat, football, or hockey stick.)

Every athlete has to work hard to improve his or her skills and to hone his or her game. If you think for a minute that you can improve your play without individual work—drills, conditioning, shooting—you're in for a big surprise! Sure, practices and scrimmages are a lot more fun. (You're actually competing against someone.) But the real improvement and growth comes from individual practice time.

A consistent walk of faith is similar. In order to live out your Christian faith, you've got to put in some alone time with God. That's where your faith is nurtured and developed.

Our Lord Jesus revealed the importance of this alone time with God in Matthew 14 when He went to a mountainside to pray by Himself.

Yes, practicing your faith among friends is important, but so is developing and nurturing it—alone.

—ROB BENTZ

SPORTS NOTE: Some think star relief pitcher Dennis Eckersley coined the term "walk-off home run" in 1993.

FROM THE PLAYBOOK: Read Matthew 14:13–21.

GAME PLAN: Practice the following prayer exercise. Spend 20 minutes of your time in prayer. Use the first 5 minutes to praise God for who He is and for His amazing attributes. Use the next 5 minutes to thank Him for specific blessings in your life. Use the next 5 to pray for specific needs and requests. Then take the final 5 minutes to be still before God and listen.

JULY 30

DUAL CITIZENSHIP

POINT OF EMPHASIS:
Heaven and earth

"But our citizenship is in heaven." PHILIPPIANS 3:20

During the 1992 Olympic Games, swimmer Martin Zubero competed while holding a dual citizenship. He was born in the United States, where he had lived nearly all of his life. He attended the University of Florida and trained for competition in the US. However, he was swimming under the colors of Spain. Why? His father is a citizen of Spain and so Martin is too. At the Olympics, he chose to represent his father's nation, to which he felt greater allegiance.

SPORTS NOTE:
Martin Zubero set a new world record in the 200m backstroke with a time of 1:57:30.

FROM THE PLAYBOOK:
Read Philippians 3:17–4:1.

As believers in Christ, we too have dual citizenship. We're citizens of this world, no matter what nation we live in, and as followers of Christ we are also citizens of heaven (Philippians 3:20). We have all the rights and privileges that accompany being a child of God. He is not only our heavenly Father but also our King, and our first loyalty must be to His kingdom.

Sometimes our dual citizenship presents us with a crucial choice. With whose "flag" will we identify? There should be no doubt about it. We are no longer to live for "earthly things" (v. 19) but give allegiance to our heavenly Father.

Do people who observe us know that we are marching under the flag of the King of kings and Lord of lords?

—DAVE EGNER

GAME PLAN: Name three things you can do in the next few days to serve as an ambassador for Christ.

ONCE AND FUTURE GLORY

POINT OF EMPHASIS:
Looking forward to God's glory

"I saw the glory of the God of Israel coming from the east."
EZEKIEL 43:2

The 1976 baseball season was glorious for Mark (The Bird) Fidrych. The Detroit Tiger pitcher burst onto the baseball scene like no one before. Within two months of pitching his first game, The Bird was a national phenomenon as the curly-haired, antics-driven pitcher filled stadiums across the land.

He would manicure the mound with his hands, talk to the baseball, and face every pitch as if it were a bit part in a movie. Fidrych had charisma to spare, and the fans loved him. Even better, he was a great pitcher!

He went 19–9 in 1976, leading the American League with a 2.34 ERA and—imagine this—pitching 24 complete games! It was one glorious summer for Mark Fidrych.

But after one year, the glory was gone. An injury messed up Fidrych's shoulder, and after four lackluster seasons, he was out of baseball. Glory-less.

Sports glory comes and goes. Glory experienced is not the same as glory remembered.

Not so with God's glory. The glory that God demonstrates to His people can be seen over and over. Moses saw the glory of God on Mt. Sinai. The priests experienced it in the tabernacle. The glory of God was evident in Solomon's temple. And in Ezekiel 43, we read that God's glory will someday return for God's people to see. In some future time, the temple at Jerusalem is to be rebuilt, and after it is, God's glory will shine.

We, of course, have not enjoyed the awe-inspiring presence of God's glory as did the folks in Old Testament days. Yet we can read Ezekiel 43 and imagine worshiping God in His complete majesty and glory.

God's once and future glory. That's something worth thinking about.

—DAVE BRANON

SPORTS NOTE:
When Mark Fidrych set the baseball world on fire in 1976 with his antics and his superb pitching, his salary was $16,500.

FROM THE PLAYBOOK:
Read Ezekiel 43:1–12.

GAME PLAN: What do you most expect to be thrilled about when you someday see God's glory? What passages of Scripture or what songs help you to imagine God's greatness?

AUGUST I

DIDN'T YOU USED TO BE THE PILOTS?

POINT OF EMPHASIS:
The problem of pride

"'You will never again be found,' declares the Sovereign Lord."
EZEKIEL 26:21

The Atlanta Flames. The Seattle Pilots. The Washington Senators. The Syracuse Nationals. The Montreal Maroons. The Chicago Stags. The Canton Bulldogs. The New York Cosmos. The Kentucky Colonels. The Memphis Sounds. The Anaheim Amigos.

Do you root for any of these teams?

You may have at one time, depending on your age. At various stages in pro sports history, these teams were full-fledged professional sports teams. But because of failing management, lack of money, poor fan support, or other reasons, these teams have all gone the way of the XFL.

SPORTS NOTE:
On May 21, 1980, the Atlanta Flames became the Calgary Flames.

FROM THE PLAYBOOK:
Read Ezekiel 26:19–21; 27:3; 28:2.

Here's another one: Tyre. Who knows, maybe they once had a team called the Tyre Repairs or the Tyre Tigers. But no more. Tyre is gone. Not just a team from Tyre, but the whole town. Tyre, as prophesied by Ezekiel, has vanished from the face of the earth.

Why did Tyre fall? Why is Tyre a member of the obsolete cities of the world? Pride.

Tyre said of itself, "I am perfect in beauty" (27:3). And Tyre's ruler said, "I am a god; I sit on the throne of a god" (28:2).

One thing Tyre found out and we should know is that God hates pride. He tells us in Proverbs 8:13, "I hate pride and arrogance." The problem with pride is that it gets in the way of our view of God.

Pride can easily skew our concept of who we are in God's eyes—and even who God is in our eyes. Tyre was great and knew it—which led to destruction. It's better to reflect onto God any glory we achieve. When we don't, like Tyre, we're headed for trouble (Proverbs 16:18). —DAVE BRANON

 GAME PLAN: How do you know where to draw the line between feeling good about what God is doing and being prideful? How does that relate to whatever role you have in sports?

IT'S ALL ABOUT . . . OTHERS

POINT OF EMPHASIS:
Loving others

"Love never fails." I CORINTHIANS 13:8

"I have to look out for my own interests. I have to do what's best for me. If I don't look out for myself, no one else will." How many times have we heard those words from a free-agent athlete who has made more than enough money to last most people a couple of lifetimes? We've almost come to expect this "me-centered" approach to life, and not just from athletes. I think we've all bought into looking at life selfishly more than we'd like to admit.

Which is what makes the "others-centered" nature of what Esther Kim did at the US Olympic Taekwondo Trials in Colorado Springs so exceptional. At the start of the flyweight final match, Esther conceded, allowing her best friend and training partner, Kay Poe, to win. Kay, top ranked in the world, had injured her left knee in the semifinal and could barely stand up. "If we clashed hard enough, her knee might have been permanently injured," Esther said. Esther Kim forfeited a spot on the US Olympic taekwondo team so her friend could go to the 2000 Games in Sydney. She later commented, "I wasn't throwing my dreams away; I was handing them to Kay."

In John 13 Jesus said that His followers could be identified by the way they loved each other. He said, "Love one another. As I have loved you, so you must love one another. By this all men will know that you are my disciples, if you love one another" (vv. 34–35).

Have you done any "others-centered" loving lately? It's a great way to let friends and loved ones know that you are a follower of Christ.

—BRIAN HETTINGA

SPORTS NOTE:
Taekwondo was first used in 50 BC in the area that is now Korea.

FROM THE PLAYBOOK:
Read about love in 1 Corinthians 13.

GAME PLAN: Do a random act of kindness for someone today. Thinking of a kindness and doing it will be a step toward becoming an "others-centered" representative of Jesus Christ.

THE SILENT SEASON

POINT OF EMPHASIS:
Getting spiritually fit

"Be prepared in season and out of season." 2 TIMOTHY 4:2

Preseason.

It's weight training, strength training, speed training. It's drills, plyometrics, nutrition.

It's going to the camps for exposure, to the gym for conditioning, and to Foot Locker for the new shoes.

Preseason is not just about getting ready for a new start; it is also about putting last season behind you. And the grueling thing about preseason is that there aren't any fans. There is no one watching to see if you went hard your last 10 minutes or if you finished each set. There is no one cheering you on as you complete each workout. But after the time of preparation, there will come a time when it will all pay off.

SPORTS NOTE:
Sometimes preseason causes problems as when star quarterbacks Michael Vick and Chad Pennington were hurt before the season began in 2003.

Preseason is like spiritual life. The apostle Paul reminds us to "forget what is behind and strain toward what is ahead" (Philippians 3:13). No matter what your "last season" looked like spiritually, you have to set it aside and strive toward a life of faith and obedience. Peter reminds us to always be prepared to give an answer for the hope that we have (1 Peter 3:15). Always be in "spiritual shape" to tell others about what Christ has done in your life. Paul again challenges us to "be prepared in season and out of season," to preach the Word and instruct others (2 Timothy 4:2).

FROM THE PLAYBOOK:
Read Philippians 3:12–4:1.

Spiritual exercise is very grueling, and often no one will notice the time you spend behind closed doors with your Savior. No one is counting; no one is cheering. But, a time is coming when preseason will be over, the game will be on, and "your reward will be great" (Luke 6:35).

—MOLLY GRETZINGER

GAME PLAN: Are you "in shape" spiritually? What is holding you back? Pray and ask God for discipline and strength. Then whip your spiritual self into shape.

MALIGNED FOR CHRIST

POINT OF EMPHASIS:
Surviving persecution

"If you are insulted because of the name of Christ, you are blessed."
I PETER 4:14

Perhaps you can identify with Roger Maris, the man whose home run record Mark McGwire, Sammy Sosa, and Barry Bonds passed in recent years. Back in 1961, when Maris was chasing Babe Ruth's record, he was maligned by the New York press. They said:

- Maris played in a 162-game season, while Ruth played only 154.
  Fact: Maris had only 5 more at-bats than the Babe.
- Maris hit only one homer off a Cy Young winning pitcher.
  Fact: Ruth hit only two off Cy Young winners.
- Maris was gunning for the short right-field fence in Yankee Stadium.
  Fact: Both were left-handed hitters. Ruth hit 30 home runs in Yankee Stadium; Maris 31.
- Maris had Mickey Mantle hitting behind him in the lineup.
  Fact: Ruth had Lou Gehrig hitting behind him.

Sometimes people are negative, critical, and categorically unfair—as was the New York sports press.

Maybe a similar thing is happening to you. You're being criticized and your efforts downplayed. Facts are being misinterpreted, untruths are being spread, and you're being hurt.

Join the club. It happened to the apostles. And it happened to Jesus, culminating in His execution for our sins.

Peter told us this would happen. He told us not to be surprised (1 Peter 4:12), but to rejoice at the opportunity to suffer as Jesus suffered (v. 13). As we endure it, we are blessed (v. 14), and the Holy Spirit is always with us.

Are you being attacked? Call on the Lord to help you bear it patiently and without bitterness—as Jesus did.　　　　　　　　　　　—DAVE EGNER

SPORTS NOTE:
Roger Maris hit 275 home runs during his major league career.

FROM THE PLAYBOOK:
Read 1 Peter 4:12–19.

 GAME PLAN: Have you ever been the victim of an unfair attack on your character or reputation? How did you respond? What can you learn from Jesus about dealing with people who you think are doing you wrong?

WHAT HAVE WE DONE?

POINT OF EMPHASIS:
Jesus' greatness

"We preach Christ crucified." I CORINTHIANS 1:23

Sometimes, Englishman Jonathan Edwards wakes up in the middle of the night in disbelief. "I pinch myself and say, 'I can't believe it. Nobody in the world has jumped farther than I have.'"

On August 7, 1995, Edwards went where no athlete had gone before. While competing in the World Track & Field Championships in Goteborg, Sweden, the triple-jumper became the first person to pass the 18-meter barrier (18.29). Then, just a few minutes later, he became the first triple-jumper to go past 60 feet (60-01/4).

Edwards began jumping seriously in 1984 after he won the triple jump at the All-English Schools Championship. He continued competing for one reason.

"I had a strong sense that this was what God wanted me to do." It was an idea his father planted in his mind. "He was saying to me, 'God has given you a gift.' He told me he thought God was going to use this ability for His glory."

That's part of how he puts his world records in perspective. "I think, 'What I've done pales in comparison to what Jesus Christ has done. He influenced the world more than anyone else in history. Yet He died on the cross for me so I can be forgiven.' For that I am truly grateful."

That perspective is helpful to us when we start thinking about the "great" things we've done! When we consider instead what Jesus did, all of our efforts—as astounding as they may seem—mean little compared with what our Savior did for us.

—DAVE BRANON

SPORTS NOTE:
Jonathan Edwards, who lives in England, retired from competitive sports in 2002 to be with his family.

FROM THE PLAYBOOK:
Read John 19:17–37.

GAME PLAN: List your three greatest accomplishments in life. How can each of those be given to God as a way of honoring Him for what He has done for you?

TEMPORARY VS. PERMANENT

POINT OF EMPHASIS:
Eternity

"For what is seen is temporary, but what is unseen is eternal."
2 CORINTHIANS 4:18

When evangelist Pat Kelly played major league baseball for the Baltimore Orioles, his manager was the fiery, successful Earl Weaver. Weaver, like many top sports skippers, kept his mind on one thing—winning baseball games. One day Kelly stopped to talk with his manager. "Weave," Pat said, "it sure is good to walk with Jesus." "That's nice," the manager replied, "but I'd rather you would walk with the bases loaded."

That exchange is a good example of the difference between two views of life—the temporary and the permanent. When we have the first, we can become pre-occupied with the things of this earth. We can forget that this life is only a time to prepare for eternity. With the permanent view, however, we recognize the importance of getting ready for eternity by trusting in and living for Jesus Christ.

There are advantages to viewing life in terms of eternity. The apostle Peter talked about a living hope (1 Peter 1:3), an incorruptible inheritance (v. 4), the assurance of spending eternity with God (vv. 5, 9), and an inexpressible joy (v. 8). That's what we get when we walk with Jesus.

How would you label your outlook? Is it temporary or permanent?

—DAVE BRANON

SPORTS NOTE:
Pat Kelly's brother LeRoy was a star running back for the Cleveland Browns during the 1960s and 1970s. LeRoy is in the Pro Football Hall of Fame.

FROM THE PLAYBOOK:
Read 1 Peter 1:3–25.

GAME PLAN: How often in a day do you think about the eternal instead of the temporary things of life? What can you do to be more eternal minded?

HARDSHIP IS INEVITABLE, MISERY IS OPTIONAL!

POINT OF EMPHASIS:
Handling trials

"Consider it pure joy, my brothers, whenever you face trials of many kinds." JAMES 1:2

Ask any Tour golfer if hardship is inevitable, and you'll get a resounding, "No kidding."

Whether it is bad bounces on the golf course, injuries, financial pressures, or even the pressing demands to play more tournaments at the expense of the family, touring pros face hardships of many kinds.

As I search the Scriptures, I see that God knows we will have to face hardships, but God also knows that through hardship we benefit from His all-mighty power and sovereignty.

Do we have a choice of response when hardship hits, or are we destined to be controlled by the circumstances? Can God play a part in our response? Hardship is inevitable, but misery is optional in golf and in life. The Word of God gives us hope that we are not to be controlled by the circumstances, but rather we have a choice of response.

James knew hardship. Yet he also knew that the first response to hardship is to view it joyfully—as something good.

Consider the message of the Word of God, which says that we are to view difficulties with a joyful and thankful heart since they reap something far greater in the end.

We have hope that our trouble will result in God's good. Therefore, hardship is inevitable, but misery is optional.

—BOBBY CLAMPETT, TV GOLF ANALYST

SPORTS NOTE:
A good illustration of how things can go wrong in golf. Retief Goosen led the 2005 US Open going into the last day—only to shoot an 11-over-par 80.

FROM THE PLAYBOOK:
Read James 1.

GAME PLAN: Next time hardship strikes, on the course or in the game of life, ask yourself some pointed questions: What is God trying to teach me about myself through this experience? What response does God want me to have? Am I willing to trust Him in this experience?

SECOND-PLACE VICTORY

POINT OF EMPHASIS:
Victory in Jesus

"Thanks be to God! He gives us the victory." I Corinthians 15:57

For Kevin Asano, judo silver medalist in the 1988 Summer Olympic Games, the Olympics will forever be a reminder of total victory.

Yep, second place for Kevin was like winning it all!

In fact, when the bell sounded in Kevin's finals match, his silver-celebration said it all. The Korean competitor who had won fell to the mat, covering his crying eyes. But Kevin, who had been beaten, raised his fists in the familiar victory pose normally reserved for solid-gold accomplishments.

Kevin was celebrating in defeat. Why? Because of a remarkable turn of events in his life that only God could direct. Before the Olympics, he had twice retired from judo, only to be drawn back by God's persistent direction. Kevin barely won the match that allowed him to get into the Games—beating a man who always had his number before.

But something happened just before Kevin's first match in the Olympics. As he prayed to God, peace and joy swept over him. He showed the joy of the Lord by smiling before and after his matches.

When he raised his hands in victory, it was the final act of a man who had done his best in God's strength. He had shown ultimate victory!

When you compete, whether it's on an exam or at work or in sports, do you exhibit the joy of the Lord? Kevin could do this because he understood that real victory is found in a relationship with Christ.

With our victory already won, we can grasp the fullness of the words, "Let nothing move you. Always give yourselves fully to the work of the Lord" (I Corinthians 15:58). Raise your hands. You're a winner!

—TOM FELTEN

SPORTS NOTE:
Kevin Asano is a member of the Hawaii Sports Hall of Fame. He was the national collegiate judo champion in 1987 and 1988 while at San Jose State University.

FROM THE PLAYBOOK:
Read 1 Corinthians 15:42–58.

GAME PLAN: Take a prayer break and thank God for all the victories He has promised: over sin, over death, over sorrow.

THE VALUE OF FRIENDSHIPS

POINT OF EMPHASIS
Friends

"Encourage one another and build each other up."
I THESSALONIANS 5:11

Christian artist Michael W. Smith says that many of his life principles have been shaped by what he's learned from sports, particularly through his friendships with three star athletes: Orel Hershiser, Brett Butler, and David Robinson.

"Those guys spurred me on in my Christian faith as I watched them speak boldly about their relationship with Jesus Christ," Smith said. "It seems that a lot of us who speak about Jesus Christ are often misread. It's frustrating when things we say are taken out of context. But I noticed that Orel, Brett, and David weren't afraid of the press. As a 'Christian artist,' I'm expected to speak out about my faith. Yet there are some days when it's harder for me to do this than others. From the standpoint that Orel, Brett, and David have also been in the public eye, we understand each other in a unique way. There's kind of a bond there. We're praying for each other that God will use us in a big way. I'm a fan of those guys, and they're fans of my music. We have a lot of respect for each other. We encourage each other. It's always nice to have someone you're comrades with—whether you're in music or sports—and our friendships go much deeper than our professions."

Make it a goal for your life to surround yourself with friends who encourage you and help you to know God better and to make Him known. In return, be that type of friend to others.

—ROXANNE ROBBINS

SPORTS NOTE:
NBA legend David Robinson posted career averages of 21.1 points, 10.6 rebounds, and 2.5 blocks per game and won two NBA championships.

FROM THE PLAYBOOK:
Read 1 Thessalonians 5:1-11.

 GAME PLAN: Call a friend today and tell them how they've helped you grow in your Christian faith.

EXCUSES, EXCUSES, EXCUSES

POINT OF EMPHASIS:
Making excuses

"She gave me some fruit from the tree, and I ate it.'" GENESIS 3:12

The manager of a minor league baseball team was tired of watching his center fielder play poorly in practice, according to a story by Don McCullough in *Discipleship Journal.* So he grabbed a glove and headed for the outfield to show the player how it should be done.

The first ball batted toward him took a bad hop and hit the manager in the mouth. Next came a high fly ball that he lost in the sun—only to find when it smacked him on his forehead. Later a hard line drive missed his glove and hit him in the face. That was enough. Furious, the manager grabbed the center fielder by the uniform and shouted, "You idiot! You've got center field so messed up, even I can't do a thing with it!"

That may be one of the worst excuses ever given for failing. But then we humans have had a lot of practice with alibis. It began with Adam and Eve. When God confronted them about eating the forbidden fruit, Adam blamed God for giving him Eve, and Eve blamed the serpent for giving her bad advice.

Adam and Eve found out that excuses don't hide guilt. When we sin—or even make an innocent mistake—how much better to face up to our failures before both God and man.

Don't waste your time making excuses. They always fall apart.

–DAVE BRANON

SPORTS NOTE:
To learn all about minor league baseball, go to www.minorleaguebaseball.com.

FROM THE PLAYBOOK:
Read Genesis 3:1–24.

 GAME PLAN: Have you been making excuses recently for things you should have done—or shouldn't have done? Begin to take responsibility and stop making excuses.

OVERCOMING A BAD START

POINT OF EMPHASIS:
Overcoming a bad start

"They took him and threw him into the cistern." GENESIS 37:24

When Wilma Rudolph was four years old, she got a bad case of scarlet fever, and she lost the use of her left leg. She didn't learn to walk again until she was seven years old.

In 1960, this same determined young woman, now twenty years old, won three gold medals at the Summer Olympic Games—in running events. She overcame a slow start in life and became a champion.

Old Testament hero Joseph had some obstacles too. Although his were not physical like Wilma's, they were huge roadblocks. As a boy reared in a blended family, he was favored by his father and hated by his jealous half-brothers. They thought they got rid of him by selling him into slavery. And when he got to Egypt, he was falsely accused of trying to seduce his master's wife and thrown into prison.

Yet Joseph became a model of courage and dependence on God. Despite many setbacks, he rose to become governor of Egypt. Under God's providence he became the "savior" of his family—including those very brothers who had treated him so cruelly.

Perhaps you're off to a bad start spiritually. Maybe you've made some bad choices and now have huge difficulties to overcome. Don't live in pity, wishing you were someone else. Start where you are, lean on God, and see what He will do in you.

The same God whose grace and power took Joseph to the top can also help you work your way past the worst spiritual obstacles. Call on Him for His forgiveness and help. With God on your side, you can overcome a bad start.

—MART DE HAAN

SPORTS NOTE:
When Wilma was born, she became the 20th of 22 children in the Rudolph family.

FROM THE PLAYBOOK:
Read Genesis 37:12–28.

GAME PLAN: What are the two biggest roadblocks to spiritual success in your life? What would be the best approach to overcoming them?

DISSOLVED DREAMS

POINT OF EMPHASIS:
God's perspective

"In all things God works for the good of those who love him."
ROMANS 8:28

My Olympic dream was formed when I was a young girl playing basketball at a small village school in rural Alberta. For the next fourteen years the desire to one day become an Olympic athlete set the course of my life. My focus never wavered in times of struggle or failure. Rather, my resolve grew stronger, giving purpose to every challenge I faced along the way.

In the summer of 2003, as a member of the Canadian National Basketball Team, I came within two games of seeing my dream become reality at a qualifying tournament in Mexico. We needed a first-place finish to qualify. Instead, we lost by six points to Brazil in the semifinal. To make matters worse, although I had been a key player throughout the tournament, a change in strategy for the Brazil game left me on the sideline. Six points. Three baskets were all we needed. My heart broke as I was forced to helplessly watch my lifelong dream dissolve before me.

Filtering through the frustration, confusion, and crushing discouragement, I clearly sensed God reassuring me that He was still in control. Our view of any situation is so limited, and yet we let our hopes rise and fall on the whim of circumstances. From God's perspective, He sees the big picture—the beginning and the end all at once—and He "works in all things for the good of those who love Him." I have to trust that, even as I live with my dissolved dreams.

—LEIGHANN REIMER, PRO BASKETBALL PLAYER

SPORTS NOTE:
Leighann was voted the most outstanding player in Canadian college basketball in 2000 and 2001.

FROM THE PLAYBOOK:
Read Romans 8.

GAME PLAN: Consider a time before you were a Christian when you were disappointed. How did you handle it? Since becoming a Christian, has your response to disappointment changed? What can you do to help yourself see the "big picture" in the middle of a disappointing situation?

AUGUST 13

KIDS AND SPORTS

POINT OF EMPHASIS:
God's glory

*"Whatever you do, work at it with all your heart,
as working for the Lord."* COLOSSIANS 3:23

In my twenty-six years of playing on the Ladies Professional Golfers Association (LPGA) Tour, I've seen many things that I like, but I've also observed things that bother me.

One thing that upsets me is the way some parents push their children to play golf. Too often, there is an over-emphasis on winning at an early age. It's as if a child is encouraged to start a pro career at age ten. Kids ought to be having fun playing golf at that age. It's not that youngsters shouldn't be encouraged to get better, it's just that winning shouldn't get blown out of proportion.

SPORTS NOTE:
Betsy King was born on this date in 1955. She was born in Reading, Pennsylvania.

FROM THE PLAYBOOK:
Read Colossians 3.

I've been taught to give my best with the talent God has given me—to be obedient to Him day-by-day. I think that's what we should be teaching our young people—not that they have to be a pro someday to be successful.

Kids are taught that if they want anything bad enough, they can have it. I don't believe that. Many other factors are involved. For example, you have to have some measure of talent. And you have to have the right temperament.

I don't think God wants us to think that way either. He wants us to give 100 percent, but that's it! We don't have to get all caught up in being "No. 1." If we're highly talented and become No. 1, fine. But if we give our best and we're No. 100, that's fine too.

As long as we do our best for God's glory, we will be pleasing God and honoring Him—which is what we're supposed to be doing anyway.

—BETSY KING, LPGA GOLFER

GAME PLAN: Do you know any youth sports athletes? How can you encourage them without pressuring them into thinking that they have to be the next Kobe Bryant or Betsy King or Cobi Jones?

JASON & MO

POINT OF EMPHASIS:
Compassion and love

"Love each other." I Thessalonians 4:9

Jason Leader was sick. The twelve-year-old had neuroblastoma, a cancerous tumor that attacks the adrenal glands and nervous system. But Jason also had someone special who gave him hope: Mo Vaughn, who then played for the Boston Red Sox.

Mo was Jason's favorite pro baseball player.

Through the efforts of The Jimmy Fund, a charity that helps kids with cancer, Mo met Jason. They connected instantly and became great friends.

When Mo first met Jason, he promised to try to hit a home run for him in his next game. And just like in the movies, in the seventh inning of the next Red Sox contest, Vaughn smoked a 3–1 pitch for a round-tripper.

There were other special moments in the friendship between this young fan and his caring major league friend— including the day Jason threw out the first pitch for a game at Fenway Park in Boston.

But a year and a half after Vaughn hit his special home run for Jason, the young man took his last breath. And Mo was in attendance at the funeral for Jason in Niverville, New York.

Mo had demonstrated what brotherly love is all about:

- Showering love on someone (1 Thessalonians 4:9).
- Showing it in an ever-increasing way (v. 10).
- Not depending on nor disturbing others (v. 11).
- Living and loving in a consistent way that affects others (v. 12).

That's the kind of love believers in Christ should have for each other. By showing "brotherly love," we become a better witness for Him. And in the process we may lift the spirits of someone who needs hope.

How do you show brotherly love? Mo knows.

—Tom Felten

SPORTS NOTE: Jason Leader died on August 14, 1994.

FROM THE PLAYBOOK: Read 1 Thessalonians 4:9–12.

 GAME PLAN: Is there a fellow Christian I know who could use a dose of brotherly love? What can I do?

AUGUST 15

HOW GOOD IS GOD?

POINT OF EMPHASIS:
God's goodness

"For it is by grace you have been saved, . . . it is the gift of God."
EPHESIANS 2:8

I was present in Montreal in 1989 when Dave Dravecky pitched the second game of his comeback after cancer surgery.

While Dravecky was pitching to Tim Raines, his arm snapped, and he fell in a heap on the mound. Later, as he was being lifted into the ambulance, Dave looked at me with a pained smile and said, "David, God is good!" How could he make this statement in the face of such adversity? His career was over, yet he had bold confidence in God's plan.

SPORTS NOTE:
Dave Dravecky is president of Outreach of Hope, a ministry to people who have been affected by amputation and cancer.

FROM THE PLAYBOOK:
Read John 15 and discover how much we depend on God.

Several years later, Dave spoke at the All-Star Game chapel service in Baltimore. His left arm had been amputated since I'd seen him last. I greeted him at the door and he asked if I'd do him a favor. He needed me to fasten the button on his right shirt sleeve. He had left in a hurry that morning and needed someone to come alongside and do for him what he could never do himself. Have you ever tried doing up a button with one hand? It's almost impossible!

Yes, God is good! He is good because He sent His Son to come alongside us when we were incapable of helping ourselves. No amount of effort or hard work could buy our salvation. We needed Christ to pay the penalty for our sins. Jesus Christ did for us what we could never do ourselves. We are saved by grace through faith. Have you experienced God's goodness?

—DAVID FISHER, MAJOR LEAGUE CHAPLAIN

GAME PLAN: Do you sometimes feel self-sufficient? Think about how impossible it would be to do anything without God's intervention in your life.

AUGUST 16

WHAT ARE YOU LOSING?

POINT OF EMPHASIS:
Personal value

"The younger son . . . squandered his wealth." LUKE 15:13

Anyone who would throw away a baseball autographed by Babe Ruth gets what he deserves.

That's exactly what a couple of Florida teenagers did a few years ago, proving once again that you don't have to be intelligent to be a thief.

The two boys, who should have been out practicing baseball, broke into a baseball card store and stole sports collectibles worth $45,000. Apparently, as they were sorting through their hot stuff, they took one look at the baseball, decided it was worthless, and threw it in a dumpster.

After the boys were arrested and spilled their story, authorities rushed to the dumpster in question. It was too late. The baseball, which had been signed by Babe Ruth, had met with the same fate as banana peels, old Kleenex, and discarded milk cartons: the incinerator.

Before we are too hard on the boys for tossing out this piece of baseball history, consider other valuable things people throw out all the time.

Young people throw out their virginity in the rush for pleasure. God's will gets tossed aside because of a misconception of what brings happiness. Good health gets trashed in the pursuit of some perceived enjoyment from cigarettes, alcohol, or drugs. A growing knowledge of God gets dumped by a schedule that makes no time for God's Word.

In Luke 15, we read about the son who threw away his youth, thinking he'd enjoy the fun of the party life. Well, he may have had a few good times, but it led straight to destruction. It wasn't worth throwing away his inheritance and good name for.

Consider the value of what God has given you. Then vow not to throw it out. Don't trash the good things in life.

—DAVE BRANON

SPORTS NOTE: In 2002, a Babe Ruth game-worn jersey was purchased for $264,000.

FROM THE PLAYBOOK: Read Luke 15:11–32.

GAME PLAN: Think about your health. What is something you've been doing that is not benefiting the body God gave you? Write that thing down, vow to stop it, and put the paper in a prominent place as a reminder.

AUGUST 17

READY FOR THE FALL

POINT OF EMPHASIS:
Humility

"God opposes the proud but gives grace to the humble." JAMES 4:6

After graduating from Henry Foss High School in Tacoma, Washington, in 1992, I headed to Walla Walla Community College. It was a 5-hour drive from home. I thought I was headed to the middle of nowhere.

Football practice was grueling—not because I wasn't in shape or lacked great work ethics, but it was so very hot. And my position coach was also a guard at the penitentiary. Need I say more?

Despite the difficult times, I became a standout and leader on the team. I was named captain. My first quarter I made the Dean's List with a perfect 4.0 GPA in six classes.

I was getting only a partial scholarship, so I had to pay for most of my schooling. I also played basketball and helped my team get to the state championships both years I attended. I was doing better than I had ever imagined.

After two years I transferred to Washington State University, and I was doing outstanding. Trouble was, I also became very big-headed. I wasn't rude to people; I just had a built-up ego that filled my head.

It was then that God decided to deflate my head. It was the last day of training camp, and by then I had caught fan and media attention. From my position at defensive end, I was routinely chasing down one of our fastest running backs. Then I felt a snap in my left foot, and I went crashing to the ground. I had broken my fifth metatarsal, and I was out for the season.

My wife, Brenda, who I had married that summer, had just made the trip to Pullman with her parents and brother David. They came into the apartment to find me sitting on the floor with a brace wrap around my foot. They had to set up the apartment without me.

I discovered that pride certainly goes before a big fall.

—DORIAN BOOSE, PRO FOOTBALL PLAYER

SPORTS NOTE:
In 2002, Dorian Boose played in the Canadian Football League championship game, the Grey Cup. His team, the Edmonton Eskimos, lost to the Montreal Alouettes 25–16.

FROM THE PLAYBOOK:
Read 1 Corinthians 4:6–10.

GAME PLAN: What is humbling you these days? Is God doing this to you to make you worse or better?

TAKING A STAND

POINT OF EMPHASIS:
Not ashamed of God

"Whosoever believeth on him shall not be ashamed."
ROMANS 9:33 (KJV)

In 1924, Eric Liddell made headlines when he refused to compete in his strongest Olympic event, the 100 meters, because the qualifying heats were held on Sunday.

Liddell was a deeply committed Christian. Like many in his day, he believed that Sunday should be set aside for worship, not worldly pursuits. While those who agreed with his convictions supported him—and the British Olympic Association unsuccessfully attempted to get the International Olympic Committee to change the date of the 100-meter heats—Liddell was not universally praised.

Yet Liddell was prepared to sacrifice his dreams of a 100-meter gold medal for the sake of his convictions.

Like Eric, we live in a world that can be hostile toward our convictions. Behavior once considered shameful is now thought of as "normal." We're constantly confronted with profanity, sexually suggestive material, opportunities to cheat or steal. It's not easy to take a stand for the things that we believe in. But Jesus said, "Whoever acknowledges me before men, I will also acknowledge him before my Father in heaven" (Matthew 10:32). Clearly, God honors those who honor Him.

It's a truth Eric Liddell understood.

When officials couldn't convince him to run the 100 meters on Sunday, Eric agreed to train for the 200 and 400 meter events. In true storybook finish, Liddell won two Olympic medals, the bronze in the 200 meters and the gold in the 400 meters—setting an Olympic record in the process.

As he ran, Eric Liddell recited Romans 9:33 over and over again: "Whosoever believeth on him shall not be ashamed" (KJV).

That's a verse we can draw strength from today!

—CHRISTIN DITCHFIELD

SPORTS NOTE:
The definitive book on Eric Liddell is *Pure Gold,* by David McCasland, published by Discovery House Publishers.

FROM THE PLAYBOOK:
Read Matthew 5:3–12 and 10:32–33.

 GAME PLAN: Think of an area in your life where you need to take a stand for Christ. Plan now to make that stand.

HOW TO BE A PEACEMAKER

POINT OF EMPHASIS:
Peacemaking

"Blessed are the peacemakers, for they will be called sons of God."
MATTHEW 5:9

I had the privilege of competing against one of the greatest female athletes of all time. Her name is Jackie Joyner-Kersee. Jackie was a phenomenal athlete. She competed in the heptathlon, which is a grueling two-day, seven-event competition. Jackie participated in four Olympics and was a five-time Olympic medalist.

SPORTS NOTE:
Jackie Joyner-Kersee won three gold medals, one silver, and one bronze in the Olympics. She was the first woman to earn more than 7,000 points in the heptathlon.

FROM THE PLAYBOOK:
Read and contemplate the Beatitudes: Matthew 5:1–12.

Apart from her athletic abilities, what impessed me the most about this remarkable woman was her welcoming and encouraging attitude. Often I would compete against Jackie in a hurdle race, and she would always approach me as a friend first, then as a competitor. Now don't get me wrong. She was a fierce competitor who always pursued the attitude of winning. But her attitude toward the athletes was always friendly. This posture was unusual because many athletes prefer to look at competitors as an enemy in order to gain the necessary edge needed for victory.

In my opinion, Jackie demonstrated the elements of peacemaking. Many times I found myself seeking her out at competitions because the aroma of love was prevalent. Her attitude helped me to compete better and treat my competitors with the same respect.

Similarly, our attitude is to be pleasing to the Lord. Our energies should be focused on winning His approval. Our efforts and desires to be peacemakers often act as a sweet fragrance that others, even our enemies, are drawn toward—and then are drawn toward Him.

—LaVONNA MARTIN-FLOREAL, OLYMPIC SILVER MEDALIST, TRACK

GAME PLAN: Would your friends call you a peacemaker? What are some things you can do in the next couple of days to show yourself to have the attitude of a peacemaker, even in tense situations?

BEARING THE NAME

POINT OF EMPHASIS:
Witnessing

"Since we live by the Spirit, let us keep in step with the Spirit."
GALATIANS 5:25

I can still remember the first day I put on that USA jersey. I was so proud. It was a dream come true; an amazing honor to travel around the world, playing volleyball, and representing my country.

Everywhere we went, we bore the USA name. Because we represented the most powerful country in the world, fans and opposing teams watched us and held us to high standards. For some, we might be the only Americans they would ever encounter. People watched us closely on and off the court.

In order to uphold this high standard, we had team rules that everyone followed. Good sportsmanship was showcased by being respectful to the opponents and the officials. We had a no-swearing policy, and it was always important to portray a disciplined, organized, and clean-cut image.

As Christians we hold similar responsibilities as being a part of a team. We bear the name of Christ. People hold us to high standards and watch us closely. Some may think Christianity is about obeying a bunch of rules, but it is so much more. To bear Christ's name is an amazing honor. He has given us the ultimate gift of eternal life. Because of His amazing grace, we should always strive to please Him and represent His name to the best of our abilities.

Wear the name of Christ with pride for the amazing gift He has given. You just never know who's watching.

—VAL KEMPER, FORMER MEMBER, US NATIONAL VOLLEYBALL TEAM

SPORTS NOTE: Val was a pioneer in pro women's volleyball as a member of the Grand Rapids Force in the United States Professional Volleyball league in 2002. The USPV had teams in Grand Rapids, Minneapolis, St. Louis, and Chicago.

FROM THE PLAYBOOK: Read Galatians 5:16–6:10.

GAME PLAN: Think back over the past couple of days. Did you represent Jesus Christ well? If not, what can you do better tomorrow to make sure people see Jesus in you?

THE HARD WORK IS ALREADY DONE

POINT OF EMPHASIS:
Faith, not works

"So then, just as you received Christ Jesus as Lord, continue to live in him." COLOSSIANS 2:6

As a child I was diagnosed with ADD and extreme hyperactivity. That's a bad combination for strict schooling by nuns and parents who are just hoping their son can fall asleep at night.

In the arena, however, it was a much different story. I loved sports, so I would practice and work really hard to succeed. Any sport I was playing at the moment was my passion. In baseball, I forced myself to concentrate on the mound, and I worked hard. Although I was small, I was able to go to college on a baseball scholarship and eventually turn pro after my junior year at LSU. Nonetheless, I was empty.

After four years of hearing people share the gospel with me, I collapsed. I had worked hard to be a good person, but my attempts and my walls of self-sufficiency caved in.

I thought working hard was the answer to Christianity. So off to work I went—performing for Jesus. More Bible study. More memorization. More "how to" books. More sharing. More scratching my head. Was I missing something?

I was exhausted, which was a good thing. Finally, I got it. I realized I needed to be redeemed, and I trusted Jesus as Savior. I realized there was nothing I could do—only what He could give me. Instead of trusting that He was big enough to change me and live through me, I had tried to attain my goal by human effort. As we learned from Simon (read Acts 8:1–25), we cannot receive God by giving money. And we can't receive Him by hard work (Ephesians 2:8–9).

Do you want Jesus as your Savior? Faith, not works, is what He wants. Then He'll take care of the rest.

—PAUL BYRD, MAJOR LEAGUE PITCHER

SPORTS NOTE:
In his best seasons as a major league pitcher, Byrd won 15 games for Philadelphia in 1999 and 17 for Kansas City in 2002.

FROM THE PLAYBOOK:
Read Romans 3 and 4.

GAME PLAN: Does this "faith, not works" idea sound too good to be true? Examine the verses in Ephesians 2:8–9 and then act on them.

ONE LITTLE GIRL, ONE BIG GOD

POINT OF EMPHASIS:
God's abundant grace

"[God] is able to do exceeding abundantly above all that we ask or think." EPHESIANS 3:20 (KJV)

A mother's heart was crushed when the doctors reported that her little three-year-old daughter was not responding to treatment and would die. She had contracted spinal meningitis and didn't even know her mother.

No amount of comfort could stop the little girl's crying. She was in great pain and too young to understand why. Her mother knew the only thing to do was pray and trust God for her little girl's life.

She stayed by her daughter's bedside and prayed through the night. Her daughter's cry turned to a wimper and finally was silenced. The doctors returned the next morning expecting her to have died in the night. To their surprise, she was peacefully sleeping. They rediagnosed her and told the mother, "She seems to be doing a little better. She has a 50–50 chance of making it, but if she comes through this, she will be mentally retarded and physically, she will never do what the normal child does."

The mother looked at the doctors with a slight smile across her face and nodded, "Uh-huh!" She knew that if God had brought her daughter out of death through the night, He had so much more for her in life.

This little girl grew up to become a world champion in track and win the gold and silver medals at the Olympic Games. She gave her life to Jesus at the age of six years old and today travels the world to minister to diversified people and world-class athletes. I know this because that little girl was me.

The promise of God is given to all believers. He will give you much more than you can ask or think because He wants His glory to be revealed in the lives of His children. Oh, how He loves you and me.

—MADELINE MIMS, OLYMPIC MEDALIST, TRACK

SPORTS NOTE:
Madeline Mims is a part of Life Athletes, a group of premiere athletes who endorse Virtue, Abstinence, and Respect for Life. You can find out about Life Athletes at www.lifeathletes.org.

FROM THE PLAYBOOK:
Read: Philippians 3:7–14; Malachi 3:10; Luke 6:38.

GAME PLAN: "Father, I am Yours to do with as You will. Your will over my life be done, not mine. May my life glorify You in all that I do, say, and am. In Jesus' name. Amen."

THE SUCCESS OF DESIRE

POINT OF EMPHASIS:
Overcoming discouragement

"[Don't] grow weary and lose heart." HEBREWS 12:3

I'm inspired every time I recall the story of a remarkable female athlete named Wendy Stoker. In high school, she diligently practiced for four years to improve her skills as a diver. As a senior, she placed third in the Iowa girls state diving championship.

Wendy went on to attend the University of Florida, where she continued her hard work. While carrying a full load of classes, she earned the No. 2 position on the varsity diving squad. Her hard work was recognized in 2002 when she was inducted into the Iowa High School Swim Coaches Association Hall of Fame.

Perhaps the most amazing thing about Wendy Stoker, however, was her typing skills. She pounded out 45 words a minute on her typewriter—with her toes.

You see, Wendy Stoker was born without arms.

Wendy's physical limitations could have held her back, but they didn't. Why? Because she possessed a main component to success—desire. Absolutely nothing of human greatness is achieved without it. With desire, we can succeed despite overwhelming limitations. Without it, we limit ourselves even though we may possess great capabilities.

Although most of us will never know the challenges Wendy Stoker faces each day, we all have our limitations, real or perceived. Our limitations can tempt us to give up desire. But when we lose desire we lose heart. That is one reason why the Bible encourages us to fix our eyes on Jesus so that we don't "grow weary and lose heart" (Hebrews 12:2–3).

Desire is the secret to success. Knowing Jesus is the secret to desire.

—JEFF OLSON

SPORTS NOTE:
Wendy was inducted into the Iowa Swim Hall of Fame in 2002.

FROM THE PLAYBOOK:
Read Galatians 6:9.

GAME PLAN: Identify where you are tempted to give up desire because your limitations seem too great. Ask God for help in pressing forward.

PRAYING STREAK

POINT OF EMPHASIS:
Effective prayer

"Always pray and [don't] give up." LUKE 18:1

Few people in life have shown the mental discipline and tenacity that marks the life of Edwin Moses. Moses won his first Olympic gold medal in the 400-meter hurdles during the 1976 Montreal Games. But his greatest achievement came in the year following the Olympics and beyond, when he began the most remarkable winning record in track history. For ten years, Edwin Moses won 122 straight hurdles races, breaking his own world record several times in the process.

How did he do it? What was his strategy? Well, Edwin was an engineer, and he broke the race down into its components, calculating the precise length and number of strides to take between hurdles and the exact pace he needed to maintain to achieve maximum efficiency. Edwin knew the importance of details. He made a habit of the daily execution of those details. The great philosopher Aristotle once said, "We are what we repeatedly do; excellence, then, is not an act, but a habit."

In the same way, the greatest achievement of a Christian's life can be marked by the daily execution of prayer. Prayer is a discipline. Paul reminded us to "be joyful always; pray continually; give thanks in all circumstances . . ." (1 Thessalonians 5:16–18). Prayer is the hallmark of the devoted life to Christ. Find that quiet place and go there each day, the same way, and lay your requests before God. "The prayer of a righteous man is powerful and effective" (James 5:16). We have access to the very throne room of God! Begin your prayer track record today and make your mark in spiritual history!

—MOLLY GRETZINGER

SPORTS NOTE:
Edwin Moses has a bachelor's degree in physics and a master's degree in business administration.

FROM THE PLAYBOOK:
Acts 4:24–31. See how the early church prayed.

GAME PLAN: Try each of these things for 5 minutes: Praise, wait, confess, read the Word, intercede, petition, pray the Word, thanksgiving, singing, meditation, listen, praise. See how one hour can be spent praying!

"PLEASE FORGIVE ME!"

POINT OF EMPHASIS:
Forgiveness

"For it is with your heart that you believe and are justified, and it is with your mouth that you confess and are saved." ROMANS 10:10

Before the 2001 football season began, Napoleon Kaufman retired to devote himself to Christian ministry. Here's his account of how he first became interested in spiritual things.

Once I reached the NFL, I got the money, got those cars, and women too—supposedly everything anyone could possibly want.

Yet I was still empty inside.

SPORTS NOTE:
Kaufman graduated from the University of Washington as the all-time rushing leader in Huskies history.

It must have showed because, although I'm normally a very upbeat person, I had people sending me Bibles and other things. I'd check them out, but eventually just shrug it off. Looking back, I realize that the Lord was calling me.

In June 1996, I began to take heed of some of the things people were saying. I began to read my Bible. I realized how far off the mark I was.

I began to read that the peace you receive—the true peace, the everlasting peace—comes through Jesus and not through wealth, cars, women, or any other material possession. He's the only One who can give you true peace.

FROM THE PLAYBOOK:
Read Romans 10.

At the same time, I was approached in training camp by a teammate who said, "Man, you know what? You don't even seem like the type of person who would be cussin' and acting like the rest of these guys."

That was all it took. That night I went to my room and said, "God, I want to repent for the stuff I've done. Please forgive me!" I asked Jesus to come into my heart and make me a new creature.

That was August 1996, and ever since then I've been dedicated to serving God and growing spiritually.

Have you repented and turned your life over to God?

—NAPOLEON KAUFMAN, FORMER NFL RUNNING BACK

 GAME PLAN: What major spiritual decision do you know you need to make? Should you do it right now before you forget?

WHAT'S IN YOUR WALLET?

POINT OF EMPHASIS:
Controlling money

"A man is a slave to whatever has mastered him." 2 PETER 2:19

In 1968, Denny McClain was one of the finest pitchers in the major leagues. After going 31–6 with a 1.96 ERA, baseball granted him the American League Cy Young Award. He topped off his extraordinary season by helping the Detroit Tigers capture the 1968 World Series. Although he lost his first two starts, he won Game 6 on only two days of rest, pushing the series to a decisive Game 7.

After the 1968 championship, the Tigers rewarded McClain, the last pitcher to win 30 games in a season, with the team's first $100,000 contract. Although he played before the era of multi-million dollar deals, McClain made the kind of money that, if handled properly, would have left him financially set for life. Instead, the money handled him.

Since leaving baseball, McClain has been in constant financial trouble. He's even spent time in prison for racketeering and bilking $3 million from the pension fund of a company he owned. Not long ago, the best pitcher in baseball in 1968 was out of jail on parole, working at a 7-Eleven selling Slurpees.

It's only one sad story, but it represents what can happen when money controls a person. Money is a wonderful servant, but it can also be a horrible master that will drive us to places we don't want to go. The Bible says that "the love of money is a root of all kinds of evil. Some people, eager for money, have wandered from the faith and pierced themselves with many griefs" (1 Timothy 6:10).

So what's in your wallet—a servant or a master?

—JEFF OLSON

SPORTS NOTE:
Denny McClain won 31 games in 1968—and 100 others the rest of his career, which totaled 10 seasons.

FROM THE PLAYBOOK:
Read Hebrews 13:5.

GAME PLAN: Examine your finances to see where money might be mastering you.

THAT NAME

POINT OF EMPHASIS:
The great name of Jesus

"At the name of Jesus every knee should bow." PHILIPPIANS 2:10

Lou Brock is one of baseball's all-time greats. Back in the 1960s and 70s the St. Louis Cardinals speedster changed the way the game was played. His prowess on the base paths created havoc for opposing teams. Brock's 118 steals in 1974 set a major league record and earned him *The Sporting News* Man of the Year Award.

When Brock retired after the 1979 season, he left the game as baseball's all-time stolen base leader with 938 steals. He also amassed 3,023 hits during his 18-year career, making him an easy choice for baseball's Hall of Fame. To close out his baseball record, Brock was elected to the Hall in 1985.

Yet in spite of his status as one of baseball's all-time greats, Lou Brock knows his place. Brock understands that his accomplishments in America's pastime are a blessing. He has a firm grasp on the fact that his eternity is secure because of the accomplishment of his Lord, Jesus Christ, on the cross. Christ's victorious achievement is the lone action that has transformed his life.

"Jesus Christ is the name greater than any other name. It's the only name that will get you into heaven," explains Brock. "When you look at the Old Testament, it was about the coming of Jesus Christ. When we look at the New Testament, we get to John the Baptist who was the first prophet to say 'Repent!' because He [the Messiah] is no longer just coming–He's here!"

Even Hall of Famers with legendary accomplishments—superstars such as Lou Brock—must acknowledge and submit to Jesus Christ as Lord. Have you?

—ROB BENTZ

SPORTS NOTE:
Lou Brock is second all-time in career stolen bases in major league history. Only Rickey Henderson swiped more bases than Brock (1,406).

FROM THE PLAYBOOK:
Memorize Philippians 2:10–11.

GAME PLAN: Have you acknowledged the amazing accomplishment of Jesus Christ on the cross of Calvary? Have you bowed your knee to the One who died to redeem you from the eternal punishment that you deserve?"

WHO'S ON THE PEDESTAL?

POINT OF EMPHASIS:
Practicing humility

"Do nothing out of selfish ambition or vain conceit, but in humility consider others better than yourselves." PHILIPPIANS 2:3

As an athlete, I find Philippians 2:3 to be an extremely challenging verse. It seems to dictate the opposite of what I tend to believe about myself, especially going into competition. In fact, when an athlete considers her opponent to be better than herself, there is much sports psychology literature that states she has already lost before she has begun. A closer look at this verse, though, can help us see the heart of its message.

Webster defines *humility* as "respectful deference," that is, "courteous respect for another's opinion or judgment." I have always respected my opponents, so that's not a problem.

Considering them to be better than myself, however, is where my difficulty lies. Another verse helps us here. We are told in I Corinthians 1:31, "Let him who boasts boast in the Lord." There's my problem! Typically, I am far from boasting in the Lord. Considering others better than myself moves me off the pedestal I tend to put myself on and helps me realize I am the person God created me to be, nothing more and nothing less.

Whether in competition or otherwise, learn how to humbly consider others better than yourself. Do not degrade yourself or compromise your personal beliefs, but merely develop a respect for those against whom you compete or hold differing views. And always remember that your gifts—even your athletic skills—come from God, not yourself.

—JEAN DRISCOLL, EIGHT-TIME BOSTON MARATHON CHAMPION

SPORTS NOTE:
Jean won the silver medal in the 1992 and 1996 Olympics in the 800-meter women's wheelchair race.

FROM THE PLAYBOOK:
Read Philippians 2:1–11.

GAME PLAN: Why should you consider others better than yourself? What does it mean to "boast in the Lord"?

MAKING THE TURN

POINT OF EMPHASIS:
Turning to Jesus Christ

"The old has gone, the new has come!" 2 Corinthians 5:17

A huge turnaround in the life of hard-partying University of Texas at El Paso college golfer Paul Stankowski began in 1988 when he was invited to a series of College Golf Fellowship dinners.

"The first dinner I went to, [former US Open champion] Scott Simpson spoke and shared what Jesus Christ had done for him. I went because there was free food yet heard something that changed my life."

For the next two years, Paul read through the book of John and slowly began to feel God's touch in his life.

"God really pricked my heart. I started understanding what grace was, and I started understanding the fact that I was a sinner and the only way for me to be saved was through Jesus Christ."

On March 9, 1990, Stankowski received Christ as Savior. His college roommates knew little about Christ, and Paul admits that his initial commitment faltered in that atmosphere. He put his Bible away and returned to his party lifestyle.

Things changed a year later at his brother's wedding.

"My brother was a believer," Stankowski recalls, "and I hung out with his Christian friends during the weekend. I had a great time. I recommitted my life to the Lord and decided to follow Him."

When he arrived back at UTEP, Stankowski's college teammates saw a new person.

"I started going to Fellowship of Christian Athletes and to church, and these guys were blown away. I met people who loved me, and it was amazing. They took me under their wing. When I got home at night or woke up in the morning, I wasn't hung over. I didn't have to think, what did I do last night?"

He made the turn in his life, and Paul Stankowski, now in his 13th year on the PGA Tour, has been living for Jesus ever since.

—ART STRICKLIN

SPORTS NOTE:
Paul Stankowski's hobbies include hunting and music.

FROM THE PLAYBOOK:
Read 2 Corinthians 5:11–6:2.

GAME PLAN: Where are you on the journey? Are you a professing Christian who lives like everyone else, or have you decided to truly follow Christ?

GETTING THROUGH THE DAY

POINT OF EMPHASIS:
The Spirit-filled life

"I will boast . . . about my weaknesses, so that Christ's
power may rest on me." **2 CORINTHIANS 12:9**

When Orel Hershiser talks, people listen.

For the former major league pitcher, that fact alone helps drive him to a humility from which we can all learn.

"I fall short. I fall short so far, it's unbelievable," says the 1988 World Series MVP. "So I'm humbled just to be listened to, just for people to be hearing what I have to say.

"I think it's humbling to be able to think clearly and look at certain situations and get the essence of them and be able to communicate it. A lot of it stems from knowing who you are in God's eyes. You can honestly evaluate yourself and the portion you've been given—your placement in life and how you relate to other human beings in the world. It's so much easier when you know who you are."

Hershiser, who retired from baseball in 2000 and is now the pitching coach for the Texas Rangers, continues. "I'm not some unbelievable person who has it all together. I am completely flawed, and I am asking to be put back together on a daily basis. The days that I think I've got it all together, I'm probably closer to the pit than on the days that I don't think I have it all together. Through my weakness, He is strong.

"A Spirit-filled life is not a self-filled life. A self-filled life is a self-consumed, selfish life. A spiritual life is an emptying, where you say, 'God, get me ready for another day.' "

See why people listen to the man they called "Bulldog"?

—ADAPTED FROM AN ARTICLE IN *SPORTS SPECTRUM* MAGAZINE,
JULY–AUGUST 2000

SPORTS NOTE:
Orel Hershiser won 204 games during his career, which extended from 1983 through 2000.

FROM THE PLAYBOOK:
Read
2 Corinthians
12:1–10.

GAME PLAN: If you were to do the kind of self-evaluation Orel Hershiser gave above, what would you say about yourself?

THE TOP 10 LIST

POINT OF EMPHASIS:
Living by God's rules

"Love the Lord your God with all your heart and with all your soul and with all your mind." MATTHEW 22:37

USA Today recently compiled a list of the ten hardest things to do in sports.

10. Skiing in the downhill
9. Saving a penalty kick in soccer
8. Riding a bicycle in the Tour de France
7. Running in a marathon
6. Figure skating's quad spin toe loop
5. A return of serve in tennis
4. Hitting a long straight tee shot in golf
3. Pole vaulting
2. Driving a race car
1. Hitting a baseball at 95 mph

SPORTS NOTE:
The Top 10 baseball cards of all time, according to Forbes.com: Honus Wagner, Ty Cobb, Joe Jackson, Nap Lajoie, Babe Ruth, Joe DiMaggio, Satchell Paige, Willie Mays, Mickey Mantle, Ted Williams.

FROM THE PLAYBOOK:
Read Matthew 22:34–40, 2 Timothy 3:10–17.

God has a Top 10 list too. The ten laws or commandments are really the most basic things a person should do just to be a decent human being. Don't kill, steal, or lie are just a few. But we fail to master the ten rules. God's guidelines are too tough, too hard. Like trying to hit a major league fastball. We strike out. In Matthew 22:37–40 Jesus summed up the ten rules into two important ones. First, love God with all your heart, soul, and mind. Second, love your neighbor as yourself. Still, those are pretty hard to do.

Second Timothy 3:16 says that the Bible can teach, correct, and train you to be the person God wants you to be. In sports or life, there are some things that will be too hard for you to do. But what God wants you to do comes with a training program guaranteed to work. It's in the Bible.

—DAN DEAL

GAME PLAN: Maybe you've given in to temptation recently and you feel really discouraged and down about it. Tell God you're sorry and continue with the training program. Sinning doesn't mean you stay away from the Bible. Sinning means you read even more of the Bible to help you win against sin the next time.

WHAT GOD IS LOOKING FOR

POINT OF EMPHASIS:
Faithfulness

"A faithful man will be richly blessed." PROVERBS 28:20

When it comes time for NFL teams to cut their rosters from 80 to 53 players each season, it brings back bad memories.

It is difficult to watch players' dreams shattered, see the course of their lives severely altered, and—maybe worst of all—see them told they just weren't good enough. Most coaches are sympathetic to the players and find no pleasure in releasing them, but despite their best efforts the message is the same: "You just didn't make the grade."

Throughout life, we will inevitably be measured according to the world's standards. We must resist allowing this to define who we are and how we perceive ourselves. Instead, we must hold firmly to our identity as children of God, knowing that by his grace, He has labeled us "saints." If we understand how God views us, we are then able to put into perspective our "failures" in attaining the world's standards.

The basis for this perspective comes from the fact that God's economy is radically different from the world's. God is not looking for greatness as our culture describes it; instead, He is looking for faithfulness. So, it is possible to suffer a loss, endure a failure, or face a disappointment—or even get cut from a team—and still be a champion in God's eyes.

SPORTS NOTE: After his NFL career ended, Frank Reich became president of Reformed Theological Seminary in Charlotte, North Carolina.

FROM THE PLAYBOOK: Read Philippians 1:15–21.

Our perception of self must be grounded in our relationship to God through faith in Jesus Christ. That is our motivation to give our best effort and remain faithful—no matter what the circumstances.

—FRANK REICH, FORMER NFL QUARTERBACK

 GAME PLAN: How does God's love help you overcome a failure in life? What does He do for you when you suffer a loss?

CONQUERING THE BEAST

POINT OF EMPHASIS:
The help of the Holy Spirit

"We take captive every thought to make it obedient to Christ."
2 CORINTHIANS 10:5

Each of us has gone through a time when it seemed that there was an all-out battle taking place in our soul. That's why we can relate to Paul when he said, "For what I want to do I do not do, but what I hate I do" (Romans 7:15). Let's call these wars inside us the battle of the beasts.

As a pro bull rider, I faced enormous beasts daily on the way to establishing myself as a world champion. Bull riding has been classified as one of the most dangerous sports in the world, and I've been greatly blessed of the Lord to be used by Him as an ambassador for His kingdom.

Let's turn from the rodeo ring to the arena of life. If you are going to succeed in the Christian life, you must conquer the beast within. You will need every tool the Lord has given you (prayer, faith, courage). This "beast" can be anything that opposes God's will for your life.

Remember the moment you surrendered your life to Jesus? That decision instantly made you a world champion in Christ and you became His ambassador. When you entered into the light (through a personal relationship with God through Jesus), you left the kingdom of darkness behind. In doing so, you became a huge threat to your former landlord, the devil.

He then launched a massive attack against your soul. The devil desires to entangle you to believe his lies.

You can conquer anything he sends your way. By the Spirit of the Lord, you are a conqueror! Through His mighty power, you can defeat any beast that stands in the way of fulfilling your God-given destiny!

—SCOTT MENDES, FORMER WORLD-CHAMPION BULL RIDER

SPORTS NOTE:
The advantage is clearly with the bull in a bull-riding event. The rider weighs about 165 pounds while the bull weighs about a ton.

FROM THE PLAYBOOK:
Read Galatians 5, Romans 8, and Colossians 3:1–10.

GAME PLAN: Seek God's face today, and allow His Spirit to reveal the beasts in your life that need to be evicted and destroyed. Most people know that God is a conqueror, but you must see yourself as one as well, for you are created in His image (Genesis 1:26).

SUMMER SAINT?

POINT OF EMPHASIS:
Living for Jesus

"Know . . . the riches of his glorious inheritance in the saints."
EPHESIANS 1:18

In what has to be one of the wackiest sports promotions ever, the St. Paul Saints minor league baseball team made a fan their "Saint for a Summer" a few years ago.

It's not what you think.

The "winner" of the promotion was a 24-year-old named Nick Cichowicz, who moved into an 8-foot x 20-foot trailer for the whole baseball season at the team's ballpark! When he arrived, the only items in the Ford Custom Camper were an iMac computer and a printer.

He was given a $5,000 stipend to buy anything he needed, but it had to be purchased over the Internet. By making it through the September 3 finale without leaving Midway Stadium, Nick was given another $5,000.

He called his experience, "A great summer job."

Being named a "Saint" for a summer may be a nice gig, but there's something a lot better out there: Christ has called you to be a saint for a lifetime. By the work of the Holy Spirit, you have been led into a personal relationship with Christ.

As a saint, this means you are identified with the Lord Himself. You are a CHRIST-ian.

How should you then live? By spending each day growing closer to your Lord. By learning more each day so that you can represent Him in truth and someday finish well in His strength.

By His grace, Christ has allowed you to know the "glorious riches" (v. 18) of salvation and eternal life. Follow Him and be a saint for all seasons.

—TOM FELTEN

SPORTS NOTE:
The Saints are a member of the Northern League, an independent baseball league not affiliated with major league teams.

FROM THE PLAYBOOK:
Read Ephesians 1:1–21.

GAME PLAN: Look up the word "saint" in the dictionary and consider how the definition represents your life.

COURT VISION

POINT OF EMPHASIS:
Choosing wisely

"Stop judging by mere appearances, and make a right judgment."
JOHN 7:24

During orientation week as a freshman at North Carolina State, I ran into Joe Cafferky, one of the members of the varsity basketball team. With him was a guy in cut-off jeans who looked to be all of thirteen years old.

Joe introduced him, saying, "This is your new teammate Monte Towe. He's a freshman too." I was stunned. He had to be kidding. This guy was 5'7" in his sneakers. There is no way this guy could be in college. There is no way he could actually play ball!

SPORTS NOTE:
David Thompson was named the Most Outstanding Player of the 1974 NCAA Finals.

FROM THE PLAYBOOK:
Read John 7.

Later that day we played some pick-up games and Monte's team won every game because he controlled the tempo. Throughout our time at North Carolina State, Monte proved not only that he could play ball but also that he was a leader and a winner. Monte was a great point guard who could shoot from downtown and distribute that ball at the right time to the right guy; he made all of us better. Under his leadership we won the NCAA national championship in 1974. Monte was an All-American and continued his career playing professional basketball for two years. Needless to say, my first impression of him was completely wrong.

In life, it is easy to make stark judgments and quick assumptions. We often rely on what we see on the outside and never take the time to really understand things before forming an opinion. Appearances can be deceiving, and that is why Jesus encourages us to "stop judging by mere appearances" so we may make the "right judgment." It is important to understand things before making rash decisions or reaching faulty conclusions. Jesus encourages us so that we may seek knowledge and ultimately obtain truth.

—DAVID THOMPSON, FORMER COLLEGE AND NBA STAR

GAME PLAN: Is there anyone in your circle of acquaintances that you've been looking at the way David saw Monte—with less than a favorable impression? How can you discover the good in that person instead of relying on negative assumptions?

BEYOND MY WILDEST DREAMS

POINT OF EMPHASIS:
God's plan

"'For I know the plans I have for you,' declares the Lord."
JEREMIAH 29:11

When I graduated from Northwestern University, I dreamed of playing football in the NFL.

I was drafted in the 12th round of the 1991 draft by the Atlanta Falcons. After training camp, the Falcons released me. I sat out of football that year, hoping to get another chance. The next spring I got a tryout with the London Monarchs of the World Football League, but after one week of camp, they said I wasn't good enough to make their team.

After that, it was hard to get another tryout anywhere. I was seriously wondering what God's plan for my life was, or if He even had a plan. Miraculously, I got a tryout with the San Diego Chargers that summer, but pulled my hamstring in camp and couldn't compete—so they released me at the end of camp.

I thought my football career was all over, but God had a plan I didn't know about. On Labor Day 1992, the Bears called me up out of the blue and signed me to their team. I knew this was a miracle of God. I ended up playing two more years with the Bears, and then two years with the Carolina Panthers. Then, in 1997, the Atlanta Falcons signed me to be their starting fullback. I played ten years in the NFL, five with the team that first released me back in 1991.

I laugh when I think of how awesome God has been to me. He taught me to trust Him through hardships, setbacks, and disappointments, and then He blessed me with a career more wonderful than my wildest dreams.

—BOB CHRISTIAN, NFL RUNNING BACK

SPORTS NOTE:
Bob played for the Bears from 1992 through 1994. His best years were with Atlanta, where he scored 12 touchdowns.

FROM THE PLAYBOOK:
Read Jeremiah 29:10–14.

GAME PLAN: How are plans developing in your life? Does it help to know that as we read in Jeremiah, God has plans for your life? When was the last time you asked God to give you clear direction as to what He wants you to do?

POINT OF EMPHASIS:
Trusting God

"In God I trust; I will not be afraid. What can man do to me?"
PSALM 56:11

John Matuszak was a 6-foot-8, 280-pound football player for the Oakland Raiders. His public image was that of a havoc-wreaking, heavy-drinking, hard-hitting player who was as much a threat off the field as on. Friends, however, knew "Tooz," as he was called, as a 280-pound puppy dog just begging to be stroked.

According to *Los Angeles Times* writer Mark Heisler, John Matuszak was "beset by fears he couldn't acknowledge." As a young boy, he was ridiculed for his gawky, beanpole appearance. Two brothers died of cystic fibrosis. The image of the Tooz was a fortress he had created to hide in. But he got trapped there by his hidden fears. He died at age 38 of a massive heart attack. His body had been weakened by years of alcohol and drug abuse.

SPORTS NOTE:
John Matuszak played for the Oakland Raiders in Super Bowl XV in New Orleans.

FROM THE PLAYBOOK:
Read 1 Samuel 18:28–19:12.

The story of King Saul bears some striking similarities. He too was a monster of a man, a fighter. He was also driven by fears (1 Samuel 18:29). Because he tried to cope with them in his own strength instead of turning to the Lord for help, his life came to an untimely end (31:4).

"Heavenly Father, no matter how big we may appear on the outside, sometimes we feel very small on the inside. Forgive us for putting up a false front and pretending we're strong enough to handle life on our own. Help us to trust You more."

—MART DE HAAN

GAME PLAN: You can admit it here. What are you afraid of? Have you ever tried handing that fear over to God?

THE BIG D: DISAPPOINTMENT

POINT OF EMPHASIS:
Disappointment

"Put your hope in God." PSALM 42:5

You don't have to be a Chicago Cubs fan to understand disappointment. But it helps.

Every sports fan understands the pain. Losing key players in trades. Dropping key playoff games. We suffer. We agonize. We hate it.

Sometimes the frustration of losing a big game, so irritating for us as fans, is too overwhelming for athletes to handle.

One former major leaguer was deeply troubled because he gave up a home run that cost his team a chance at World Series glory. A few years later, this pitcher took his own life—unable to cope with the letdown. The disappointment was too much for him.

Both in sports and out, disappointment can crush us. It can take away our joy of living. It can make each day look like a long, dark tunnel to nowhere.

Perhaps you are dealing with a major disappointment in your life. If so, you need hope.

Not Chicago hope, Cubs' style. That's just spring-training wishful thinking. No, you need **real** hope. Hope that there is a reason behind the disappointment. Hope that something can be done about it. Hope in God.

Listen to the words of an ancient writer—someone who knew about true disappointment. "Why are you downcast, O my soul? Why so disturbed within me? Put your hope in God" (Psalm 42:5).

Think about it. Doesn't it make sense to turn your disappointment over to Someone who is all-powerful and full of love? Try it. Talk to God about your disappointment. Ask Him to help you get through the tough times.

—DAVE BRANON

SPORTS NOTE:
The Chicago Cubs won the World Series in 1907 and 1908—and not since.

FROM THE PLAYBOOK:
Find how the psalm writer seeks help when he is down by reading Psalm 42.

GAME PLAN: Think of your deepest disappointment. Write it down on a piece of paper. Now get alone and talk to God about it, giving it to Him and asking Him to give you hope. Then throw the paper away to remind yourself that you've given the disappointment to God.

THE LADAINIAN LIMBO

POINT OF EMPHASIS:
Love others more than self

"Dear friends, let us love one another." I JOHN 4:7

What is it with NFL end zone celebrations? When did all this silliness become an integral part of the game? Lambeau Leaps and impromptu dance steps are one thing. But Mr. Universe poses, Sharpies, and cell phones? Come on!

How about that latest craze—the LaDainian Limbo? Never heard of it? That's because LaDainian Tomlinson doesn't *do* end zone celebrations. He simply hands the ball to the nearest official and jogs to the sideline. No grandstanding. No look-at-me theatrics. Just great football.

LaDainian refuses to fall victim to one of life's greatest temptations. It's the temptation of pride. And that's a struggle I dare say we all have.

The apostle John warned against "the cravings of sinful man, the lust of his eyes and the boasting of what he has and does" (1 John 2:16). These things "[come] not from the Father but from the world."

Our unhealthy desire to draw attention to ourselves runs counter to what God desires for us. The only antidote is love—love for God and love for others. John constantly exhorted us to love each other. (Check out 1 John 4:7–21). It's the constant theme of the New Testament. And it is embodied in the life of Jesus.

If you ever find yourself scoring a touchdown (I never did), toss the pigskin to the nearest striped-shirt. Then celebrate with your teammates and thank them. That will grab attention! More important, it will honor Jesus, who loved us so much that He gave up the glory of heaven for us.

—TIM GUSTAFSON

SPORTS NOTE: Tomlinson owns a restored red 1964 Chevy Impala.

FROM THE PLAYBOOK: Read 1 John 2:15–17.

GAME PLAN: What do your goals say about your pride? Do they glorify you? Or God? Do you find yourself dwelling on how well you do certain things? How can this be a danger? During Satan's temptation of Jesus in the wilderness (see Luke 4:5–8), how did Jesus handle the devil's appeal to His ego? (v. 8).

LEARNING THE HARD WAY

POINT OF EMPHASIS:
Christian discipline

"No discipline seems pleasant at the time." HEBREWS 12:11

Tennis star Pete Sampras was asked to name the most important match he had ever played at the US Open. The four-time Open champ had plenty to choose from—including the match in 1990 that gave him his first Grand Slam title at age nineteen. Instead, Sampras chose the 1992 final, a match he lost to Stefan Edberg in a tough four-setter.

It was a terrible disappointment—one that most of us would choose to forget if it had happened to us. But Sampras sees that loss as a major turning point in his career. As he explains, "Before that match, I didn't hate to lose." The bitterness of the loss provided Sampras with the motivation he needed to get his game into full gear. It inspired him to discipline himself and give his best effort all the time. Before the Edberg match, Pete was a "one hit wonder." But when he retired from tennis in 2003, he had 14 Grand Slam titles and was considered by some to be the best player in the history of the game.

Hebrews 12:11 says, "No discipline seems pleasant at the time, but painful. Later on, however, it produces a harvest of righteousness and peace for those who have been trained by it."

There are some things we all have to learn the hard way, and one of those things is that we need discipline. We need the correction of losses and of helpful advice from others. In the Christian life, the true champions are the ones who can learn from these experiences—and then allow Christ to help them grow stronger because of the tough times.

— CHRISTIN DITCHFIELD

SPORTS NOTE: Pete Sampras' best Grand Slam event was Wimbledon, which he won in 1993, 1994, 1995, 1997, 1998, 1999, and 2000.

FROM THE PLAYBOOK: Read Hebrews 12:1–13.

 GAME PLAN: Think of a recent situation when you felt God's correction. How did you learn from that? How do you discipline yourself?

THE KICKER GETS KICKED AROUND

POINT OF EMPHASIS:
Enduring trouble for God's glory

"God works for the good of those who love him." ROMANS 8:28

A few years ago, my team acquired a new head coach. He and I got off to a rough start when I missed several field goals. I had to remember that God had placed him in authority over me (Hebrews 13:17)—even as he humiliated me in front of my teammates and 68,000 fans.

Jesus endured the ultimate humiliation before the resurrection, and later He sat at the right hand of the throne of God. This should encourage us as we face opposition.

SPORTS NOTE:
Matt Stover began his NFL career in 1991 with the Cleveland Browns, who moved to Baltimore and became the Ravens in 1996.

During my struggle, the team brought in another kicker to replace me. I submitted the situation to God and prayed that His will would be served. It's easy to be willing to be used by God during good times, but now I had to be willing to be used through my hard times.

The other kicker was gone after five weeks.

God was faithful. He gave me strength to persevere through the most difficult circumstances of my career (Philippians 4:13). He allowed me to make 18 straight field goals to finish the season and keep my job.

FROM THE PLAYBOOK:
Read Hebrews 12:1–3.

All eyes were on me during this trial, but my eyes were fixed on Christ. I was encouraged as my teammates later told me that an inner peace had shone through me and that my ability to handle my coach with self-control spoke volumes to them. I am confident that God used this incident to further His Kingdom.

Are you willing to be used, even if it could cost you your career? Trust that God has it all under control and that "God works for the good of those who love Him" (Romans 8:28).

—MATT STOVER, KICKER, BALTIMORE RAVENS

GAME PLAN: List three struggles that you are enduring right now. How can you use each one to bring glory to God?

A PLACE TO TURN

POINT OF EMPHASIS:
The Bible, our book of helps

"If your law had not been my delight, I would have perished."
PSALM 119:92

In 2001, several years after losing his arm to cancer, former major leaguer Dave Dravecky and his wife Jan collaborated with Joni Eareckson Tada to produce the *Encouragement Bible*. It's an NIV version of the Bible that contains sidebars with anecdotes, personal testimonies, and Scripture indexes that point to God's love and promises for His children in times of suffering.

"Many people don't turn to the Bible because they feel unqualified to read and understand it," Dravecky explained. "Part of the beauty and the genius of Scripture is that it's alive, empowered by the Holy Spirit of God. And when you're suffering, God's words are more precious than anything else. We also know the challenges of reading the Bible when your life is turned upside-down. That's why we've put lots of helpful features in this edition.

"We want [people] to know that our greatest discovery in the Bible wasn't that we found answers to some of our questions about suffering," Dave and Jan say in the preface, "Rather, our greatest discovery was the gradual and wondrous unveiling of our awesome God, the one who holds all of the answers. Through these pages [of the Bible], we discovered the God who is the Answer to every question, yearning, and desire of the human heart. Our hope and prayer is that you too, will make that same wonderful discovery."

The Bible. It's still the place to turn to for help.

—ROXANNE ROBBINS

SPORTS NOTE:
Dave and Jan Dravecky's son Jonathan played first base for the Azusa Pacific University baseball team.

FROM THE PLAYBOOK:
Read Psalm 119.

GAME PLAN: Write a letter to a friend who is going through a difficult time. Include some Bible verses that will provide them with encouragement.

DISCOVERING LIFE AFTER DEATH

POINT OF EMPHASIS:
Handling death

"By prayer and petition, with thanksgiving, present your requests to God. And the peace of God, which transcends all understanding, will guard your hearts and your minds in Christ Jesus." PHILIPPIANS 4:6–7

There is such a thing as life after death. When a loved one dies, we might feel that our own life has been taken away from us. But the peace of God will restore the goodness of our life to us.

I had to travel through a time when I had to face and conquer the doubts that my mom's death brought into my life. Once I realized that this is possible only through Christ, I began to live again.

I was devastated by the death of my mom in 1996. Never once had she been sick. I lost my mom to what doctors call Legionnaire's disease (double pneumonia). I was saddened, I was angry, I was bitter, and I was mad at God. I turned away from Him and refused to acknowledge that spiritually I was dying. I shut the Holy Bible with no intentions of opening it anytime soon.

There were moments when I could not breathe when I thought about her not being a part of my life. I would almost feel as if I was having a nervous breakdown. As time passed, I realized that I was only sinking further into despair—so I began to turn to my only hope. As I began to pray and seek God's face, I found myself being more able to handle the fact that my mother was gone.

God began to instill a peace inside of me. That kind of peace "surpasses all understanding, [and] will guard your hearts and minds through Christ Jesus" (Philippians 4:7 NKJV).

We must rely on God to see us through life's difficult situations.

When I did that, I began to live again and see that there was life for me after my mom's death.

—CHARLOTTE SMITH-TAYLOR, WNBA FORWARD

SPORTS NOTE:
During one off-season, Charlotte worked for the company that owns *Sports Spectrum* magazine.

FROM THE PLAYBOOK:
Read Psalm 23 if you need any comfort that relates to death.

GAME PLAN: What is seeming to take the joy out of your life? How can I let Philippians 4:7 help me with that? Have you experienced grief recently? Is it possible to gain God's peace?

DON'T FLINCH

POINT OF EMPHASIS:
Becoming a brave Christian

"Stand firm in the faith; be men of courage; be strong."
I CORINTHIANS 16:13

The psalmist said, "I will speak of your statutes before kings and will not be put to shame" (Psalm 119:46). In essence, the psalmist is saying to us: "Don't flinch!"

The dictionary defines the word *flinch* as "to withdraw or shrink from, as if from pain." If we let pain cause us to flinch in our Christian walk, we will definitely lose impact.

Football players also have to learn not to flinch. One fearless player who has that down is Mike Brown of the Chicago Bears. I had the opportunity to recruit Mike Brown from high school to the University of Nebraska. Mike was only 5'8" and barely 180 pounds in high school, but he moved around the football field like a rocket! There was never any hesitation when he tackled another player. Not once did I see him flinch when driving his body into a ball carrier.

Not many players tackle like Mike Brown. That's why he is such a great player. Some players, just before they make contact, flinch and turn their head and shoulders a little bit. They don't want to take the full blow. The natural tendency is to wince and avoid pain.

Coaches teach that it's better to initiate the blow at full speed with proper technique than to avoid the contact by flinching.

That is exactly what God wants from us. He needs full-speed players who are willing to think, walk, and talk in a way that helps them live out their relationship with Jesus Christ to a world that opposes them. God wants brave men and women to tackle the opposition in the name of Jesus Christ at all costs. Don't flinch!

—RON BROWN, FORMER COLLEGE FOOTBALL COACH

SPORTS NOTE:
Ron Brown was an assistant football coach at the University of Nebraska for 17 years. After leaving the Huskers, he became president of the Nebraska Fellowship of Christian Athletes.

FROM THE PLAYBOOK:
Read 2 Timothy 1:1–9.

 GAME PLAN: What makes you want to flinch in your Christian life? Why do you sometimes lack courage? How can your close fellowship with God give you courage not to shrink back—but to attack the challenge?

SEPTEMBER 14

STANDING OUT IN THE CROWD

POINT OF EMPHASIS:
Standing out for God

"'They neither serve your gods nor worship the image.'" DANIEL 3:12

It would have been impossible to do the wave at the college football game between the Washington State Cougars and the San Jose State Spartans in Pullman, Washington, on November 12, 1955.

Why? Because the paid attendance for this contest was one. Not one hundred thousand, not one thousand, not one hundred.

Just one.

It seems that a bitter snowstorm made the faithful stay away in droves, leaving a single fan to root the team on.

Although college football games are not usually where it happens, life is full of instances where you have to stand alone. And it is seldom easy.

Perhaps you recall the old TV commercial in which the nerdy bicyclist mistakenly shows up for a race all decked out in his helmet and racing spandex, only to be met at the starting line by a bunch of grizzly-looking guys on REAL bikes—Harley-Davidsons. He was all alone because he forgot to "phone first." That's another picture of how it feels when you are all alone.

Despite the inconvenience and the anxiety that standing alone causes, the Bible indicates that those who do stand up for what is right will receive God's approval and help. For instance, it wasn't easy for Shadrach and his two buddies to stand when everybody around them was bowing down to an idol. But they were protected by the Lord.

SPORTS NOTE:
The largest crowd in college football has historically been at Michigan Stadium, home of the Michigan Wolverines, where more than 111,000 fans can watch a game.

FROM THE PLAYBOOK:
Read Daniel 3.

Although you won't face a fiery furnace for your stand, there are consequences. Refusing to participate in fraudulent practices may cost you a job. Espousing creation might raise the ire of a science instructor. Witnessing might anger fellow workers. Standing alone and standing out is tough, but it might be the only way to show others that you're not afraid of standing up for God.

—DAVE BRANON

 GAME PLAN: Have you had a tough "stand alone" situation recently? How did you handle it? How could you have handled it better?

THE VALUE OF ACCOUNTABILITY

POINT OF EMPHASIS:
Accountability

"Carry each other's burdens." GALATIANS 6:2

During their four years at Florida State, Peter Boulware and Andre Wadsworth became best friends. When they entered the pros, Wadsworth played for the Arizona Cardinals and Boulware suited up for the Baltimore Ravens.

Despite geographical distance, their friendship stayed strong. They continued to share the same spiritual beliefs and values. They helped each other grow in their Christian faith by talking about things in the Bible and sharing what God was doing in their lives. They also helped each other make wise choices. There are a lot of temptations in the NFL and life in general to do the wrong things.

"It's tough by yourself when you're trying to live right and to do the right thing," Boulware said. "But Andre and I would encourage each other and keep each other accountable. When we would see the other person do something that violated biblical standards, we would say, 'I don't think you should be doing that,' or 'I see that you're struggling here. How can I help? The accountability Andre and I had with each other paid off. It helped us to make choices that had a positive impact on our lives."

Boulware and Wadsworth strongly believe in living out the verse that says, "Brothers, if someone is caught in a sin, you who are spiritual should restore him gently. But watch yourself, or you also may be tempted. Carry each others burdens, and in this way you will fulfill the law of Christ" (Galatians 6:1–2).

As pro football players, they valued accountability. If you haven't done this, open yourself up to someone who will challenge you when you make decisions that violate God's standards.

—ROXANNE ROBBINS

SPORTS NOTE:
Peter Boulware helped the Baltimore Ravens win Super Bowl XXXV 34–7 over the New York Giants.

FROM THE PLAYBOOK:
Read Galatians 6:1–10.

GAME PLAN: Think of a time a friend advised you not to do something that he or she thought was wrong or would bring you harm. Write out how that counsel benefited you.

THROWING IN THE KNEEPADS?

POINT OF EMPHASIS:
Trusting God

"Run in such a way as to get the prize." I CORINTHIANS 9:24

It had been a long trip. Ten days in Switzerland with eight volleyball matches down and one to go.

After playing eleven years of competitive sports, for the first time ever I was "riding the pine." Not only did I sit the bench, I was the only player who had not played the entire trip. My confidence level was at an all-time low. I was ready to throw in the kneepads, put volleyball behind me, and forget my Olympic dreams.

SPORTS NOTE:
In April 2005, Val's husband Hunter Kemper became the first American to be rated the No. 1 triathlete in the world.

FROM THE PLAYBOOK:
Read 1 Corinthians 9:19–27.

The night before our final match was a night I'll never forget. I sat out on the terrace of our hotel overlooking Lake Geneva and surrounded by the Swiss Alps. In the midst of God's amazing creation I felt His presence. I opened my Bible and cried out to Him through all of my hurt and frustration. He spoke to me strongly through His Word: "Do you not know that in a race all the runners run, but only one gets the prize? Run in such a way as to get the prize" (I Corinthians 9:24).

I began to realize that I was in the same race as my teammates. We were all running together. We all wanted to play. We all wanted to win. However, which of us played was up to the coach. Was I about to quit over one disappointing tournament? No! Through God's inspiring Word, my attitude did a 180-degree turn that night in Switzerland. I began to accept my role, and I continued to press on.

It's amazing how similar our spiritual journey is to the ups and downs in athletics. In sports and in life, when we face hardship and trials, it is tempting to quit. We must be encouraged to change our attitude. We must trust that God will strengthen us as we continue to run for our eternal prize. We must not quit.

—VAL KEMPER, FORMER MEMBER, US NATIONAL VOLLEYBALL TEAM

GAME PLAN: Are you ready to quit something important because you are discouraged? Have you spoken with God about this and asked Him to give you strength? Can you see how God's name can be glorified if you stick with it?

TELL YOUR FRIENDS!

POINT OF EMPHASIS:
Witnessing to friends

"[Jesus] said unto them, 'Go into all the world and preach the good news to all creation.'" MARK 16:15

Jesus commands Christians to "go into all the world and preach the good news to all creation. Whoever believes and is baptized will be saved, but whoever does not believe will be condemned" (Mark 16:15–16).

Before the 2000 Olympics began, I knew that if I made the team I was going to give all the glory to my Lord and Savior Jesus Christ. I had the opportunity to play in front of the world in the gold medal game in Sydney and relied on God's strength to play and be a witness for Him.

Since bringing home Olympic gold medals with the USA Softball Team, all of us on the team have had many opportunities for speaking engagements and media events. Some of my teammates have endorsements with shoe companies, most of us have contracts with bat companies like Worth Inc., we have had some appearances on TV, and we have been featured in magazines.

SPORTS NOTE: Leah's husband Tommy has been a representative of BWP Bats, a wooden bat manufacturer.

FROM THE PLAYBOOK: Read Acts 8:26–40.

But let me tell you about a special opportunity. A couple weeks after I was home, I had the opportunity to speak at the church my husband Tommy and I attend, Harvest Christian Fellowship in Riverside, California. As I stood up in front of a couple thousand people and started to share what God has done in my life and about my Olympic experience, I knew that this was the greatest opportunity I could have.

The media appearances are great for a short time, but it's God's message of eternal life that truly matters. Sharing that message is something we can all do.

Struggling with wondering how to spread the good news? Just tell the people in your world about Jesus. That's all you're expected to do.

—LEAH O'BRIEN-AMICO, OLYMPIC GOLD MEDALIST, SOFTBALL

GAME PLAN: Is there someone who needs to hear the gospel from you via conversation, e-mail, letter, or phone call? Why not give yourself a deadline to spread the good news with that person?

SEPTEMBER 18

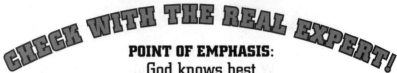
CHECK WITH THE REAL EXPERT!

POINT OF EMPHASIS:
God knows best

"Trust in the Lord with all your heart and lean not on your own understanding; in all your ways acknowledge him, and he will make your paths straight." PROVERBS 3:5–6

A few years ago, as I was looking to purchase a cellular phone, a salesperson allowed me to take one of the phones home for a week to try it out. Attempting to be a good consumer, I quickly studied the brochures to learn about the features as well as the coverage and service the company offered. I became an expert in wireless communication—at least in my own mind.

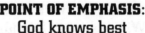

SPORTS NOTE:
Danny Wuerffel won the Heisman Trophy in 1992 while playing for the University of Florida.

FROM THE PLAYBOOK:
Read Job 10:8–12.

Later that week I met a gentleman who obviously needed my technical expertise based on his use of a far inferior phone. As I presented this cellular-deficient man the scoop on wireless services and phone options, he tried to interrupt me. Not to be deterred, I continued my informative presentation—I was certain the company would have hired me on the spot as their spokesperson had they heard my spiel.

Moments later, I asked the man what he did for a living. I was shocked when he said, "I just retired from the company that built your phone. I helped design your phone and the services you tried to tell me about."

An embarrassing moment for sure.

But don't we do the exact same thing with God? He designed us and He knows how we work. Yet how often do we assume we know best and don't even need His input? When we try to run our own lives and seek no guidance from God, we are as foolish as I was with my cell phone.

May God give us the strength to admit our foolishness and humbly learn that He always knows what's best. After all, He made us.

—DANNY WUERFFEL, FORMER NFL QUARTERBACK

GAME PLAN: What area have you been keeping from God, thinking you know better? Today, turn this area over to Him.

HE LOVES THIS GAME!

POINT OF EMPHASIS:
Wrongs don't make things right

"The Lord . . . understands every motive." I CHRONICLES 28:9

Seven years is a long time to play college football.

Sure, there are redshirt guys who can squeeze five years out of a scholarship, but they are just rookies compared to Ron Weaver. This guy set a record that will probably never be broken.

He played seven years of college football. Not legally, you understand. First, he played two years at a junior college before transferring to Sacramento State for his junior and senior years. That's four years, which is pretty much the limit on the number of college years you can suit up.

But hey, when you love football, you just can't stop. Using a "borrowed" social security number and an assumed name to match, "Don't call me Ron" enrolled as a freshman in another junior college, where he played two more years. If you're keeping score, that's six years.

If that wasn't gutsy enough, the guy then moved on to the University of Texas—one of the most famous football schools in the land. There, at age thirty, he played defensive back for the Longhorns. Finally, as Texas was preparing to play in the 1995 Sugar Bowl, the ruse was discovered, and the long-in-the-tooth Longhorn was sent packing.

SPORTS NOTE: Historically, college football players have been allowed to participate in football for four years out of a possible five years at the college.

FROM THE PLAYBOOK: Read Genesis 12:10–20.

Although you can't fault Weaver's dedication, what he did points out a common error: Doing wrong to produce good results. It's the old "going over the speed limit to get to church on time" scenario. Cheating on taxes so the family can afford a new dishwasher just won't wash. It's still wrong, even if good comes from it.

Doing wrong is never right.

—DAVE BRANON

GAME PLAN: What have you done wrong that you have justified by claiming good motives? Does someone need an apology?

KEEPING NO RECORDS

POINT OF EMPHASIS:
Forgiveness

"For I will forgive their wickedness and will remember their sins no more." HEBREWS 8:12

There are few things in the NFL more excruciating than the day after the game when we watch the game film, and our coaches correct our every mistake from the game—in front of all our teammates.

One week in particular, I was dreading watching the film. On one play, as I was covering a punt, my opponent blocked me so hard that no matter what I tried, I could not get off the block. It is no shame to get blocked, but to stay blocked is unacceptable, and I was getting knocked backward almost as fast as the returner was running forward. Our opponent had a big return, and I was nowhere near the play.

The next day, I could barely stand thinking about watching my failure in front of all my teammates. I wished there was some way out of the impending judgment, but I knew I was guilty and there was no way out. However, as the play developed, the cameraman had starting zooming in on the returner, and I wasn't even on the film. No, I didn't get credit for the tackle on that play, but I didn't get condemned for not getting off the block. There was no record of my failure.

What an example of the grace Jesus bought for us on the cross! We were guilty—with no way out from the judgment we deserved—but Jesus shed His blood so that our sins would be washed away. When we accept His free gift of forgiveness, then there is no record of those sins. God, through Jesus, forgives us.

—BOB CHRISTIAN, FORMER NFL RUNNING BACK

SPORTS NOTE:
Bob Christian retired from the NFL on March 12, 2003.

FROM THE PLAYBOOK:
Read Romans 4.

GAME PLAN: Have you had your sinful record forgiven? Do you know that Jesus has washed away your sin with His forgiveness? Until you have, you have a record that will keep you out of heaven. Make sure you have your record wiped clean.

OWN UP TO YOUR "FUMBLES"

POINT OF EMPHASIS:
Owning up to our mistakes or failures

"He who conceals his sins does not prosper." PROVERBS 28:13

I recently watched a football game in which a quarterback fumbled a snap from center on a critical fourth-down play. Rather than falling on the ball, the startled signal-caller made the unfortunate mistake of trying to pick it up—knocking the ball farther behind the line of scrimmage. As he lunged for the football a second time, he inadvertently kicked it backward another 20 yards. Eventually one of his teammates ended the mishap by falling on the ball at the 2-yard line.

If you were that quarterback, how would you respond after the play?

If it were me, I might blame the center for a bad snap. Maybe I would mutter something about my teammates or my coach's play-calling ability. His response was noteworthy. He immediately owned up to his mistake and shouldered the blame for putting his team in a terrible position. Rather than engaging in finger-pointing and causing divisions, he united his team with his ownership and displayed the kind of attitude that made a comeback possible.

We all have our own versions of fumbling the ball. Like the quarterback, sometimes we fumble unintentionally. Other times we fumble the ball on purpose. We not only say and do things that are harmful to others but we also make it difficult for others to trust us. Or we cause others to be afraid.

It's never easy to own up to our mistakes. We all have a bit of Adam in us—wanting to blame others and even God for our mistakes (Genesis 3:11–12). But imagine the fears we can begin to calm and the trust we can begin to restore in our relationships when we own up to the "poor field position" our failures have created.

—JEFF OLSON

SPORTS NOTE: The most fumbles ever in a single pro game by one player was seven by Len Dawson of the Kansas City Chiefs against the San Diego Chargers on November 15, 1964.

FROM THE PLAYBOOK: Read Psalm 32:1–5.

 GAME PLAN: Are you troubled over a time when you didn't own up to hurting a friend? Go to your friend and apologize for any struggles you've created for him or her.

STRONG AND COURAGEOUS

POINT OF EMPHASIS:
Courage from God

"Be strong and very courageous." JOSHUA 1:7

I remember like it was yesterday. Sunday, September 22, 2002. Final round of the Solheim Cup.

Individual singles matches were all that were left to decide the team winner. I drew Annika Sorenstam, the world's No. 1 female golfer. The media and world thought this was the biggest mismatch of the day. But not for me or my US teammates. Though my support seemed small, it was plentiful. I knew God would never give me anything He and I could not face together. So with confidence, I entered the match the underdog and played with the strength and fire only the Holy Spirit could ignite. My husband, Nate (who was also my caddie), my captain, my team, my family, and friends all offered me the support and encouragement I would need to face this challenge.

SPORTS NOTE:
Wendy Ward started playing golf when she was seven years old living in San Antonio.

FROM THE PLAYBOOK:
Read 1 Samuel 17.

I remember going to sleep the night before this final match and being inspired by the great story of David and Goliath (1 Samuel 17). David, like me, was certainly the underdog taking on the big, mighty giant Goliath. Outsized and destined to be defeated, David stood strong and with the hand of God on his side, successfully defeated Goliath.

Now, David did not have the support of his teammates as I did, but he did prevail—thanks to his faith and trust in God. I was fortunate to have the support of my teammates, plus the power of God working through me to match Annika shot for shot. We went on to halve the match, which was like a victory for me—and eventually it helped lead to the win for the US team.

The essence of my story is standing strong in the face of challenges and battles. With God's help, you can be victorious in every thing you do, even when the deck is stacked against you. Be strong and courageous! (Joshua 1:7).

—WENDY WARD, LPGA GOLFER

GAME PLAN: What is your huge opposition today? A meeting with the boss? A job interview? A huge test? A big game? An illness? We all face Goliaths in life. The question is whether we go up against our problems alone or with God next to us.

MIKE'S EYES

POINT OF EMPHASIS:
Fixing our eyes on the Lord

"My eyes are fixed on you, O Sovereign Lord." PSALM 141:8

Mike Singletary, Hall of Fame inductee in 1998, was a legendary NFL competitor whose eyes told it all. The man who went to ten Pro Bowls and won a Super Bowl in 1985 was so intense during games that his peepers seemed to be straining right out of their sockets!

One thing that Mike is even more passionate about is telling people about Jesus Christ. Here's a two-pronged message for youth that he delivered to listeners of *Sports Spectrum* radio: "Young men, find out what is the truth of God. You hear a lot of things, you see a lot of things, and it's important that you know who you are in Christ and who you represent. Be willing to stand up for what's right, no matter what the cost.

"Young women, know that you do not have to do anything to prove that you are in with the 'in crowd.' Jesus Christ is faithful. You don't have to be a 'trophy' for any guy. In Christ you will always be victorious."

Where we place our eyes *is* important. Mike Singletary was constantly scanning the field during games.

Now he implores young men and women to realize that they must keep their eyes fixed on Christ (Hebrews 12:2).

When our eyes are in the right place, we don't have to do anything to prove who we are. The right vision keeps us ready to stand up and do what's right.

Sage 20–20 advice from the Bears' insightful No. 50.

—TOM FELTEN

SPORTS NOTE: Mike is a member of the College Hall of Fame, the Baylor Hall of Fame, the Southwest Conference Hall of Fame, and the Pro Football Hall of Fame.

FROM THE PLAYBOOK: Read Hebrews 12:1–12.

GAME PLAN: Choose today to turn your eyes away from things that are detrimental to your spiritual health. Silently say to yourself throughout the day, "My eyes are on Christ."

WHAT'S YOUR GOAL?

POINT OF EMPHASIS:
Setting the best goal

"We make it our goal to please him." 2 CORINTHIANS 5:9

Paul Henderson lit the lamp and ignited a firestorm of frenzied fans. In 1972, during the final seconds of the eight-game Soviet-Canada series, it was Paul's poke that became the winning goal and caused Canadians to jump and cheer throughout the land.

Looking back on that moment, he states, "Talk about boyhood dreams—that was the highlight of my 18-year hockey career!" What a thrill that must have been for Henderson—to make the play that decided that game and brought glory to the homeland.

SPORTS NOTE:
Paul hit his big shot to help Canada beat Russia on this date in 1972.

Henderson will forever be remembered in the halls of hockey lore for his mighty score. However, he finds the great goal to be a pale-puck comparison to his real victory on earth.

"Coming to know Jesus Christ as my personal Lord and Savior was truly the pinnacle of my entire life," he says. "Giving Him first place in my life has put everything else in its proper perspective."

FROM THE PLAYBOOK:
Read 2 Corinthians 5:1–10.

So what goals in life light your fire? It's not wrong to have objectives and dreams, but the key is understanding where they fit into your ultimate purpose in this world.

Paul Henderson knows that purpose. So did the apostle Paul. In 2 Corinthians 5 he made it clear that our goal must be to please God. He also wrote, "For we must all appear before the judgment seat of Christ, that each one may receive what is due him for the things done while in the body, whether good or bad" (v. 10).

This solemn truth is a reminder for us today to choose the best goal—living in a way that brings glory to Jesus Christ. Is that your goal?

—TOM FELTEN

 GAME PLAN: Write down three life goals. How do they fit into the ultimate goal of glorifying God?

SEPTEMBER 25

BATTLING BACK FROM THE BRINK

POINT OF EMPHASIS:
Trust God through trials

"We rejoice in our sufferings, because we know that suffering produces perseverance." ROMANS 5:3

My softball teammates and I felt confident as we headed into the 2000 Olympics in Sydney, Australia. As reigning Olympic Champions and World Champions, we knew what it took to win.

We never would have believed that halfway through the Games we would be on the brink of elimination.

After winning 112 games in a row, including the first two games in Sydney, we lost three straight games. One more loss and our team would be eliminated before the medal round.

After our third loss, a teammate read to the team out loud on the bus Romans 5:3–4, which says, "We also rejoice in our sufferings because we know that suffering produces perseverance; perseverance, character; and character, hope." We needed to persevere, and we needed hope.

We did persevere. We went on to beat Japan in the championship game, and we received the gold medals after the game.

In life you can receive a prize much greater than an Olympic gold medal, the prize of eternal life. After persevering through life's trials, you, like the apostle Paul, will be able to declare, "I have fought the good fight, I have finished the race, I have kept the faith. Now there is in store for me the crown of righteousness, which the Lord, the righteous Judge, will award to me on that day"(2 Timothy 4:7–8).

Despite the setbacks you might face today, keep trusting the Lord. He has a fantastic reward waiting for you in heaven.

—LEAH O'BRIEN-AMICO, OLYMPIC GOLD MEDALIST, SOFTBALL

SPORTS NOTE: Softball and soccer made their Olympic debut in the 1996 Olympics in Atlanta. The US won both.

FROM THE PLAYBOOK: Read James 1:2–18.

 GAME PLAN: What is your biggest struggle this week? Does it sometimes make you want to stop trusting God? Remember, that would be the worst thing you could ever do. Hold on.

EXTREME IRONERS?

POINT OF EMPHASIS:
The joy of giving

"Their extreme poverty welled up in rich generosity."
2 CORINTHIANS 8:2

Most extreme sports are way cool. They combine athleticism with some fresh events that sometime border on the danger zone. Then there's the extreme sport that involves an ironing board!

I'm serious.

Around the globe, enthusiasts of Extreme Ironing do their thing, according to a recent news report, "in remote, inhospitable, dangerous, or unusual locations."

The photo included with the report shows a guy suspended by a cable between two tall rock cliffs, ironing a piece of clothing. The board is somehow attached to him.

From Mount Rushmore to Times Square, you'll find these impressive (sorry) athletes getting the wrinkles out. In fact, if Phil Shaw of the Extreme Ironing Bureau has his way, Extreme Ironing will one day be an Olympic Sport.

The apostle Paul was into extreme stuff too. No, not ironing—he was into extreme giving. He commended the churches of Macedonia (like Philippi, Thessalonica, Berea) for their incredible generosity.

He put it this way: "Out of the most severe trial, their overflowing joy and their extreme poverty welled up in rich generosity" (2 Corinthians 8:2). Paul was proud of these believers in Jesus who had chosen to deny their own needs to help others.

They were in poverty, but they gave their stuff away like a rich person.

Is this the way you give to God and His work? Are you giving out of poverty or out of abundance?

God calls us to be extreme in our giving. When we take this step of faith, He is glorified and we are blessed. Take it to the extreme today. Press on!

—TOM FELTEN

SPORTS NOTE:
Do you think Tom is making this up? Go to www.extremeironing.com.

FROM THE PLAYBOOK:
Read 2 Corinthians 8:1–9.

GAME PLAN: Review your giving over the past month. Consider one person or work that is worthy of an extreme gift and send it off today.

GODLY INSPIRATION

POINT OF EMPHASIS:
Modeling Christ

"Follow my example, as I follow the example of Christ."
I CORINTHIANS 11:1

All coaches, whether they embrace the responsibility or not, play a role in directing and shaping the athletes they work with. Coaches either build up or tear players down. They empower or weaken others by their words and the example they set. They create an environment that inspires a person to excel or fail. Coaches demonstrate how to handle success and how to deal with losses; in short, they set the tone for the team.

Great coaches tap hidden potential and get the best investments on obvious talent. They give their athletes a vision of something larger than themselves and define a mission worth pursuing. They turn doubters into believers. Great coaches are strong leaders and inspire great results.

NFL punter Josh Bidwell says, "Without a question, my high school coach had the biggest influence on my life from a football perspective. He knew the game and brought out the best in the players. But the biggest factor for me was that he was a strong man of God with a tremendous amount of integrity that I admired. He never compromised his faith—that was first and foremost in his life. I think that spoke louder than anything. He was available to meet with me one-on-one to talk about my growth as a player, a Christian, and a person."

In I Corinthians 11:1 Paul says, "Follow my example as I follow the example of Christ." Josh Bidwell found an example in his coach of a man who follows Christ. Who in your life models a consistent Christian walk? What can you learn from that person?

—ROXANNE ROBBINS

SPORTS NOTE:
Josh spent the first five years of his NFL career with the Green Bay Packers.

FROM THE PLAYBOOK:
Read Titus 2.

GAME PLAN: Write a letter to a person who has influenced you to walk more closely with God because of their example. Thank them and give specific ways they have helped you mature in your own faith.

SEPTEMBER 28

WHEN I AM AFRAID

POINT OF EMPHASIS:
God's care

"The Lord is my helper; I will not be afraid." HEBREWS 13:6

Laura Wilkinson surprised everyone in Sydney, Australia, at the 2000 Olympic Games. She entered the finals of the platform diving competition of the Games in fifth place. There seemed to be no way Laura could reach the top of the field.

But as Wilkinson watched her competitors begin making major errors with their dives, she began to believe there was still a chance for her to win.

"I decided not to pay attention to the scoreboard," she says. "I was going to just put together my best list and do the best I could."

That was just the strategy Laura needed. She strung together five solid dives, and she won the gold medal.

SPORTS NOTE:
In 2000 Laura Wilkinson became the first American to win the gold in platform diving since 1964.

FROM THE PLAYBOOK:
Read Psalm 46.

What proved to be the greatest surprise of the night was still to come. While being interviewed following her final dive for Olympic glory, Laura was asked what she was thinking as she stood on the platform. She responded, "I can do all things through Christ who strengthens me" (Philippians 4:13 NKJV).

Wilkinson saw the power of God carry her through a time when she needed strength. "There are several Bible verses I keep close to me," she says. "When I get nervous or scared, I think of Isaiah 41:10. God promises to always be with me when I'm afraid. That means the impossible is possible," she says. "During the Olympics it was especially true."

We're not talking magic words here. We're talking about asking the God of the universe to work, through the Holy Spirit, in our lives. There is nothing that we cannot get through when we allow God's awesome presence to accompany us.

—DAVE BRANON

GAME PLAN: What do you fear the most? How often do you step back and pray, asking for God to calm your heart when that fear strikes?

GOD HAS A PLAN FOR YOU

POINT OF EMPHASIS:
God's plan

"All the days ordained for me were written in your book before one of them came to be." PSALM 139:16

For I know the plans I have for you,' declares the Lord, 'plans to prosper you and not to harm you, plans to give you a hope and a future'" (Jeremiah 29:11). Those words have taken on special meaning for me because they remind me how much God cares.

At the 2000 Olympic Games in Sydney, Australia, we had a very special batgirl for our game against Cuba. Katie, a sixteen-year-old from Texas, and her family were flown out to Australia to watch us play.

Although she looked completely healthy and wore a smile on her face, Katie had undergone the battle of her life. She had fought cancer, and when she was in Australia, Katie was in remission. She was involved in the Make-a-Wish Foundation, which had granted her wish to meet the United States Olympic softball team.

Before the game against Cuba, I asked her if she wanted to join our team in our pregame prayer, and she accepted. As I knelt down and prayed to the Lord, I was humbled by the peace of this young girl. The biggest worry for myself was winning a softball game, and this girl was and is fighting for her life.

Her strength, along with an important verse in God's Word, has taught me much about life. I can rejoice daily because I know that "all of the days ordained for me were written in [His] book before one of them came to be" (Psalm 139:16).

God has a plan for each person. I am thankful that I can trust each day to Him—both on earth and in eternity.

—LEAH O'BRIEN-AMICO, OLYMPIC GOLD MEDALIST, SOFTBALL

SPORTS NOTE:
In 2005, Leah planned to play for the Chicago Bandits of the National Pro Fastpitch League, but she had to miss the season while awaiting the birth of her second child.

FROM THE PLAYBOOK:
Read Psalm 139.

 GAME PLAN: What troubles you about today? Pray this prayer: "Lord, thank You for today. I know You've given it to me for a reason. Help me to enjoy it as a special gift from You. And help me to live for You today."

WHY ME IN 2003?

POINT OF EMPHASIS:
God's mysterious work

"Consider it pure joy, my brothers, whenever you face trials."
JAMES 1:2

When life is good, happiness is easy to find. But what about when times are difficult? How can we focus on the joy of the Lord when we are trying to deal with challenging times?

In 2003 I became the first major league pitcher to lose 20 games in one season since 1980. I cannot tell you why God chose me to go through that trial, but I can tell you that my faith is stronger because of it. When we are faced with trials, we can *attempt* to deal with it on our own, or we can draw closer to God. God does not allow us to struggle for punishment; rather, He desires to teach us. Trials are an opportunity to discover how God can work through our lives for good.

I learned how He is able to work through His children in the midst of challenging circumstances. Those around me watched to see how I would respond to the losses, and He provided many opportunities to share my faith with them. Although it was difficult, I remained close to the Lord and was able to handle my challenge in a way that was pleasing to Him. It required a daily commitment to pray and study His Word. Plus, the encouragement from other Christians was a blessing.

No matter what trial you are facing, let your joy be found in the knowledge that God is continually molding you into who He desires you to be. Be comforted by the fact that He will use you in a mighty way. Let your strength through trials bring glory to Christ!

—MIKE MAROTH, MAJOR LEAGUE PITCHER

SPORTS NOTE:
The Detroit Tigers lost 119 games in 2003, the second most losses ever by a major league team.

FROM THE PLAYBOOK:
Read James 1.

GAME PLAN: Your trials may be much worse than losing 21 baseball games or they may be not as troubling as that. List your top three trials and then see how God can be glorified even through them.

"THE THRILL OF VICTORY, THE AGONY OF DEFEAT"

POINT OF EMPHASIS:
Spiritual training

"No discipline seems pleasant." HEBREWS 12:11

If you ever played high school football, you'll appreciate this story, which comes from the 1930s—long before it was deemed illegal to offer monetary incentives to high school kids.

As psychologist and author James Dobson tells the story, a small-town team in Oklahoma had felt the agony of defeat all too often over the years. Finally a local car dealer decided the community had suffered enough. He asked to speak to the boys in the locker room following a Friday night loss. He gave one of the most dramatic and powerful locker room speeches of all time. He told the young men and their coaches that if they won the next game, he would give them each a brand new Ford. All they had to do was beat their bitter rivals. The team went wild with anticipation. For seven days the boys dreamed of winning and their new car. In fact, the entire school was caught up in it all.

Finally, the fateful Friday night arrived. The electricity of the moment sent a tingle through the stands as the boys ran onto the field. The coach gave them some last-minute instructions. Emotions and expectations were high as they kicked off. The final score? They lost 38 to 0.

What happened? The team was so pumped up, how could they possibly lose? In reality, a seven-day emotional high didn't make up for the team's lack of discipline. They had a losing record because they didn't do their conditioning drills or study their playbooks. So, without training and practice to back up their newfound emotion, they were still the same pitiful team.

On the field of our spiritual lives, it's the same. Second Timothy 2 says pursuing godly traits isn't always easy. But we need to work hard to achieve them—or we'll miss the thrill of daily spiritual victory.

—DAN DEAL

SPORTS NOTE: In 2004, there were 1,032,682 high school football players in the United States.

FROM THE PLAYBOOK: Take a look at Hebrews 12:11–12.

GAME PLAN: Ask the Lord to help you link the emotion and the discipline in your spiritual life. It will help you live a more successful and happier life in God.

LIVE A FRUITFUL LIFE

POINT OF EMPHASIS:
Fruitfulness

"The seed on good soil stands for those with a noble and good heart." LUKE 8:15

When Darrell Green entered the NFL as a young Christian kid, he immediately built friendships with some men of God on his team and made sure he planted himself with those people. As a result, his faith and maturity grew like that of a tree planted in fertile soil. His friends, who also desired to walk with God, helped provide nourishment and the pruning he needed and still needs in his life.

SPORTS NOTE:
Among the companies under the umbrella of Darrell Green Enterprises are the Darrell Green Youth Life Foundation and the Darrell Green Mortgage Company.

FROM THE PLAYBOOK:
Read Luke 8:1–15.

Green is thankful for the maturing process God continues to work in him as he grows in the fertile soil consisting of godly counsel, godly fellowship, and time in Scripture and prayer. Of course, it's not always easy. He still falls short and has to be set straight—as we all do. Each of us has to, on occasion, go to someone and admit a fault and turn to God for help. Green is thankful he has an advocate with God. If we confess our sins, God is faithful and just to forgive us.

As our lives and actions are motivated by the biblical principles of living, dealing with finances, loving others, training our children, and serving others, we will produce a crop that brings glory to God. Consider the type of crop your life is producing. Today, make an effort to spend time with people who help you grow in fertile soil. Pray that God will prune away the weeds that are choking your faith.

—ROXANNE ROBBINS

GAME PLAN: Today, thank a friend who has helped provide spiritual nourishment and pruning in your life.

COLBY AND KRISPY KREME

POINT OF EMPHASIS:
Knowing Jesus

"Here I am! I stand at the door and knock." REVELATION 3:20

My son Colby's favorite part of our family's trip to Disney World was stopping at the Krispy Kreme doughnut shop before we even left our hometown.

Colby's my buddy and he loves to eat. Even at the age of three he could spot the "HOT" sign inside the Krispy Kreme shop from quite a distance away. Upon his arrival, though, the sign (which indicates freshly cooked doughnuts have just been put out) gets little attention as he sprints inside to the greater reality . . . or the best things—fresh doughnuts.

Jesus flashed signs as well. They were wonders and miracles that proved his messiahship. He finished with the ultimate sign of defeating death on a cross, an act that separates Him from all other religious leaders and qualifies Him as who He said He was—God.

Although the signs are great, they are not the best things. The best things are the greater realities that the signs themselves point out. The fact is, trusting in Him gives us access to the Father, who is crazy about us and accepts us with all our baggage. The greater reality is that Jesus calls us His home and fellowships with us as a friend, lover, and brother. The truth is, we can listen to the comforting instincts of the Holy Spirit, who reveals to us that we can rest from our works of trying to be a good person and trust in the finished work of the cross.

Early in my walk with the Lord, I desired knowledge and I memorized the signs like the back of my hand. But as I grew, I began to seek the "doughnuts" or intimate fellowship with Him. I desperately desired the greater realities of eating with a person who laid down His life for me.

—PAUL BYRD, MAJOR LEAGUE PITCHER

SPORTS NOTE:
While at LSU, Paul Byrd set the record for most wins by a pitcher in one season (17). It was at LSU that Byrd trusted Jesus as Savior.

FROM THE PLAYBOOK:
Read Ephesians 2.

GAME PLAN: What realities of your relationship with Christ have you enjoyed recently? List three things about that relationship that you especially enjoy.

INVITE GOD IN

POINT OF EMPHASIS:
Giving God the glory

"In him and through faith in him we may approach God with freedom and confidence." EPHESIANS 3:12

Throughout my football career at the University of Florida, the annual game against our Southeastern Conference (SEC) rival Georgia was always a heated contest.

In the pregame of the 1995 contest, I couldn't seem to loosen up properly. My mechanics were off, and my arm just never seemed to get on track. I tried everything, but nothing seemed to help. The receivers and coaches were obviously concerned as we returned to the locker room moments before kickoff.

Filled with anxiety, I knelt by my locker to pray. I confessed, "Lord, I've tried everything, and it hasn't worked. I desperately need Your help. Whatever happens, good or bad, will be all for Your glory."

That day I learned a far more subtle and much deeper lesson than I could have imagined.

Statistically speaking, I played the best game of my career, throwing four touchdowns and leading us to an incredible victory. Now, I know that God can and sometimes will answer prayers in that manner, but I also know that God isn't a genie—granting us our every desire. I have also prayed and then played poorly. What I *really* learned is an incredible truth about being a follower of Christ in life.

At some point in our lives, we have to come before Him and confess, "Lord, I've tried my best at this game of life, and it's not working as I know it should. I need you to come in, transform me, and work through me. And whatever happens, good or bad, will be for Your glory."

May God bless us as we invite Him in and turn our lives over to Him.

—DANNY WUERFFEL, FORMER NFL QUARTERBACK

SPORTS NOTE:
Danny is director of development at Desire Street Ministries, an organization with a school, a pediatric clinic, and an outreach program in New Orleans' inner city.

FROM THE PLAYBOOK:
Read about dedicating yourself to being committed to God in Psalm 40:1–8.

GAME PLAN: Are you willing to turn each part of your life over to God? Write down three areas that you need to hand over to Him right away.

TOUGH CHRISTIANS

POINT OF EMPHASIS:
Toughness and faith

"Everyone who competes in the games goes into strict training. They do it to get a crown that will not last; but we do it to get a crown that will last forever." I Corinthians 9:25

Every year there comes a part of the season that is truly tough, and that time is training camp. Someone may look at what basketball players do at the beginning of the season and ask, "Why do they call it 'training camp'?"

It's simple. This is the time when all the hard work that was put in during the summer comes to fruition. This is the beginning of a very long season, but it brings all the hard work together so that the outcome will be good.

It takes time, dedication, and some pain to insure that everything will be right for the season. In sports, we train our minds and bodies very hard for something that will come to an end one day.

But what about our souls, which will last forever? When conviction or spiritual warfare brings pain, do we quit or do we endure? When we can't see our dreams further than tomorrow, do we quit or do we endure?

We need training camp for the soul. Training camp for the soul is the renewing of the heart, mind, and spirit through prayer, Bible study, and fellowship with other believers. This type of training brings toughness that will overcome the barriers we face on an everyday basis—barriers that seemingly tear down our bodies. Plainly and simply, the Word of God makes you tough.

Are you training to be a tough Christian? Don't slack off. The hard work will be worth it!

—Charlie Ward, former NBA guard

SPORTS NOTE:
Despite winning the Heisman Trophy, Charlie Ward was not drafted by an NFL team. So, he went to the NBA.

FROM THE PLAYBOOK:
Read 2 Corinthians 9:24–27.

 GAME PLAN: Are you training with a purpose? Are you training to be tough? Study your Bible, memorize Scripture, and get plugged in with a Bible-believing church. Learn toughness from the toughest guy this universe will ever know: Jesus Christ!

TACKLING TEMPTATION

POINT OF EMPHASIS:
Temptation

"He will . . . provide a way out." I CORINTHIANS 10:13

If you follow sports closely, you know that temptation has tripped up many good athletes. Even some who profess to know Jesus Christ as Savior have stumbled along the way by succumbing to a temptation.

One former NFL player who is concerned about this is Ken Ruettgers, who played for the Green Bay Packers for twelve seasons. And he has an idea why it happens to some athletes. "Everyone around you tells you how great you are. But there's so much insecurity in sports. One day you're a hero, and the next day you're a zero. Players are looking for affirmation. It lends itself to being vulnerable to temptation."

SPORTS NOTE:
Many Christian pro athletes develop accountability partners to help them deal with on-the-road temptations that could draw them from their relationship with God.

FROM THE PLAYBOOK:
Read Genesis 39:1–12.

The same thing that threatens pro athletes threatens the rest of us, and we need to know how to avoid trouble. Here is what some pro athletes suggest can help us tackle temptation:

Bob Christian, former NFL running back: "Everyone needs people to go to and to be honest with. In the body of Christ we need people to ask us tough questions."

Jason Elam, NFL kicker: "More than anything, you've got to set aside time every day to pray. You've got to read and study the Word."

Travis Fryman, former major league infielder: "The best way to avoid temptation is to try not to be subjected to it. There are obvious situations and places to avoid and conversations you don't need to be in."

And finally, Paul, first-century clean-up man: "No temptation has seized you except what is common to man. God is faithful; he will not let you be tempted beyond what you can bear" (1 Corinthians 10:13).

Tackle temptation before it tackles you.

—DAVE BRANON

GAME PLAN: What tempts you the most? Do you find ways to gravitate toward that temptation or away from it? Each time you step toward it, ask God to turn you around.

PRACTICING THE BASICS

POINT OF EMPHASIS:
The basics of the faith

"So then, just as you received Christ Jesus as Lord, continue to live in him." COLOSSIANS 2:6

In golf, it helps me to watch players like Tiger Woods swing the golf club. I think if I devoted enough time to observing the truly great players, my golf game would dramatically improve. Once I envision what a good swing looks like, it gives me a new perspective when I look at my own swing.

But there is more to it than watching. Tiger's coach, Butch Harmon, says there is really no secret to Tiger's success. He says Tiger, for the most part, has been working on the same things for the past seven years. Butch says there are problem areas Tiger has a tendency to slip back into if he is not continually working on the fundamentals of his swing.

Just like Tiger Woods has certain tendencies in his swing that, if left unchecked, can become a problem, so does each of us have a tendency to sin—and that will result in disaster.

Our desire and vision for Christlike living should not be focused on our own "swing." Instead it must be focused on Jesus Christ who is perfect in every way. Paul told us, "Just as you received Christ Jesus as Lord, continue to live in him, rooted and built up in him" (Colossians 2:6). Our imitation of Jesus is not merely found in outward acts of kindness and mercy, but it is first an inward attitude of humility toward God—which brings confidence, peace, and hope that the "world" does not know.

Tiger is continually working on his swing. In the same way we would do well to pursue with intensity a continual improvement of our relationship with Jesus Christ.

—FRANK REICH, FORMER NFL QUARTERBACK

SPORTS NOTE:
Tiger Woods has a book called *How I Play Golf* in which he shares some of his secrets to mastering the links.

FROM THE PLAYBOOK:
Read Colossians 2:6–12.

 GAME PLAN: Write down three steps you would like to take to enhance your relationship with Jesus Christ.

OCTOBER 8

GIVING BACK

POINT OF EMPHASIS:
Christian charity

"From everyone who has been given much, much will be demanded." LUKE 12:48

Many professional and Olympic athletes around the country have taken the essence of Luke 12:48 to heart and are using their gifts and talents to invest in the lives of others.

Former Denver Bronco player Steve Fitzhugh, for example, uses the leadership skills he cultivated as a professional athlete to direct "The House," an after-school center for underserved youth in southeast Washington, DC.

FROM THE PLAYBOOK:
Read Luke 12:35–48.

Retired San Antonio Spurs center David Robinson and his wife Valerie put up $7 million of their own money to start the Carver School, a charter school serving needy families in San Antonio.

Derrick Brooks, who played a big role in helping the Tampa Bay Buccaneers clinch Super Bowl XXXVII, started "Brooks Bunch." Derrick partners with the local Boys and Girls Clubs to conduct an after-school educational program. He secures certified teachers to teach the students about various parts of the world. At the end of each school year, Derrick takes qualified students on a field trip as a reward. A few summers ago Derrick took 21 kids to South Africa! And he recruited former Bucs head coach Tony Dungy and Tony's wife Lauren to go along as chaperones.

Former World Series pitcher Dave Dravecky and his wife Jan founded and direct a ministry called "Outreach of Hope," which offers resources and biblical encouragement for cancer patients and amputees.

Former tennis star Andrea Jaeger is reaching out to cancer patients [children] through the "Silver Lining Foundation" she established and directs in Aspen, Colorado.

What are you doing with the gifts and talents you've been given? Are you blessing others by sharing what God's given you? — ROXANNE ROBBINS

GAME PLAN: Think of people who inspire you by their example of serving others. How can you follow in their footsteps?

IT'S A DOG-EAT-DOG WORLD

POINT OF EMPHASIS:
The battle within

"The fruit of the Spirit is love." GALATIANS 5:22

Once upon a time, as the story goes, two big, bad dogs happened upon each other in a city alley. These two dogs had controlled the turf in their area of the city. They knew they could not co-exist in this neighborhood, so they began to brace for a bloody duel.

People began to ask, "Which dog will win?"

One man stated, "The dog that wins is the dog that's fed!" When you parallel his answer to our spiritual condition, you see that this man was truly wise.

Before I became a Christian, I had one big, bad dog living inside of me. I call him the "Flesh Dog." Flesh Dog is bent on evil from the get-go. He growls out demands that his fleshly desires be satisfied. Read Galatians 5:18–21, which describes what I call the "Flesh Dog."

When I trusted Jesus Christ as my Savior for eternal life, I found a better companion. His name was the Spirit, and He (God the Holy Spirit) took residence inside of me. The Spirit is perfect. He produces beautiful fruit inside—the attitudes of Jesus Himself. Read Galatians 5:22–23 describing what I like to call the "Spirit Dog."

These two "dogs" square off at each other inside of me every day of my life. Which will win? The one that's fed! To live in victory for Christ I must continually feed the Spirit by

- Daily studying God's Word and praying—don't miss.
- Surrounding myself with godly people.
- Continually thinking, speaking, and doing God's Word day and night.

Since you woke up this morning, have you been feeding the flesh or the Spirit?   —RON BROWN, FORMER COLLEGE FOOTBALL COACH

SPORTS NOTE: Ron Brown has a Christian sports radio program on the ESPN radio station in Lincoln, Nebraska. It is called *Goin' Deep*.

FROM THE PLAYBOOK: Read Galatians 5.

GAME PLAN: The work of being saved was done by Jesus Christ on the cross, and the work of giving us power to live daily for Him is done by the Holy Spirit. Are you allowing the Spirit to be your guide, or is something else controlling your life?

OCTOBER 10

KEEP YOUR EYES ON THE PRIZE

POINT OF EMPHASIS:
Keep Christ in sight

"I press on toward the goal to win the prize for which God has called me heavenward in Christ Jesus." PHILIPPIANS 3:14

In 1 Corinthians 9:24–27, Paul depicts a race worth running and a prize worth receiving. In that passage, he gives us some incredible insights into the race, the rules of competition, and the finish.

When entering any type of competition, such as life, we need to understand what we are competing for. For example, if I go into a football season without knowing that my goal is the playoffs or the Super Bowl, the games every week become monotonous and insignificant.

Paul states that in the race God calls us to run there is a prize to be won. It is essential that we as Christians understand what that prize is. Paul proclaimed, "To live is Christ" (Philippians 1:21) and "I press toward . . . the upward call of God in Christ Jesus" (Philippians 3:14 NKJV). We must know that the prize is Christ Himself. Yes, we can receive eternal life. Yes, we can receive forgiveness. Yes, we can receive peace. Yes, we experience love. But the ultimate prize to obtain is Christ alone.

Jesus Christ represents all righteousness and all that is good on earth and in heaven. HE is eternal life. HE is love. HE is peace. HE is in control of all things. Jesus said I AM, and He is!

SPORTS NOTE:
John Burrough played three seasons for the Atlanta Falcons and two seasons for the Minnesota Vikings.

FROM THE PLAYBOOK:
Read John 10:14–16.

Knowing that He is the prize is an awesome wonder. It gives us the ultimate goal to strive for. It gives our life meaning.

Running this race called life becomes breathtaking when we understand what is at stake. In Philippians 3:13 Paul says we should be "forgetting those things which are behind and reaching forward to those things which are ahead." Look ahead to the prize. Look ahead to Christ!

—JOHN BURROUGH, FORMER NFL DEFENSIVE END

GAME PLAN: If you live by the motto "To live is Christ," what are three areas of your life that will be affected?

WHAT'S YOUR FOCUS?

POINT OF EMPHASIS:
Focus on Christ

"Do you not know that in a race all the runners run, but only one gets the prize? Run in such a way as to get the prize." I CORINTHIANS 9:24

In the passage we are examining in these four devotional articles for October 10 through 13 (1 Corinthians 9:24–27), the apostle Paul illustrates the importance of running a race with the end goal in mind at all times.

In yesterday's devotional, we saw that we are running the race with Christ as the ultimate prize. Life can be difficult at times, and it can be even harder if your concentration is always focused on your present situation. A friend once told me, "Obstacles are what you see when you take your eyes off your goal."

Often we are so consumed with where we are that we have no opportunity to see where we are going.

If the object of focus is on you, it creates a selfish perspective. But your success cannot be determined by looking inwardly and comparing yourself with others. This philosophy takes your focus away from God, where it must be, and places it on you. When you take your eyes off Jesus, you lose sight of the significance of your life.

If Paul, Timothy, Barnabas, and Luke are playing a round of golf in which Paul and Luke both shoot 86, Barnabas shoots 79, and Timothy shoots 75, who wins? In reality no one wins. Why? Because the goal is par—and no one achieved it!

My encouragement for you is that you avoid comparing yourself with others around you. Always look to the prize ahead, which is Christ alone. Comparing yourselves with others is foolishness, and it causes you to embrace the wrong standard.

Christ is the standard, and nothing less will do! Keep your focus on Christ! That will give you the proper perspective.

—JOHN BURROUGH, FORMER NFL DEFENSIVE END

SPORTS NOTE: John Burrough transferred to Wyoming after one year at Washington State. He was a second team all-Western Athletic Conference selection during his senior year.

FROM THE PLAYBOOK: Read Luke 9:23–27.

GAME PLAN: What are some ways you compare yourself with others spiritually? How can you stop doing that and concentrate on Jesus?

DON'T GIVE UP!

POINT OF EMPHASIS:
Diligence

"Everyone who competes in the games goes into strict training."
1 CORINTHIANS 9:25

In 1 Corinthians 9:24–27 Paul writes about preparing for the great race of life with diligent determination and perseverance. Because we know that Christ is the prize, our focus throughout must remain on Him.

The illustration Paul is referring to when he writes about "the games" in verse 25 is the Isthmian or Corinthian Games. The Olympic Games were the most celebrated, but the Isthmian Games were of the same style. Athletes persevered through intense, yearly training to compete, as do athletes today.

SPORTS NOTE:
John Burrough graduated from the University of Wyoming with a degree in geophysics.

FROM THE PLAYBOOK:
Read about Jesus' example in Mark 10:43–45.

In Paul's illustration, he teaches us to approach the Christian life in the same manner. We must train our minds and bodies through perseverance and determination for the call of Christ. *The New Ungers Bible Dictionary* describes *perseverance* as "the duty and privilege of a Christian to continue steadfastly in obedience and fidelity to Christ, not in order to inherit eternal life, but to demonstrate our love and gratitude for Christ."

Here are some ways you can do that: Persevere in seeking God's will daily. Diligently determine the course God has chosen for you each day. Run the race in this manner; know that Christ is the prize, focus your perspective on Christ throughout the race, and prepare with perseverance and determination. This allows you, as a Christian, to experience the risen Lord in all His majesty.

Paul's whole passion is his focus on Christ. In life's race, our focus must always be on Jesus! Our daily preparation for living must focus on Him. Our race strategy must focus on Him. Our perspective must focus on Him. The prize we are reaching for must be Jesus.

Getting the picture? It's all about JESUS!

—JOHN BURROUGH, FORMER NFL DEFENSIVE END

GAME PLAN: What aspects of the Christian life take the most perseverance for you? Make those challenges a part of your daily goal of drawing closer to Jesus.

GO FOR THE LASTING POWER!

POINT OF EMPHASIS:
God's power

"I will boast all the more gladly about my weaknesses, so that Christ's power may rest on me." 2 CORINTHIANS 12:9

We've been talking about I Corinthians 9:24–27, which describes the preparation, perspective, and perseverance for the race of life. We know the prize is Christ himself, and we understand that the focus must remain on Him. The remaining question is this: How do we maintain focus during the race?

Athletes receive inspiration from the crowd's roar while competing, but when the game is over the applause ceases.

Where does our validation, inspiration, and true strength come from? What can we trust in that will sustain us through all of the games of life? The applause of heaven must be what we seek. Why? Because how much more do you think your Father cheers for you than does your fellow man?

The strength to sustain and excel must come from the only "true" Power—the same Power that breathed the heavens and earth into existence! The same Power that made you and me! The same Power that sent His only Son to be crucified! The same Power that raised Jesus on the third day and allowed Him to ascend into heaven! The same Power that defeated death, hell, and the grave! The same Power, through faith and trust in Jesus Christ, now resides in us through the Holy Spirit!

You want lasting power? You want supernatural strength? Trust in God's power that lives within you. Then, and only then, will you have the ability to sustain and maintain focus in the race of life?

When you stop living just *for* Him and truly start living *from* Him, His power and majesty become the unyielding inspiration that drives you daily!

—JOHN BURROUGH, FORMER NFL DEFENSIVE END

SPORTS NOTE:
In 1999 John Burrough was voted one of the 50 top players in Wyoming sports history.

FROM THE PLAYBOOK:
Read 2 Corinthians 12:7–10.

GAME PLAN: How has God's power been manifest in your life recently?

"ONLY GOD CAN HELP"

POINT OF EMPHASIS:
God's help

"Set your minds on things above." COLOSSIANS 3:2

Imagine you're an eight-year-old with dreams of playing pro ball one day.

Imagine you are gifted in football and you have a great high school and college career.

Imagine you then become the first African-American to start at quarterback in the NFL.

Imagine twenty years later being homeless and living on the streets.

Stop imagining. It happened.

Just a few years ago, former Pittsburgh Steelers quarterback Joe Gilliam Jr. was discovered begging on the streets of Nashville. His life, since leaving the game back in 1975 after four seasons, was difficult. His police record—several arrests—was more imposing than his football records are impressive.

How does someone sink so low? "Sometimes I like myself and sometimes I don't," said Joe, who admitted to continued drug abuse. Then he said, "Only God can help."

A long time ago, another man needed help—Amaziah, king of Judah. He had made the bad choice to hire 100,000 Israelite mercenaries to do battle for him. But a man of God told him this was wrong and that "the Lord can give you much more than that" (2 Chronicles 25:9).

Amaziah listened and obeyed. At first. But a short time later he began worshiping pagan idols. His life became a nightmare. First he lost his throne—then his life.

Joe Gilliam Jr. was right when he said, "Only God can help." But recognizing who God is (which King Amaziah did at one time) and choosing to obey Him are two different things.

If you want to keep your life in the game and out of the gutter, set your mind on things above. Strive to obey God. He will give you so much more than anything the world can offer.

—TOM FELTEN

SPORTS NOTE:
Joe Gilliam Jr. died in early 2001 at the age of 49.

FROM THE PLAYBOOK:
Read 2 Chronicles 25.

GAME PLAN: Take your biggest problem and give it to God. Write a note to yourself about this, seal it, and don't look at it for a week. Then open it and see how God has helped you with it.

WATCH YOUR MOUTH

POINT OF EMPHASIS:
Controlling the tongue

"The Lord said to [Moses], 'Who gave man his mouth?'" Exodus 4:11

It is commonplace these days to be watching a televised sporting event in which the cameras zoom in on two athletes "trash talking" one another. Often the exchange is examined in a replay so the announcers can get a sense of how it started. Words can certainly draw attention to the individuals involved in the verbal skirmish.

There are many verses in the Bible that address the significance of the words we speak. For example, Ephesians 4:29 says, "Do not let any unwholesome talk come out of your mouths, but only what is helpful for building others up according to their needs, that it may benefit those who listen." Clearly, Paul's words tell us that God cares what we say and how our words affect those around us.

Isn't it interesting, though, as James pointed out, that "out of the same mouth come praise and cursing"? (James 3:10). We praise God and curse men (or vice versa) with the same mouth. What an irony!

During the course of our lives, there will inevitably be situations that test our self-control, especially in the midst of heated sports competition. Sometimes, we lose control of our thoughts and then our mouths when we are tired, off-guard, and vulnerable.

That's why we must train ourselves now—in the cool sensibility of a calm moment far from the heat of battle—to be pure in speech and deed. People are watching, and your example could either be cause for praising or cursing. It could lead them to or away from the Savior.

That's why we must watch what we say.

—Jean Driscoll, eight-time Boston Marathon champion

SPORTS NOTE:
A young man with a very accurate arm once said to his very tall and strong opponent, "I'll strike you down and cut off your head." David trash-talked Goliath and then delivered on his words.

FROM THE PLAYBOOK:
Read James 3:4–11.

GAME PLAN: Can you think of a time when you lost control of your words? What kind of damage did you cause? Why are the words you speak important to God?

OCTOBER 16

WITNESSING WHEREVER

POINT OF EMPHASIS:
Witnessing

"Then the disciples went out and preached everywhere." MARK 16:20

It was the seventh game of the 1962 World Series. The San Francisco Giants had a man on second base, which put him near New York Yankee second baseman Bobby Richardson. When the Yanks decided to change pitchers, Richardson, who was a Christian, saw a unique opportunity. While the new pitcher was warming up, he walked over to the man on second base and asked him if he knew Jesus as his Savior.

When the runner reached the dugout later, he asked teammate Felipe Alou, who was also a Christian, what was going on. "Even in the seventh game of the World Series," he said to Felipe, "you people are still talking about Jesus." That runner couldn't understand what made Christians so eager to talk about Jesus Christ, even in highly unusual situations.

Bobby Richardson's World Series witness is a 20th-century example of what Mark was writing about when he said that the disciples "went out and preached everywhere." We sometimes think pulpits are the only places from which to tell the good news of Christ. But our message is too important to keep quiet. Richardson witnessed at second base during a break in a baseball game.

Are we as ready and willing to show with our life and tell with our lips the difference Jesus can make?

"Lord, help us see and seize opportunities to witness wherever we are."

—DAVE BRANON

SPORTS NOTE:
Bobby Richardson, MVP of the 1960 World Series, set a record in that Series with 12 runs batted in. Richardson's New York Yankees lost the Series to the Pittsburgh Pirates when Bill Mazeroski hit a game-winning home run in Game 7.

FROM THE PLAYBOOK:
Read Mark 16:14–20.

GAME PLAN: When was the last time you shared the good news of Jesus Christ with someone? How can you improve and increase your witness for the Lord?

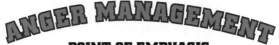

POINT OF EMPHASIS:
Controlling anger

"Anyone who is angry with his brother will be subject to judgment."
MATTHEW 5:22

Skirmishes. As a sports fan, we've all seen more than a few "dust-ups." Perhaps it was a bench-clearing brawl in baseball following a brush-back pitch, or maybe it was a gloves-off showdown on the ice after a hard check into the boards. Whatever the battle, the world of sports is often punctuated with anger-filled, fists-flying, bloody-nose action.

While sports fans seem to thrive on the excitement of an old-fashioned brouhaha, the core issue of an on-field battle is much more serious than we often recognize.

As followers of Jesus Christ, you and I must look deeper than the action that entices a fight. The core issue doesn't begin with a tight pitch or a tough check. These are symptoms of a problem that's rooted much deeper—it's called anger. And it's rooted in our heart.

What does the Bible teach us about anger?

Simply stated, anger is dangerous. According to Jesus, a heart filled with anger is sinful. In the gospel of Matthew 5:21–22, Jesus talks about the severity of anger. "You have heard that it was said to the people long ago, 'Do not murder, and anyone who murders will be subject to judgment.' But I tell you that anyone who is angry with his brother will be subject to judgment."

We often overlook the severity of anger. Yet it is subject to judgment. That's why we must be careful to manage anger properly. We must deal with it in our lives and make sure it does not lead us to actions worthy of God's judgment on us.
—ROB BENTZ

SPORTS NOTE: The NBA rules regarding players and spectators says, "Any coach, player or trainer who deliberately enters the spectator stands during the game will be automatically ejected and the incident reported by e-mail to the Commissioner."

FROM THE PLAYBOOK: Read Matthew 5:21–26.

GAME PLAN: How do you respond when someone wrongs you? How do you handle the brush-back pitch or the hard checks that you face every day? Do you respond with anger? If you do, here's a biblical response. Recognize your anger-filled response as sin, repent of it, ask for God's forgiveness, and pray that God will give you a pure heart.

FIRE AND ICE

POINT OF EMPHASIS:
God's leading

"[God] sent His Son." 1 JOHN 4:9

Bob Bassen enjoyed a respectable career in the NHL, playing for several teams until he retired in 2000. His career on the ice was also marked by an exceptional story of love. While he was with the Dallas Stars but recuperating from a knee injury, he was sitting near the arena ice watching a game when he met a woman who worked in the Stars' office. Her name was Holly Yarbrough.

They struck up a conversation, then a friendship, and then a romance. They eventually married, and Bob moved on to play his final two years—one in Canada and one in St. Louis.

While the ice played a key part in Bob's life, fire also had its role. It was at a bonfire at his church when he was 12 that he trusted Jesus Christ as His Savior.

On that night, the pastor had preached a message from John 3:16.

Bob tells what happened. "I heard that verse, 'For God so loved the world that he gave his one and only Son, that whoever believes in him shall not perish but have eternal life.' I mean, everybody knows that verse. But when the pastor explained eternal life, I couldn't understand it. But I wanted it. I don't think anyone can really fathom everlasting life, but it sounded good. At that bonfire service I accepted Christ."

On the ice, Bassen found a career and his wife. At the fire, he found eternal life.

Fire and ice were a pretty good combination for Bob. God leads us to Himself and to the really important things in life in a variety of ways, doesn't He? It's up to us to look for them—to listen for His voice as He calls us wherever we are.

—DAVE BRANON

SPORTS NOTE:
Bob Bassen played in 767 NHL games and scored 232 points.

FROM THE PLAYBOOK:
Read John 3.

GAME PLAN: Have you found the eternal life Bob was talking about? Nothing you can ever do is more important than to trust Jesus and have your sins forgiven.

THE BIG HOUSE

POINT OF EMPHASIS:
Looking forward to heaven

"That I may dwell in the house of the Lord." PSALM 27:4

Although the University of Michigan has laid claim to the term "The Big House" for its gargantuan stadium in Ann Arbor, every team knows what it means to have home-field advantage.

Of course at Michigan it helps to have 111,000 of your closest friends screaming for you to succeed, but it goes beyond that. When you go into your own version of The Big House, you have numerous advantages.

For one, when you're home, the enemy is not welcome. For another, you'll have a hoard of people supporting your efforts. You have your own pep band, your own announcers, your very own locker in your own locker room. There's nothing quite like home field-advantage in your version of The Big House.

Well, except in what we might call The Really Big House.

David talked about it. He said, "I love the house where you live, O Lord, the place where your glory dwells" (Psalm 26:8). To the people of Israel, The Big House was the temple, because God with all His glory, strength, power, love, and caring was there. If the Israelites left Jerusalem, they knew that when they returned, they could visit the temple and be at the advantage over their enemies.

One day, we who have trusted Christ will live in the glory and majesty of which the Israelites received a taste. When we go to God's Ultimate Big House, to heaven, we will be in His presence. No enemy can defeat us there, and we will have every advantage of being at home—forever.

There's no bigger home-field advantage than to be in the very presence of God in the place He has built for us.

—DAVE BRANON

SPORTS NOTE: When Michigan Stadium was built in 1927, it held 72,000 people. In the first game at the stadium, Michigan beat Ohio Wesleyan 33–0.

FROM THE PLAYBOOK: Read Psalm 27.

GAME PLAN: You don't go to a temple; you go to a church. Is your church a little bit of heaven, where Christians love each other? What can help you to look forward to heaven?

CAPTAIN ENCOURAGEMENT

POINT OF EMPHASIS:
Encouraging others

"Speaking the truth in love, we will . . . grow up." EPHESIANS 4:15-16

In 2003 I was selected as the new captain of the Phoenix Coyotes, which is both a great honor and a great responsibility.

When it comes to team motivation, there is a range of styles. I could jump on every little mistake and tear guys apart in front of the team, or I could pat everyone on the back and say "Good job," no matter what. But neither approach helps a team be the best. The first one chips away at the players' confidence; the second excuses any need for improvement.

SPORTS NOTE:
In 2004, Shane Doan was runner-up to Jarome Iginla of the Calgary Flames for the NHL Foundation Player Award, given to the player who does the most to enhance life in his community.

FROM THE PLAYBOOK:
Read 1 Thessalonians 5:11–15.

I found it difficult at first to be more vocal with the players about their game. By nature I am an encourager. I'd love to be able to just highlight the positives and tell everyone they are doing great. But if I am going to do the best for my team, sometimes that requires talking with a player about areas where he is struggling, and challenging him to improve.

In Ephesians 4:15–16, Paul wrote about the need for us to grow up as believers and grow together as one body in Christ, each depending on the other. This is a great model for team building. As believers, we will never grow into a complete body unless we are willing to speak God's truth to one another—not to find fault and tear down in judgment, but to counsel and encourage, in humility and *in love*.

Who are the people that have most encouraged your growth in the Lord? What was it they said or did that was most effective? Is there someone in your circle of believers who needs that encouragement from you?

—SHANE DOAN, CENTER

 GAME PLAN: Are there some people you need to send an e-mail to today, just to let them know you think they are pretty important? Make a note of it, and be an encourager.

WHAT GOD CAN BUILD

POINT OF EMPHASIS:
God's incredible creation

"O Lord my God, you are very great." PSALM 104:1

A re you proud of your favorite team's stadium?

Many sports fans are, but perhaps the proudest were the folks in Houston in the mid-1960s when they saw The Eighth Wonder of the World—the Houston Astrodome. It was a brand-new concept back then—an indoor place to play football and baseball. It was an awe-inspiring structure.

We're pretty clever when it comes to designing sports stadiums. We've even got retractable domes now. We've built some great monuments to sports.

But our efforts are puny compared with what God has built using His creative power. Psalm 104 reminds us what God can build, and it's a far cry better than Paul Brown Stadium or the Pepsi Center. Consider what God builds:

SPORTS NOTE: The Houston Astrodome was built in 1965 for about $35 million.

FROM THE PLAYBOOK: Read Psalm 104.

- He stretches out the skies like a tent.
- He built a home for Himself in the heavens.
- He created the wind, the rain, and fire.
- He divided the waters into rivers and oceans.
- He created watering places for the animals, which are his handiwork.
- He planted food to feed His animals and His special creation: mankind.
- He decorated His world with trees and birds, and He made special animals to inhabit harsh places.

No matter what great sports structures we create—even Wrigley Field—let us not for a moment forget that we are subcontractors to the master builder. We are not even rough-in guys compared to the great designer. We cannot approach for a moment the unmatchable creativity of our creator-God. That reality made the psalmist say, "I will sing praise to my God as long as I live" (Psalm 104:33).

He created the first dome—and he called it the heavens. Praise God!

—DAVE BRANON

GAME PLAN: Have you ever sat back and really contemplated the majesty of God's creation? What are some of the most awe-inspiring, worship-causing elements of our Creator's design in your thinking?

BUCHAREST PERSPECTIVE

POINT OF EMPHASIS:
Helping others

"Has not God chosen those who are poor in the eyes of the world to be rich in faith?" JAMES 2:5

*H*all of Fame golfer Betsy King has given of herself for the past few years travel-ing to Europe—especially to Romania—to help children and provide spiritual assistance. She tells about one such experience.

Eight other players on the LPGA Tour and I first went to Romania not knowing exactly what we would be doing. We were with a group that had been involved in adoptions of children in the United States.

The first time we went, we stayed with families and visited orphanages. We got to meet quite a few children, and we played with the kids and supplied some support to the ministry that was working there.

SPORTS NOTE:
In 1989, Betsy was named *Golf World* magazine's Player of the Year.

FROM THE PLAYBOOK:
Read James 2:1–13.

The second time we went, we again went to some orphanages and to a hospital. We sang for the children, which wasn't our forte. We sang for youth groups and at a formal church service in Bucharest.

The thing that stands out as we take these trips is the word *perspective*. We have to put things into perspective in terms of what's really important in life.

The first year, I went to Romania after winning a tour-nament in Japan, and within 48 hours I was on the streets of Bucharest, meeting street kids—kids as young as five years old who had no place to live. God used that to show me that winning a golf tournament isn't all that important.

We sang the song, "Give Thanks," and one of the lines is "let the poor say I am rich," and for them, it is so true. They're so financially poor, yet they're rich in their faith and commitment to the Lord.

Now, that's a great perspective!

—BETSY KING, LPGA GOLFER

GAME PLAN: Have you thought about being involved in some kind of missions trip? Why not plan to see if you can put that in your schedule for next year.

LIFE OVER FOOTBALL

POINT OF EMPHASIS:
Keeping right priorities

"Now may the Lord of peace himself give you peace at all times."
2 THESSALONIANS 3:16

After battling injuries throughout his college career, California-Davis placekicker David Forester was healthy and looking forward to his senior season in 2001. Finally, he would be able to contribute the way he had hoped.

Then younger brother Tommy's body rejected the kidney their father gave Tommy in 1993. Dialysis was required. A new donor was needed. Mom wasn't a good match. The Foresters had hoped Tommy's siblings—Jimmy, David, and Beth—would not be needed as donors, at least for many years.

"I felt the Lord calling me to pursue this," David says. "I talked with my mom, and we decided we'd all test. If we got a really close match, maybe we'd never have to do this again. I was by far the closest tissue match."

When the test results came back, David was done with football.

"It was never a hard decision to make," David says. "It was a little hard being out of football, but the fact that I know the Lord makes it a lot easier. The closer you walk with the Lord—and I've really been close to Him through this process—the more you see that His plan becomes your plan. And once you've been in His plan, there's no place you'd rather be."

David says, "It has made people ask, 'What is your source of peace?' That's the kind of opportunities we've been praying for—chances to tell people about Christ."

That's a sacrifice! Giving up a kidney was a chance to witness for Jesus.

—VICTOR LEE

> **SPORTS NOTE:**
> Two NBA players competed after having received a kidney transplant: Sean Elliott and Alonzo Mourning.

> **FROM THE PLAYBOOK:**
> Read 1 Corinthians 10:33; 11:1.

GAME PLAN: When you have faced a difficulty in your life, were you able to experience God's peace? If not, have you thought about why you could not sense God's help?

DAVID'S KIDS

POINT OF EMPHASIS:
The value of helping others

*"If anyone . . . sees his brother in need but has no pity on him,
how can the love of God be in him?"* 1 JOHN 3:17

Now that David Robinson is done playing basketball, he can concentrate on his pet project: Carver Academy. This school, which he founded, has blossomed into a pre-kindergarten-through-eighth-grade independent school specializing in teaching of the highest order for low-income families who live on San Antonio's East Side.

SPORTS NOTE:
In addition to running the Carver Academy, David Robinson serves on the staff of his church in San Antonio.

"We have five basic pillars we teach the students: discipline, integrity, initiative, faith, and service," says Robinson. "This was a concept I've always wanted to see instilled in kids. I've always been big on education, and, coming from the Naval Academy, I love discipline. I just love the whole education process, the sense of being a part of something greater than yourself."

Carver Academy is based on a foundation of Judeo-Christian Scripture and values, and it uses the small-classroom setting to give students high-tech instruction emphasizing leadership, family values, and high student achievement. It helps the kids focus on achieving greatness in whatever they choose to do.

FROM THE PLAYBOOK:
Read 1 John 3:11–20.

"That's what we loved about life in the military," says Robinson. "You didn't care about your salary. That wasn't what you were studying for. You were studying to accomplish something great. That was the heart I wanted to put in this school. The thing I'm most proud of is that the vision has been caught by all the teachers, administrators, and everyone here. The atmosphere here is so sweet toward doing something positive for those students."

David Robinson has illustrated how to incorporate his faith and his fame into something worthwhile. He's a big guy with a big heart for kids. His efforts can remind us of our responsibility to come alongside and help others.

—DARRYL HOWERTON

GAME PLAN: Think about a situation you know of where someone needs help. What can you do to meet the need? Create a plan to do something about it.

WASN'T GOD WATCHING?

POINT OF EMPHASIS:
Coping with death

"Precious in the sight of the Lord is the death of His saints."
PSALM 116:15

When Payne Stewart boarded his final flight in October 1999, he was getting on a plane you would think God would spend a little extra time protecting. After all, this was not a group of boozing buddies sneaking off to a party. These were God-fearing, Jesus-loving people.

So what happened up there between earth and heaven? Did God look the other way? Was He not watching? Don't you get anything for trusting God? Why didn't He save those good people?

If living on this earth were all there is to life, we'd be hopeless in answering those questions. But this is not all there is. Our time here is only a short prelude to an amazing eternal existence for those who know God through faith in Jesus Christ.

When it came time for Payne's eternal existence in heaven to begin, we saw things only from this side. We missed the remarkable homecoming Payne and his friends experienced when God ushered them into His presence, but we can imagine it was fantastic: "Precious in the sight of the Lord is the death of his saints" (Psalm 116:15).

That's small consolation. When death takes what matters most, it's not easy to say, "That's okay, God, we'll get along fine down here." But that's when we turn to Him and His promises. The same God who welcomes His children into heaven has promised to surround us with His arms of comfort. And He has promised never to leave us.

Was God watching? Yes, He was watching . . . and waiting with open arms. The same loving arms that on this side of heaven give us comfort.

—DAVE BRANON

> **SPORTS NOTE:**
> Payne Stewart won the 1999 US Open. It was his third victory in a PGA major.

> **FROM THE PLAYBOOK:**
> Read Psalm 23 for an incredible experience in comfort.

GAME PLAN: Have you had someone in your life taken from you through death? What were some of the things you discussed with God during this time?

FREE OR BOUND?

POINT OF EMPHASIS:
Freed by Christ

"He has sent me to bind up the brokenhearted." ISAIAH 61:1

Have you ever experienced a broken heart? I love how the Lord lets us know that He not only came to save the lost but also to heal the brokenhearted! (See Psalm 34:18.) He cares about our wounds and wants to bring us healing.

Many of us have wounds that we cover with the bandage of sports. We work out like crazy, we drive ourselves beyond where others would stop, and we carry anger inside and it manifests as aggression.

Oh, I've been there. For years the game was the thing that saved me from going over the edge. We all find something to deal with our hurts. I used softball and baseball. But the problem is, it is all temporary. We continue to reapply a new bandage because the wound just seems to keep splitting open. The healing never takes place.

But Jesus has come to heal our hearts. When we allow him to apply His medicine, we find healing. There will forever remain a scar, but that scar tells a story, a testimony of the healing power of Jesus.

So if you struggle with sin that afflicts you from the outside or sin you've committed, allow Jesus and His truth to bring healing to your bones. Galatians 5:1 says, "It is for freedom that Christ has set us free. Stand firm, then, and do not let yourselves be burdened again by a yoke of slavery." When we allow God to free us up, we live and play with more joy and have more peace.

Are you bound by sin or free in Christ?

—KIM VOISARD, FORMER PRO BASEBALL PLAYER

SPORTS NOTE:
Kim's husband Mark is a former pitcher in the Colorado Rockies organization.

FROM THE PLAYBOOK:
Read 2 Corinthians 3:7–18.

 GAME PLAN: Does something seem to have its grip on you? Have you asked Jesus to free you from its clutches—and then depended on His Holy Spirit to give you the strength to remain free?

CLIMB ON

POINT OF EMPHASIS:
Trusting God's commands

"Love the Lord your God and keep His requirements."
DEUTERONOMY 11:1

"Climb on." With those two words the instructor at the camp's climbing tower gave me permission to begin ascending a 40-foot tower. Prior to my climb, I had watched as a number of wiry, athletic campers scaled the wall like spiders—some making it look effortless.

My climb would not look that way.

After several minutes of huffing and puffing, my 40-something body was still 10 feet from the top and ready to stop. The instructor would have none of it. "Use your skeleton," He barked. "You're hunched over. Stand up and hug the wall!"

I wanted to point out to him that I was hauling 225 pounds up the massive structure, but fortunately I listened and learned.

With his helpful words I soon found myself at the top of the wall. It's amazing what you can accomplish when you follow the right instruction.

Trying to ascend a climbing tower is symbolic of our relationship with God. Sometimes we find ourselves struggling and feeling as if we have no answers. We're tired, burned out, and ready to give up.

During these desperate moments we may be inclined to blame God. *Why is this happening to me? Haven't you seen all the good things I've done?*

Instead, we need to return to the basics. God's requirements are plainly written on the pages of the Bible. Your struggles may be the result of your failure to follow His instruction. He says to you, "Faithfully obey the commands I am giving you today" (Deuteronomy 11:13).

When we do that, the climb of life becomes a whole lot better.

—TOM FELTEN

SPORTS NOTE:
If you want to find out more about rock climbing, go to www.rockclimbing.com.

FROM THE PLAYBOOK:
Read Deuteronomy 11:1–15.

GAME PLAN: Write three important instructions God gives us in the Bible. Pull out these instructions several times today and consider how well you're following them.

NO ROOM FOR FEAR

POINT OF EMPHASIS:
Casting out fear

"But perfect love drives out fear." I JOHN 4:18

Fear is one of the deadliest forms of warfare that threatens the Christian. In our country today, the spirit of fear has been released in an unprecedented way.

That's the bad news. The good news is that we as God's children should not fear (2 Timothy 1:7). Instead, we can live to the fullest each day by doing what God has called us to do—and by doing it with all our heart to God's glory.

SPORTS NOTE:
In bull riding, the rider must stay on the bull for eight seconds, and the rider's free hand cannot touch himself, the bull, or his equipment.

FROM THE PLAYBOOK:
Read Psalm 91; Proverbs 9:10; 29:25; Isaiah 41:10; Matthew 10:28; Romans 8:15; and Hebrews 2:15.

As you can imagine, fear is the driving force behind my professional sport of bull riding. Every time we compete, we have a choice. We can either accept fear or use it to our advantage. Notice that I didn't say we get rid of it. What we are doing is, by its very nature, dangerous and scary. As riders, though, we can't let fear drive us under its own terms. I know personally speaking that my ability to put the spirit of fear under my feet (when I was preparing to ride a bull) was because I had confidence in knowing that I was doing what I was born to do.

As a result, a deep love was born in me for both the Lord and for the sport. There is no greater satisfaction in this world than knowing that you are in your perfect place with God and in life. (Psalm 37:4). On the other hand, many people succumb to the spirit of fear in their lives, which causes them to reject the very life Jesus purchased for us when He suffered and died on the cross.

How do we get rid of fear? We need to know the Word (Proverbs 4:20–23) and refuse to give in to the devil (Ephesians 4:27). God wants to perfect us in His love so that we will have no room for fear in our lives.

—SCOTT MENDES, FORMER WORLD-CHAMPION BULL RIDER

GAME PLAN: God has done His part in Jesus (1 John 3:8), and now it's your responsibility to take action and fight to rid yourself of the spirit of fear. God will empower you all the way as you learn to trust Him.

PROCLAIM CHRIST WITH CONFIDENCE

POINT OF EMPHASIS:
Inviting others to meet Jesus

"Hope does not disappoint us." ROMANS 5:5

Prior to making the 1992 and 1996 Olympic teams, racewalker Allen James experienced success at the collegiate level. The All-American recalls that at this point life was just cruising along.

One evening while spending time with his teammates, out of the blue, one of them suggested they all go to church together the next day. James had spent little time in church but decided it was a good idea. He went and noticed something really different about most of the people in the church. "They had something that I didn't seem to have," James said. "They had a contentment and love in their life. The difference was so clear that I continued to go back to the church.

"After the fourth visit, I realized what I lacked was a personal relationship with God through His Son Jesus Christ." James added, "I learned that I could respond to God's love for me through the payment Christ made on my behalf when He died on the cross for my imperfections by praying and asking Him to enter my heart as Lord and Savior."

After putting his trust in Jesus, James said things were different. "God had become my foundation. I found that the circumstances of my life did not shake God up. That gave me the confidence and hope I needed. It also provided me with a great sense of purpose as I understood that God created me and had a plan for my life."

A big reason James learned about God's love for him was that a teammate invited him to church. When is the last time you invited someone to your church?

—ROXANNE ROBBINS

SPORTS NOTE:
After retiring from race-walking, James became the director of marketing and special events at Niagara Falls State Park.

FROM THE PLAYBOOK:
Read Romans 5.

GAME PLAN: Make a list of three people you'd like to invite to attend services with you. Then think of the best way to invite them to join you at church.

NAYSAYERS

POINT OF EMPHASIS:
Listening to the right people

"Trust in the Lord with all your heart." PROVERBS 3:5

Think about a sports team you've been on or are currently a part of. Visualize the faces of your teammates and reflect on their personalities. Who were the people who worked the hardest? Who had the best attitude? Who lacked talent but made up for it by practicing longer hours than everyone else? Which teammate treated the coach with the greatest respect? Was there a player who had a hard time respecting authority? If so, how did his or her attitude affect your team? Which people on your team helped you excel?

SPORTS NOTE:
Kevin played for the New York Jets from 2001 through 2003. A wide receiver, he caught 20 passes and scored one touchdown in the NFL.

FROM THE PLAYBOOK:
Read Proverbs 3.

Former New York Jets player Kevin Swayne did all those things. Kevin was told by many that he wouldn't make it to the NFL. Some said he was too skinny. He was only a junior college player, and so on. But Kevin learned not to listen to the detractors. Instead he put his trust in God. From growing up in a troubled Los Angeles neighborhood to excelling in the NFL, Kevin says he often reflects on his life. "I look back on my life, and the neighborhood I came from," he says. "It would have been so easy for me to have turned out like so many others—drugged out, hopeless, or dead. But God had His hand on me. I haven't been perfect, but I know who my blessings come from, and who the Lord of my life is."

Kevin says he has learned to live by Proverbs 3:5–6, which says, "Trust in the Lord with all your heart . . . in all your ways acknowledge him and he will make your paths straight."

Are you trusting God with all your heart or listening to the naysayers?

—ROXANNE ROBBINS

GAME PLAN: When did God help you accomplish something despite people telling you it couldn't happen?

OCTOBER 31

WHAT IT'S LIKE

POINT OF EMPHASIS:
Understanding the seriousness of sin

"A good name is more desirable than great riches." PROVERBS 22:1

It's not like we grabbed clothes and ran out. It's not like that at all." That was Laveranues Coles' defense when he and Florida State teammate Peter Warrick were arrested for stealing $400 worth of merchandise from a department store in 1999.

"It's not like I killed the President," added Warrick.

So what was it like? It was like . . . stealing! The method didn't matter, and comparisons to murder are irrelevant when the charge is theft.

Even offensive superstars get defensive when caught breaking the law. But what if they never learn that honesty is far more valuable than the seven-figure salaries they now enjoy in the NFL?

King David never stole anything from Dillard's. He was far more foolish than that! The shepherd king, the one of whom God said, "I have found David son of Jesse a man after my own heart" (Acts 13:22), had a fling with a trusted soldier's wife and then arranged his death. Yet David provides us with a model of genuine repentance.

Interestingly, David didn't say, "Hey, it's not like I killed Uriah myself." He didn't say, "It's not like I haven't done a lot for this country." He said, "I have sinned against the Lord" (2 Samuel 12:13). His honest response to God is contained for us in Psalm 51, a heartfelt cry for forgiveness of what could not be undone.

"He who conceals his sins does not prosper," said the wise man in Proverbs 28:13. "But whoever confesses and renounces them finds mercy."

Have you blown it recently? Remember—it's not like God can't make a bad thing good! He can!

—TIM GUSTAFSON

SPORTS NOTE:
Both Peter Warrick and Laveranues Coles overcame their college troubles and made careers for themselves in the NFL.

FROM THE PLAYBOOK:
Read Psalm 51 or 2 Samuel 12:1–13.

 GAME PLAN: Are you defensive when you're wrong? Why? Is there anyone who has not sinned? How should this change your attitude toward others caught in wrongdoing? What should your reaction be when you've sinned?

THE IMPACT ZONE

POINT OF EMPHASIS:
Make an impact for God

"Suddenly there was the sound of a violent wind." ACTS 2:2

Paul Zimmerman is an author and physicist who made some discoveries about the forces that take place on the football field. For example, when a 240-pound lineman hits a 240-pound running back, the collision is equal to 1,000 times the force of gravity.

One thousand times! Astronauts experience 10 Gs on lift-off. Jet fighter pilots pass out at 20 Gs. It appears that the force of collision on the football field is far more than what the human body can handle. No player can go into the impact zone and not feel the physical ramifications.

There's also a spiritual impact zone, and the hit there can never be strong enough. In fact, the bigger the better. Moses entered the impact zone in Exodus 7 when he took on the Egyptians. Peter felt the force of the spiritual Gs in Acts 2 when he preached a powerful sermon under the Spirit's guidance. These men and many others made an impact for the Kingdom of god in the lives around them. You can too. Here's how:

Be consistent. Be reliable and strong by staying on track spiritually.

Be real. Don't be a hypocrite. Be real to your very core.

Be unselfish. You may make an impact that no one else notices.

Be determined. Refuse to quit; never lose your enthusiasm.

You don't need to be huge, strong, and fast with a helmet and shoulder pads to make an impact. You can be an impact in someone else's life when you let God put you in the impact zone.

—DAN DEAL

SPORTS NOTE:
How hard do they hit? According to one report, between 1994 and 2001, there were 182 incidences of concussions suffered by NFL players.

FROM THE PLAYBOOK:
Read Acts 2, which tells the story of Peter making a big hit.

GAME PLAN: How much of an impact have I had on others spiritually? What are two things I can do to improve my impact?

BRINGING THE ARK HOME

POINT OF EMPHASIS:
The cost of disobedience

"The Lord's anger burned against Uzzah because of his irreverent act." 2 SAMUEL 6:7

What would your teammates think of you if you lost the World Cup of Soccer? Not the game—the trophy.

It happened. The great trophy that mesmerizes the world of soccer every 4 years was at one time on the lam. Once called the Jules Rimet Trophy, the World Cup symbol of greatness was stolen when it was in the possession of Brazil. Eventually it was recovered, and its discovery soothed many frayed nerves and assuaged volumes of angry people.

If losing a sports trophy is a bad idea, imagine what it must have felt like to the people of Israel when they lost the Ark of the Covenant. And imagine how excited they were to see it return.

It had been 100 years since the Philistines had captured the sacred box, and now David was endeavoring to bring it home to Jerusalem. It was a glorious celebration for the Jewish people as David and 30,000 companions traveled to Baalah of Judah to fetch the ark.

They placed the sacred box on a cart and prepared to escort it home in full glory. But there was a problem. The ark was not supposed to be on a cart; it was to be carried on two rods with Levites bearing the burden. When the cart hit a rough spot and appeared ready to tip—and the ark with it—Uzzah reached out to steady it. Big mistake! He was struck dead immediately.

Understandably, David was filled with fear after this, and he refused to transport the ark back to Jerusalem. He ordered it left behind at the house of Obed-Edom. Disobedience takes its toll.

What is disobedience costing us? It could cause us to lose something far more valuable than the Jules Rimet Trophy.   —DAVE BRANON

SPORTS NOTE: Between 1930 and 2002, Brazil won the World Cup five times; Italy, three times; West Germany, three times.

FROM THE PLAYBOOK: Read 2 Samuel 6.

GAME PLAN: Disobedience to God can come in *specific* defiance of His biblical standards or in refusal to do the things the Holy Spirit prompts us to do. In what ways have you neglected to act on God's commands recently?

PREPARING FOR VICTORY: 1. KNOW YOUR ENEMY

POINT OF EMPHASIS:
Looking out for Satan

"Your enemy the devil prowls around like a roaring lion looking for someone to devour." I PETER 5:8

It amuses me when people approach us and say, "You play games on Sunday. What do you do all week?" They don't understand the meticulous details and the hard work that go into preparation for victory. The physical conditioning is strenuous, and it takes self-discipline. But there's also mental preparation. You have to know your plays, and you have to know your enemy—your opponent.

SPORTS NOTE:
Kyle Brady went to Penn State University. He was drafted in 1995 by the New York Jets.

FROM THE PLAYBOOK:
Read John 8:44.

As a football player, it would be ludicrous for me to go out on the field if I hadn't studied my opponents. The same is true in our Christian lives. If we don't know our enemy, we cannot be victorious.

Who is our enemy? He is Satan. Scripture tells us he is real. First Peter 5:8 says, "Be self-controlled and alert. Your enemy the devil prowls around like a roaring lion looking for someone to devour."

We must take a firm stand against him. The Bible calls Satan a liar—the father of lies—and it tells us he's been lying from the beginning. He lied to Adam and Eve, tricking them into believing they would be like God if they ate the forbidden fruit.

How is Satan lying to us today? One way is by saying there are many ways to God—that worshiping Buddha, Mohammed, and Jesus all lead to the same place. But the Bible says in Acts 4:12, "There is no other name under heaven given to men by which we must be saved." In John 14:6 Jesus said, "I am the way and the truth and the life. No one comes to the Father except through me."

So, that's our enemy. We must be prepared to battle him with the truth that comes from our heavenly Father and His Word, the Bible.

—KYLE BRADY, NFL TIGHT END

GAME PLAN: What are four things you know about Satan and his lying ways? How can you counter his attacks on your life?

NOVEMBER 4

PREPARING FOR VICTORY: 2. BEWARE OF THE WORLD

POINT OF EMPHASIS:
Recognizing worldliness

"Among you there must not be even a hint of sexual immorality."
EPHESIANS 5:3

In my job as a football player, I have to spend a lot of time preparing mentally for the games we play. I have to study the playbook and make sure I know all our patterns. But I also have to know what kind of tendencies my opponents have. What will they do to stop me, and how can I avoid allowing them to do those things?

Similarly, as Christians we have to be aware of the traps and tricks that are in our world—things that can bring us down or make us ineffective as witnesses for Christ. That's why I say that our second enemy is the world—specifically the wrong cultural values and assumptions that are out there.

If you watch TV or movies for long, you'll see what our culture says is worth living for. We're told you can't be happy or content unless you are wealthy, popular, beautiful, or have a nice car.

Also, we are told that sexual relationships outside of marriage are acceptable. Our world tries to make us think we are wrong to believe that marriage is pure and the exclusive place for sexual relationships.

We must be aware that the values of our culture clash head-on with the values of our God. Every one of us has been influenced to some degree by these values—me included.

I pray that God will call us to love and value the things He does. First Timothy 6:6 says, "But godliness with contentment is great gain."

Godliness. That's what we must value the most.

—KYLE BRADY, NFL TIGHT END

SPORTS NOTE:
In 1997, his last season with the New York Jets, Kyle Brady caught 30 passes and scored 5 touchdowns.

FROM THE PLAYBOOK:
Read Ephesians 4:17–32.

GAME PLAN: It is hard to realize how much the world influences us—especially through the media. Next time you watch, look for three of the world's values that you know are opposed to God's values. Then begin to look for them all the time. You may find yourself changing the channel more often.

PREPARING FOR VICTORY: 3. KNOW YOURSELF

POINT OF EMPHASIS:
Man's sin

"I have the desire to do what is good, but I cannot carry it out."
ROMANS 7:18

When I get ready to play a football game, as I said, I have to know my opponent and I have to avoid his tricks and traps. But there's another person I have to watch out for: Me.

I have to know that if I'm not careful, I will be my own worst enemy.

In the Christian life, we have a bit of that going on because when we were saved, our sinful nature was not taken from us. It is still lurking in us. That can be enemy No. 3 if we're not careful.

SPORTS NOTE:
Kyle Brady was a first alternative to the Pro Bowl in 2001.

FROM THE PLAYBOOK:
Read Romans 7:7–25.

Some people say, "Well, I think mankind is generally good." I ask them if they've watched the evening news lately. Scripture says in James 4:1, "What causes fights and quarrels among you? Don't they come from your desires that battle within you?" In Romans 7 the apostle Paul describes his own desperate struggle with sin. This man, who was Christianity's greatest missionary, said, "For what I do is not the good I want to do; no, the evil I do not want to do—this I keep on doing" (Romans 7:19). Then he cried out, "What a wretched man I am!" (Romans 7:24).

It's a pretty bleak picture—with enemies all around. Opponents and their sneaky ways. Ourselves and our tendency to sin despite God's love and salvation. What can we do?

Paul asks this key question: "Who will rescue me from this body of death?" (v. 24). And then he supplies the answer: "Thanks be to God—through Jesus Christ our Lord!" (v. 25). We can have victory over each of our enemies by clinging to Christ and trusting His power to save us and keep us close to Him.

—KYLE BRADY, NFL TIGHT END

GAME PLAN: How do you trip yourself up in your Christian life? Have you given your sinful ways over to Jesus and asked Him to keep you pure and holy? Perhaps you should write down three problem areas you need to surrender to Him.

PREPARING FOR VICTORY: 4. KNOW GOD

POINT OF EMPHASIS:
Knowing God

"My help comes from the Lord." PSALM 121:2

Once we know who our enemies are, the next thing we must know is our God.

Most important, we must believe in His Son. Romans 10:9 says, "That if you confess with your mouth, 'Jesus is Lord,' and believe in your heart that God raised Him from the dead, you will be saved." God gives us the strength for victory through knowing His Son. It's only through repentance and coming to Jesus that we can have victory in this life. First John 5:4 says, "For everyone born of God overcomes the world. This is the victory that has overcome the world."

These verses are true, but the life of victory is not passive. As Christians, we must exercise our faith if we want victory. Here are some vital spiritual exercises:

1. We must read, study, and meditate on God's Word. "I have hidden your word in my heart that I might not sin against you" (Psalm 119:11).
2. We must be in fellowship with other believers for encouragement, instruction, and rebuke.
3. We must be obedient. When Jesus would heal someone and that person would trust in Him, He would tell him or her, "Go and sin no more." Are you stealing? Stop. Are you sexually involved with your boyfriend or girlfriend? Stop. Disobedience leads only to defeat.

SPORTS NOTE: Through 2004, Kyle Brady was the third-leading receiver in Jacksonville Jaguars history.

FROM THE PLAYBOOK: Read Psalm 121.

Each season, my team and I prepare for victory. In my Christian life I hope to be victorious as well. I will do that by knowing my God and protecting myself against my enemies. Praise God for the victory!

—KYLE BRADY, NFL TIGHT END

GAME PLAN: How are you doing with those three spiritual exercises? It's not too late to know God better through reading, fellowshiping, and obeying.

GOING TO EXTREEEEEEMES

POINT OF EMPHASIS:
Step out for Jesus

"I have come that they may have life, and have it to the full."
JOHN 10:10

Bored? Tired of the same old predictable routine day and night? Looking for a rush of adrenaline to slap your brain cells silly and make you feel alive?

If so, you might want to try one of the extreme sports that are the craze these days.

I have to admit that I'm not into the more extreme sports—though I've gotten a rush from jumping off a high ledge into a cold Canadian lake, tried to stay upright while water-skiing, and pushed my tired body to the brink of collapse during a 25K run. All that sounds pretty tame, though, compared to base-jumping the New River Gorge Bridge in West Virginia.

Why do people risk life and limb in extreme sports? Philosopher William James wrote, "It is only by risking our persons from one hour to another that we live at all."

Jesus had a bit of a different take. He seemed to say that we aren't really living unless we're risking our lives— for His sake. He said, "If anyone would come after me, he must deny himself and take up his cross and follow me. For whoever wants to save his life will lose it, but whoever loses his life for me will find it" (Matthew 16:24–25).

In Hebrews 11 we read about a number of people who went to extremes—even died—in their devotion to the Lord. They found a life that was full (John 10:10) in a life of faith, in living on the edge for Jesus.

I'd like to rephrase an old "X Games" slogan: "If you're not living on the edge, you're taking up too much room!" I prefer, "If you're not living on the edge for Christ, you're not really living."

—KURT DE HAAN

SPORTS NOTE:
The New River Gorge Bridge, site of popular base-jumping by many thrill seekers, was completed in 1977. It is 3,030 feet long and 876 feet high.

FROM THE PLAYBOOK:
Read Hebrews 11:23–40.

 GAME PLAN: Do you like to "play it safe" spiritually, not risking rejection by people you know? What would happen if you took a stand for Christ and biblical values?

NOT QUITE GOOD ENOUGH

POINT OF EMPHASIS:
Salvation

"For all have sinned and fall short of the glory of God." ROMANS 3:23

As an NBA rookie, there were times when I felt everyone was pulling me in different directions. The coach wanted more practice time, my wife wanted me to talk to her more, my family needed more money, and my friends wanted me to "hang out" with them.

It was during this time that someone approached me about the claims of Christ. However, I felt I didn't have time for Christ. My life was already overflowing with things to do. Christianity seemed like just another thing to add to my busy life!

God had to show me the value of the gospel over a period of three to four years. I had always thought I was basically a good person with a good heart, and I had never cheated on my wife.

However, being good will not get me into heaven. Let me illustrate. God blessed me with good shooting skills. I consistently placed in the Top 10 in free throw percentage in the NBA, usually shooting between 86 and 88 percent. That's better than most NBA players. So, if I compared myself with others, I rated very well. But I'm still not perfect.

In life, God says we have to be perfect (Matthew 5:48), and we have to keep all His laws (James 2:10). God is the standard, not others. We all break God's laws and fall short of God's glory (Romans 3:23). The Bible says in Romans 6:23 that "the wages of sin is death, but the gift of God is eternal life." This is why we all need a Savior. He could give me the eternal life I don't deserve.

I had to admit that I am a sinner, and I had to ask God to forgive me—and He did!

—HERSEY HAWKINS, FORMER NBA GUARD

SPORTS NOTE:
Hersey Hawkins led the NCAA in scoring as a college senior in 1988 by averaging 36 points a game.

FROM THE PLAYBOOK:
Read Romans 3:9–26.

GAME PLAN: What is keeping you from enjoying the eternal benefits of salvation? If there's something about the gospel you don't understand, seek out some help.

WHO'S TO BLAME?

POINT OF EMPHASIS:
Taking responsibility

"A man's . . . heart rages against the Lord." PROVERBS 19:3

It was a great afternoon for a Mid-American Conference football showdown. During the 2001 football season, Ball State and Toledo were set to tangle in a game that was supposed to be all about the Rockets. But Ball State had other ideas, and the Cardinals upset the visiting conference opponent. Students streamed onto the field. The ensuing celebration toppled the goal posts in both end zones. Ball State student Andrew Bourne was in the middle of it all. When one of the goal posts fell, it hit Andrew, breaking one of his legs and some vertebrae in his back. He's still paralyzed today.

SPORTS NOTE:
Akron, Kent State, Ohio University, Central Michigan, Eastern Michigan, Marshall, Bowling Green, Northern Illinois, Toledo, Western Michigan, Buffalo, Miami, and Ball State are all members of the Mid-American Conference.

FROM THE PLAYBOOK:
Read Proverbs 19 and Galatians 6 from *The Message*.

Andrew and his parents filed a lawsuit against the goal post maker, Gilman Gear. The family claimed that the aluminum posts were "designed and constructed in a manner which allowed them to suddenly snap and collapse." Now, I'm truly sorry for what happened to this 23-year-old. It's an awful thing to endure. But why blame the manufacturer when it was the celebrating students who caused the problem?

A spokesman for Gilman Gear said the lawsuit was without merit. The company thought it was a case of personal responsibility.

A man named Solomon had a few things to say about blame and responsibility in the Bible. Speaking in general terms of the trouble people bring on themselves, he says in Proverbs 19:3 that people ruin their lives by their own stupidity—but then blame God for their trouble. It's human nature for us to blame someone or something else instead of taking responsibility for our own actions.

We all will have to answer someday for our actions. We might as well start taking responsibility now .
—DAN DEAL

GAME PLAN: What situation are you facing that you want to blame on someone else, when in reality the problem is of your own making? How can you change your thinking on this?

UNPROTECTED

POINT OF EMPHASIS:
Armor of God

"Put on the full armor of God." EPHESIANS 6:13

As an athlete, I put on my protective equipment every time I go on the ice. Every piece serves a purpose. I learned the hard way that there are no spare parts.

At the end of practice one day, there were just two of us left out on the ice. I removed my mouth guard to speak with the equipment manager—just as my teammate took one last slap shot. Unbelievably, the puck deflected off the cross bar and smacked me in the mouth, knocking out my two front teeth.

I was not pleased. My teeth had survived almost twenty years of hockey, since I first laced on skates as a small boy. Now I had to endure countless dentist appointments, root canals, even false teeth—all because I let down my guard and did not have on the equipment necessary to protect my teeth.

As believers, we need to be clothed daily in protective equipment, such as the belt of truth, the shield of faith, and the helmet of salvation to name just a few. This armor of God protects our hearts and minds, just as sports equipment protects our body. And every piece is vital. If we neglect even a seemingly small area of our lives, we can leave ourselves open to things that will hinder our walk with God.

Study the armor of God in Ephesians 6:12–17. Put it on every day. Be smart and remember that there are no spare parts—that way you won't get your teeth knocked out.

—SHANE DOAN, NHL HOCKEY

SPORTS NOTE:
Shane and Andrea Doan have three children: Gracie, Joshua, and Karys.

FROM THE PLAYBOOK:
Read Ephesians 6:13–17.

GAME PLAN: Can you think of a specific example where you let down your guard and allowed something to hinder your walk with God? Can you identify the piece of God's armor that would have protected you in that situation? What things can you do to "put on the full armor of God"?

THE INVITATION

POINT OF EMPHASIS:
Salvation

"Salvation is found in no one else." ACTS 4:12

Veteran NHL goaltender Dominic Roussel was in junior hockey when he received "The Invitation."

It wasn't a formal calligraphy-and-parchment-paper-type invitation to the most prestigious social event in town. This invitation, sent from then-NHL star Ryan Walter, was just a normal piece of paper written from one hockey player to another.

The letter Roussel received was an invitation to attend a Billy Graham Crusade where Walter was to speak. Roussel was interested immediately. He had been reading his Bible and searching for the way to heaven, but he had yet to find it. So Roussel accepted the invitation.

At the crusade, the young goalie listened intently as Walter detailed how putting his faith in Jesus Christ had changed his life and the lives of other players in the NHL. Walter told of the eternal life he now possessed because of forgiveness offered by Christ.

Roussel had found the way to heaven!

That night, Dominic Roussel made an invitation of his own: he asked Jesus Christ to forgive his sins and be his Savior.

If you're looking for the way to heaven, the Bible teaches us that Jesus is the only way. Have you invited Jesus into your life? Receive eternal life today by talking with God. Say something like this:

God, I confess that I am a sinner. I accept the forgiveness that Your Son Jesus offers me because of what He did on the cross. Beginning today, I want to live for You. I want to spend eternity with You in heaven. I invite Jesus Christ to be the Lord of my life. Thank you for saving me. Amen!

—ROB BENTZ

SPORTS NOTE:
Dominic Roussel played for Philadelphia, Winnipeg, Anaheim, and Edmonton during his NHL career.

FROM THE PLAYBOOK:
Read John 3:1–16.

GAME PLAN: Plan now to extend an invitation to Jesus to a friend. Then ask someone to pray for you that it will go well.

DAD'S SCRAPBOOK

POINT OF EMPHASIS:
God's unconditional acceptance

"But God demonstrates his own love for us in this: While we were still sinners, Christ died for us." ROMANS 5:8

When I was about ten, my parents stepped out of the house for a while, and I thought it would be a good time to do some investigating.

Mom and Dad's closet seemed like a good place to start.

I dug out a couple of old paper bags that contained scrapbooks. To my astonishment, I found photos and newspaper clippings about my dad's football career.

Even though my dad was a high school football coach, I knew virtually nothing about his playing days. You can imagine my shock to discover that Dad was the captain of the Penn State football team, selected to play in the East-West College All-Star Game, and drafted by the NFL.

When I asked my dad why he had not told me about this really cool stuff, he told me he never wanted me to feel the pressure of having to play sports. He said he would love me and support me whether I ever picked up a ball or not. Not until much later did I realize the strength and power of those words. That was unconditional acceptance and love!

All the years I played sports, Dad's unconditional acceptance gave me the motivation, strength, and confidence to achieve to my highest level.

Now I see how clearly this reflects the gospel. God's unconditional love and acceptance of us that is found in His Son, Jesus Christ is the basis for our motivation, strength, and hope as we seek to honor Him. Because of Jesus, He accepts and loves us—unconditionally.

—FRANK REICH, FORMER NFL QUARTERBACK

SPORTS NOTE: As a quarterback, Frank Reich orchestrated the largest comeback in a game in both college and NFL history.

FROM THE PLAYBOOK: Read Luke 15:11–32.

GAME PLAN: What does God's unconditional love mean to you? What are three advantages it gives you as you move into a new day?

NOVEMBER 13

FROM BAD TO GOOD

POINT OF EMPHASIS:
God's help in trials

"In all things God works for the good of those who love him."
ROMANS 8:28

A t the end of my first year of racing, I was invited to a triathlon in Japan—all expenses paid. I was the only US female representative, so it was quite an honor. There was one catch: The race was almost three times as long as any race I had ever done. It would be a challenge just to finish, but I was game!

When I arrived in Japan, I decided to loosen up in the hotel pool. On my last flipturn, as my feet came over I whacked my heel down hard on the edge. I had never in twelve years of swimming hit my heel. It hurt just to walk on it, let alone run sixteen miles at the end of the triathlon.

At first I cried out to God and asked why this happened. In reading the Bible that night, I discovered today's verse. "In all things"—including racing a triathlon with a hurt heal—"God works for the good of those who love him." All I could do was put my faith in God that He would turn this situation around to His good, because I loved Him and trusted Him.

On race day I swam and biked well, but the real test was the run. When I put on my shoes, I felt no pain. Skeptics might say it was adrenaline, but I ran for sixteen pain-free miles—four miles longer than my longest run ever. Adrenaline can't do that, but the Lord can.

The Lord created a situation that I thought was bad. He did it so my faith and trust in Him could be strengthened. That's for my good. But He also gave me a story of triumph (well, second place in this case), to encourage others that "in all things God works for the good of those who love him."

—BARB LINDQUIST, WORLD-CLASS TRIATHLETE

SPORTS NOTE:
In college, Barb competed on the Stanford swim team. She won gold medals in the 1987 and 1991 Pan American Games.

FROM THE PLAYBOOK:
Read Romans 8:28–39.

 GAME PLAN: What is happening in your life this week that looks bad but that God can turn into good? It takes real faith and trust to see that happen. Are you willing to try?

NOVEMBER 14

BETWEEN HEARTBEATS

POINT OF EMPHASIS:
The need for forgiveness

"Be kind and compassionate." EPHESIANS 4:32

Josh sat in silence. Each beat of his heart rammed relentlessly inside his chest. He was crying. His mind was racing. He was scared.

Josh had just seen a fellow teen die.

Hockey can be a violent game. But what happened to 16-year-old Matthew Messing was not about a brutal hit. Josh had cleanly checked Matthew in a high school hockey game.

It was an accident. Everyone knew it, but Josh Wingate was having a hard time accepting it.

The doctor's report was not easy to understand, but it said that Matt had likely been hit at precisely the right place at the exact millisecond between heartbeats, causing his death. Josh was devastated.

Then came the phone call. Josh picked up the receiver and listened to some of the sweetest words he had ever heard. It was Matt's dad. He told Josh not to blame himself, and that he loved him.

The tears were still in Josh's eyes, but the heavy load was lifted. He was forgiven. Mr. Messing's response to Josh is a dramatic example of how we need to forgive others—even when it really, really hurts.

Paul implored Philemon to have this kind of forgiving heart. Onesimus, Philemon's slave, had stolen from his master and then run away. In a letter to Philemon, Paul implored him to forgive Onesimus and take him back. Maybe even set him free.

The appeal was based on love—the love Paul and Philemon shared in Jesus. Paul told Philemon that his act of forgiveness would refresh his "heart in Christ" (v. 20).

Do you need to forgive someone today? Out of love for Jesus, grant that forgiveness. You'll be surprised at how much refreshment it will bring.

— TOM FELTEN

SPORTS NOTE:
The actual name of the injury that took Matthew's life is commotio cordi. It has also claimed the lives of young baseball players struck in the chest with a ball.

FROM THE PLAYBOOK:
Read the story of Philemon. It's between Titus and Hebrews.

 GAME PLAN: I need to forgive _____ today.

RUN THE RIGHT PLAY

POINT OF EMPHASIS:
Preserving sexual purity

"Among you there must not be even a hint of sexual immorality."
EPHESIANS 5:3

A few years ago, a study of prime-time TV shows (7:00 to 10:00 PM) revealed that approximately 2,000 TV episodes illustrated sexual behavior. Of these episodes, 80 percent of them depicted people who were unmarried.

Let's talk about one popular show during that time: *Coach.* The coach was living with his girlfriend—and their sexual relationship was assumed and accepted. The message was clear: You have permission to engage in sex outside of marriage.

God does not give this permission. In the Bible, the message is clear: Don't run that play (sexual intimacy) until you are married. Scripture is plain on this matter—sex is designed for a man and a woman within the confines of marriage (Genesis 2:24). Within marriage God's Word says in essence: Run that play. Run it often (read Hebrews 13:4).

Sex is a beautiful gift designed by God. It has always been a big deal to Him. He created it for basically three reasons:

1. Procreation. Precious children created in God's own image with an eternal soul (Genesis 9:1).

2. Marital pleasure. That special bond of security and intimacy reserved for a husband and wife (Song of Songs).

3. Symbolizing the union of Christ. The Bridegroom becoming one with His bride: the church (Ephesians 5:25).

Every time we think or act on a sexual impulse, we ought to be reminded of our spiritual intimacy with Jesus Christ.

Run the only play that results in true sexual intimacy—within marriage.

—RON BROWN, FORMER ASSISTANT COLLEGE FOOTBALL COACH

SPORTS NOTE:
At one time, Coach Brown was considered for the head coaching job at a major university but was turned down because the school didn't think his Christian convictions would mesh at the school.

FROM THE PLAYBOOK:
Read
1 Corinthians
7:12–20.

GAME PLAN: Where are you getting your information about what is acceptable sexual behavior? From TV? The movies? Songs? Or from the Word of God?

ONLY AS A RESULT OF FAITH

POINT OF EMPHASIS:
Faith to overcome

"Faith is being sure of what we hope for." HEBREWS 11:1

Jean Driscoll was born with spina bifida. Doctors predicted she would never walk and that she would most likely remain dependent on her parents her entire life.

Despite the odds, Jean became one of the world's most decorated athletes. She won the wheelchair division of the prestigious Boston Marathon eight times and medaled in three Olympic games. Jean says her success in racing was built on the foundation of her faith and a passage of Scripture that has become her personal creed: "Faith is being sure of what we hope for and certain of what we do not see" (Hebrews 11:1). "That verse helped me see my disability through different lenses," Jean says. "Walking is overrated. Jesus Christ suffered and died on the cross for my sin. I now know, by faith, that He lives in me and gives me grace day by day."

For most of Jean's life, people placed limitations on her. "I went from feeling worthless to having Olympic medals and a fan base. It blows me away that people recognize me when I go to the grocery store." With her success has come responsibility. Jean welcomes the opportunity to be a role model who shows how to live up to the motto she includes with her autograph: "Dream Big and Work Hard."

"For young people and adults," Jean says, "the biggest limitations are the ones you place on yourself. You have to experience failure before you can appreciate success."

Like Jean did, take time to reflect on a trial or failure that helped you appreciate the success God has given you.

—ROXANNE ROBBINS

SPORTS NOTE:
Jean was named the Women's Sport Federation Sportswoman of the Year in 1991.

FROM THE PLAYBOOK:
See who made the "Hall of Faith" in Hebrews 11.

GAME PLAN: Take a step of faith this week. Do something you know you should do but have been afraid to do. Afterward, write down what God taught you about faith through this exercise.

CHECK YOUR ATTITUDE

POINT OF EMPHASIS:
The value of a Christlike attitude

"Your attitude should be the same as that of Christ Jesus."
PHILIPPIANS 2:5

A first-round draft choice of the San Diego Chargers in 1983, Gill Byrd had an outstanding NFL career. He was selected to the All-Pro team four times, inducted into the Charger Hall of Fame (1998), and named to the Charger All-Time Team (2000).

SPORTS NOTE:
In 2003, Gill Byrd became an assistant defensive coach for the St. Louis Rams.

FROM THE PLAYBOOK:
Read 1 Peter 4:1–5.

As I grew up in San Francisco, my mom always asked me if my attitude was right. I never really grasped the significance of her question until I became heavily involved in sports, specifically in the National Football League. While talent got me by in Pop Warner, high school, and college, my attitude played a much bigger role in my overall development once I entered the NFL. First Peter 4:1–2 states that we need to have the same attitude that Christ had. Let me share one incident with you.

During my rookie season, my attitude surrounded me—and me alone. I thought I could *want* to be the best without having the *will* to be the best and still have success on and off the field. My coach asked me if I knew the difference between *activity* and *productivity*. He explained that it all started with the proper attitude in believing in your teammates and carrying out your assignments. As I took the field before that game, my attitude didn't reflect it all being about me. It reflected how my attitude could impact my teammates.

The same is true when it comes to our walk with God. Jesus' attitude was to serve. Our attitude should also be to serve. As a Christian, our first priority should be a willingness to give up any liberty that we have so we can lead someone to Christ. What's *your* attitude today?

—GILL BYRD, FORMER NFL CORNERBACK

GAME PLAN: Sometimes it's good to have an attitude check. And the best way to do that is to see if your attitude about life is at all like Jesus' attitude would be.

CHECK YOUR ACTIONS

POINT OF EMPHASIS:
Doing the right thing

"Let us not love with words or tongue but with actions." 1 JOHN 3:18

Gill Byrd's teammates voted him their most inspirational player (1987-1992). He also won the 1988 Ed Block Courage Award and the 1993 Bart Starr Award for exemplary leadership on and off the field.

In yesterday's devotional, we touched on our attitude. Next we move on to our actions, which are a reflection of our attitude. First Peter 4:2–3 says our actions are consistent with what God wants us to do.

In about my fourth year in the NFL, I thought I had the right attitude regarding a couple of my teammates. The team wanted to replace me with a younger cornerback. He was a great guy, but I knew my job was in jeopardy. One side of me wanted to help the young buck develop into the best possible player he could be. The other side said, "No way! This is my job." My attitude was to do whatever I needed to do in order to show that I was the best player, even if it meant not doing what was best for the team.

A more mature Christian challenged me, saying that if I truly had the attitude and belief that Jesus was in control of my life, I needed to have the right actions—actions reflecting the fact that God was in control.

When you are faced with a situation that involves doing the right thing but you lack the right attitude, how do you respond? As a Christian, it's easy to get caught up in the pleasures of the world and justify doing the wrong thing because everybody else is doing it. Don't get caught in that trap!

—GILL BYRD, FORMER NFL CORNERBACK

SPORTS NOTE:
Gill Byrd was inducted into the San Diego Chargers Hall of Fame in 1998.

FROM THE PLAYBOOK:
Read 1 John 3.

GAME PLAN: How do your attitudes result in actions? Are your actions sometimes not pleasing to God but instead pleasing to you or to others? How can you change that?

CHECK YOUR ASSOCIATES

POINT OF EMPHASIS:
Picking friends

"Bad company corrupts good character." I CORINTHIANS 15:33

After serving as head of player development for the Green Bay Packers (1999-2001), Byrd founded Players Chapel Program, a non-profit Christian organization that uses Christian professional athletes to help raise funds for organizations that disciple youth.

We have all heard the saying, "Birds of a feather, flock together." When it comes to being obedient to what the Bible teaches, our associations play a vital role in our attitudes and actions.

SPORTS NOTE:
Gill Byrd holds the San Diego Chargers all-time record for interceptions (42).

As a player in the National Football League, it was critical for me to have individuals around me who had the same goals I did. I needed people who would encourage me, who would show me what it meant to serve others, and who would challenge me to be more than I thought I could be. One friend named Tim Ware showed me the type of attitude and actions I needed to have to be the best player on the field. We worked out together and we studied the Bible together.

FROM THE PLAYBOOK:
Read 1 Samuel 20, the story of two true friends.

It's the same when it comes to being a Christian. Who are you hanging out with? What attitudes do your friends possess? What actions are seen consistently in their lives?

There is a big difference between *belief* and *behavior*. I can believe all I want about being the best player in the NFL. But if I'm not hanging around the right people and turning that belief into behavior in how I challenge and love others, I will not achieve my ultimate goals.

First Peter 4:4 clearly supports the fact that "Birds of a feather" do indeed "flock together." Don't doubt it for a second!

—GILL BYRD, FORMER NFL CORNERBACK

GAME PLAN: Do you have any friends who will keep you in check as Gill was talking about? What kinds of questions do you ask each other as you try to stay accountable?

CHECK YOUR ACCOUNTABILITY

POINT OF EMPHASIS:
Being accountable

"I opposed him to his face, because he was clearly in the wrong."
GALATIANS 2:11

It's a fact of human nature: We don't want to be held accountable for our actions! But that's the world of the professional athlete.

I hated being critiqued every day in practice and then every week about my performance in the game. When you have the mentality that you want to be a straight A student in life, you realize that having the right attitude, actions, and associates means being able to accept being held accountable. It also means you need the courage to hold others accountable.

You see, when I played there were a number of athletes who would look you straight in the eye and say, "Who do you think you are that you can hold me accountable for my actions?" Isn't it the same in our walk with God? First Peter 4:5 tells us that God will hold us accountable for the things we do.

The biggest misconception is that we can't, in love, hold our brothers and sisters accountable for their attitude, actions, and associates. As a player, understanding the importance of accountability was a scary proposition. Once I was able to live out that principle with my teammates, we were all on the same page and became a more effective and efficient organization.

When we begin to grasp the importance of accountability, the body of Christ will become a functional, thriving presence in whatever community we live.

—GILL BYRD, FORMER NFL CORNERBACK

SPORTS NOTE:
Gill and Marilyn Byrd have two sons, Gill II and Jarius, who both have played college football.

FROM THE PLAYBOOK:
Read Galatians 2.

GAME PLAN: Are you opposed to accountability? What dangers can that lead to? What dangers does that bring a person in leadership? How have we seen a lack of accountability bring people down?

YOU AND GOD MAKE A TEAM

POINT OF EMPHASIS:
With God, you're never alone

"You will seek me and find me when you seek me with all your heart."
JEREMIAH 29:13

God has taught me many precious lessons through playing basketball in Europe. Most important, though, He has taught me to rely solely on Him to meet my needs.

I have lived in Italy for several years, and during this time many obstacles have arisen to halt my spiritual growth. First, there is a language barrier that at times seems impossible to overcome. There are no English-speaking churches here, and I have yet to meet an American Christian in this small city of Italy. Second, my teammates are good men, but none of them know the Lord the way I do. It would be easy for me to make up excuses for becoming stagnant in my spiritual walk, but I have chosen another route. That route is to seek God with all my heart. The Lord tells us in Jeremiah 29:13, "You will seek me and find me when you seek me with all your heart."

If you feel as if you are living the Christian life on your own, take heart. Continue to obey the Lord and seek Him with all your heart. Like the tree that flourishes in a drought, the godly person who delights in God's Word can survive a spiritual desert as well.

C. S. Lewis described it magnificently in *The Screwtape Letters*. He said, "Satan's cause is never more in danger than when a human being no longer desiring, but still intending to do God's will, looks around upon a world from which every trace of God seems to have vanished and asks why he has been forsaken, yet still obeys." Standing alone? Keep this in mind: God is still there, and He wants you to lean on him.

—CASEY SHAW, PRO BASKETBALL PLAYER

SPORTS NOTE:
Casey Shaw's brother-in-law, Scott Drew, took over the embattled Baylor University basketball program in 2003.

FROM THE PLAYBOOK:
Read C. S. Lewis's book, *The Screwtape Letters*.

GAME PLAN: If you are stuck in a spiritual desert, refocus your attention on God and His Word. That will bring hope and help.

IN A FOG

POINT OF EMPHASIS:

"In all your ways acknowledge him, and he will make your paths straight." PROVERBS 3:6

Dense fog and sailing are not a good mix. A few summers ago, on the last day of a week-long youth group trip, our ten-boat flotilla woke up to thick fog. The final leg of our journey was a long one that required careful navigation to avoid running aground.

Fortunately, several of the captains were prepared for just such an event. So we pulled up anchors and ventured out, closely following the captains who knew exactly where they were going.

How did they know? They were using Global Positioning System (GPS) instruments, which use satellites positioned around the globe. Signals from space enable people on earth to determine their exact position.

After we had motored (no wind for the sails) for a long time through the fog across a vast bay, able to see only the boat ahead of us, suddenly the key buoy appeared just to the port side of our boat. We were right on course!

Since that day I have often wished I had that kind of foolproof system of finding my way through life when it seemed I was in a fog. At those times I have concluded that often all we can do is faithfully follow the One leading the way. We can trust Him to bring us right where He wants us to be (Proverbs 3:5–6).

We may not be able to see very far ahead, but we are able to keep Christ in view, talk with Him, seek His wisdom, ask for His protection from poor choices, and live in obedience to Him.

He will get us through those foggy decision-making situations and take us exactly where He wants us to be.

—KURT DE HAAN

SPORTS NOTE: The most famous sailing race in the world is the America's Cup, which has been contested since 1851.

FROM THE PLAYBOOK: Read Proverbs 3:1–6.

 GAME PLAN: At what times in your life has it seemed as if you were in a fog? How have you followed God through those times? What key decisions will you be facing soon? How will you know what God wants you to do?

NOVEMBER 23

REPLACE COMPLAINTS WITH THANKS

POINT OF EMPHASIS:
Thankfulness

"Give thanks in all circumstances." I THESSALONIANS 5:18

During my junior year at Northwestern University, I learned an important lesson about thankfulness. It was midseason, and we had yet to win a game. Our homecoming game was very close—going back and forth right down to the last seconds. Trailing by 2 with 7 seconds left, we called a timeout on the 17-yard line and sent the field goal unit out for the game-winning field goal. The kick was tipped, however, and it went just wide. Instead of an exhilarating win, we suffered a bitter defeat.

That loss hurt badly. It didn't seem fair that we never seemed to catch a break. Our chances of winning a single game that year started to look grim. The next week I was sitting in church and started complaining to God about how life was unfair. When I finally stopped, God quietly spoke to me. He asked me how many people would love to be in my shoes? How many would love to have a scholarship to Northwestern? How many would love to start for a Division I team? How many would just love the chance to play football? How many would just love to be able to walk?

Thinking about those questions made me ashamed of complaining. I had a lot to be thankful for. I started approaching each day, each practice, and each game with thankfulness. It didn't change my circumstances, but it changed me within the circumstances. I ended up working harder and enjoying life more in the midst of a difficult season.

—BOB CHRISTIAN, FORMER NFL RUNNING BACK

SPORTS NOTE:
Bob Christian, who supports the organization Life Athletes, says abstinence before marriage is best because "God, who loves us and is all knowing, intended it that way."

FROM THE PLAYBOOK:
Read Psalm 118:1–16.

GAME PLAN: How about making a things-to-be-thankful-for list. Add to it each day, and when crummy things happen, go to the list and remind yourself of reasons to give thanks.

POINT OF EMPHASIS:
Thanksgiving

"Give thanks to the Lord, for he is good." PSALM 107:1

Thanksgiving Day is special! (And not solely because of turkey and stuffing and family and football.)

Thanksgiving Day is special because it is the one day each year that our nation sets aside to pause and give thanks. Why is this so special? Because our country is giving us an entire day to follow a biblical teaching that, as Christians, we should be living out every day of the year—to give thanks in all circumstances.

This Thanksgiving, thank God for the beautiful sunrise you saw this week. Thank God for His grace. Thank God for your junior varsity basketball coach. Give thanks for your ankle sprain. Give thanks for your best friend on the basketball team. Thank God for the warm bed you sleep in each night. Thank God for the athletic trainer who tapes that injured ankle.

Thank God for the forgiveness you have in Jesus Christ. Give thanks for Mom and Dad and for their support of all your athletic endeavors. Give thanks that you're riding the bench and not playing as much as you'd like. Give thanks for all the safe bus rides to and from your athletic contests. Thank God for your athletic director. Give thanks for the school whose name is emblazoned across your jersey. Thank God for good nutrition. Thank God for the assistant coach who has helped you become a better player.

Thank God for His Son, Jesus Christ. Thank God for Christ's death on the cross that saves you from the penalty of your sin. Thank God for eternal life.

—ROB BENTZ

SPORTS NOTE: The National Football League played its first Thanksgiving Day game in 1934 when the Chicago Bears played the Detroit Lions at University of Detroit Stadium.

FROM THE PLAYBOOK: Read and memorize Psalm 7:17.

GAME PLAN: Make a list of ten things—good and bad—that you are thankful for right now. Share them with your family and/or friends at the Thanksgiving meal.

NOVEMBER 25

SAY THANKS ANYWAY

POINT OF EMPHASIS:
Thankfulness

"Thanks be to God! He gives us the victory." I CORINTHIANS 15:57

A friend sent me an e-mail that suggests some new ways to look at thankfulness. According to the note:

• If you have food in the refrigerator, clothes on your back, a roof overhead, and a place to sleep, you are richer than 75 percent of this world.

• If you have money in the bank, in your wallet, and spare change in a dish some place, you are among the top 8 percent of the world's wealthy.

SPORTS NOTE:
Casey Shaw played in 2005 for a team in Italy after spending time on a team in Spain.

FROM THE PLAYBOOK:
Read 1 Thessalonians 5:16–18.

• If you woke up this morning with more health than illness, you are more blessed than the million who will not survive this week.

• If you have never experienced the danger of battle, the loneliness of imprisonment, the agony of torture, or the pangs of starvation, you are ahead of 500 million people in the world.

• If you can attend church meetings without fear of harassment, arrest, torture, or death, you are more blessed than three billion in the world.

It is easy to be thankful when things are going our way, but a Christian can rise above any situation—even the ones mentioned above—to thank God for causing all things to work together for good.

Paul, the apostle, was a man who suffered much pain, yet he wrote, "Be joyful always; pray continually; give thanks in all circumstances, for this is God's will for you in Christ Jesus" (1 Thessalonians 5:16–18). Paul's thankfulness was not conditioned on any circumstance. He gave great praise to God because of His wonderful attributes, works, and words.

Paul knew that all eternity would not be enough time to thank God for His tender mercies. We should all follow Paul's example of thankfulness today.

—CASEY SHAW, PRO BASKETBALL PLAYER

GAME PLAN: What are the Top 5 things you are thankful for? Make a note to pray for these things faithfully in the next few days.

GOD'S PLAN

POINT OF EMPHASIS:
God's Plan

"And who knows but that you have come to royal position for such a time as this." ESTHER 4:14

For as long as I can remember, I always aspired to be a basketball star. After many years of hard work, I accomplished my goal—I made it to the pros! At the pinnacle of my career, I was the highest paid professional athlete. David Thompson was a household name; little kids patterned their games after "Skywalker." The fame felt good. But then it all ended.

Through my trials and tribulations God stood His ground and carried me through. He was my refuge. After I had recovered, my basketball days were over—I was no longer able to play, but I was able to tell my story and share how without God's grace I would have never overcome my problems. And although I missed inspiring people on the basketball courts, I was motivating people in a much more important way. I was encouraging them to grow in their relationship to Christ.

In the Bible, Esther was placed in the kingdom "for such a time" to save her people. God places us in a variety of situations and circumstances, and although we may be unsure of His reasoning, God is always in control. He has a plan for our lives. So in each situation you find yourself in, think of how you can use it to help others grow in the Lord.

Maybe you were placed there for such a time as this!

—DAVID THOMPSON, FORMER NBA STAR

SPORTS NOTE: David Thompson's autobiography *Skywalker* tells the story of his troubled NBA career and his rise from the destruction of drugs.

FROM THE PLAYBOOK: Read Esther 4.

GAME PLAN: Think about where you are today and what you are scheduled to do. How can you make sure what you accomplish today is done for God's glory?

PARRY'S PERSEVERANCE

POINT OF EMPHASIS:
Enduring life's hardships

"Trust in God; trust also in me." JOHN 14:1

Neil Parry is a guy with a lot of stick-to-it-iveness. Several years ago, the San Jose State football player had his lower right leg amputated after a serious injury.

Game over, right? No more football, correct?

Wrong.

Neil set a goal to make it back to the gridiron. He wanted to play again.

What he endured along the way is hard to believe: 25 operations, 15 prosthetic legs, and a lot of setbacks.

In September of 2003, however, Neil Parry lined up for a San Jose State punt return. The ball was hiked, and Parry hit two players at the line and proceeded downfield—looking for a block.

Parry played just that one play during the game, and his team lost to Nevada 42–30, but the crowd cheered for him—having witnessed his amazing example of guts and determination.

Life can often hit us with some devastating results. Our first reaction may be to fight back out of anger—or to curl up and shut off the rest of the world.

Jesus, however, has a better plan. He tells us to "Trust in God; trust also in me" (John 14:1). His words helped calm the troubled hearts of disciples like Peter, who were unsure they could endure what lay ahead.

As we trust in Jesus, with a deep belief in His faithfulness, we are better equipped to endure life's hardships. Make it your goal to trust Him with all your heart (Proverbs 3:5–6), and you'll be amazed at your ability to persevere—whatever comes your way.

—TOM FELTEN

SPORTS NOTE:
The NCAA had to revamp its insurance coverage to accommodate Neil Parry's return to football, something the organization did to acknowledge and honor Parry's courageous comeback.

FROM THE PLAYBOOK:
Read John 14:1–14.

GAME PLAN: Take a few minutes to write down the names of some believers in Jesus you know who have gone through great trials and persevered. How did trusting in Jesus help them along the way?

QUITTERS CAN BE WINNERS

POINT OF EMPHASIS:
The value of godliness

"Godliness has value for all things." I TIMOTHY 4:8

Is there life after football? On many campuses at this time of year, that may be a debatable issue!

Bo Schembechler, who was the head coach of the Michigan Wolverines for twenty years, learned early in his career that football is only part of life. When he came to Michigan, his coaches put up a sign above the locker-room door. It said, "Those Who Stay Will Be Champions."

Some time later, Bo noticed that someone had scribbled underneath, "And those who quit will be doctors, lawyers, and captains of industry."

Although quitting is often seen as a coward's escape hatch, quitters can sometimes be winners. Quitters become winners when they rearrange their priorities in life and stop spending too much time on things that have no lasting benefit.

The apostle Paul told Timothy that physical training has some value, but when compared with spiritual pursuits it's way down the list. Godliness, though, has value "for both the present life and the life to come" (I Timothy 4:8). That's why Paul told young Timothy to make his spiritual life a high priority.

SPORTS NOTE:
While the football coach at Michigan, Schembechler won 194 games and lost just 48.

FROM THE PLAYBOOK:
Read 1 Timothy 4:7–16.

Your efforts to read the Bible today and even to read this devotional show that you are interested in developing your spiritual life. You're on the right track. But some days it's hard to know which activities to quit so you have time to "train yourself to be godly" (v. 7). Those are the issues of life that really last.

Make choices that reflect a long-range, eternal view of life. Quit whatever blocks your spiritual progress. Then in God's record book you'll be a true champion!

—KURT DE HAAN

GAME PLAN: What activities crowd out time for prayer or church or service to others? Is the way you choose to use your time a good example to those around you? God never plays games with us.

POSITIVELY HOWARD

POINT OF EMPHASIS:
Glorifying God through troubles

"[God] comforts us in all our troubles, so that we can comfort those in any trouble with the comfort we ourselves have received from God." 2 CORINTHIANS 1:4

Tim Howard did something rather unusual. This American-born soccer goalie has made the big move from US pro soccer to the English Premier League by joining the world-famous Manchester United team.

Howard's success in the US before he left in 2003 to play in England not only benefited his teammates, but it also served as an example to children with Tourette's Syndrome, an incurable neurological disorder producing uncontrollable tics.

SPORTS NOTE:
To sign Tim Howard when he first joined ManU, the team had to pay a fee of 2.3 million pounds.

FROM THE PLAYBOOK:
Read
2 Corinthians
1.

"I'm trying to let these kids know that they can look to me as a role model," says Howard, who has Tourette's. "I've achieved an amazing dream of being a pro athlete, and I'm letting them know they can do anything they want."

While playing in Major League Soccer, Howard treated more than 200 children with Tourette's Syndrome to a MetroStars' home game at Giants Stadium. After the game, Howard stayed for two hours to answer questions.

"One kid was so afraid to try out for his high school team that he never even bothered to try," Howard recalls. "He was so afraid of his tics and being made fun of. After seeing me and hearing me speak, he said he was going to try out."

Former teammate Steve Shak admires Howard's courage.

"He turned what most of society believes to be a negative into a positive and used his influence to glorify God," Shak says. "He has shown me what it means to be fearless in life. The world has been made a better place because Tim successfully lives with Tourette's Syndrome."

What difficulty has God given you that you can use to glorify Him?

—DAVE BRANON

GAME PLAN: Think about what God has allowed to happen in your life. Do you think others have gone through the same thing? How can you help others through what God has taught you?

NEVER GIVE UP

POINT OF EMPHASIS:
Winning through perseverance

"Be strong and do not give up." 2 Chronicles 15:7

The LA crowd was stunned. Its mighty USC Trojan football team was being blown away by Notre Dame. It was 24–6 at halftime. The Irish, then defending national champions, had made the Trojans look like chumps.

The second half began with a kickoff to USC's Anthony Davis. Suddenly, on this bleak November day in 1974, the stadium erupted as Davis took the ball from two yards deep in his end zone all the way to pay dirt. 102 yards! Touchdown, USC!

Davis scored another TD on the Trojan's next possession. The score was now 24–19, and Notre Dame was wondering where the famous "luck of the Irish" had gone.

By the time the smoke had cleared, the Trojans had annihilated the Irish, 55–24. USC's coach John McKay called it, "probably one of the wildest things that ever happened on a football field."

The bottom line? USC never gave up.

In our lives, there are times when we've been beaten down. Maybe we've "blown it" over the first half of this month—or this life. Perhaps we feel inept in our relationships or careers.

If so, listen to this: "Be strong and do not give up" (2 Chronicles 15:7). The Lord gave those words to a man named Azariah, who delivered them to a troubled king by the name of Asa.

Az also told him, "The Lord is with you when you are with him. If you seek him, he will be found by you" (v. 2).

Regardless of your situation, seek God and His will. Never give up. If you've trusted Christ, God is on your side—and that's all you need.

—Tom Felten

SPORTS NOTE: Trailing 31–0 at halftime, the Maryland Terrapins came back to defeat Miami 42–40 in the greatest comeback in college football history.

FROM THE PLAYBOOK: Read 2 Chronicles 15:1–7.

GAME PLAN: Write down what you feel are the biggest failures in your life. Next, write down how you feel God views you in spite of your challenges. Pray to Him for renewed strength and commitment.

MORNING READING

POINT OF EMPHASIS:
Morning devotions

"In the morning, O Lord, you hear my voice." PSALM 5:3

When is the best time to read the Bible and spend time with God? If you're like some people who think the morning is some kind of daily punishment, you'll say evening. Although we can't say for sure, the morning certainly does get its fair share of biblical mention as a good time to meet with God.

Psalm 90:14 gives us a pretty good rationale for doing so. It says, "Satisfy us in the morning with your unfailing love, that we may sing for joy and be glad all our days." It's kind of a get-ready-for-the-day philosophy, and it seems to make sense.

SPORTS NOTE:
In 1995, Bill Brooks caught a team-record 11 touchdowns for the Buffalo Bills.

FROM THE PLAYBOOK:
Read Psalm 90:13–17.

Former NFL player Bill Brooks would agree with that practical guidance. About his own God-directed moments he said, "I like to get up every morning and read. I think that's the only way I can start my day—get up and read the good Word the Lord has given us and try to use that in my everyday walk of life and apply it to my life."

Morning reading is good because it can set the tone for the rest of the day. And, as Brooks pointed out, it makes application of God's Word throughout the day that much easier.

Are you a morning Bible reader? If not, try it. You just might find it a good way to "be glad all [y]our days."

—DAVE BRANON

GAME PLAN: Morning, nighttime, or not at all? Where do you stand on the devotions scale? What plan can you create to help you develop the habit of meeting with God each day?

TRUSTING GOD'S PLAN

POINT OF EMPHASIS:
Trusting God

"Trust in the Lord with all your heart." PROVERBS 3:5

Trust is a difficult concept to grasp. It is even harder when the chips are down.

I remember the second time I made it through Qualifying School for the LPGA Tour. I had shot 83 the first day, and the prospects of keeping my card on Tour weren't looking very bright. After much prayer and reflection, I decided that there wasn't much I could control, and I decided that I would give the rest of the week over to God.

The only thing I could control was to discipline myself to stay committed and play every shot to the best of my ability. How the rest of the field did was something that I could not control. I knew that God held my future in His hands and that no matter what happened, He knew what was best for me. After deciding that I would yield control to God, a tremendous burden was lifted from me because I knew that I no longer had to worry. All I had to do was my very best and trust that God knew the best plan and way for me.

The next day I shot a 67, and I picked up my first career hole-in-one. I also played well the remaining two days, and I was able to keep my card for the following season.

There is something freeing about letting go and letting God handle your concerns. It is hard to do, because we all want to exercise some form of control in our lives. If we could just learn to let God be in charge, we would have less to worry about in our lives. After all, He's our Maker. Of course He knows the best plan for our lives.

—SIEW AI LIM, LPGA GOLFER

SPORTS NOTE:
Siew Ai's name is pronounced "See-you I."

FROM THE PLAYBOOK:
Read Proverbs 16:1–9.

GAME PLAN: What area of your life are you having trouble giving up to God? Is it a matter of trust or a matter of simply not wanting to let go?

THE ESSENCE OF LEADERSHIP

POINT OF EMPHASIS:
Training for leadership

"Train yourself to be godly. For physical training is of some value, but godliness has value for all things." I TIMOTHY 4:7–8

In my younger years of playing sports, I could not understand the reason for everything being so structured. The coach would make us run grueling wind sprints for not practicing well or enthusiastically. We would continue to run even if only one player was out of position on a play. We would have to run these plays over and over—again and again.

But later I discovered that in this was the essence of leadership. Leadership is a repetitive pattern practiced the right way. As humans we know that we can practice bad habits, so practice does not necessarily make perfect—it only makes the habit we practice permanent. However, perfect practice makes perfect.

Let's think of a clothing pattern for a moment. If the pattern is not correct, then everything that follows it will be out of order. The sleeves may be too short or the length may be too long. We don't want to fall short of the promises God has for our lives, and certainly we don't want to wait too long to capture God's glory.

In I Timothy 4:12, the apostle Paul challenges Timothy to be a pattern to believers in word (keeping your word when you give it), in conduct (the way you handle conflict at crucial moments), in love (giving something that is really precious to you, like your time), in faith (allowing the Holy Spirit to lead you somewhere that is uncomfortable), and in purity (putting your hope in Him, because "everyone who has this hope purifies himself, just as he is pure"—I John 3:3).

If we too follow that pattern, we'll begin to understand what God wants us to do as we train to be leaders for him.

—CHARLIE WARD, NBA GUARD

SPORTS NOTE:
College Football News named Charlie Ward as one of the 100 best college football players of all time.

FROM THE PLAYBOOK:
Read 1 Timothy 4:6–16.

GAME PLAN: Leadership takes a lot of hard work, dedication, and repetition to make sure your pattern and lifestyle are leading people to Christ. Check your own pattern to see if it is worth duplicating. What areas of improvement are necessary?

DEATH OF A DREAM

POINT OF EMPHASIS:
Giving dreams to God

"You intended to harm me, but God intended it for good."
GENESIS 50:20

When Jean-Guy Talbot took a two-hander at a member of the Junior Canadiens in a 1952 hockey game, the bloody result resembled a scalping. Talbot's target never amounted to much after that assault—not on the ice anyway.

Yet that victim has hoisted the Stanley Cup a record nine times. He has more wins than any head coach in NHL history. His name is Scotty Bowman—a sure-fire Hall of Fame coach.

That injury meant the death of a dream. But it gave rise to another dream, with fantastic results.

The Bible is full of ordinary guys who became heroes after their dreams died. Accused of a crime he didn't commit, Joseph the dreamer endured slavery and then imprisonment. Yet he became second in command to Pharaoh and rescued his own family. He graciously told his brothers, "You intended to harm me [by selling me into slavery], but God intended it for good" (Genesis 50:20).

Moses went from a basket in the Nile to Pharaoh's palace. Then he fled the palace because of a crime he *did* commit. Tending sheep in the Arabian Desert for 40 years, his dreams evaporated—until he led the greatest escape in history. Psalm 105:26 says, "[God] sent Moses his servant . . . whom he had chosen."

Whom He had chosen! Moses must have felt his life slipping away after he left the palace. But God's plans are always greater than our dreams.

Are your dreams dying? Give them to God. Then hang on! With the Creator, the ride is usually a wild one.

—TIM GUSTAFSON

SPORTS NOTE:
As an NFL coach, Scotty Bowman won 1,244 games, including 223 in the playoffs.

FROM THE PLAYBOOK:
Read Psalm 105:16–41.

GAME PLAN: Write down a couple of your dreams. How do they line up with the priorities God wants you to have? Do you really trust God with your future?

THE GIRLS HAVE GAME

POINT OF EMPHASIS:
The fallout from prejudice

"Don't show favoritism." JAMES 2:1

My daughter's first basketball game of the season was going to be brutal to watch.

At least that's what I thought. In my mind I saw a mix of soccer and rugby being played on a basketball court. This brand of basketball was hardly ready for a debut on the X-Games. More like the Z-Games. Zzzzzzzzzz. Wake me up when it's over.

But to my utter amazement I saw bounce passes, picks being set, and even a made 3-pointer. The girls do have game. The problem was my prejudice. I didn't even realize it at first.

I think a lot of us are that way. I'm all for my daughter playing sports. Girls have talent, no question about it. But I had pre-judged this group of eighth-grade girls. Yeah, I was bad and I admit it. Sometimes I'm not too smart.

This whole thing got me thinking deeper. About me, about us as humans, and about those of us who say we're Christians. Are we willing to admit the prejudice that may be in our spiritual lives?

In his book *Growing Slowly Wise*, author David Roper expounds on the subject of pre-judging. He says, "Prejudice, whether elitism, sexism, ageism, or racism, is not a minor fault. It's serious sin. To justify and defend it, rather than repent of it suggests that I may not be a Christian at all. James minces no words. I can't be a bigot and call myself a believer."

I told my daughter I was sorry for thinking all I'd see at her game was a rugby scrum on a basketball court.

—DAN DEAL

SPORTS NOTE:
In 2004, the number of girls who played high school basketball in the United States stood at 457,070.

FROM THE PLAYBOOK:
Read James 2:1–13 and Matthew 5:7.

 GAME PLAN: Jesus tells each of us to act and speak in mercy. The reason is, we're judged by the same standard that we use to pre-judge others.

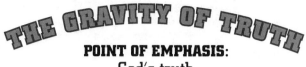

THE GRAVITY OF TRUTH

POINT OF EMPHASIS:
God's truth

"I am the way and the truth and the life." JOHN 14:6

Let's say I took you to the top floor of New York City's tallest building—the Empire State Building. What if I then opened the window and said, "Jump!" Would you do that? I don't think so! You understand the law called "gravity." The one God created and Isaac Newton discovered. Because of gravity, jumping would be a long fall to your death.

But what if someone said, "Wait a minute, Brown, that's *your* truth. Who says there's only one truth? We believe that with proper technique you could actually float!"

Then what if the whole world started to trust in this lie—that one could float after jumping out of a tall building? What if I were the only person left in the whole world who believed that one would fall—not float? Would that change the truth?

Does the majority rule here? NO! Truth is not Silly Putty that can be shaped however we want. Trust the truth regardless of how the majority votes.

Jesus made a definitive statement in John 14:6. He said, "I am the way and the truth and the life. No one comes to the Father except through me."

Most of the world has rejected that statement and the One who made it. Many believe there are other roads to God. They feel they can believe what they want and "float" into the arms of God one day. That, however, is trusting a lie.

Truth—like gravity—is not about numerical majority. Count on this—there is one truth. That truth is in Jesus Christ alone. Don't jump to the majority. Stand on the truth.

—RON BROWN, FORMER COLLEGE FOOTBALL COACH

SPORTS NOTE:
Ron Brown has written two books: *The Mark of a Champion* and *The First Kingdom War.*

FROM THE PLAYBOOK:
Read John 1.

GAME PLAN: What are some areas of truth that you've been wondering about recently? How do you test man's teachings vs. God's truth? How do you know which is which?

DECEMBER 7

THE DAY THEY RETIRED MY JERSEY

POINT OF EMPHASIS:
Honoring Christ

"I can do everything through him who gives me strength."
PHILIPPIANS 4:13

In December 2004 I was so excited to return to my high school in Michigan to have a ceremony to retire my high school jersey. The problem was that the day before my jersey was to be retired, I had an NBA game in Los Angeles.

So, I had to take a "red-eye" flight from LA to Michigan. While on the plane, I started to feel a sharp pain in my side. I tried to sleep it off but just couldn't get rid of the feeling. When I got home, my mom even tried to make me some chicken and rice before the ceremony to make me feel better. But the pain continued.

The jersey retirement ceremony had been planned for a long time, and I did not want to disappoint my high school coaches and fans. Although I felt awful, I decided to go through with it. I prayed that Jesus would give me the strength to make it through. The ceremony went great, but toward the end I had to ask my brother to take me to see a doctor.

When I got to the hospital, I was told I needed an emergency appendectomy. That was tough because as an NBA player I did not want to miss any games and let my team down. It was Wednesday, and I knew we had a game in three days. I was so bummed when the doctor told me I would probably need at least a few weeks to heal after the surgery.

My family began to pray for me that it would be a successful surgery and recovery. God blessed me, because on Saturday I was back in Los Angeles trying to help my Clippers teammates to a victory. I made a behind-the-back pass that electrified the crowd. I think the fans felt that God had given me the extra strength and healing I needed.

In the end, I wanted Jesus Christ to be honored and glorified on that day, and I know He was.   —CHRIS KAMAN, NBA CENTER

GAME PLAN: In hard times, ask for perfect strength from the Lord in prayer, and He will give you the strength to endure.

LESSONS FROM LOSING

POINT OF EMPHASIS:
God's purposes

"In all things God works for the good of those who love him."
ROMANS 8:28

I am a competitive person. Every time I step on the ice, the goal for my team is to win.

One season we were off to a great start, winning our first three games—just the way I like it. But before we knew it, we were struggling through an ugly winless streak.

Losing is no fun. But for me to think that we can win all 82 games in an NHL season is simply unrealistic. I have had to learn a few things about how to handle a loss. So I choose to become more focused on winning the next game, and to play with more intensity and determination. I try to encourage our players and bring out their strengths. I purpose to become a better teammate and player in spite of defeat.

In life we can feel defeated by circumstances that come at us. In the midst of the struggle, it is hard to imagine that good will come out of difficult times. But God says it will. The Bible says that God causes everything to work for the good of those who love Him. He will take our times of defeat and work them out to give us something better.

Our team may not finish high in the standings—despite how hard we will play. But I can still trust that God has a purpose for me in this—just as He has for every detail of my life, because I love Him and am "called according to *His* purpose."

—SHANE DOAN, NHL CENTER

SPORTS NOTE:
Through the 2003–2004 season, Shane Doan had scored 351 NHL points in 648 games.

FROM THE PLAYBOOK:
Read James 1:2–8.

 GAME PLAN: Is there a situation in your life today that seems to be defeating you? Is there anything you can do to change the situation? When the situation is out of your hands, what can you do to place it in God's hands?

THEY CALL ME COACH

POINT OF EMPHASIS:
The importance of biblical teaching

"Your word is a lamp to my feet." PSALM 119:105

There they were, 12 girls waiting for the coach (me!) to start our first soccer practice. I was expecting a great year; we had some talented young ladies on the team.

So, filled with hope, I blew my whistle. There was that one little problem though. I'd never played organized soccer . . . ever! But I had an ace up my sleeve. These girls didn't need much coaching, I thought. They've all played for years, I figured. It would be simple. Or so I hoped.

I had only one drill to work on at our first practice. It took about 20 minutes. That left 1 hour and 40 minutes to kill. So I handed out jerseys. We drank some water. I handed out the schedule. We got another drink. It got so bad that half the girls sat down on the field and started talking about which boys they liked at school. Then one girl quit the team. Where was that ace again?

I had to take action. I went to the library and checked out a book on soccer. As I read, I learned some of the basic rules, simple strategies, and most important for me, coaching drills. I needed the book.

A couple of months later, I saw a parallel between my coaching experience and my life. I think it applies to each of our lives. We need help to live this life or it soon spirals out of control. There's a Book that will give you everything you need. It's called the Bible. As you read the Bible, you'll find a strategy for life that really works. We all need the Book.

—DAN DEAL

SPORTS NOTE:
In 2004, 309,032 girls competed on high school soccer teams across the United States.

FROM THE PLAYBOOK:
Read 2 Timothy 3:16–17.

GAME PLAN: Find your Bible and turn to the book of Proverbs. Start reading, and when you see a good coaching tip, write it down. You can begin your own personal playbook from the Bible.

A THANKS REMINDER

POINT OF EMPHASIS:
Thankfulness

"I have learned the secret of being content in any and every situation." PHILIPPIANS 4:12

During a recent basketball game, I observed the variety of fans gathering in the stands. One man in particular caught my eye; his crumpled hands, shriveled and weakened body made him quite unlike those around him. I watched him weave his way closer to the court, awkwardly steering his wheelchair as he maneuvered a joystick with his chin.

I was struck by this image. Here was a man who, without an obvious miracle, would never leave the chair he was sitting in, and here I was running freely without pain, enjoying an activity that I quite often take for granted.

I was humbled by the thought. How many times have I complained about running too many lines or having sore muscles or even the inconvenience of traveling for a game? Despite this man's circumstances, he sat there with a smile on his face enjoying every moment of the game.

We have received from God blessings beyond our imagination, yet somehow we manage to find something to complain about. God has asked us to be content in all circumstances, whether in plenty or in want. Often I need to remind myself that God has placed me where He wants me, and I am to be thankful for all He has given me.

No matter what your lot is in life, take a moment to think about all the blessings in your life. Learn to rely on God; He knows what is best for each of us, and He promises to give us strength to joyfully live each day.

— LEIGHANN REIMER, PRO BASKETBALL PLAYER

SPORTS NOTE: Leighann Reimer is the younger sister of NHL hockey star Shane Doan.

FROM THE PLAYBOOK: For more on this topic see 1 Timothy 6:6, 8 and Hebrews 13:5.

 GAME PLAN: What blessings has God placed in your life today? How can you find true contentment where you are right at this moment? Have you taken the time to thank God for all He has given you?

DECEMBER 11

SIN IN THE CAMP

POINT OF EMPHASIS:
Getting rid of sin

"It is true! I have sinned against the Lord." JOSHUA 7:20

As I think back on my days as a basketball coach at a Christian high school, I remember vividly one of my students coming to me after we had lost a couple of games and saying, "Coach, I think I know why we're losing. There's sin in the camp."

This astute and spiritually observant player was suggesting that some of his teammates were doing things they shouldn't be doing and that God would not honor our team. His "sin in the camp" line was a reference to the story of Achan, whose sin caused the Israelites to lose a battle at Ai. In that case, God was clearly upset with the sin, and He allowed the enemy to conquer Joshua's men.

SPORTS NOTE:
In 2004, there were 544,811 teenage boys who played on high school basketball teams in the United States.

FROM THE PLAYBOOK:
Read Joshua 7–8.

Although I was never convinced that our players' alleged indiscretions were why we were having trouble—I could see that it was often weak defense and poor free-throw shooting that were our problems—there is truth in the concept that sinful activity does cause trouble.

Think about what happened a few years ago with a football player who was arrested the night before his team was to play in the Super Bowl. The indiscretion of that player upset his teammates greatly, and neither he nor his fellow warriors performed well the next day. They were soundly defeated.

Here's the point. Whether our sin leads to a direct defeat because of God's discipline or not, we know that going against God's commands is a bad idea.

If there is sin in your camp, don't worry about whether it will lead to a defeat—worry about getting back into a strong, vibrant relationship with God. First John 1:9 says, "He is faithful and just and will forgive us our sins and purify us from all unrighteousness."

—DAVE BRANON

GAME PLAN: Be honest. What is it? What sin is in your camp? If there is something that you have been doing that violates God's standards, confess it to Him and find the joy of forgiveness.

NO GREATER TREASURE

POINT OF EMPHASIS:
The supremacy of Christ

"I consider everything a loss compared to the surpassing greatness of knowing Christ Jesus my Lord." PHILIPPIANS 3:8–9

As a football player, I certainly have been blessed. When I reflect on my career, I often wonder if it really happened or if I am only dreaming.

Whether it be a high school, college, or NFL Europe championship ring or even the Heisman Trophy, I'm extremely fortunate to possess such coveted awards and such fond memories. Yet in the midst of it all, I have also acquired another treasure so great that all of the football accolades, trophies, and memories pale in comparison. I have found a living and loving relationship with my Creator through His Son, Christ Jesus.

In the book of Philippians, Paul lists all of his accomplishments—and it is quite a list. Yet when he encountered Christ and the good news of the gospel, he considered "everything a loss compared to the surpassing greatness of knowing Christ Jesus." Compared to a relationship with Christ, he even called all of those good things he had done "rubbish."

As we think over our lives—the things we've done and the good things we've received—can we truly share in Paul's perspective? Have we truly encountered a God whose love so affects us that everything else pales in comparison?

May we dare pray that God would ravish us with the reality of His love and so transform us to live life in the fullness in which we were created? God certainly will bless those who do.

—DANNY WUERFFEL, FORMER NFL QUARTERBACK

SPORTS NOTE:
Danny Wuerffel is the only college quarterback who ever put together back-to-back seasons with quarterback ratings over 170.

FROM THE PLAYBOOK:
Read Philippians 3:1–11.

 GAME PLAN: List your five greatest accomplishments in life. Can any compare with knowing Jesus Christ personally? Are you sure you do know Him personally?

FEAR THE COACH

POINT OF EMPHASIS:
God's chastisement

"I consider that our present sufferings are not worth comparing with the glory that will be revealed in us." ROMANS 8:18

I spent most of my freshman year at the University of Kentucky living in fear. It wasn't the pressure of playing in front of 24,000 fans or playing on national television. It was the fear of being chastised by coach Rick Pitino.

Have you ever had a coach or boss who could make you feel one inch tall and put the "fear of God" in you? Coach Pitino could do that! He was never afraid to tell you what he really thought. As a matter of fact my first interaction with him sent me home crying. I was eighteen years old.

Why would anyone want to play for someone like that? Well, you wouldn't unless you wanted to be the absolute best basketball player you could be. With Pitino, it wasn't personal. It was coaching, and he expected you to take it as such. Listen, learn, and get better. Even if it hurt.

Similarly, there have been times in my life when God seemed unfair. What He was allowing to go on in my life seemed like too much for me to handle. It didn't seem to be something a loving Father would let His son go through.

But in His sovereignty and His love, God guides us through those times. Hebrews 12:7–11 tells us that God disciplines His children. It is for our good and growth that we endure trying and difficult times. It is because God loves His children that He refuses to leave us where we are. He wants us to share in His holiness.

God's chastising may seem difficult, but He does not want us to continue in our stagnant lives. Just like a coach, God wants us to be better.

— CAMERON MILLS, FORMER COLLEGE BASKETBALL PLAYER

SPORTS NOTE:
Cameron Mills, who played for the Kentucky Wildcats, runs a basketball camp in Lexington, Kentucky.

FROM THE PLAYBOOK:
Read Romans 8:1–27.

GAME PLAN: What is God speaking to you about? What does He want you to change for His glory and honor? Are you willing to be disciplined?

LEARNING IN LEAPS AND BOUNDS

POINT OF EMPHASIS:
Pleasing God

"In the same way, faith by itself, if it is not accompanied by action, is dead." JAMES 2:17

Growing up in Shelby, North Carolina, I spent most of my days on the basketball court. It was a small dirt court behind my house—but nevertheless it was a court.

As a ball player I was always noted for my jumping ability, hence the nickname "Skywalker." People would ask me, "How did you get to be such a great leaper?" Sure, some of it was genetics, but most of the ability came from the time I spent on that little dirt court in my backyard.

As a kid, I always dreamed of dunking a basketball, so every day I did jumping drills wearing ankle weights. I went to the gym, lifted, and then did more drills—all wearing my ankle weights. I would jump around the house knocking over plants, lamps, and anything else that got in my way. Needless to say, my mother wasn't too pleased. But if that was what it took, that was what I was going to do. Anything to accomplish my goal!

Later in life I realized that I needed to be that dedicated and devoted to God and His Word. Because Jesus died for our sins, we all have that "natural ability"; we are saved if we've trusted Him. But to have a lasting, strong relationship with Christ, we have to cultivate it. We have to read the Bible, pray continually, seek God in all our doings, and encourage others in Christ.

I may have been a good jumper without all the extra drills—but to become a *great* jumper I had to work. This is true of all Christians; we must put in that extra work for Christ in service, in faith, and in prayer. Our ultimate goal is to be pleasing to the Lord; we should do any and everything to accomplish that goal.

—DAVID THOMPSON, FORMER NBA PLAYER

SPORTS NOTE:
David Thompson's niece is Charlotte Smith-Taylor, who has had a long career in the WNBA.

FROM THE PLAYBOOK:
Read James 2.

GAME PLAN: Think of some goals you've set for yourself. Think of how hard you worked to achieve those goals. Did you ever have any spiritual goals for which you worked that hard?

DECEMBER 15

THE POWER OF THE WORD

POINT OF EMPHASIS:
God's Word

"The words I have spoken to you are spirit and they are life."
JOHN 6:63

Have you ever had a coach who hurt you with harsh words? Or did you have a coach who spoke carefully and lifted you up? It's been said that it takes ten positive phrases to knock out a negative one.

During my many years of coaching, I've come across a number of stories that demonstrate how powerful an encouraging word can be. Recently, I was told about a young girl who attended a basketball camp. She was participating in a one-minute shooting contest and was the least talented player on the court, but she put forth her best effort. After several attempts, she was close to beating her previous best score with time left on the clock. Her counselor shouted out, "You're dangerous!" She heard those words and proceeded to drain the last few buckets. Afterward, she reported her new best score to the head coach and said with a straight face, "Coach, I'm dangerous."

That's a humorous story, but it illustrates trust. That girl believed what her counselor told her. And we can believe Christ, who said, "The words I have spoken to you are spirit and they are life" (John 6:63).

We can trust that what God says in His Word is the truth for all. One day, the entire world will realize it. For now, let's speak words that build up those around us—strangers and friends alike. Mark my word, there will come a time when we will be very glad that we spoke words full of the Spirit and life.

—SUE SEMRAU, WOMEN'S COLLEGE BASKETBALL COACH

SPORTS NOTE:
In her Web site biography, Sue says, "Our lives are not determined by what happens to us, but by how we react to what happens."

FROM THE PLAYBOOK:
Read Psalm 119:89–96.

 GAME PLAN: Who needs you to speak up to them so you can share with them the power of God's Word?

FOR BETTER, FOR WORSE

POINT OF EMPHASIS:
The promise of marriage

"Marriage should be honored by all." HEBREWS 13:4

You have to admire the commitment and integrity reflected in a statement made by one of sport's brightest stars. He is possibly his game's best player, but he's under contract to a team that has finished either last or second to last in their division the past few years. Commenting on his situation, this recently married young man said, "Right now, it's like a marriage. You're going to go through ups and downs. My allegiance is to this team. I'm hoping with all my heart that we turn this around." That speaks well of his perspective of his professional life, and of the future health of his newly established marriage.

Knowing that there will be "ups and downs" is an important fact to remember about how we approach the commitments we make in life, especially the vows made at a wedding. Author David Roper, in his book *Out of the Ordinary* says, "The words 'for better, for worse; for richer for poorer; in sickness and in health' take into account the possibility that keeping that promise will be difficult and that circumstances and our spouse's needs will change over time."

Those promises aren't for the five-year length of a professional sports contract. Those promises, made before God to love, honor, and cherish, are "till death us do part."

So even when "worse," "poorer," or "in sickness" describe the phase your marriage is in, integrity means that you'll keep your word even when doing so costs you a great deal.

—BRIAN HETTINGA

SPORTS NOTE:
One of the longest marriages among sports figures today is Ernie and Lulu Harwell. The legendary baseball announcer and his bride were married in 1941.

FROM THE PLAYBOOK:
Read about how marriage is based on the principled practice of love and commitment, not feelings (Ephesians 5:21–33).

GAME PLAN: Remember that you promised to be committed to your spouse's good "for better, for worse; for richer for poorer; in sickness and in health." What can you do today for him or her to follow through on that promise?

MUGGSY'S TRUST

POINT OF EMPHASIS:
Christian influence

"You are the salt of the earth." MATTHEW 5:13

During my first two-and-a-half years in the NBA, I played for the Golden State Warriors.

The morning of most home games, we had a light practice. Toward the end of each of these practices, we had a friendly shooting competition. The older veterans always kept score and if a dispute arose, they would resolve it. However, on one particular morning they lost track of the score.

I seldom say much during practice; however, this time I spoke up and mentioned the score. Muggsy Bogues, one of the older veterans, reinforced what I said by saying that I was a Christian, and I would never lie.

Well, I do make my share of mistakes, and I have lied in the past. Nonetheless, Muggsy's comment not only flattered me but it also made me aware that by our actions those around us notice what we are about on the inside, even if we do not say much.

In the Bible, the inspired writers sometimes used metaphors to say something is similar to but not exactly the same as something else. For instance, we read in Matthew 5:13 that Christians are the salt of the earth. This metaphor equates Christians and salt. Real salt provides flavor. Similarly, Christians should be a positive influence on those around them, being the "salt" in any given situation. The verse also says real salt is thrown out if it loses its flavor. This is not true of Christians. Believers can be restored through God's forgiveness and grace.

If you have a positive influence on the people around you—if you are salt—they will notice. Your good example can point those people to Christ.

—TODD FULLER, FORMER NBA PLAYER

SPORTS NOTE:
Muggsy Bogues, at 5' 3", was the smallest player ever in NBA history.

FROM THE PLAYBOOK:
Read Romans 8:5–10.

GAME PLAN: What are three situations you are involved in that allow you to be the kind of lifestyle witness that Todd was when he played for the Warriors?

USING YOUR HEAD

POINT OF EMPHASIS:
Protect your relationship with God

"Why do you persist in rebellion? Your whole head is injured."
ISAIAH 1:5

A professional football player—a quarterback no less—scored a crucial touchdown and then celebrated by banging his head against a padded concrete wall. That's a TD dance he won't repeat.

Why? Because of his self-imposed head-cracking, he missed the second half of the game and ended up in the hospital for a check-up. Medical folks X-rayed his head and diagnosed the head-butting quarterback as having a sprained neck. And probably a bruised ego.

I've done a few stupid things in my life too. We all have. The words said in anger. The temptation that should have been resisted. The act of compassion that went undone. The apathy in our relationship with God.

Stupid. Worse yet—sinful and self-defeating.

Through the prophet Isaiah, the Lord spoke tough but loving words to the rebellious Israelite people of about 2,700 years ago. He told them that they were not using their heads in the right way. Instead, they were inflicting injury upon themselves. He asked them, "Why do you persist in rebellion? Your whole head is injured, your whole heart afflicted" (1:5). They just couldn't understand how much they were hurting themselves by their disobedience.

The good news for Israel was that God was willing to forgive them (vv. 18–19). That's still true today. When we do something really stupid—like sin against a holy God, He can forgive us. If we turn from our sin and back to the Lord, He will forgive us and give us a bright future.

So let's use our heads—in the right way, that is—and we'll protect our heart relationship with the Lord. —KURT DE HAAN

SPORTS NOTE: Speaking of sports injuries, more than half of the injuries that occur with high school girls in sports happen to cheerleaders.

FROM THE PLAYBOOK: Read Isaiah 1:1–20.

GAME PLAN: What stupid things have you done lately? Are there sinful attitudes or actions in your life that you have not been willing to give up? Why? How are you hurting yourself and others? How good does it feel when you know that you are right with God?

DECEMBER 19

POINT OF EMPHASIS:
Honoring Jesus

"Do this in remembrance of me." I CORINTHIANS 11:24

When Brett Hull skated onto the ice in a Red Wings intra-squad game a few years ago, he wasn't wearing his familiar No. 17. Instead, he was wearing No. 80 in honor of Herb Brooks.

Brooks, who is most famous for coaching the 1980 US Olympic hockey team to its "Miracle on Ice" gold medal, died in a car accident in August 2003. Hull, who had actually spoken with Brooks the night before his untimely death, said about wearing the former coach's number: "It's just kind of to honor a great man and a great coach, just to keep him on people's minds."

One of the fears that took me by surprise when I lost a close family member a few years ago was that she would drift from our minds. I feared that people (including myself) would forget the special and kind-hearted person she was. I've sensed the same concern as I've witnessed friends and co-workers lose a child, a husband, a dad, a brother.

Remembering those who meant so much to us is critical. They are forever linked to our story and will always be a part of who we are. To forget what they meant to us is to forget a part of who we are.

I believe this is one reason Jesus, within hours of His death and resurrection, instructed His disciples and all who followed Him to make it a habit to remember Him (1 Corinthians 11:23–25). Remembering our Lord's life, death, and resurrection isn't only a part of us—it's the very heart of who we are.

—JEFF OLSON

SPORTS NOTE:
After Herb Brooks led the US team to their improbable win over the Russians in the 1980 Olympics, he quickly went into the locker room so his players would get all the attention.

FROM THE PLAYBOOK:
Read 1 Corinthians 15:3–4.

GAME PLAN: If you don't already, make time to remember and reflect on the life, death, and resurrection of Jesus Christ.

A HAPPY RETIREMENT

POINT OF EMPHASIS:
Thankfulness

"Give thanks in all circumstances." I THESSALONIANS 5:18

For twelve years, Paul Gruber lined up on the left side of the Tampa Bay Buccaneers' offensive line. And for those twelve seasons the Bucs' starting left tackle successfully protected the quarterback, opened holes for ball carriers, and anchored the offensive line.

He was long recognized as one of the best tackles in the business. Unfortunately, his personal success was rarely matched by his team's success. The Bucs were, shall we say, less-than-stellar during Gruber's tenure in the trenches for Tampa Bay.

In 1999, after a serious leg injury, Paul Gruber retired from the game of football.

Was Paul Gruber bitter about a career filled with far more losses than wins? Was he angry that although he had the respect of his peers, he never received personal achievement awards? Was he mad that an injury ended his career before he was ready to end it?

No!

Instead, Gruber, a Christian, put I Thessalonians 5:18 into action. At a press conference announcing his retirement, he said his retirement wasn't a sad thing. Rather he looked back on his twelve-year NFL journey as a "blessing." In a situation where he could have complained, Gruber was thankful.

What can we learn from Gruber's actions? As followers of Jesus Christ, we have reason to be thankful *all* the time—regardless of the circumstances. Even when things don't work out the way we think they should, we can give thanks.

—ROB BENTZ

SPORTS NOTE:
Considered one of the best players in the history of the Tampa Bay Buccaneers, Paul Gruber started every game he appeared in for the Bucs.

FROM THE PLAYBOOK:
Read about the thankfulness of someone who went through some trials of his own: Psalm 34.

 GAME PLAN: Think of an instance when something happened that you didn't want to happen. Now list three blessings that have resulted from your difficult circumstance. Pray to God and tell Him how thankful you are for your previously unwelcome situation.

DECEMBER 21

RUN AND JUMP

POINT OF EMPHASIS:
Handling pressure

"The wolf attacks the flock and scatters it." JOHN 10:12

The basketball huddle: "Okay, here's the plan. Full-court pressure; run and jump. We're looking for the steal or the turnover. Force them to dribble. Push them beyond their limit of control. Remember—jump only when the dribbler is out of control or they have lost their downcourt vision! Don't let up; this game is ours."

The enemy's huddle: "Okay, here's the plan. Full-court pressure; run and jump. We're looking to steal, kill, and destroy. Force them to go it alone. Force them away from help. Push them beyond their limit to resist temptation. Remember—attack only when the opponents are already weakened or when they have lost sight of their purpose. Don't give up. We're not far behind; this game is ours!"

I find it interesting how much the sports tactics we talk about and watch are similar to the tactics of the spiritual realm.

Think about it. Can you identify with full-court pressure in your life? The Bible clearly explains that the enemy is real and "prowls around like a roaring lion looking for someone to devour" (1 Peter 5:8). Satan and his team are constantly conjuring up plans to lead the whole world astray (Revelation 12:9). If you are finding yourself rattled by Satan's pressure, remember to keep your head up, look for your teammates, and protect yourself with the heavenly armor (Ephesians 6:10–18).

"Thanks be to God! He gives us the victory through our Lord Jesus Christ" (1 Corinthians 15:57).

—MOLLY GRETZINGER

SPORTS NOTE:
Looking for a good basketball strategy book by a master coach? Try *Practical Modern Basketball* by John Wooden.

FROM THE PLAYBOOK:
Read Ephesians 6:10–18 and put on each piece of armor before you leave your house this week!

 GAME PLAN: In what specific area of your life do you feel Satan's pressure? When in that situation, memorize and recite James 4:7, "Resist the devil, and he will flee from you."

GO WITH THE GOSPEL

POINT OF EMPHASIS:
Taking on a challenge

"As you go, preach this message: The kingdom of heaven is near."
MATTHEW 10:7

One of the most exciting things I've ever done was to travel with a college basketball evangelism team. It was a thrill to take the gospel to thousands and thousands of people through a game I love to play.

For more than a month, we traveled throughout the Philippines, playing more than thirty basketball games in front of large crowds of people. At halftime, we gave our testimonies of faith in Christ, we sang (as a singer, I was a good point guard), and we explained the gospel. After the game, we would go into the crowd and help people who had been led to pray to trust Jesus Christ as Savior.

As thrilling as that was, imagine the excitement that must have coursed through the hearts of the very first gospel team God ever sent out.

In Matthew 10, we read about the commissioning of the original twelve gospel-spreaders—a dozen hand-picked disciples who Christ Himself sent out to do His bidding.

Their work was ground-breaking and dangerous, for they were proclaiming a counterculture message. Yet they were equipped with the power of God as their main weapon.

Have you ever been involved in a gospel team? Opportunities abound to escape your comfort zone and touch a world that needs the countercultural message that Jesus saves.

God will give you the strength, the wisdom, and the power to succeed. Perhaps it's time to step out and get involved in a gospel team.

—DAVE BRANON

SPORTS NOTE: One organization that takes many people on sports evangelism trips is Score International, found at www. scoreinternational. org.

FROM THE PLAYBOOK: Read Matthew 10.

GAME PLAN: What is your area of interest? Can you find an organization that can use your God-given skills and abilities to help a group of people learn about Jesus? Set a timetable, investigate, and go.

THE SCAPEGOAT

POINT OF EMPHASIS:
Jesus' sacrifice for us

"It is better for you that one man die for the people." JOHN 11:50

The company was losing money. The price of its stock was sliding, and the corporate board was grumbling. So the president, desperate to do something, fired the vice-president in charge of sales.

In a similar situation, a college basketball team was mired in a losing season after six consecutive successful years and three visits to the NCAA tournament. Attendance was down and the alumni were howling. So the university fired the coach.

In both cases, good people were released because the organization needed a scapegoat. They focused the blame on one person, even though many were at fault.

That's what happened to Jesus. The high priest Caiaphas, without knowing the full import of his words, said it would be best to sacrifice one man, Jesus. He thought it would save the nation from the oppressive Romans (John 11:47–50). What he didn't realize was that Jesus was bearing the guilt and penalty for the sins of the world in fulfillment of the Old Testament picture of the two goats—one a sacrifice for sin, the other a scapegoat that symbolically carried their sins away (Leviticus 16).

We deserve eternal death. How grateful we can be that God made Jesus our scapegoat.

—DAVE EGNER

SPORTS NOTE:
College football coaches such as Ron Zook and Tyrone Willingham were given just three years to make a difference, and then they were fired because some were not happy with the results.

FROM THE PLAYBOOK:
Read Leviticus 16:1–10, 20–22.

GAME PLAN: Why did Jesus need to die for you? What are some of the blessings you can experience because of Christ's sacrifice for you?

THE GREATEST MOMENT IN HISTORY

POINT OF EMPHASIS:
The Christmas miracle

"Let's . . . see this thing that has happened." LUKE 2:15

- US Hockey's "Miracle on Ice"
- Mary Lou Retton's "Vault Without Fault"
- Mark McGwire's record-breaking 62nd home run.

Those are some of the greatest moments in the history of sports. If you were fortunate enough to witness one of these phenomenal events, you know you'll never forget that thrilling moment. We still get chills when we see video of Mary Lou's remarkable vault or when we hear Al Michaels exalt, "Do you believe in miracles? Yes!"

But no matter how awesome the sports moment, no "miracle" can ever compare to the truly supernatural miracle we celebrate each December 25.

On that stupendous day 2,000 years ago, in a little town called Bethlehem, a few shepherds were given a first-hand announcement of the greatest moment in the history of the world—the birth of Jesus!

Since the Garden of Eden, God's people had been waiting for the Messiah. For thousands of years, the prophets had predicted it. Finally the moment had arrived: "When the time had finally come, God sent his Son . . ." (Galatians 4:4).

What a mind-boggling experience for these shepherds! To be among the first to see the baby Jesus, God in the flesh! He had come to set us free from the bondage of sin and death—to reconcile us to God. He brought hope and peace —and the promise of everlasting life. Now that's a moment to celebrate!

Do you believe in miracles? There's never been one like what happened on that first Christmas day. —CHRISTIN DITCHFIELD

SPORTS NOTE:
According to ESPN, the greatest moment in Super Bowl history was when Joe Namath and the New York Jets beat the Baltimore Colts in Super Bowl III.

FROM THE PLAYBOOK:
Read Luke 2:1–20; Matthew 2:1–12.

 GAME PLAN: This Christmas, don't miss the reason for the season. Before opening your presents, take time to re-read the story of Jesus' birth in Luke 2. Then thank God for His "indescribable gift!"

CHRISTMAS DAY 1980

POINT OF EMPHASIS:
The meaning of Christmas

"The gift of God is eternal life in Christ Jesus." ROMANS **6:23**

Christmas Day has different meanings for different people. For many, it's all about gifts. Some big. Some small. Gifts needed, and some, well, not really needed at all.

On Christmas Day 1980, I got a gift that I didn't truly *need*. But WOW! was I excited to get it!

I got the first baseman's mitt that I had wanted for so long. You see, this was no ordinary baseball glove. This was the one piece of equipment that would make me the best first baseman in all of Little League. This was the mitt I had begged my parents to get me for more than a year. And on December 25, 1980, the mitt was mine.

Looking back, the mitt was a great Christmas gift. It received more than its fair share of time "around the bag." (Once, it even made the first two outs of a Little League triple play.) But as great a gift as my first baseman's mitt was, it wasn't something that I really *needed*. Rather, it was a gift I *wanted*.

This Christmas Day, consider receiving a gift that is far better than any gift you could ever want.

God is offering you the gift of eternal life in Jesus Christ. To receive it, simply confess your sin, ask God for His forgiveness, acknowledge Christ's sacrifice on the cross as payment for your sin. Grab hold of the greatest gift ever—a relationship with God through His Son, the Lord Jesus Christ. That's a gift we all truly *need*.   —ROB BENTZ

SPORTS NOTE:
One of the most popular baseball gloves is the Wilson A2000, which will cost about $160 to put under the tree.

FROM THE PLAYBOOK:
Read Romans 10:9–11.

GAME PLAN: To receive God's gift of eternal life, talk with God in the following prayer: "God, I am a sinner. I need Your forgiveness. I know that Your Son, Jesus Christ, lived a perfect life and gave that life on a cross to pay the penalty of my sin. I accept His sacrifice on my behalf. Today, I confess Jesus as Lord of my life! Thank You for forgiving me and for making me a new creation."

WHAT GOD HATES

POINT OF EMPHASIS:
God's guidelines

"There are six things the Lord hates." PROVERBS 6:16

There are six things the Lord hates, seven that are detestable to him: haughty eyes, a lying tongue, hands that shed innocent blood, a heart that devises wicked schemes, feet that are quick to rush into evil, a false witness who pours out lies, and a man who stirs up dissension among brothers" (Proverbs 6:16–19).

What enters your mind as your read these words, knowing that God *hates* these behaviors? Do you find yourself thinking of times, perhaps even recently, when you did the very thing God abhors? It's convicting that the Lord puts "shedding innocent blood" and spreading "dissension among brothers" in the same list. One clearly seems more heinously wrong than the other. But let's focus on the seventh thing listed: spreading dissension among brothers. What does this mean? "Dissension," which is translated "strife" in some Bible versions, is defined as "a bitter, sometimes violent conflict. An act of contention. Exertion for superiority."

On a sports team, it could take the form of turning your teammates against another player so you'll end up on top. Even if the argument or hard feelings only exist between you and the other person, everyone on your team feels the tension, and that is strife. Consider how you're treating your teammates and the other people in your life. If you're creating strife, ask the Lord for wisdom to behave differently and act on the guidance He gives you.

SPORTS NOTE:
Does character count in sports? Read about an organization that is attempting to help young athletes develop good character at http://characterthat counts.gospelcom.net

FROM THE PLAYBOOK:
Read Proverbs 6:12–19.

—ROXANNE ROBBINS

GAME PLAN: Reflect on a relationship that's been difficult for you. Ask God to bring healing and then write out steps you can take to make things better.

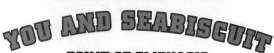

YOU AND SEABISCUIT

POINT OF EMPHASIS:
Reflecting Christ's glory

"The Lord looks at the heart" 1 SAMUEL 16:7

There were three major sports in America in the 1930s—baseball, boxing, and horseracing. In the late 1930s, a race horse named Seabiscuit, who had been written off as a loser, came from nowhere to capture the hearts of America. In the fall of 1938, 40 million fans (1 out of 3 Americans) gathered around the radio and listened to the long-awaited matchup between the underdog, Seabiscuit, and the Triple Crown winner, War Admiral. Seabiscuit won by 4 lengths.

Seabiscuit didn't look like a champion. From birth, his trainers considered him too small and nothing like his thoroughbred descendants. So he wasn't given much of a chance to show his true potential. He lost his first 17 starts and was eventually trained to lose in order to bolster the confidence of other horses.

SPORTS NOTE:
Seabiscuit was one of the Top 10 newsmakers of 1938.

But that all changed when a new owner and trainer saw in him what no one else did. They saw his *heart* and gave him a second chance. Laura Hillenbrand, author of the book *Seabiscuit*, says, "He didn't look the part, but you can't see a horse's heart by looking at its frame."

FROM THE PLAYBOOK:
Read 1 Samuel 16.

The world may judge us by how we look, but God values what is in our heart (1 Samuel 16:7). Inside the heart of every Christian is an unveiled glory that is meant to be discovered and revealed. The Bible says that all Christians "reflect the Lord's glory . . . with ever-increasing glory" (2 Corinthians 3:18).

Find the glory of Christ in your heart and put it on display! No matter what you look like, you can be a winner for Him!

—JEFF OLSON

GAME PLAN: What are some things that might keep you from finding or reflecting the glory of Christ in you?

WHY AM I HERE?

POINT OF EMPHASIS:
Great commission

"Therefore go and make disciples." MATTHEW 28:19

"Why am I here?"

I was asked this question once, and I answered the question rather hurriedly, yet correctly. My response was, "To make an impact on this world, to change lives. We were not put here just to exist or to gain personal satisfaction from the many things of this world. But we were put here to be an extension of Christ."

Before Jesus ascended into heaven shortly after His resurrection, He gave what we have come to call "The Great Commission." It says that we were put here to continue what Christ started while on earth—to be ministers of God's Word and to lead people to Christ throughout the world.

In 2001, the WNBA gave a T-shirt to all players that read, "The WNBA: This is who I am." As athletes, many of us believe this slogan. We spend countless hours preparing our body and mind to meet next season's athletic challenges, and that's okay.

But what about us as Christians? We fail to spend twenty minutes a day getting connected with Christ to make sure we are prepared to meet life's daily challenges. The sport world is so enticing that we forget that we are disciples first and athletes second. And we forget that our sport is not why God put us here, but it is the avenue He gave us to bring glory to Him through our play and our discipleship to others.

If you are an athlete, begin to use the platform God has given you as your place of ministry. Be an extension of Christ and fulfill His Great Commission. It's the reason you are here.

—KEDRA HOLLAND-CORN, PRO BASKETBALL PLAYER

SPORTS NOTE:
Kedra's husband, Jesse, has an MBA from Tulane University. Jesse and Kedra both speak multiple languages.

FROM THE PLAYBOOK:
Read Matthew 28:16–20.

 GAME PLAN: Why are you where you are? Do you know how God can use you where you are to glorify Him? What would have to change for that to happen?

WHAT IS YOUR LEGACY?

POINT OF EMPHASIS:
Leaving a legacy for Christ

"For to me, to live is Christ and to die is gain." PHILIPPIANS 1:21

A legacy might be defined in a dictionary as anything that is handed down from an ancestor. It could be described by what you are remembered for. Perhaps the best description that I have heard is that your legacy is the dash or hyphen that sits between your date of birth and the date of death on your tombstone.

What is it that you are living for? Is it for professional progress, personal glory, or personal possessions? Are you striving to be the best employee or the best athlete or the best "something else" that one day will mean nothing? What is life to you?

The apostle Paul stated his purpose in Philippians 1:21 when he said, "For to me, to live is Christ and to die is gain." I believe it was Paul's desire and sole aim in life to glorify Jesus Christ in all that he did. Paul made it his purpose to imitate Christ and to emulate the humility, love, and compassion of Jesus. Paul desired and purposed to spread the gospel of Jesus Christ. He wanted others to know of God's love and gift of grace.

Paul had committed to make Jesus Christ his life. To him, Christ was life. What a legacy!

—BILL SAMPEN, FORMER MAJOR LEAGUE PITCHER

SPORTS NOTE:
For baseball players, a baseball card is part of the legacy they leave behind. You can get a Bill Sampen baseball card at Internet baseball card sites.

FROM THE PLAYBOOK:
Read Philippians 1.

 GAME PLAN: Which of these verses best describes you, Philippians 1:21, "For to me, to live is Christ" or Philippians 2:21, "For everyone looks out for his own interests, not those of Jesus Christ." One of these verses most accurately describes our life and the legacy that we are preparing to leave. Are you comfortable with the legacy you are preparing to hand down? Are you willing to change it?

THE PROBLEM WITH LOOKING BACK

POINT OF EMPHASIS:
Pressing on

"Let us run with perseverance." HEBREWS 12:1

It's been years since the first runner broke through the four-minute barrier for the mile run. That runner was Roger Bannister, who ran a 3:59.4 mile on May 6, 1954.

Soon others were challenging Bannister. John Landy was next to crash through the four-minute mark, running a 3:58 mile just two months after Bannister's landmark race.

So, what was the next logical thing to take place? A showdown between Landy and Bannister. On August 7, the two went head-to-head. "The Mile of the Century," it was called, and the world's only two runners who had traveled that distance in less than four minutes faced off.

The gun sounded, and Bannister and Landy took off. At first, they ran together. As the race went into the final lap, Landy edged into the lead. Closer and closer the two drew toward the finish line. The leader, though, wondered where his opponent was. So he turned his head to look over his shoulder. As he did, Bannister blew past Landy and took the lead. He raced home with the title as the world's fastest miler.

Landy later told a reporter, "If I hadn't looked back, I would have won!"

Is it possible that we sometimes find ourselves in the same situation John Landy was in? We are racing through life, eager to make an impact. But then we turn around to see what is behind us—what we've already passed. We lose our focus.

First Corinthians 9:24–27 tells us that discipline is the key to winning. And that discipline may mean that we let go of what is past and press ahead. In Philippians 3:12–13, the apostle Paul said, "I press on, . . . forgetting what is behind and straining toward what is ahead."

As we think of next year, let's keep in mind that God wants us to keep looking ahead, not dwelling on the past. Let's press on. —DAVE BRANON

SPORTS NOTE: By 1999, the world record for the mile run had been reduced to 3:43.13.

FROM THE PLAYBOOK: Read Hebrews 12:1–2.

GAME PLAN: What past thing is haunting me? How can I keep it in the past and eliminate it from my future?

LOOKING AHEAD

POINT OF EMPHASIS:
God's future glory

"I press on toward the goal to win the prize." PHILIPPIANS 3:13–14

When I reflect on my twenty-year career as a track and field athlete, what sticks with me the most is facing the challenging transition of moving from competitive life to regular life.

I have struggled with being a "normal" person. Many of these struggles include the normalcy of everyday living. My role as a wife, mother, and full-time working woman—combined with the lack of notoriety, international travel, and the thrill of competition—has presented many challenges. Sometimes it has even created fear in me.

But there is one future transition coming—one that I am certain will contain no fear. I am speaking of my transition someday into the presence of my heavenly Father. Although I am challenged by this life, I look forward to seeing my Savior face to face. Although the desire for death is not imminent for me, I am secure in knowing that the current challenges I face will cease to exist on the day I enter heaven. The longing and voids I sometimes feel because of no longer being an elite level athlete will be transformed into joy.

I rejoice in knowing that I am secure in this knowledge because of the blood Jesus shed for me. His death assures me of eternal life. It causes me to no longer dread what I miss, but to focus on what's to come.

—LaVonna Martin-Floreal, Olympics silver medalist, track

SPORTS NOTE:
While competing in track for the University of Tennessee, LaVonna set school records in four events and is the all-time Lady Vol leader with 12 Southeast Conference titles.

FROM THE PLAYBOOK:
Read Revelation 21:1–4.

 GAME PLAN: What fears of this life get you down? Does it help to spend some time thinking about the future home in heaven that God has prepared for you?

Here are brief biographical notes about the sports people who contributed articles to *Power Up*.

Kyle Abbott, baseball

Kyle is one of a number of baseball players who became a major league chaplain after their careers ended. Abbot, who pitched for 4 years in the early 90s (Angels, Phillies), later became the Baseball Chapel representative for the Texas Rangers.

Tricia Bader-Binford, basketball

Tricia Bader-Binford played guard for the Utah Starzz and the Cleveland Rockers in the WNBA between 1998 and 2002. In April 2005, she was named the women's basketball coach at Montana State University. She and her husband Todd have a son, Justin.

Dorian Boose, football

Dorian has had two pro football careers—one in the NFL and one in the Canadian Football League. He spent five seasons in the NFL before moving north to play in the CFL for the Edmonton Eskimos.

Kim Braatz-Voisard, baseball, softball

Kim has the distinction of being the very first woman to hit an over-the-fence home run against a team of professional men players. She did that while playing for the Colorado Silver Bullets baseball team. Kim is married to Mark Voisard, a former pitcher in the Colorado Rockies organization.

Kyle Brady, football

The New York Jets drafted Kyle after his successful career at Penn State. He spent four seasons with the Jets before moving to Jacksonville in 1999. When not playing football, he is active with the Fellowship of Christian Athletes.

Jenny Boucek, basketball

An injury ended Jenny Boucek's WNBA dreams early—after one year with the Cleveland Rockers. After that, she became a coach, and in 2004 she helped lead the Seattle Storm to its first WNBA title. She played college basketball at the University of Virginia.

Ron Brown, football
For 17 years, Ron was a valued assistant football coach at Nebraska. But when a new regime took over in 2003, he was let go. Because of his heart for ministry, he took over as the director of the Fellowship of Christian Athletes in Nebraska.

Erin Buescher, basketball
Erin Buescher began her college basketball career at the University of California at Santa Barbara, where she was an all-conference player. She then transferred to The Master's College to take advantage of that school's Christian atmosphere. After college, she was drafted by the Minnesota Lynx of the WNBA. She has played for Minnesota, Charlotte, and Sacramento.

John Burrough, football
John Burrough played for the Atlanta Falcons, Minnesota Vikings, and St. Louis Rams from 1995 to 2002. He appeared in the Super Bowl for Atlanta in 1999.

Gill Byrd, football
Gill Byrd spent 10 years in the NFL with the San Diego Chargers. He became the team's all-time leader in interceptions. After he retired, he was inducted into the Chargers' Hall of Fame. He enjoys working with young Christians in discipleship situations. In 2003, he became an assistant coach for the St. Louis Rams.

Paul Byrd, baseball
After pitching for Louisiana State University, Paul signed with the Cleveland Indians in 1991. Since then, he has played in the major leagues for the Mets, the Braves, the Phillies, the Royals, and the Angels. He won 17 games for Kansas City in 2002.

Bob Christian, football
After playing at Northwestern University, Christian spent 10 years in the NFL as a running back for the Chicago Bears, the Carolina Panthers, and Atlanta Falcons.

Bobby Clampett, golf
Bobby Clampett spent 15 years on the PGA Tour, finishing 17th in 1981. He won the 1982 Southern Open. He joined CBS Sports as a course reporter in 1991. He and his wife Marianna have five children.

Tanya Crevier, basketball
Tanya Crevier is one of the premier basketball ball-handlers in the world. Tanya played college basketball at South Dakota State, and then she played in the pioneer women's pro league—the Women's Basketball League. She has been performing

ball-handling shows since then, making her name known at NBA halftimes, college basketball games, and at schools and businesses.

Amanda Cromwell, soccer

At one time, Amanda Cromwell was pulling off a difficult dual career as a soccer player in the WUSA and as a coach at the University of Central Florida. Before that, she was a member of the US National soccer team. She was an alternate on the 1996 team that won gold at the Olympics. Amanda began coaching Central Florida in 1999.

Josh Davis

Josh Davis was the only Olympian in 1996 to win three Olympic gold medals. In his career, he has won three gold and two silver medals. Josh and Shantel Davis have five children.

Pat Day

When he retired from racing in 2005, Pat Day had amassed the most wins ever by a jockey: more than 8,000 career victories. He retired to spend more time on his ministry—a chaplaincy to fellow jockeys.

Shane Doan, hockey

Shane Doan is a center for the Phoenix Coyotes in the NHL. He grew up at the Circle Square Ranch in Canada. He and his wife have three children.

Jean Driscoll, marathons

Jean Driscoll was born with spina bifida, but that did not stop her from being one of the premier athletes of the 1990s. She became a world-class wheelchair marathon champion, capturing the Boston Marathon eight times and winning two silver medals in the Olympics. She has written a book about her life. It is called *Determined to Win*.

David Fisher, chaplain

Not many people have been with one team as long as David Fisher has been with the Toronto Blue Jays. He began offering spiritual assistance to the team in 1977. He is also chaplain for other sports teams in the Toronto area.

Todd Fuller, basketball

While in high school at Charlotte Christian in Charlotte, North Carolina, Fuller was coached by former NBA All-Star Bobby Jones. After high school, Todd played at North Carolina State before being drafted by the Golden State Warriors. In his 5-year NBA career, he played for the Warriors, Utah, Charlotte, Miami, and Orlando.

Paul Grafer, soccer

Paul Grafer was a goalkeeper for the MLS MetroStars before retiring from Major League Soccer. While with the MetroStars, he was backup goalkeeper to Tim Howard, who moved on to play for Manchester United.

Tracy Hanson, golf

Tracy Hanson began her LPGA career in 1995. In 2001, she was finished 44th on the LPGA money list. A graduate of San Jose State University, she lives in Ormond Beach, Florida.

Kedra Holland-Corn, basketball

After a successful career at Georgia, Kedra spent seven seasons in the WNBA—from 1999 through 2004. Twice she averaged more than 10 points a game for the Sacramento Monarchs. She also played pro basketball overseas.

Hersey Hawkins

In 1988, Hersey Hawkins led the NCAA in scoring, averaging 36.3 points a game for the Bradley Braves. His 1,125 points that season was the seventh best ever by a Division I player. He played in the NBA for 13 years.

Amber Jacobs, basketball

Amber grew up around basketball, as her dad was a longtime coach and instructor. She went to Boston College and led the Lady Eagles to the NCAA Sweet 16 twice. Her three-point shooting skill led to a WNBA career. Amber was drafted by the Minnesota Lynx in 2004.

Chris Kaman, basketball

After playing high school basketball for a tiny Christian school in Grand Rapids, Michigan, Chris attended Central Michigan and developed into a first-round draft pick. He was drafted in 2003 by the LA Clippers.

Napoleon Kaufman

A first-round draft pick of the Oakland Raiders, Napoleon Kaufman gained nearly 5,000 yards as an NFL running back. He retired after the 2000 season at the age of 27 to pursue ministry opportunities. He pastors a church in California.

Val Kemper, volleyball

After an All-American career on the volleyball court at Michigan State University, Val joined up with the US National team. She seemed destined to compete for the US women in the 2000 Olympics, but in the final weeks before the Games, she was cut from the team. That day, she had her first date with triathlete Hunter Kemper, whom she married in 2004.

Betsy King, golf
Betsy is a member of the LPGA Hall of Fame. During her distinguished career, she has won six majors and a total of 34 tournaments.

Siew-Ai Lim, golf
Born in Malaysia, Siew-Ai (See-you-I) came to the United States to attend the University of South Carolina. She stayed and now is a part of the LPGA Tour. She had her best year in 2004, when she finished 63rd on the Tour.

Barb Lindquist, triathlon
Barb Lindquist turned a successful swimming career at Stanford into a wildly successful triathlon career. In the early years of the 21st century, she was named the No. 1 female triathlete in the world. In 2004, she competed for the US in the Olympic Games.

Kevin Malone
During the 1990s, Kevin Malone was the general manager of two major league baseball teams—first the Montreal Expos and later the Los Angeles Dodgers. After leaving baseball, he began working with The Master's College in California. He also takes periodic missions trips overseas with major league baseball players.

Mike Maroth, baseball
In 2003, Mike Maroth was part of an awful baseball season. He was a member of the Detroit Tigers as they suffered through 119 losses. Mike lost 21 of those games. Yet he never complained—and he won the hearts of many. He and his wife Brooke are very active in helping homeless people get enough to eat.

LaVonna Martin-Floreal, track
In 1992, LaVonna won the silver medal at the Olympics in the 100-meter hurdles. She competed in two Olympics for the United States. She is now a schoolteacher, and her husband, Edrick, is women's track & field coach at Stanford.

Scott Mendes, rodeo
In 1997, Scott reached the pinnacle of his sport when he won the bull riding world championship. He has taken his fame in this sport and turned it into ministry with an organization called Spur'n With Jesus.

Cameron Mills, basketball
After helping the Kentucky Wildcats win the 1998 NCAA national championship, Cameron began Cameron Mills Ministries, which includes basketball camps and speaking engagements.

Madeline Manning Mims, track

Madeline Manning was a member of the US Olympic track team four times (1968, 1972, 1976, and 1980). She won gold in the 1968 Olympics, setting a new Olympic record in the 800-meter race (2:00.9), and she is in the National Track & Field Hall of Fame. Madeline is in full-time Christian ministry as a singer and motivational speaker. She wrote an autobiography called *The Hope of Glory*.

Leah O'Brien-Amico, softball

Leah O'Brien Amico has earned three Olympic gold medals as a member of the US softball team. When she won gold in 2004, she was the only mom on the team. She and her husband Tommy have two children.

John Register, track

In 1994, hurdler John Register made a misstep that would change his life. As he was practicing the hurdles, he fell, causing serious damage to his left leg. The injury caused him to have the leg amputated. Two years later, he was in the Atlanta Paralympics. John now competes as a disabled athlete and works with the US Olympic committee.

Frank Reich, football

Frank Reich owns the distinction of being the quarterback behind the two largest comebacks in college and NFL history. While with Maryland, he led the Terps back to a huge win over Miami. With the NFL Buffalo Bills, he engineered a huge comeback over the Houston Oilers. After his NFL career ended, Frank went into Christian ministry, eventually becoming president of Reformed Theological Seminary in North Carolina.

Leighann Reimer, basketball

Leighann is Shane Doan's sister. She was twice named the best women's college basketball player in Canada. After college she went to Europe to play professional basketball. Leighann is married to Chad Reimer. They have a daughter, born in 2005.

Bill Sampen, baseball

Bill Sampen pitched in the major leagues from 1990 through 1994 with Montreal, Kansas City, and California. He finished his career with a winning record (25–21) and an ERA under 4 (3.75). After leaving baseball, he became an associate pastor of a church in Indiana.

Sue Semrau, basketball

When Sue Semrau took over the women's basketball team at Florida State University, the team was not very good at all. She turned the team around and had the team in the Top 25 within three years. She has been named the SEC Coach of the Year.

Casey Shaw, basketball
Casey Shaw played college basketball at the University of Toledo, where his wife, Dana Drew, also played. Casey played briefly with the Philadelphia 76ers before moving on to play in Europe.

Charlotte Smith-Taylor, basketball
Charlotte Smith-Taylor will be forever remembered for hitting the winning shot in the 1995 NCAA women's basketball tournament as North Carolina won the title. She played in both the American Basketball League and the WNBA. Charlotte spent six years with the Charlotte Sting. She is David Thompson's niece.

Matt Stover, football
Matt Stover was drafted by the Cleveland Browns in 1991 after he attended Louisiana Tech. By 2005, Stover had scored 1,481 points, putting him in the Top 20 of all-time in NFL history. Matt also had the longest tenure of any player with the Baltimore Ravens, moving with the team from Cleveland in 1996.

David Thompson, basketball
One of the greatest college basketball players of all-time, David Thompson is known for his 44-inch vertical leap and for leading the North Carolina State Wolfpack to a national championship in the middle of UCLA's long run in the 1970s. Thompson now lives in North Carolina. He has written an autobiography called *Skywalker*.

Charlie Ward, basketball
Charlie Ward won the Heisman Trophy in 1993 as the top college football player. He was drafted by the New York Knicks, and he scored nearly 4,000 points and handed out more than 2,500 assists in his NBA career.

Wendy Ward, golf
When she is not helping her husband Nate tend the cattle on their ranch in Washington state, Wendy is one of the top players on the LPGA Tour. Through 2005, she had won four LPGA titles. She competed twice for the US in the Solheim Cup.

Danny Wuerffel, football
Danny Wuerffel won the Heisman Trophy in 1994 as the top college football player. He played in the NFL with New Orleans, Green Bay, Chicago, and Washington. After retiring, he began working with Desire Street Ministries in New Orleans.

Here are brief biographical notes about the writers who contributed articles to *Power Up*.

Rob Bentz
A longtime staff member for *Sports Spectrum* magazine, Rob is completing a Masters of Divinity course at Reformed Theological Seminary in Orlando, Florida.

Dave Branon
Managing editor of *Sports Spectrum* magazine since 1990 and a contributing writer to the devotional booklet *Our Daily Bread*.

Barb Cash
An occasional freelance writer for *Sports Spectrum*, Barb lives near Atlanta. She and her husband, Tim, chaplain for the Atlanta Braves, have five children.

Lorilee Craker
A transplanted Canadian living in Michigan, Lorilee has written several books about being a mom and other family-related issues. She has written many feature articles for *Sports Spectrum*.

Dan Deal
Dan is a radio producer at RBC Ministries. He can be heard occasionally on *Sports Spectrum* radio and other RBC programs.

Kurt De Haan
Kurt was managing editor of *Our Daily Bread* until his death in 2003. An avid sailor and runner, Kurt died while running in August of that year.

Mart De Haan
Mart is president of RBC Ministries and Kurt's brother. Their grandfather, Dr. M. R. De Haan, was the founder of Radio Bible Class (RBC Ministries) in 1938.

Del Diduit
Del is a freelance writer who has penned several articles for *Sports Spectrum* magazine. He lives in Wheelersburg, Ohio.

Christin Ditchfield
Christin began her writing career with articles on tennis players for *Sports Spectrum*. She has written several books and has her own radio ministry.

Dave Egner
Dave is a longtime writer for *Our Daily Bread*. During his career at RBC Ministries, he was managing editor of *Campus Journal* (now called *Our Journey*), and he at one time had a regular column in *Sports Spectrum*.

Tom Felten
Tom worked with *Sports Spectrum* in a management role for a number of years. He is currently managing editor of *Our Journey*, a devotional publication of RBC Ministries.

Molly Gretzinger
Molly's first exposure to *Sports Spectrum* was as an intern for the magazine while she was in college. Now she works with the ministry Youth for Christ in Denver and writes for *Power Up*.

Tim Gustafson
Tim serves RBC as managing editor of the *Our Daily Bread* devotional. He also serves the United States as a chief gunner's mate in the Navy Reserve.

Brian Hettinga
Brian is the host and producer of the weekly radio program *Discover the Word*, produced by RBC Ministries.

Darryl Howerton
An occasional writer for *Sports Spectrum*, Darryl has covered the NBA for the now-defunct *Sport* magazine and for *Hoop* magazine for a number of years.

Victor Lee
Victor spent many years covering major league baseball for major newspapers. Now he is a pastor in Knoxville. He writes a regular column for *Sports Spectrum* magazine.

Jeff Olson
Jeff is a biblical counselor at RBC Ministries. He dispenses spiritual advice to readers and listeners of RBC publications and programs.

Roxanne Robbins

Longtime *Sports Spectrum* writer Roxanne Robbins lives in Washington, DC, where she has worked for a variety of communications organizations. She has covered several Olympic Games for Christian media outlets. She is a regular writer for *Power Up.*

Art Stricklin

Art works with Marketplace Ministries of Dallas, Texas. He also is a noted golf writer for top golf publications as well as a frequent writer of articles for *Sports Spectrum* magazine.